HERODOTUS

IV

LCL 120

HERODOTUS

BOOKS VIII–IX

WITH AN ENGLISH TRANSLATION BY
A. D. GODLEY

HARVARD UNIVERSITY PRESS
CAMBRIDGE, MASSACHUSETTS
LONDON, ENGLAND

First published 1925
Reprinted 1930, 1946, 1961, 1969, 1981, 1997

LOEB CLASSICAL LIBRARY® is a registered trademark
of the President and Fellows of Harvard College

ISBN 0-674-99134-6

Printed in Great Britain by St Edmundsbury Press Ltd,
Bury St Edmunds, Suffolk, on acid-free paper.
Bound by Hunter & Foulis Ltd, Edinburgh, Scotland.

CONTENTS

INTRODUCTION

THE following is a brief analysis of the contents of Books VIII and IX, based on the summary in Stein's edition :—

BOOK VIII

Ch. 1–5. The Greek fleet at Artemisium ; question of supreme command ; bribery of Themistocles by the Euboeans.

Ch. 6–14. Despatch of a Persian squadron to sail round Euboea, and its destruction by a storm. Effect of the storm on the rest of the Persian fleet ; first encounter between the two fleets.

Ch. 15–17. Second battle off Artemisium.

Ch. 18–23. Retreat of the Greeks ; Themistocles' attempt to tamper with the Ionians ; Persian occupation of Euboea.

Ch. 24–33. Visit of Persian sailors to the field of Thermopylae. Olympic festival (26). Feuds of Thessalians and Phocians ; Persian advance through Phocis (27–33).

Ch. 34–39. Persian march through Boeotia, and unsuccessful attempt upon Delphi.

Ch. 40–48. Abandonment of Attica by the Athenians ; the Greek fleet at Salamis.

Ch. 49–55. Greek council of war ; Persian invasion of Attica and occupation of Athens.

INTRODUCTION

INTRODUCTION

BOOK IX

INTRODUCTION

In the eighth and ninth books the central subjects are the battles of Salamis and Plataea respectively. Herodotus describes the preliminaries of Salamis, and both the operations prior to Plataea and the actual battle, with much detail; and his narrative has given rise to a good deal of controversy. Sometimes it is difficult to reconcile his story with the facts of geography. Sometimes, it is alleged, he is contradicted by the only other real authority for the sea fight at Salamis, Aeschylus. More often, he is said to sin against the laws of probability. He makes generals and armies do things which are surprising; and this is alleged to detract from his credit; for a historian, who allows generals and armies to disregard known rules of war, is plainly suspect, and at best the dupe of camp gossip, if not animated by partiality or even malice.

As to the battle of Salamis, a mere translator has no desire to add greatly to the literature of controversy. But it is worth while to review Herodotus' account. On the day before the battle, the Persian fleet, apparently, lay along the coast of Attica, its eastern wing being near Munychia; the Greeks being at Salamis, opposite to and rather less than a mile distant from Xerxes' ships. During the night, Persian ships were detached to close the two entrances of the straits between the mainland and Salamis. At dawn of the following day, the Greeks rowed out and made a frontal attack on the Persians facing them.

This account is questioned by the learned, mainly on two grounds; firstly, because (it is alleged) the Persians, if they originally lay along the Attic coast, could not have closed the two entrances of the straits without the knowledge of the Greeks; secondly, because Herodotus' narrative differs from that given by Aeschylus, in the Persae, a play produced only eight years after the battle. As to the first objection, the Persian manoeuvre was executed in darkness, and by small vessels, not modern battleships: it is surely not incredible that the Greeks should have been unaware of its full execution. As to the second ground of criticism,— that Herodotus and Aeschylus do not agree, and that Aeschylus must be held the better authority,— it still remains to be shown in what the alleged discrepancy consists. It is a fact which appears to escape the observation of the learned that Aeschylus is writing a poetic drama, and not a despatch. His manner of telling the story certainly differs from that of Herodotus; but the facts which he relates appear to be the same: and in all humility I cannot but suggest that if commentators would re-read their Herodotus and their Aeschylus in parallel columns, without (if this be not too much to ask) an *a priori* desire to catch Herodotus tripping, some of them, at least, would eventually be able to reconcile the historian with the tragedian. For Aeschylus no- where contradicts what is apparently the view of Herodotus,—that the Persians, or their main body, lay along the Attic coast opposite Salamis when the Greeks sailed out to attack them. Messrs. How and Wells (*quos honoris causa nomino*) say that this was probably not so, because, according to Aeschylus, "some time" elapsed before the Persians could see the Greek advance, and the strait is only one thousand five hundred yards wide. But as a matter of fact, Aeschylus does not say that some time elapsed. His expression is θοῶς δὲ πάντες ἦσαν ἐκφανεῖς ἰδεῖν—"*quickly* they were all plain to view."

INTRODUCTION

Herodotus' narrative of the manœuvres of Mardonius' and Pausanias' armies near Plataea is, like most descriptions of battles, not always very clear. It is full of detail; but as some of the localities mentioned cannot be quite certainly identified, the details are not always easy to understand; and it must be confessed that there are gaps in the story. For instance, we must presume (though meritorious efforts are made to explain the statement away) that Herodotus means what he says when he asserts in Ch. 15 that Mardonius' army occupied the ground "from Erythrae past Hysiae"; the Persians, therefore, were then on the right bank of the Asopus; yet soon afterwards they are, according to the historian's equally plain statement, on the left bank. Hence there are real obscurities; and the narrative is not without picturesque and perhaps rather surprising incidents; which some commentators (being rather like M. About's gendarme, persons whose business it is to see that nothing unusual happens in the locality) promptly dismiss as "camp gossip." Altogether, what with obscurity and camp gossip, scholars have given themselves a fairly free hand to reconstruct the operations before Plataea as they must have happened—unless indeed "someone had blundered," an hypothesis which, apparently, ought only to be accepted in the very last resort, and hardly then if its acceptance implies Herodotus' veracity. Reconstruction of history is an amusing game, and has its uses, especially in places of education, where it is played with distinguished success; yet one may still doubt whether rejection of what after all is our only real authority brings the public any nearer to knowing what did actually happen. Strategists and tacticians do make mistakes; thus, generally, are battles lost and won; and unreasonable incidents do occur. However, it is fair to say that most of the reconstruction of Salamis and Plataea was done before August, 1914.

But here, as elsewhere in his history, Herodotus' authority is much impaired by the presumption, popular since Plutarch, of a pro-Athenian bias which leads him to falsify history by exaggerating the merit of Athens at the expense of other states, especially Sparta. Now we may readily believe that if Herodotus lived for some time at Athens, he was willing enough to do ample justice to her achievements; but if he is to be charged with undue and unjust partiality, and consequent falsification, then it must be shown that the conduct which he attributes to Athens and to Sparta is somehow not consistent with what one would naturally expect, from the circumstances of the case, and from what we know, *aliunde*, about those two states. Scholars who criticise Herodotus on grounds of probability ought to be guided by their own canon. If a historian is to be discredited where his narrative does not accord with what is antecedently probable, then he must be allowed to gain credit where antecedent probability is on his side; and there is nothing in Herodotus' account of Athenian and Spartan actions during the campaigns of 480 and 479 which disagrees with the known character of either people. *Pace* the socialistic conception of an unrelieved similarity among all states and individuals, the Athenians of the fifth century, B.C., were an exceptional people; their record is not precisely the record of Boeotia or Arcadia; it seems fair to say, without appealing to Herodotus' testimony, that they were more gifted, and more enterprising, than most. The spirit of the Hellenic world is general,—intense local patriotism, intense fear and hatred of Oriental absolutism and strange worships,—was more alive among the Athenians, probably, than in any other Greek state. Sparta also had her share of these qualities; she too would make no terms with the Persian; only her methods of resistance were different. Primarily, each state was interested in its own safety. To Spartans—disinclined to methods other than traditional, and as yet unaccustomed to naval warfare—it seemed that Sparta could be best defended by blocking the land access to the Peloponnese; they would defend the Isthmus successfully, as they had tried and failed to defend Thermopylae. This meant, of course, the sacrifice of Attica; and naturally that was a sacrifice not to be made willingly by Athenians. Their only chance of saving or recovering Attica lay in fighting a naval action close to its coasts; nay, the abandonment of Salamis meant the exposure of their dependents to fresh dangers; therefore, they pressed for the policy of meeting and defeating the Persian where he lay by the Attic coast. This policy was to prove successful; and thereby, the Athenians incidentally accomplished what was undoubtedly also their object, the salvation of Hellas; but the primary purpose of both Sparta and Athens, both before Salamis and before Plataea (when the Athenians were naturally displeased by a plan which left Attica a prey to the enemy) was undoubtedly to do the best they could for themselves.

INTRODUCTION

This, in fact, was always the desire of all Greek states, as of most others in the history of the world; and as the actions of both Athens and Sparta were the natural outcome of that desire, there is no need to suspect Herodotus of unduly favouring the Athenians when he credits them with the plans which led to victory, or of unduly disparaging the Spartans when he describes their delays and hesitations before their march to Boeotia.

If the charge of an excessively pro-Athenian bias is to be sustained, it must be shown that Herodotus is prone to deny credit to the great rival of Athens. But there is no evidence of that. Sparta receives full measure from Herodotus. No Spartan could conceivably have been dissatisfied with the chapters on Thermopylae. Plataea is represented as a Spartan victory; it was the Spartans and Tegeans who in Herodotus' story were the real heroes of the day; the glory of winning "the greatest victory ever won" is definitely given to the Spartan commander-in-chief. On the other hand Themistocles, the typical Athenian, is treated with a severity which even appears to be rather gratuitous. It is true that Herodotus does not take pains to praise two other Greek states which at various times were at feud with Athens. He tells us that the Thebans "medized," a fact which has not, I believe, been denied, even by Plutarch; it is difficult to see what else he could have said. True, he reports a damaging story about the Corinthians and their failure to take part in the action of Salamis; but he adds, in his candid way, that nobody believes the story outside Attica.

The hypothesis of Herodotus' "obvious pro-

Athenian bias" is one which is bound to appeal to readers who are laudably afraid of being led away by hero-worship; but it has one fault—it lacks evidence.

With the crowning victory of Mycale, where for the first time a Persian army was defeated by a Greek within the boundaries of the Persian empire, the history of the war comes to an end. But the chapters which conclude Book IX are no anti-climax; they are congruous with the whole, part and parcel of the narrative, and as striking an example of Herodotus' supreme art as any passage in his history. What was it after all (a reader might be supposed to ask) that nerved most of the Greeks to resist Darius' and Xerxes' powerful armaments? The answer is plain; it was fear of the caprice and cruelty of Oriental despots, and desire to protect Greek temples from sacrilege. These concluding chapters illustrate and justify the Greek temper. The methods of Persian absolutism are vividly portrayed in the gruesome story of Xerxes' love and Masistes' death; and the crucified body of Artaÿctes, the defiler of temples, hangs by the Hellespontian shore, overlooking the scene of Xerxes' proudest achievement and display, as a warning to all sacrilegious invaders; so perish all who lay impious hands on the religion of Hellas! . . . The story is now complete. The play is played; and in the last chapter of the book, Cyrus the great protagonist of the drama is called before the curtain to speak its epilogue.

[Besides the authorities enumerated at the beginning of Vol. I of this translation, the following

INTRODUCTION

sources are recommended to the students of the campaigns of Salamis and Plataea :—

G. B. Grundy, *The Great Persian War*.

J. A. R. Munro, *Journal of Hellenic Studies*, xxii. 323–32 and xxiv. 144–65.

Prof. Goodwin, *Harvard Studies of Classical Philology*, 1906, pp. 75 ff.]

BIBLIOGRAPHICAL ADDENDUM

H. R. Immerwahr, *Form and Thought in Herodotus*, Chapel Hill 1966

J. L. Myres, *Herodotus: Father of History*, Oxford 1953

J. E. Powell, *Lexicon to Herodotus*, Cambridge 1938 (repr. 1960)

HERODOTUS

BOOK VIII

ΗΡΟΔΟΤΟΥ ΙΣΤΟΡΙΑΙ

Θ

1. Οἱ δὲ Ἑλλήνων ἐς τὸν ναυτικὸν στρατὸν ταχθέντες ἦσαν οἵδε, Ἀθηναῖοι μὲν νέας παρεχό-μενοι ἑκατὸν καὶ εἴκοσι καὶ ἑπτά· ὑπὸ δὲ ἀρετῆς τε καὶ προθυμίης Πλαταιέες ἄπειροι τῆς ναυτικῆς ἐόντες συνεπλήρουν τοῖσι Ἀθηναίοισι τὰς νέας. Κορίνθιοι δὲ τεσσεράκοντα νέας παρείχοντο, Μεγαρέες δὲ εἴκοσι. καὶ Χαλκιδέες ἐπλήρουν εἴκοσι, Ἀθηναίων σφι παρεχόντων τὰς νέας, Αἰγινῆται δὲ ὀκτωκαίδεκα, Σικυώνιοι δὲ δυοκαί-δεκα, Λακεδαιμόνιοι δὲ δέκα, Ἐπιδαύριοι δὲ ὀκτώ, Ἐρετριέες δὲ ἑπτά, Τροιζήνιοι δὲ πέντε, Στυρέες δὲ δύο, καὶ Κήιοι δύο τε νέας καὶ πεντηκοντέρους δύο· Λοκροὶ δέ σφι οἱ Ὀπούντιοι ἐπεβοήθεον πεντηκοντέρους ἔχοντες ἑπτά.
2. Ἦσαν μὲν οὗτοι οἱ στρατευόμενοι ἐπ' Ἀρτε-μίσιον, εἴρηται δέ μοι καὶ ὡς τὸ πλῆθος ἕκαστοι τῶν νεῶν παρείχοντο. ἀριθμὸς δὲ τῶν συλλεχθει-σέων νεῶν ἐπ' Ἀρτεμίσιον ἦν, πάρεξ τῶν πεντη-κοντέρων, διηκόσιαι καὶ ἑβδομήκοντα καὶ μία. τὸν δὲ στρατηγὸν τὸν τὸ μέγιστον κράτος ἔχοντα παρείχοντο Σπαρτιῆται Εὐρυβιάδην Εὐρυκλείδεω·

2

HERODOTUS

BOOK VIII

1. THE Greeks appointed to serve in the fleet were these: the Athenians furnished a hundred and twenty-seven ships; the Plataeans manned these ships with the Athenians, not that they had any knowledge of seamanship, but of mere valour and zeal. The Corinthians furnished forty ships, and the Megarians twenty; and the Chalcidians manned twenty, the Athenians furnishing the ships; the Aeginetans eighteen, the Sicyonians twelve, the Lacedaemonians ten, the Epidaurians eight, the Eretrians seven, the Troezenians five, the Styrians two, and the Ceans two, and two fifty-oared barks; and the Opuntian Locrians brought seven fifty-oared barks to their aid.

2. These were they who came to Artemisium for battle; and I have now shown how they severally furnished the whole sum. The number of ships that mustered at Artemisium was two hundred and seventy one, besides the fifty-oared barks. But the admiral who had the chief command was of the Spartans' providing, Eurybiades, son of Euryclides;

οἱ γὰρ σύμμαχοι οὐκ ἔφασαν, ἢν μὴ ὁ Λάκων
ἡγεμονεύῃ, Ἀθηναίοισι ἕψεσθαι ἡγεομένοισι, ἀλλὰ
λύσειν τὸ μέλλον ἔσεσθαι στράτευμα.
3. Ἐγένετο γὰρ κατ᾽ ἀρχὰς λόγος, πρὶν ἢ καὶ
ἐς Σικελίην πέμπειν ἐπὶ συμμαχίην, ὡς τὸ ναυτικὸν Ἀθηναίοισι χρεὸν εἴη ἐπιτράπειν. ἀντιβάντων
δὲ τῶν συμμάχων εἶκον οἱ Ἀθηναῖοι μέγα πεποιη-
μένοι περιεῖναι τὴν Ἑλλάδα καὶ γνόντες, εἰ στα-
σιάσουσι περὶ τῆς ἡγεμονίης, ὡς ἀπολέεται ἡ
Ἑλλάς, ὀρθὰ νοεῦντες· στάσις γὰρ ἔμφυλος
πολέμου ὁμοφρονέοντος τοσούτῳ κάκιον ἐστὶ ὅσῳ
πόλεμος εἰρήνης. ˉἐπιστάμενοι ὦν αὐτὸ τοῦτο
οὐκ ἀντέτεινον ἀλλ᾽ εἶκον, μέχρι ὅσου κάρτα ἐδέοντο αὐτῶν, ὡς διέδεξαν· ὡς γὰρ δὴ ὠσάμενοι τὸν
Πέρσην περὶ τῆς ἐκείνου ἤδη τὸν ἀγῶνα ἐποιεῦντο,
πρόφασιν τὴν Παυσανίεω ὕβριν προϊσχόμενοι
ἀπείλοντο τὴν ἡγεμονίην τοὺς Λακεδαιμονίους.
ἀλλὰ ταῦτα μὲν ὕστερον ἐγένετο.
4. Τότε δὲ οὗτοι οἱ καὶ ἐπ᾽ Ἀρτεμίσιον Ἑλλήνων ἀπικόμενοι ὡς εἶδον νέας τε πολλὰς κατα-
χθείσας ἐς τὰς Ἀφέτας καὶ στρατιῆς ἅπαντα
πλέα, ἐπεὶ αὐτοῖσι παρὰ δόξαν τὰ πρήγματα τῶν
βαρβάρων ἀπέβαινε ἢ ὡς αὐτοὶ κατεδόκεον, κα-
ταρρωδήσαντες δρησμὸν ἐβουλεύοντο ἀπὸ τοῦ
Ἀρτεμισίου ἔσω ἐς τὴν Ἑλλάδα. γνόντες δὲ
σφέας οἱ Εὐβοέες ταῦτα βουλευομένους ἐδέοντο
Εὐρυβιάδεω προσμεῖναι χρόνον ὀλίγον, ἔστ᾽ ἂν
αὐτοὶ τέκνα τε καὶ τοὺς οἰκέτας ὑπεκθέωνται. ὡς
δ᾽ οὐκ ἔπειθον, μεταβάντες τὸν Ἀθηναίων στρατηγὸν πείθουσι Θεμιστοκλέα ἐπὶ μισθῷ τριήκοντα

---

[1] After the capture of Byzantium in 476 B.C.

4

for the allies said, that if the Laconian were not
their leader they would rather make an end of the
fleet that was preparing than be led by the
Athenians.

3. For in the first days, before the sending to
Sicily for alliance there, there had been talk of
entrusting the command at sea to the Athenians.
But when the allies withstood this, the Athenians
waived their claim, deeming the safety of Hellas
of prime moment, and seeing that if they quarrelled
over the leadership Hellas must perish; wherein
they judged rightly; for civil strife is as much
worse than united war as war is worse than peace.
Knowing that, they gave ground and waived their
claim, but only so long as they had great need of
the others, as was shown; for when they had driven
the Persian back and the battle was no longer for
their territory but for his, they made a pretext of
Pausanias' highhandedness and took the command
away from the Lacedaemonians. But all that befel
later.[1]

4. But now, the Greeks who had at last come to
Artemisium saw a multitude of ships launched at
Aphetae, and armaments everywhere, and contrary
to all expectation the foreigner was shown to be
in far other case than they had supposed; wherefore
they lost heart and began to take counsel for flight
from Artemisium homewards into Hellas. Then
the Euboeans, seeing them to be thus planning,
entreated Eurybiades to wait a little while, till they
themselves should have brought away their children
and households. But when they could not prevail
with him, they essayed another way, and gave
Themistocles, the Athenian admiral, a bribe of

ταλάντοισι, ἐπ' ᾧ τε καταμείναντες πρὸ τῆς
Εὐβοίης ποιήσονται τὴν ναυμαχίην.

5. Ὁ δὲ Θεμιστοκλέης τοὺς Ἕλληνας ἐπισχεῖν
ὧδε ποιέει· Εὐρυβιάδῃ τούτων τῶν χρημάτων
μεταδιδοῖ πέντε τάλαντα ὡς παρ' ἑωυτοῦ δῆθεν
διδούς. ὡς δέ οἱ οὗτος ἀνεπέπειστο, Ἀδείμαντος
γὰρ ὁ Ὠκύτου ὁ Κορίνθιος στρατηγὸς τῶν λοιπῶν
ἤσπαιρε μοῦνος, φάμενος ἀποπλεύσεσθαί τε ἀπὸ
τοῦ Ἀρτεμισίου καὶ οὐ παραμενέειν, πρὸς δὴ τοῦτον
εἶπε ὁ Θεμιστοκλέης ἐπομόσας " Οὐ σύ γε ἡμέας
ἀπολείψεις, ἐπεί τοι ἐγὼ μέζω δῶρα δώσω ἢ βασιλεὺς ἄν τοι ὁ Μῆδων πέμψειε ἀπολιπόντι τοὺς
συμμάχους." ταῦτά τε ἅμα ἠγόρευε καὶ πέμπει
ἐπὶ τὴν νέα τὴν Ἀδειμάντου τάλαντα ἀργυρίου
τρία. οὗτοί τε δὴ πάντες δώροισι ἀναπεπεισμέ-
νοι ἦσαν καὶ τοῖσι Εὐβοεῦσι ἐκεχάριστο, αὐτός
τε ὁ Θεμιστοκλέης ἐκέρδηνε, ἐλάνθανε δὲ τὰ λοιπὰ
ἔχων, ἀλλ' ἠπιστέατο οἱ μεταλαβόντες τούτων
τῶν χρημάτων ἐκ τῶν Ἀθηνέων ἐλθεῖν ἐπὶ τῷ
λόγῳ τούτῳ τὰ χρήματα.

6. Οὕτω δὴ κατέμεινάν τε ἐν τῇ Εὐβοίῃ καὶ
ἐναυμάχησαν, ἐγένετο δὲ ὧδε. ἐπείτε δὴ ἐς τὰς
Ἀφέτας περὶ δείλην πρωίην γινομένην ἀπίκατο
οἱ βάρβαροι, πυθόμενοι μὲν ἔτι καὶ πρότερον περὶ
τὸ Ἀρτεμίσιον ναυλοχέειν νέας Ἑλληνίδας ὀλίγας,
τότε δὲ αὐτοὶ ἰδόντες, πρόθυμοι ἦσαν ἐπιχειρέειν,
εἴ κως ἕλοιεν αὐτάς. ἐκ μὲν δὴ τῆς ἀντίης προσπλέειν οὔ κώ σφι ἐδόκεε τῶνδε εἵνεκα, μή κως
ἰδόντες οἱ Ἕλληνες προσπλέοντας ἐς φυγὴν
ὁρμήσειαν φεύγοντάς τε εὐφρόνη καταλαμβάνῃ·
καὶ ἔμελλον δῆθεν ἐκφεύξεσθαι, ἔδει δὲ μηδὲ

thirty talents on the condition that the Greek fleet should remain there and fight, when they fought, to defend Euboea.

5. This was the way whereby Themistocles made the Greeks to stay where they were: he gave Eurybiades for his share five talents of that money, as though it were of his own that he gave it. Eurybiades being thus won over, none of the rest was of a resisting temper save only Adimantus, son of Ocytus, the Corinthian admiral, who said that he would not remain but sail away from Artemisium; to him said Themistocles, adding an oath thereto: "Nay, you of all men will not desert us; for I will give you a greater gift than the king of the Medes would send you for deserting your allies"; and with that saying he sent withal three talents of silver to Adimantus' ship. So these two were won over by gifts, the Euboeans got their desire, and Themistocles himself was the gainer; he kept the rest of the money, none knowing, but they that had received a part of it supposing that it had been sent for that intent by the Athenians.

6. So the Greeks abode off Euboea and there fought; and it came about as I shall show. Having arrived at Aphetae in the early part of the afternoon, the foreigners saw for themselves the few Greek ships that they had already heard were stationed off Artemisium, and they were eager to attack, that so they might take them. Now they were not yet minded to make an onfall front to front, for fear lest the Greeks should see them coming and take to flight, and night close upon them as they fled; it was their belief that the Greeks would save themselves by flight, and by the

πυρφόρον τῷ ἐκείνων λόγῳ ἐκφυγόντα περι-
γενέσθαι.

7. Πρὸς ταῦτα ὦν τάδε ἐμηχανῶντο· τῶν νεῶν
ἁπασέων ἀποκρίναντες διηκοσίας περιέπεμπον
ἔξωθεν Σκιάθου, ὡς ἂν μὴ ὀφθείησαν ὑπὸ τῶν
πολεμίων περιπλέουσαι Εὔβοιαν κατά τε Καφηρέα
καὶ περὶ Γεραιστὸν ἐς τὸν Εὔριπον, ἵνα δὴ περιλάβοιεν οἱ μὲν ταύτῃ ἀπικόμενοι καὶ φράξαντες
αὐτῶν τὴν ὀπίσω φέρουσαν ὁδόν, σφεῖς δὲ ἐπι-
σπόμενοι ἐξ ἐναντίης. ταῦτα βουλευσάμενοι
ἀπέπεμπον τῶν νεῶν τὰς ταχθείσας, αὐτοὶ οὐκ
ἐν νόῳ ἔχοντες ταύτης τῆς ἡμέρης τοῖσι Ἕλλησι
ἐπιθήσεσθαι, οὐδὲ πρότερον ἢ τὸ σύνθημά σφι
ἔμελλε φανήσεσθαι παρὰ τῶν περιπλεόντων ὡς
ἡκόντων. ταύτας μὲν δὴ περιέπεμπον, τῶν δὲ
λοιπέων νεῶν ἐν τῇσι Ἀφέτῃσι ἐποιεῦντο ἀριθμόν.

8. Ἐν δὲ τούτῳ τῷ χρόνῳ ἐν ᾧ οὗτοι ἀριθμὸν
ἐποιεῦντο τῶν νεῶν, ἦν γὰρ ἐν τῷ στρατοπέδῳ
τούτῳ Σκυλλίης Σκιωναῖος δύτης τῶν τότε
ἀνθρώπων ἄριστος, ὃς καὶ ἐν τῇ ναυηγίῃ τῇ κατὰ
Πήλιον γενομένῃ πολλὰ μὲν ἔσωσε τῶν χρημάτων
τοῖσι Πέρσῃσι, πολλὰ δὲ καὶ αὐτὸς περιεβάλετο·
οὗτος ὁ Σκυλλίης ἐν νόῳ μὲν εἶχε ἄρα καὶ πρότερον αὐτομολήσειν ἐς τοὺς Ἕλληνας, ἀλλ' οὐ
γάρ οἱ παρέσχε ὡς τότε. ὅτεῳ μὲν δὴ τρόπῳ
τὸ ἐνθεῦτεν ἔτι ἀπίκετο ἐς τοὺς Ἕλληνας, οὐκ
ἔχω εἰπεῖν ἀτρεκέως, θωμάζω δὲ εἰ τὰ λεγόμενα
ἐστὶ ἀληθέα· λέγεται γὰρ ὡς ἐξ Ἀφετέων δὺς
ἐς τὴν θάλασσαν οὐ πρότερον ἀνέσχε πρὶν ἢ
ἀπίκετο ἐπὶ τὸ Ἀρτεμίσιον, σταδίους μάλιστά
κῃ τούτους ἐς ὀγδώκοντα διὰ τῆς θαλάσσης

8

Persian purpose not so much as a firebearer [1] of them must be saved alive.

7. Wherefore this was the plan that they devised. Separating two hundred ships from the whole number, they sent them to cruise outside Sciathus (that so the enemies might not see them sailing round Euboea) and by way of Caphereus round Geraestus to the Euripus, so that they might catch the Greeks between them, the one part holding that course and barring the retreat, and they themselves attacking in front. Thus planning, they sent the appointed ships on their way, purposing for themselves to make no attack upon the Greeks that day, nor before the signal should be seen whereby the ships that sailed round were to declare their coming. So they sent those ships to sail round, and set about numbering the rest at Aphetae.

8. Now at the time of their numbering the ships, there was in the fleet one Scyllias, a man of Scione; he was the best diver of the time, and in the shipwreck at Pelion he had saved for the Persians much of their possessions and won much withal for himself; this Scyllias had ere now, it would seem, purposed to desert to the Greeks, but he never had had so fair an occasion as now. By what means he did thereafter at last make his way to the Greeks, I cannot with exactness say; but if the story be true it is marvellous indeed; for it is said that he dived into the sea at Aphetae and never rose above it till he came to Artemisium, thus passing underneath the sea for about eighty furlongs.

---

[1] The πυρφόρος carried the sacred fire which was always kept alight for the sacrifices of the army; his person was supposed to be inviolable.

διεξελθών. λέγεται μέν νυν καὶ ἄλλα ψευδέσι
εἴκελα περὶ τοῦ ἀνδρὸς τούτου, τὰ δὲ μετεξέτερα
ἀληθέα· περὶ μέντοι τούτου γνώμη μοι ἀποδεδέχθω
πλοίῳ μιν ἀπικέσθαι ἐπὶ τὸ Ἀρτεμίσιον. ὡς δὲ
ἀπίκετο, αὐτίκα ἐσήμηνε τοῖσι στρατηγοῖσι τήν
τε ναυηγίην ὡς γένοιτο, καὶ τὰς περιπεμφθείσας
τῶν νεῶν περὶ Εὔβοιαν.

9. Τοῦτο δὲ ἀκούσαντες οἱ Ἕλληνες λόγον
σφίσι αὐτοῖσι ἐδίδοσαν. πολλῶν δὲ λεχθέντων
ἐνίκα τὴν ἡμέρην ἐκείνην αὐτοῦ μείναντάς τε καὶ
αὐλισθέντας, μετέπειτα νύκτα μέσην παρέντας
πορεύεσθαι καὶ ἀπαντᾶν τῇσι περιπλεούσῃσι
τῶν νεῶν. μετὰ δὲ τοῦτο, ὡς οὐδείς σφι ἐπέπλεε,
δείλην ὀψίην γινομένην τῆς ἡμέρης φυλάξαντες
αὐτοὶ ἐπανέπλεον ἐπὶ τοὺς βαρβάρους, ἀπόπειραν
αὐτῶν ποιήσασθαι βουλόμενοι τῆς τε μάχης καὶ
τοῦ διεκπλόου.

10. Ὁρῶντες δὲ σφέας οἵ τε ἄλλοι στρατιῶται
οἱ Ξέρξεω καὶ οἱ στρατηγοὶ ἐπιπλέοντας νηυσὶ
ὀλίγῃσι, πάγχυ σφι μανίην ἐπενείκαντες ἀνῆγον
καὶ αὐτοὶ τὰς νέας, ἐλπίσαντες σφέας εὐπετέως
αἱρήσειν, οἰκότα κάρτα ἐλπίσαντες, τὰς μέν γε
τῶν Ἑλλήνων ὁρῶντες ὀλίγας νέας, τὰς δὲ ἑωυτῶν
πλήθεΐ τε πολλαπλησίας καὶ ἄμεινον πλεούσας.
καταφρονήσαντες ταῦτα ἐκυκλοῦντο αὐτοὺς ἐς
μέσον. ὅσοι μέν νυν τῶν Ἰώνων ἦσαν εὔνοοι
τοῖσι Ἕλλησι, ἀέκοντές τε ἐστρατεύοντο συμφορήν
τε ἐποιεῦντο μεγάλην ὁρῶντες περιεχομένους
αὐτοὺς καὶ ἐπιστάμενοι ὡς οὐδεὶς αὐτῶν ἀπο-
νοστήσει· οὕτω ἀσθενέα σφι ἐφαίνετο εἶναι τὰ
τῶν Ἑλλήνων πρήγματα. ὅσοισι δὲ καὶ ἡδομένοισι ἦν τὸ γινόμενον, ἅμιλλαν ἐποιεῦντο ὅκως

There are many tales of this man, some like lies and some true; but as concerning the present business it is my opinion, which I hereby declare, that he came to Artemisium in a boat. Having then come, he straightway told the admirals the story of the shipwreck, and of the ships that had been sent round Euboea.

9. Hearing that, the Greeks took counsel together; there was much speaking, but the opinion prevailed that they should abide and encamp where they were for that day, and thereafter when it should be past midnight put to sea and meet the ships that were sailing round. But presently, none attacking them, they waited for the late afternoon of the day and themselves advanced their ships against the foreigner, desiring to put to the proof his fashion of fighting and the art of breaking the line.[1]

10. When Xerxes' men and their generals saw the Greeks bearing down on them with but a few ships, they deemed them assuredly mad, and themselves put out to sea, thinking to win an easy victory; which expectation was very reasonable, as they saw the Greek ships so few, and their own many times more numerous and more seaworthy. With this assurance, they hemmed in the Greeks in their midst. Now as many Ionians as were friendly to the Greeks came unwillingly to the war, and were sore distressed to see the Greeks surrounded, supposing that not one of them would return home; so powerless did the Greeks seem to them to be. But those who were glad of the business vied each with each that he might be the first to take an

---

[1] For the διέκπλους see Bk. VI. ch. 12.

αὐτὸς ἕκαστος πρῶτος νέα Ἀττικὴν ἑλὼν παρὰ
βασιλέος δῶρα λάμψεται· Ἀθηναίων γὰρ αὐτοῖσι
λόγος ἦν πλεῖστος ἀνὰ τὰ στρατόπεδα.

11. Τοῖσι δὲ Ἕλλησι ὡς ἐσήμηνε, πρῶτα μὲν
ἀντίπρωροι τοῖσι βαρβάροισι γενόμενοι ἐς τὸ
μέσον τὰς πρύμνας συνήγαγον, δεύτερα δὲ
σημήναντος ἔργου εἴχοντο ἐν ὀλίγῳ περ ἀπολαμφθέντες καὶ κατὰ στόμα. ἐνθαῦτα τριήκοντα
νέας αἱρέουσι τῶν βαρβάρων καὶ τὸν Γόργου τοῦ
Σαλαμινίων βασιλέος ἀδελφεὸν Φιλάονα τὸν
Χέρσιος, λόγιμον ἐόντα ἐν τῷ στρατοπέδῳ ἄνδρα.
πρῶτος δὲ Ἑλλήνων νέα τῶν πολεμίων εἷλε
ἀνὴρ Ἀθηναῖος Λυκομήδης Αἰσχραίου, καὶ τὸ
ἀριστήιον ἔλαβε οὗτος. τοὺς δ᾽ ἐν τῇ ναυμαχίῃ
ταύτῃ ἑτεραλκέως ἀγωνιζομένους νὺξ ἐπελθοῦσα
διέλυσε. οἱ μὲν δὴ Ἕλληνες ἐπὶ τὸ Ἀρτεμίσιον
ἀπέπλεον, οἱ δὲ βάρβαροι ἐς τὰς Ἀφέτας, πολλὸν
παρὰ δόξαν ἀγωνισάμενοι. ἐν ταύτῃ τῇ ναυμαχίῃ Ἀντίδωρος Λήμνιος μοῦνος τῶν σὺν βασιλέι
Ἑλλήνων ἐόντων αὐτομολέει ἐς τοὺς Ἕλληνας,
καὶ οἱ Ἀθηναῖοι διὰ τοῦτο τὸ ἔργον ἔδοσαν αὐτῷ
χῶρον ἐν Σαλαμῖνι.

12. Ὡς δὲ εὐφρόνη ἐγεγόνεε, ἦν μὲν τῆς ὥρης
μέσον θέρος, ἐγίνετο δὲ ὕδωρ τε ἄπλετον διὰ
πάσης τῆς νυκτὸς καὶ σκληραὶ βρονταὶ ἀπὸ
τοῦ Πηλίου· οἱ δὲ νεκροὶ καὶ τὰ ναυήγια ἐξεφέροντο ἐς τὰς Ἀφέτας, καὶ περί τε τὰς πρώρας
τῶν νεῶν εἱλέοντο καὶ ἐτάρασσον τοὺς ταρσοὺς
τῶν κωπέων. οἱ δὲ στρατιῶται οἱ ταύτῃ ἀκούοντες
ταῦτα ἐς φόβον κατιστέατο, ἐλπίζοντες πάγχυ
ἀπολέεσθαι ἐς οἷα κακὰ ἦκον. πρὶν γὰρ ἢ καὶ
ἀναπνεῦσαι σφέας ἔκ τε τῆς ναυηγίης καὶ τοῦ

Attic ship and receive gifts from the king; for it was the Athenians of whom there was most talk in the fleet.

11. But the Greeks, when the signal was given them, first drew the sterns of their ships together, their prows turned towards the foreigners; then at the second signal they put their hands to the work, albeit they were hemmed in within a narrow space and fought front to front. There they took thirty of the foreigners' ships and the brother of Gorgus king of Salamis withal, even Philaon son of Chersis, a man of note in the fleet. The first Greek to take an enemy ship was an Athenian, Lycomedes, son of Aeschraeus, and he it was who received the prize for valour. They fought that seafight with doubtful issue, and nightfall ended the battle; the Greeks sailed back to Artemisium, and the foreigners to Aphetae, after faring far below their hopes in the fight. In that battle Antidorus of Lemnos deserted to the Greeks, alone of all the Greeks that were with the king; and for that the Athenians gave him lands in Salamis.

12. When darkness came on, the season being then midsummer, there was abundance of rain all through the night and violent thunderings from Pelion; and the dead and the wrecks were driven towards Aphetae, where they were entangled with the ships' prows and fouled the blades of the oars. The ships' companies that were there were dismayed by the noise of this, and looked in their present evil case for utter destruction; for before they were

χειμῶνος τοῦ γενομένου κατὰ Πήλιον, ὑπέλαβε
ναυμαχίη καρτερή, ἐκ δὲ τῆς ναυμαχίης ὄμβρος
τε λάβρος καὶ ῥεύματα ἰσχυρὰ ἐς θάλασσαν
ὁρμημένα βρονταί τε σκληραί.

13. Καὶ τούτοισι μὲν τοιαύτη ἡ νὺξ ἐγίνετο,
τοῖσι δὲ ταχθεῖσι αὐτῶν περιπλέειν Εὔβοιαν ἡ
αὐτή περ ἐοῦσα νὺξ πολλὸν ἦν ἔτι ἀγριωτέρη,
τοσούτῳ ὅσῳ ἐν πελάγεϊ φερομένοισι ἐπέπιπτε,
καὶ τὸ τέλος σφι ἐγίνετο ἄχαρι. ὡς γὰρ δὴ
πλέουσι αὐτοῖσι χειμών τε καὶ τὸ ὕδωρ ἐπεγίνετο
ἐοῦσι κατὰ τὰ Κοῖλα τῆς Εὐβοίης, φερόμενοι τῷ
πνεύματι καὶ οὐκ εἰδότες τῇ ἐφέροντο ἐξέπιπτον
πρὸς τὰς πέτρας· ἐποιέετό τε πᾶν ὑπὸ τοῦ θεοῦ
ὅκως ἂν ἐξισωθείη τῷ Ἑλληνικῷ τὸ Περσικὸν
μηδὲ πολλῷ πλέον εἴη.

14. Οὗτοι μέν νυν περὶ τὰ Κοῖλα τῆς Εὐβοίης
διεφθείροντο· οἱ δ' ἐν Ἀφέτῃσι βάρβαροι, ὥς
σφι ἀσμένοισι ἡμέρη ἐπέλαμψε, ἀτρέμας τε
εἶχον τὰς νέας καί σφι ἀπεχρᾶτο κακῶς πρήσ-
σουσι ἡσυχίην ἄγειν ἐν τῷ παρεόντι. τοῖσι δε
Ἕλλησι ἐπεβοήθεον νέες τρεῖς καὶ πεντήκοντα
Ἀττικαί. αὗταί τε δή σφεας ἐπέρρωσαν ἀπι-
κόμεναι καὶ ἅμα ἀγγελίη ἐλθοῦσα, ὡς τῶν βαρβάρων οἱ περιπλέοντες τὴν Εὔβοιαν πάντες εἴησαν
διεφθαρμένοι ὑπὸ τοῦ γενομένου χειμῶνος. φυλάξαντες δὴ τὴν αὐτὴν ὥρην, πλέοντες ἐπέπεσον
νηυσὶ Κιλίσσῃσι· ταύτας δὲ διαφθείραντες, ὡς
εὐφρόνη ἐγίνετο, ἀπέπλεον ὀπίσω ἐπὶ τὸ
Ἀρτεμίσιον.

15. Τρίτῃ δὲ ἡμέρῃ δεινόν τι ποιησάμενοι οἱ
στρατηγοὶ τῶν βαρβάρων νέας οὕτω σφι ὀλίγας
λυμαίνεσθαι, καὶ τὸ ἀπὸ Ξέρξεω δειμαίνοντες,

recovered after the shipwreck and the storm off
Pelion, they next must abide a stubborn sea-fight, and
after the sea-fight rushing rain and mighty torrents
pouring seaward and violent thunderings.

13. Thus did the night deal with them; but to
those that were appointed to sail round Euboea that
same night was much crueller yet, inasmuch as it
caught them on the open sea; and an evil end they
had. For the storm and the rain coming on them
in their course off the Hollows of Euboea, they
were driven by the wind they knew not whither,
and were cast upon the rocks. All this was the
work of heaven's providence, that so the Persian
power might be more equally matched with the
Greek, and not much greater than it.

14. So these perished at the Hollows of Euboea.
But the foreigners at Aphetae, when to their great
comfort the day dawned, kept their ships unmoved,
being in their evil plight well content to do nothing
for the nonce; and fifty-three Attic ships came to
aid the Greeks, who were heartened by the ships'
coming and the news brought withal that the
foreigners sailing round Euboea had all perished
in the late storm. They waited then for the same
hour as before, and putting to sea fell upon certain
Cilician ships; which having destroyed, when darkness came on, they returned back to Artemisium.

15. But on the third day, the foreign admirals, ill
brooking that so few ships should do them hurt,
and fearing Xerxes' anger, waited no longer for the

HERODOTUS

οὐκ ἀνέμειναν ἔτι τοὺς Ἕλληνας μάχης ἄρξαι,
ἀλλὰ παρακελευσάμενοι κατὰ μέσον ἡμέρης
ἀνῆγον τὰς νέας. συνέπιπτε δὲ ὥστε τὰς αὐτὰς
ἡμέρας τάς τε ναυμαχίας γίνεσθαι ταύτας καὶ
τὰς πεζομαχίας τὰς ἐν Θερμοπύλῃσι. ἦν δὲ
πᾶς ὁ ἀγὼν τοῖσι κατὰ θάλασσαν περὶ τοῦ
Εὐρίπου, ὥσπερ τοῖσι ἀμφὶ Λεωνίδην τὴν ἐσβολὴν
φυλάσσειν. οἱ μὲν δὴ παρεκελεύοντο ὅκως μὴ
παρήσουσι ἐς τὴν Ἑλλάδα τοὺς βαρβάρους, οἱ
δ' ὅκως τὸ Ἑλληνικὸν στράτευμα διαφθείραντες
τοῦ πόρου κρατήσουσι. ὡς δὲ ταξάμενοι οἱ
Ξέρξεω ἐπέπλεον, οἱ Ἕλληνες ἀτρέμας εἶχον
πρὸς τῷ Ἀρτεμισίῳ. οἱ δὲ βάρβαροι μηνοειδὲς
ποιήσαντες τῶν νεῶν ἐκυκλοῦντο, ὡς περιλάβοιεν
αὐτούς.

16. Ἐνθεῦτεν οἱ Ἕλληνες ἐπανέπλεόν τε καὶ
συνέμισγον. ἐν ταύτῃ τῇ ναυμαχίῃ παραπλήσιοι
ἀλλήλοισι ἐγίνοντο. ὁ γὰρ Ξέρξεω στρατὸς ὑπὸ
μεγάθεός τε καὶ πλήθεος αὐτὸς ὑπ' ἑωυτοῦ
ἔπιπτε, ταρασσομενέων τε τῶν νεῶν καὶ περι-
πιπτουσέων περὶ ἀλλήλας· ὅμως μέντοι ἀντεῖχε
καὶ οὐκ εἶκε· δεινὸν γὰρ χρῆμα ἐποιεῦντο ὑπὸ
νεῶν ὀλιγέων ἐς φυγὴν τράπεσθαι. πολλαὶ μὲν
δὴ τῶν Ἑλλήνων νέες διεφθείροντο πολλοὶ δὲ
ἄνδρες, πολλῷ δ' ἔτι πλεῦνες νέες τε τῶν βαρβάρων καὶ ἄνδρες. οὕτω δὲ ἀγωνιζόμενοι διέστησαν
χωρὶς ἑκάτεροι.

17. Ἐν ταύτῃ τῇ ναυμαχίῃ Αἰγύπτιοι μὲν τῶν
Ξέρξεω στρατιωτέων ἠρίστευσαν, οἳ ἄλλα τε
μεγάλα ἔργα ἀπεδέξαντο καὶ νέας αὐτοῖσι ἀνδράσι
εἷλον Ἑλληνίδας πέντε. τῶν δὲ Ἑλλήνων κατὰ
ταύτην τὴν ἡμέρην ἠρίστευσαν Ἀθηναῖοι καὶ

16

Greeks to begin the fight, but gave the word and put out to sea about midday. And it so fell out that these sea-battles were fought through the same days as the land-battles at Thermopylae; the seamen's whole endeavour was to hold the Euripus, as Leonidas' men strove to guard the passage; the Greek battle word was to give the foreigner no entry into Hellas, and the Persian to destroy the Greek host and win the strait. So when Xerxes' men ordered their battle and came on, the Greeks abode in their place off Artemisium; and the foreigners made a half circle of their ships, and strove to encircle and enclose them round.

16. At that the Greeks charged and joined battle. In that sea-fight both had equal success. For Xerxes' fleet wrought itself harm by its numbers and multitude: the ships were thrown into confusion and ran foul of each other; nevertheless they held fast, nor yielded, for they could not bear to be put to flight by a few ships. Many were the Greek ships and men that there perished, and far more yet of the foreigners' ships and men; thus they battled, till they drew off and parted each from other.

17. In that sea-fight of all Xerxes' fighters the Egyptians bore themselves best; besides other great feats of arms that they achieved, they took five Greek ships and their crews withal. Of the Greeks on that day the Athenians bore themselves best;

'Αθηναίων Κλεινίης ὁ 'Αλκιβιάδεω, ὃς δαπάνην
οἰκηίην παρεχόμενος ἐστρατεύετο ἀνδράσι τε
διηκοσίοισι καὶ οἰκηίῃ νηί.
18. Ὡς δὲ διέστησαν, ἄσμενοι ἑκάτεροι ἐς
ὅρμον ἠπείγοντο. οἱ δὲ Ἕλληνες ὡς διακριθέντες
ἐκ τῆς ναυμαχίης ἀπηλλάχθησαν, τῶν μὲν νεκρῶν
καὶ τῶν ναυηγίων ἐπεκράτεον, τρηχέως δὲ περιε-
φθέντες, καὶ οὐκ ἥκιστα 'Αθηναῖοι τῶν αἱ ἡμίσεαι
τῶν νεῶν τετρωμέναι ἦσαν, δρησμὸν δὴ ἐβούλευον
ἔσω ἐς τὴν Ἑλλάδα.
19. Νόῳ δὲ λαβὼν ὁ Θεμιστοκλέης ὡς εἰ
ἀπορραγείη ἀπὸ τοῦ βαρβάρου τό τε Ἰωνικὸν
φῦλον καὶ τὸ Καρικόν, οἷοί τε εἴησαν ἂν τῶν
λοιπῶν κατύπερθε γενέσθαι, ἐλαυνόντων τῶν
Εὐβοέων πρόβατα ἐπὶ τὴν θάλασσαν ταύτην,
συλλέξας τοὺς στρατηγοὺς ἔλεγέ σφι ὡς δοκέοι
ἔχειν τινὰ παλάμην, τῇ ἐλπίζοι τῶν βασιλέος
συμμάχων ἀποστήσειν τοὺς ἀρίστους. ταῦτα
μέν νυν ἐς τοσοῦτο παρεγύμνου, ἐπὶ δὲ τοῖσι
κατήκουσι πρήγμασι τάδε ποιητέα σφι εἶναι
ἔλεγε, τῶν τε προβάτων τῶν Εὐβοϊκῶν καταθύειν
ὅσα τις ἐθέλοι· κρέσσον γὰρ εἶναι τὴν στρατιὴν
ἔχειν ἢ τοὺς πολεμίους· παραίνεέ τε προειπεῖν
τοῖσι ἑωυτῶν ἑκάστους πῦρ ἀνακαίειν· κομιδῆς
δὲ πέρι τὴν ὥρην αὐτῷ μελήσειν, ὥστε ἀσινέας
ἀπικέσθαι ἐς τὴν Ἑλλάδα. ταῦτα ἤρεσέ σφι
ποιέειν, καὶ αὐτίκα πῦρ ἀνακαυσάμενοι ἐτράποντο
πρὸς τὰ πρόβατα.
20. Οἱ γὰρ Εὐβοέες, παραχρησάμενοι τὸν
Βάκιδος χρησμὸν ὡς οὐδὲν λέγοντα, οὔτε τι
ἐξεκομίσαντο οὐδὲν οὔτε προσεσάξαντο ὡς παρε-

and of the Athenians Clinias son of Alcibiades; he brought to the war two hundred men and a ship of his own, all at his private charges.

18. So they parted and each right gladly made haste to his own anchorage. When the Greeks had drawn off and come out of the battle, they were left masters of the dead and the wrecks; but they had had rough handling, and chiefly the Athenians, half of whose ships had suffered hurt; and now their counsel was to flee to the inner waters of Hellas.[1]

19. Themistocles bethought him that if the Ionian and Carian nations were rent away from the foreigners, the Greeks might be strong enough to get the upper hand of the rest. Now it was the wont of the Euboeans to drive their flocks down to the sea there. Wherefore gathering the admirals together he told them that he thought he had a device whereby he hoped to draw away the best of the king's allies. So much he revealed for the nonce; but in the present turn of affairs this (he said) they must do: let everyone slay as many as he would from the Euboean flocks; it was better that the fleet should have them, than the enemy. Moreover he counselled them each to bid his men to light a fire; as for the time of their going thence, he would take such thought for that as should bring them scathless to Hellas. All this they agreed to do; and forthwith they lit fires and then laid hands on the flocks.

20. For the Euboeans had neglected the oracle of Bacis, deeming it void of meaning, and neither by carrying away nor by bringing in anything had

---

[1] This means, I suppose, to the seas nearer their homes.

σομένου σφι πολέμου, περιπετέα τε ἐποιήσαντο
σφίσι αὐτοῖσι τὰ πρήγματα. Βάκιδι γὰρ ὧδε
ἔχει περὶ τούτων ὁ χρησμός.

φράζεο, βαρβαρόφωνος ὅταν ζυγὸν εἰς ἅλα
    βάλλῃ
βύβλινον, Εὐβοίης ἀπέχειν πολυμηκάδας
    αἶγας.

τούτοισι οὐδὲν τοῖσι ἔπεσι χρησαμένοισι ἐν τοῖσι
τότε παρεοῦσί τε καὶ προσδοκίμοισι κακοῖσι
παρῆν σφι συμφορῇ χρᾶσθαι πρὸς τὰ μέγιστα.
21. Οἱ μὲν δὴ ταῦτα ἔπρησσον, παρῆν δὲ ὁ
ἐκ Τρηχῖνος κατάσκοπος. ἦν μὲν γὰρ ἐπ' Ἀρτεμισίῳ κατάσκοπος Πολύας, γένος Ἀντικυρεύς,
τῷ προσετέτακτο, καὶ εἶχε πλοῖον κατήρες ἕτοι-
μον, εἰ παλήσειε ὁ ναυτικὸς στρατός, σημαίνειν
τοῖσι ἐν Θερμοπύλῃσι ἐοῦσι· ὡς δ' αὔτως ἦν
Ἀβρώνιχος ὁ Λυσικλέος Ἀθηναῖος καὶ παρὰ
Λεωνίδῃ ἕτοιμος τοῖσι ἐπ' Ἀρτεμισίῳ ἐοῦσι
ἀγγέλλειν τριηκοντέρῳ, ἤν τι καταλαμβάνῃ νεώτερον τὸν πεζόν. οὗτος ὢν ὁ Ἀβρώνιχος ἀπι-
κόμενός σφι ἐσήμαινε τὰ γεγονότα περὶ Λεωνίδην
καὶ τὸν στρατὸν αὐτοῦ. οἱ δὲ ὡς ἐπύθοντο
ταῦτα, οὐκέτι ἐς ἀναβολὰς ἐποιεῦντο τὴν ἀπο-
χώρησιν, ἐκομίζοντο δὲ ὡς ἕκαστοι ἐτάχθησαν,
Κορίνθιοι πρῶτοι, ὕστατοι δὲ Ἀθηναῖοι.
22. Ἀθηναίων δὲ νέας τὰς ἄριστα πλεούσας
ἐπιλεξάμενος Θεμιστοκλέης ἐπορεύετο περὶ τὰ
πότιμα ὕδατα, ἐντάμνων ἐν τοῖσι λίθοισι γράμματα, τὰ Ἴωνες ἐπελθόντες τῇ ὑστεραίῃ ἡμέρῃ
ἐπὶ τὸ Ἀρτεμίσιον ἐπελέξαντο. τὰ δὲ γράμματα
τάδε ἔλεγε. "Ἄνδρες Ἴωνες, οὐ ποιέετε δίκαια

they shown that they feared an enemy's coming;
whereby they were the cause of their own destruction; for Bacis' oracle concerning this matter runs
thus:

"Whenso a strange-tongued man on the waves
    casts yoke of papyrus,
  Then let bleating goats from coasts Euboean be
    banished."

To these verses the Euboeans gave no heed; but
in the evils then present and soon to come they
could not but heed their dire calamity.

21. While the Greeks were doing as I have said,
there came to them the watcher from Trachis. For
there was a watcher at Artemisium, one Polyas, a
native of Anticyra, who was charged (and had a
rowing boat standing ready therefor), if the fleet
should be at grips, to declare it to the men at
Thermopylae; and in like manner, if any ill should
befall the land army, Abronichus son of Lysicles,
an Athenian, was with Leonidas, ready for his part
to bring the news in a thirty-oared bark to the
Greeks at Artemisium. So this Abronichus came
and declared to them the fate of Leonidas and his
army; which when the Greeks learnt, they no
longer delayed their departure, but went their ways
in their appointed order, the Corinthians first, and
last of all the Athenians.

22. But Themistocles picked out the seaworthiest
Athenian ships and went about to the places of
drinking water, where he engraved on the rocks
writing which the Ionians read on the next day
when they came to Artemisium. This was what
the writing said: "Men of Ionia, you do wrongly

ἐπὶ τοὺς πατέρας στρατευόμενοι καὶ τὴν Ἑλλάδα
καταδουλούμενοι. ἀλλὰ μάλιστα μὲν πρὸς ἡμέων
γίνεσθε· εἰ δὲ ὑμῖν ἐστι τοῦτο μὴ δυνατὸν ποιῆσαι,
ὑμεῖς δὲ ἔτι καὶ νῦν ἐκ τοῦ μέσου ἡμῖν ἔζεσθε καὶ
αὐτοὶ καὶ τῶν Καρῶν δέεσθε τὰ αὐτὰ ὑμῖν ποιέειν.
εἰ δὲ μηδέτερον τούτων οἷόν τε γίνεσθαι, ἀλλ᾽ ὑπ᾽
ἀναγκαίης μέζονος κατέζευχθε ἢ ὥστε ἀπίστασθαι,
ὑμεῖς δὲ ἐν τῷ ἔργῳ, ἐπεὰν συμμίσγωμεν, ἐθελο-
κακέετε μεμνημένοι ὅτι ἀπ᾽ ἡμέων γεγόνατε καὶ
ὅτι ἀρχῆθεν ἡ ἔχθρη πρὸς τὸν βάρβαρον ἀπ᾽
ὑμέων ἡμῖν γέγονε." Θεμιστοκλέης δὲ ταῦτα
ἔγραφε, δοκέειν ἐμοί, ἐπ᾽ ἀμφότερα νοέων, ἵνα ἢ
λαθόντα τὰ γράμματα βασιλέα Ἴωνας ποιήσῃ
μεταβαλεῖν καὶ γενέσθαι πρὸς ἑωυτῶν, ἢ ἐπείτε
ἀνενειχθῇ καὶ διαβληθῇ πρὸς Ξέρξην, ἀπίστους
ποιήσῃ τοὺς Ἴωνας καὶ τῶν ναυμαχιέων αὐτοὺς
ἀπόσχῃ.

23. Θεμιστοκλέης μὲν ταῦτα ἐνέγραψε· τοῖσι δὲ
βαρβάροισι αὐτίκα μετὰ ταῦτα πλοίῳ ἦλθε ἀνὴρ
Ἱστιαιεὺς ἀγγέλλων τὸν δρησμὸν τὸν ἀπ᾽ Ἀρτεμισίου τῶν Ἑλλήνων. οἱ δ᾽ ὑπ᾽ ἀπιστίης τὸν
μὲν ἀγγέλλοντα εἶχον ἐν φυλακῇ, νέας δὲ ταχέας
ἀπέστειλαν προκατοψομένας· ἀπαγγειλάντων δὲ
τούτων τὰ ἦν, οὕτω δὴ ἅμα ἡλίῳ σκιδναμένῳ
πᾶσα ἡ στρατιὴ ἐπέπλεε ἁλὴς ἐπὶ τὸ Ἀρτεμίσιον.
ἐπισχόντες δὲ ἐν τούτῳ τῷ χώρῳ μέχρι μέσου
ἡμέρης, τὸ ἀπὸ τούτου ἔπλεον ἐς Ἱστιαίην· ἀπικόμενοι δὲ τὴν πόλιν ἔσχον τῶν Ἱστιαιέων, καὶ
τῆς Ἐλλοπίης μοίρης γῆς δὲ τῆς Ἱστιαιώτιδος
τὰς παραθαλασσίας χώρας πάσας ἐπέδραμον.

24. Ἐνθαῦτα δὲ τούτων ἐόντων, Ξέρξης ἑτοι-

to fight against the land of your fathers and bring slavery upon Hellas. It were best of all that you should join yourselves to us; but if that be impossible for you, then do you even now withdraw yourselves from the war, and entreat the Carians to do the same as you. If neither of these things may be, and you are fast bound by such constraint that you cannot rebel, yet we pray you not to use your full strength in the day of battle; be mindful that you are our sons and that our quarrel with the foreigner was of your making in the beginning." To my thinking Themistocles thus wrote with a double intent, that if the king knew nought of the writing it might make the Ionians to change sides and join with the Greeks, and that if the writing were maliciously reported to Xerxes he might thereby be led to mistrust the Ionians, and keep them out of the sea-fights.

23. Such was Themistocles' writing. Immediately after this there came to the foreigners a man of Histiaea in a boat, telling them of the flight of the Greeks from Artemisium. Not believing this, they kept the bringer of the news in ward, and sent swift ships to spy out the matter; and when the crews of these brought word of the truth, on learning that, the whole armada at the first spreading of sunlight sailed all together to Artemisium, where having waited till midday, they next sailed to Histiaea, and on their coming took possession of the Histiaeans' city, and overran all the villages on the seaboard of the Ellopian [1] region, which is the land of Histiaea.

24. While they were there, Xerxes sent a herald

[1] The northern half of Euboea, including the district of Histiaea.

μασάμενος τὰ περὶ τοὺς νεκροὺς ἔπεμπε ἐς τὸν
ναυτικὸν στρατὸν κήρυκα, προετοιμάσατο δὲ
τάδε· ὅσοι τοῦ στρατοῦ τοῦ ἑωυτοῦ ἦσαν νεκροὶ
ἐν Θερμοπύλῃσι (ἦσαν δὲ καὶ δύο μυριάδες),
ὑπολιπόμενος τούτων ὡς χιλίους, τοὺς λοιποὺς
τάφρους ὀρυξάμενος ἔθαψε, φυλλάδα τε ἐπιβαλὼν
καὶ γῆν ἐπαμησάμενος, ἵνα μὴ ὀφθείησαν ὑπὸ τοῦ
ναυτικοῦ στρατοῦ. ὡς δὲ διέβη ἐς τὴν Ἱστιαίην
ὁ κῆρυξ, σύλλογον ποιησάμενος παντὸς τοῦ στρατοπέδου ἔλεγε τάδε. "Ἄνδρες σύμμαχοι, βασιλεὺς Ξέρξης τῷ βουλομένῳ ὑμέων παραδίδωσι
ἐκλιπόντα τὴν τάξιν καὶ ἐλθόντα θεήσασθαι ὅκως
μάχεται πρὸς τοὺς ἀνοήτους τῶν ἀνθρώπων, οἳ
ἤλπισαν τὴν βασιλέος δύναμιν ὑπερβαλέεσθαι."

25. Ταῦτα ἐπαγγειλαμένου, μετὰ ταῦτα οὐδὲν
ἐγίνετο πλοίων σπανιώτερον· οὕτω πολλοὶ ἤθελον
θεήσασθαι. διαπεραιωθέντες δὲ ἐθηεῦντο διεξιόντες
τοὺς νεκρούς· πάντες δὲ ἠπιστέατο τοὺς κειμένους
εἶναι πάντας Λακεδαιμονίους καὶ Θεσπιέας, ὁρῶντες καὶ τοὺς εἵλωτας. οὐ μὲν οὐδ' ἐλάνθανε τοὺς
διαβεβηκότας Ξέρξης ταῦτα πρήξας περὶ τοὺς
νεκροὺς τοὺς ἑωυτοῦ· καὶ γὰρ δὴ καὶ γελοῖον ἦν·
τῶν μὲν χίλιοι ἐφαίνοντο νεκροὶ κείμενοι, οἱ δὲ
πάντες ἔκέατο ἁλέες συγκεκομισμένοι ἐς τὠυτὸ
χωρίον, τέσσερες χιλιάδες. ταύτην μὲν τὴν
ἡμέρην πρὸς θέην ἐτράποντο, τῇ δ' ὑστεραίῃ οἱ
μὲν ἀπέπλεον ἐς Ἱστιαίην ἐπὶ τὰς νέας, οἱ δὲ
ἀμφὶ Ξέρξην ἐς ὁδὸν ὁρμέατο.

26. Ἧκον δέ σφι αὐτόμολοι ἄνδρες ἀπ' Ἀρκα-
δίης ὀλίγοι τινές, βίου τε δεόμενοι καὶ ἐνεργοὶ
βουλόμενοι εἶναι. ἄγοντες δὲ τούτους ἐς ὄψιν
τὴν βασιλέος ἐπυνθάνοντο οἱ Πέρσαι περὶ τῶν

to the fleet, having first bestowed the fallen men as
I shall show. Of all his own soldiers who had fallen
at Thermopylae (that is, as many as twenty thousand)
he left about a thousand, and the rest he buried in
digged trenches, which he covered with leaves and
heaped earth, that the men of the fleet might not
see them. So when the herald had crossed over
to Histiaea, he assembled all the men of the fleet
and thus spoke: "Men of our allies, King Xerxes
suffers any one of you that will to leave his place
and come to see how he fights against those foolish
men who thought to overcome the king's power."

25. After this proclamation, there was nought so
hard to get as a boat, so many were they who would
see the sight. They crossed over and went about
viewing the dead; and all of them supposed that
the fallen Greeks were all Lacedaemonians and
Thespians, though there were the helots also for
them to see. Yet for all that they that crossed
over were not deceived by what Xerxes had done
with his own dead; for indeed the thing was
laughable; of the Persians a thousand lay dead
before their eyes, but the Greeks lay all together
assembled in one place, to the number of four thousand. All that day they spent in seeing the sight;
on the next the shipmen returned to their fleet at
Histiaea, and Xerxes' army set forth on its march.

26. There had come to them some few deserters,
men of Arcadia, lacking a livelihood and desirous
to find some service. Bringing these men into the
king's presence, the Persians inquired of them what

25

Ἑλλήνων τί ποιέοιεν· εἷς δέ τις πρὸ πάντων ἦν
ὁ εἰρωτῶν αὐτοὺς ταῦτα. οἱ δέ σφι ἔλεγον ὡς
Ὀλύμπια ἄγουσι καὶ θεωρέοιεν ἀγῶνα γυμνικὸν
καὶ ἱππικόν. ὁ δὲ ἐπείρετο ὅ τι τὸ ἄεθλον εἴη
σφι κείμενον περὶ ὅτευ ἀγωνίζονται· οἱ δ᾽ εἶπον
τῆς ἐλαίης τὸν διδόμενον στέφανον. ἐνθαῦτα
εἴπας γνώμην γενναιοτάτην Τιγράνης ὁ Ἀρτα-
βάνου δειλίην ὦφλε πρὸς βασιλέος. πυνθανόμενος γὰρ τὸ ἄεθλον ἐὸν στέφανον ἀλλ᾽ οὐ
χρήματα, οὔτε ἠνέσχετο σιγῶν εἶπέ τε ἐς πάντας
τάδε. "Παπαῖ Μαρδόνιε, κοίους ἐπ᾽ ἄνδρας
ἤγαγες μαχησομένους ἡμέας, οἳ οὐ περὶ χρημάτων
τὸν ἀγῶνα ποιεῦνται ἀλλὰ περὶ ἀρετῆς." τούτῳ
μὲν δὴ ταῦτα εἴρητο.

27. Ἐν δὲ τῷ διὰ μέσου χρόνῳ, ἐπείτε τὸ ἐν
Θερμοπύλῃσι τρῶμα ἐγεγόνεε, αὐτίκα Θεσσαλοὶ
πέμπουσι κήρυκα ἐς Φωκέας, ἅτε σφι ἔχοντες
αἰεὶ χόλον, ἀπὸ δὲ τοῦ ὑστάτου τρώματος καὶ
τὸ κάρτα. ἐσβαλόντες γὰρ πανστρατιῇ αὐτοί
τε οἱ Θεσσαλοὶ καὶ οἱ σύμμαχοι αὐτῶν ἐς τοὺς
Φωκέας, οὐ πολλοῖσι ἔτεσι πρότερον ταύτης τῆς
βασιλέος στρατηλασίης, ἐσσώθησαν ὑπὸ τῶν
Φωκέων καὶ περιέφθησαν τρηχέως. ἐπείτε γὰρ
κατειλήθησαν ἐς τὸν Παρνησὸν οἱ Φωκέες ἔχοντες
μάντιν Τελλίην τὸν Ἠλεῖον, ἐνθαῦτα ὁ Τελλίης
οὗτος σοφίζεται αὐτοῖσι τοιόνδε. γυψώσας ἄνδρας
ἑξακοσίους τῶν Φωκέων τοὺς ἀρίστους, αὐτούς τε
τούτους καὶ τὰ ὅπλα αὐτῶν, νυκτὸς ἐπεθήκατο
τοῖσι Θεσσαλοῖσι, προείπας αὐτοῖσι, τὸν ἂν μὴ

---

[1] On the hypothesis, usually received till lately, that the
games took place at the first full moon after the summer

the Greeks were doing, there being one who put this question in the name of all. The Arcadians telling them that the Greeks were keeping the Olympic[1] festival and viewing sports and horse-races, the Persian asked what was the prize offered, wherefor they contended; and they told him of the crown of olive that was given to the victor. Then Tigranes son of Artabanus uttered a most noble saying (but the king deemed him a coward for it); when he heard that the prize was not money but a crown, he could not hold his peace, but cried, "Zounds, Mardonius, what manner of men are these that you have brought us to fight withal? 'tis not for money they contend but for glory of achievement!" Such was Tigranes' saying.

27. In the meantime, immediately after the misfortune at Thermopylae, the Thessalians sent a herald to the Phocians, inasmuch as they bore an old grudge against them, and more than ever by reason of their latest disaster. For a few years before the king's expedition the Thessalians and their allies had invaded Phocis with their whole army, but had been worsted and roughly handled by the Phocians. For the Phocians being beleaguered on Parnassus and having with them the diviner Tellias of Elis, Tellias devised a stratagem for them: he covered six hundred of the bravest Phocians with gypsum, themselves and their armour, and led them to attack the Thessalians by night, bidding them

solstice, we should have to adopt some theory such as Stein's, that the conversation here recorded took place in late June, while Xerxes was at Therma; for Thermopylae was fought in late August. But Macan says that the above hypothesis about the date of the games is exploded.

λευκανθίζοντα ἴδωνται, τοῦτον κτείνειν. τούτους
ὦν αἵ τε φυλακαὶ τῶν Θεσσαλῶν πρῶται ἰδοῦσαι
ἐφοβήθησαν, δόξασαι ἄλλο τι εἶναι τέρας, καὶ
μετὰ τὰς φυλακὰς αὐτὴ ἡ στρατιὴ οὕτω ὥστε
τετρακισχιλίων κρατῆσαι νεκρῶν καὶ ἀσπίδων
Φωκέας, τῶν τὰς μὲν ἡμισέας ἐς Ἄβας ἀνέθεσαν
τὰς δὲ ἐς Δελφούς· ἡ δὲ δεκάτη ἐγένετο τῶν
χρημάτων ἐκ ταύτης τῆς μάχης οἱ μεγάλοι
ἀνδριάντες οἱ περὶ τὸν τρίποδα συνεστεῶτες
ἔμπροσθε τοῦ νηοῦ τοῦ ἐν Δελφοῖσι, καὶ ἕτεροι
τοιοῦτοι ἐν Ἄβῃσι ἀνακέαται.

28. Ταῦτα μέν νυν τὸν πεζὸν ἐργάσαντο τῶν
Θεσσαλῶν οἱ Φωκέες πολιορκέοντας ἑωυτούς·
ἐσβαλοῦσαν δὲ ἐς τὴν χώρην τὴν ἵππον αὐτῶν
ἐλυμήναντο ἀνηκέστως. ἐν γὰρ τῇ ἐσβολῇ ἡ
ἐστὶ κατὰ Ὑάμπολιν, ἐν ταύτῃ τάφρον μεγάλην
ὀρύξαντες ἀμφορέας κενοὺς ἐς αὐτὴν κατέθηκαν,
χοῦν δὲ ἐπιφορήσαντες καὶ ὁμοιώσαντες τῷ ἄλλῳ
χώρῳ ἐδέκοντο τοὺς Θεσσαλοὺς ἐσβάλλοντας.
οἳ δὲ ὡς ἀναρπασόμενοι τοὺς Φωκέας φερόμενοι
ἐσέπεσον ἐς τοὺς ἀμφορέας. ἐνθαῦτα οἱ ἵπποι
τὰ σκέλεα διεφθάρησαν.

29. Τούτων δή σφι ἀμφοτέρων ἔχοντες ἔγκοτον
οἱ Θεσσαλοὶ πέμψαντες κήρυκα ἠγόρευον τάδε.
"Ὦ Φωκέες, ἤδη τι μᾶλλον γνωσιμαχέετε μὴ
εἶναι ὅμοιοι ἡμῖν. πρόσθε τε γὰρ ἐν τοῖσι Ἕλλησι,
ὅσον χρόνον ἐκεῖνα ἡμῖν ἥνδανε, πλέον αἰεί κοτε
ὑμέων ἐφερόμεθα· νῦν τε παρὰ τῷ βαρβάρῳ τοσοῦτο δυνάμεθα ὥστε ἐπ' ἡμῖν ἐστι τῆς γῆς ἐστε-
ρῆσθαι καὶ πρὸς ἠνδραποδίσθαι ὑμέας. ἡμεῖς
μέντοι τὸ πᾶν ἔχοντες οὐ μνησικακέομεν, ἀλλ'
ἡμῖν γενέσθω ἀντ' αὐτῶν πεντήκοντα τάλαντα

28

slay whomsoever they should see not whitened. The Thessalian sentinels were the first to see these men and to flee for fear, supposing falsely that it was something beyond nature, and next after the sentinels the whole army fled likewise; insomuch that the Phocians made themselves masters of four thousand dead, and their shields, whereof they dedicated half at Abae and the rest at Delphi; a tithe of what they won in that fight went to the making of the great statues that stand round the tripod before the shrine at Delphi, and there are others like them dedicated at Abae.

28. Thus had the beleaguered Phocians dealt with the Thessalian foot; and when the Thessalian horsemen rode into their country the Phocians did them mortal harm; they dug a great pit in the pass near Hyampolis and put empty jars therein, covering which with earth, till all was like the rest of the ground, they awaited the onset of the Thessalians. These rode on thinking to sweep the Phocians before them, and fell in among the jars; whereby their horses' legs were broken.

29. These two deeds had never been forgiven by the Thessalians; and now they sent a herald with this message: "Men of Phocis, it is time now that you confess yourselves to be no match for us. We were ever formerly preferred before you by the Greeks, as long as we were on their side; and now we are of such weight with the foreigner that it lies in our power to have you deprived of your lands, ay, and yourselves enslaved withal. Nevertheless, though all rests with us, we bear you no ill-will for the past; pay us fifty talents of silver for what you

ἀργυρίου, καὶ ὑμῖν ὑποδεκόμεθα τὰ ἐπιόντα ἐπὶ
τὴν χώρην ἀποτρέψειν."

30. Ταῦτά σφι ἐπαγγέλλοντο οἱ Θεσσαλοί. οἱ
γὰρ Φωκέες μοῦνοι τῶν ταύτῃ ἀνθρώπων οὐκ
ἐμήδιζον, κατ' ἄλλο μὲν οὐδέν, ὡς ἐγὼ συμβαλ-
λόμενος εὑρίσκω, κατὰ δὲ τὸ ἔχθος τὸ Θεσσαλῶν·
εἰ δὲ Θεσσαλοὶ τὰ Ἑλλήνων ηὖξον, ὡς ἐμοὶ δοκέειν, ἐμήδιζον ἂν οἱ Φωκέες. ταῦτα ἐπαγγελ-
λομένων Θεσσαλῶν, οὔτε δώσειν ἔφασαν χρήματα,
παρέχειν τε σφίσι Θεσσαλοῖσι ὁμοίως μηδίζειν,
εἰ ἄλλως βουλοίατο· ἀλλ' οὐκ ἔσεσθαι ἑκόντες
εἶναι προδόται τῆς Ἑλλάδος.

31. Ἐπειδὴ δὲ ἀνηνείχθησαν οὗτοι οἱ λόγοι,
οὕτω δὴ οἱ Θεσσαλοὶ κεχολωμένοι τοῖσι Φωκεῦσι
ἐγένοντο ἡγεμόνες τῷ βαρβάρῳ τῆς ὁδοῦ. ἐκ μὲν
δὴ τῆς Τρηχινίης ἐς τὴν Δωρίδα ἐσέβαλον· τῆς
γὰρ Δωρίδος χώρης ποδεὼν στεινὸς ταύτῃ κατα-
τείνει, ὡς τριήκοντα σταδίων μάλιστά κῃ εὖρος,
κείμενος μεταξὺ τῆς τε Μηλίδος καὶ Φωκίδος
χώρης, ἥ περ ἦν τὸ παλαιὸν Δρυοπίς· ἡ δὲ χώρη
αὕτη ἐστὶ μητρόπολις Δωριέων τῶν ἐν Πελοποννήσῳ. ταύτην ὦν τὴν Δωρίδα γῆν οὐκ ἐσίναντο
ἐσβαλόντες οἱ βάρβαροι· ἐμήδιζόν τε γὰρ καὶ οὐκ
ἐδόκεε Θεσσαλοῖσι.

32. Ὡς δὲ ἐκ τῆς Δωρίδος ἐς τὴν Φωκίδα ἐσέβαλον, αὐτοὺς μὲν τοὺς Φωκέας οὐκ αἱρέουσι.
οἱ μὲν γὰρ τῶν Φωκέων ἐς τὰ ἄκρα τοῦ Παρνησοῦ
ἀνέβησαν. ἔστι δὲ καὶ ἐπιτηδέη δέξασθαι ὅμιλον
τοῦ Παρνησοῦ ἡ κορυφή, κατὰ Νέωνα πόλιν
κειμένη ἐπ' ἑωυτῆς· Τιθορέα οὔνομα αὐτῇ· ἐς τὴν
δὴ ἀνηνείκαντο καὶ αὐτοὶ ἀνέβησαν. οἱ δὲ πλεῦνες
αὐτῶν ἐς τοὺς Ὀζόλας Λοκροὺς ἐξεκομίσαντο, ἐς

did, and we promise to turn aside what threatens your land."

30. This was the Thessalians' offer. The Phocians, and they alone of all that region, would not take the Persians' part, and that for no other reason (if I argue aright) than their hatred of the Thessalians; had the Thessalians aided the Greek side, then methinks the Phocians would have stood for the Persians. They replied to the offer of the Thessalians that they would give no money; that they could do like the Thessalians and take the Persian part, if for any cause they so wished, but they would not willingly betray the cause of Hellas.

31. This answer being returned to them, thereat the Thessalians in their wrath against the Phocians began to guide the foreigner on his way. From the lands of Trachis they broke into Doris; for there is a narrow tongue of Dorian land stretching that way, about thirty furlongs wide, between the Malian territory and the Phocian, which in old time was Dryopian; this region is the motherland of the Dorians of the Peloponnese. To this Dorian territory the foreigners did no harm at their invasion; for the people took the Persian part, and the Thessalians would not have them harmed.

32. When they entered Phocis from Doris, the Phocians themselves they could not catch; for some of the Phocians ascended to the heights of Parnassus; and the peak of Parnassus called Tithorea, which rises by itself near the town Neon, has room enough for a multitude of people; thither they carried up their goods and themselves ascended to it, but the most of them made their way out of the country to

Ἄμφισσαν πόλιν τὴν ὑπὲρ τοῦ Κρισαίου πεδίου
οἰκημένην. οἱ δὲ βάρβαροι τὴν χώρην πᾶσαν
ἐπέδραμον τὴν Φωκίδα· Θεσσαλοὶ γὰρ οὕτω ἦγον
τὸν στρατόν· ὁκόσα δὲ ἐπέσχον, πάντα ἐπέφλεγον
καὶ ἔκειρον, καὶ ἐς τὰς πόλις ἐνιέντες πῦρ καὶ ἐς
τὰ ἱρά.

33. Πορευόμενοι γὰρ ταύτῃ παρὰ τὸν Κηφισὸν
ποταμὸν ἐδηίουν πάντα, καὶ κατὰ μὲν ἔκαυσαν
Δρυμὸν πόλιν κατὰ δὲ Χαράδραν καὶ Ἔρωχον
καὶ Τεθρώνιον καὶ Ἀμφίκαιαν καὶ Νέωνα καὶ
Πεδιέας καὶ Τριτέας καὶ Ἐλάτειαν καὶ Ὑάμπολιν
καὶ Παραποταμίους καὶ Ἄβας, ἔνθα ἦν ἱρὸν
Ἀπόλλωνος πλούσιον, θησαυροῖσί τε καὶ ἀνα-
θήμασι πολλοῖσι κατεσκευασμένον· ἦν δὲ καὶ
τότε καὶ νῦν ἔτι χρηστήριον αὐτόθι. καὶ τοῦτο
τὸ ἱρὸν συλήσαντες ἐνέπρησαν. καί τινας διώκοντες εἷλον τῶν Φωκέων πρὸς τοῖσι ὄρεσι, καὶ
γυναῖκας τινὰς διέφθειραν μισγόμενοι ὑπὸ
πλήθεος.

34. Παραποταμίους δὲ παραμειβόμενοι οἱ βάρβαροι ἀπίκοντο ἐς Πανοπέας. ἐνθεῦτεν δὲ ἤδη
διακρινομένη ἡ στρατιὴ αὐτῶν ἐσχίζετο. τὸ μὲν
πλεῖστον καὶ δυνατώτατον τοῦ στρατοῦ ἅμα
αὐτῷ Ξέρξῃ πορευόμενον ἐπ᾽ Ἀθήνας ἐσέβαλε
ἐς Βοιωτούς, ἐς γῆν τὴν Ὀρχομενίων. Βοιωτῶν
δὲ πᾶν τὸ πλῆθος ἐμήδιζε, τὰς δὲ πόλις αὐτῶν
ἄνδρες Μακεδόνες διατεταγμένοι ἔσωζον, ὑπὸ
Ἀλεξάνδρου ἀποπεμφθέντες· ἔσωζον δὲ τῇδε,
δῆλον βουλόμενοι ποιέειν Ξέρξῃ ὅτι τὰ Μήδων
Βοιωτοὶ φρονέοιεν.

35. Οὗτοι μὲν δὴ τῶν βαρβάρων ταύτῃ ἐτράποντο, ἄλλοι δὲ αὐτῶν ἡγεμόνας ἔχοντες ὁρμέατο

32

the Ozolian Locrians, where is the town of Amphissa above the Crisaean plain. The foreigners overran the whole of Phocis, the Thessalians so guiding their army; and all that came within their power they burnt and wasted, setting fire to towns and temples.

33. Marching this way down the river Cephisus they ravaged all before them, burning the towns of Drymus, Charadra, Erochus, Tethronium, Amphicaea, Neon, Pediea, Tritea, Elatea, Hyampolis, Parapotamii, and Abae, where was a richly endowed temple of Apollo, provided with wealth of treasure and offerings; and there was then as now a place of divination there. This temple, too, they plundered and burnt; and they pursued and caught some of the Phocians near the mountains, and did certain women to death by the multitude of their violators.

34. Passing Parapotamii the foreigners came to Panopea; and there their army parted asunder into two companies. The greater and stronger part of the host marched with Xerxes himself towards Athens and broke into the territory of Orchomenus in Boeotia. Now the whole people of Boeotia took the Persian part, and men of Macedonia sent by Alexander safeguarded their towns, each in his appointed place; the reason of the safeguarding being, that Xerxes might understand the Boeotians to be on the Persian side.

35. So this part of the foreign army marched as aforesaid, and others set forth with guides for the

ἐπὶ τὸ ἱρὸν τὸ ἐν Δελφοῖσι, ἐν δεξιῇ τὸν Παρνησὸν
ἀπέργοντες. ὅσα δὲ καὶ οὗτοι ἐπέσχον τῆς
Φωκίδος, πάντα ἐσιναμώρεον· καὶ γὰρ τῶν Πανο-
πέων τὴν πόλιν ἐνέπρησαν καὶ Δαυλίων καὶ
Αἰολιδέων. ἐπορεύοντο δὲ ταύτῃ ἀποσχισθέντες
τῆς ἄλλης στρατιῆς τῶνδε εἵνεκα, ὅκως συλήσαντες
τὸ ἱρὸν τὸ ἐν Δελφοῖσι βασιλέι Ξέρξῃ ἀποδέξαιεν
τὰ χρήματα. πάντα δ᾽ ἠπίστατο τὰ ἐν τῷ ἱρῷ
ὅσα λόγου ἦν ἄξια Ξέρξης, ὡς ἐγὼ πυνθάνομαι,
ἄμεινον ἢ τὰ ἐν τοῖσι οἰκίοισι ἔλιπε, πολλῶν
αἰεὶ λεγόντων, καὶ μάλιστα τὰ Κροίσου τοῦ
Ἀλυάττεω ἀναθήματα.

36. Οἱ Δελφοὶ δὲ πυνθανόμενοι ταῦτα ἐς πᾶσαν
ἀρρωδίην ἀπίκατο, ἐν δείματι δὲ μεγάλῳ κατε-
στεῶτες ἐμαντεύοντο περὶ τῶν ἱρῶν χρημάτων,
εἴτε σφέα κατὰ γῆς κατορύξωσι εἴτε ἐκκομίσωσι
ἐς ἄλλην χώρην. ὁ δὲ θεός σφεας οὐκ ἔα κινέειν,
φὰς αὐτὸς ἱκανὸς εἶναι τῶν ἑωυτοῦ προκατῆσθαι.
Δελφοὶ δὲ ταῦτα ἀκούσαντες σφέων αὐτῶν πέρι
ἐφρόντιζον. τέκνα μέν νυν καὶ γυναῖκας πέρην
ἐς τὴν Ἀχαιίην διέπεμψαν, αὐτῶν δὲ οἱ μὲν
πλεῖστοι ἀνέβησαν ἐς τοῦ Παρνησοῦ τὰς κορυφὰς
καὶ ἐς τὸ Κωρύκιον ἄντρον ἀνηνείκαντο, οἱ δὲ ἐς
Ἄμφισσαν τὴν Λοκρίδα ὑπεξῆλθον. πάντες δὲ
ὦν οἱ Δελφοὶ ἐξέλιπον τὴν πόλιν, πλὴν ἑξήκοντα
ἀνδρῶν καὶ τοῦ προφήτεω.

37. Ἐπεὶ δὲ ἀγχοῦ ἦσαν οἱ βάρβαροι ἐπιόντες
καὶ ἀπώρων τὸ ἱρόν, ἐν τούτῳ ὁ προφήτης, τῷ
οὔνομα ἦν Ἀκήρατος, ὁρᾷ πρὸ τοῦ νηοῦ ὅπλα
προκείμεα ἔσωθεν ἐκ τοῦ μεγάρου ἐξενηνειγμένα
ἱρά, τῶν οὐκ ὅσιον ἦν ἅπτεσθαι ἀνθρώπων οὐδενί.

34

temple at Delphi, keeping Parnassus on their right. These, too, laid waste whatsoever part of Phocis they occupied, burning the towns of the Panopeans and Daulii and Aeolidae. The purpose of their parting from the rest of the army and marching this way was, that they might plunder the temple at Delphi and lay its wealth before Xerxes; who (as I have been told) knew of all the most notable possessions in the temple better than of what he had left in his own palace, and chiefly the offerings of Croesus son of Alyattes; so many had ever spoken of them.

36. When the Delphians learnt all this they were sore afraid; and in their great fear they inquired of the oracle whether they should bury the sacred treasure in the ground or convey it away to another country. But the god bade them move nothing, saying that he was able to protect his own. On that hearing, the Delphians took thought for themselves. They sent their children and women oversea to Achaia; of the men, the most went up to the peaks of Parnassus and carried their goods into the Corycian cave,[1] and some escaped to Amphissa in Locris; in brief, all the Delphians left the town save sixty men and the prophet.

37. Now when the foreigners drew nigh in their coming and could see the temple, the prophet, whose name was Aceratus, saw certain sacred arms, that no man might touch without sacrilege, brought out of the chamber within and laid before the shrine. So

[1] In the heights above Delphi and some three hours distant from it, adjacent to Parnassus. The cave is "some 200 feet long, 90 feet broad at the widest point, and 20 to 40 feet high" (How and Wells).

ὃ μὲν δὴ ἤιε Δελφῶν τοῖσι παρεοῦσι σημανέων τὸ
τέρας· οἱ δὲ βάρβαροι ἐπειδὴ ἐγίνοντο ἐπειγόμενοι
κατὰ τὸ ἱρὸν τῆς Προναίης Ἀθηναίης, ἐπιγίνεταί
σφι τέρεα ἔτι μέζονα τοῦ πρὶν γενομένου τέρεος.
θῶμα μὲν γὰρ καὶ τοῦτο κάρτα ἐστί, ὅπλα ἀρήια
αὐτόματα φανῆναι ἔξω προκείμενα τοῦ νηοῦ· τὰ
δὲ δὴ ἐπὶ τούτῳ δεύτερα ἐπιγενόμενα καὶ διὰ
πάντων φασμάτων ἄξια θωμάσαι μάλιστα. ἐπεὶ
γὰρ δὴ ἦσαν ἐπιόντες οἱ βάρβαροι κατὰ τὸ ἱρὸν
τῆς Προναίης Ἀθηναίης, ἐν τούτῳ ἐκ μὲν τοῦ
οὐρανοῦ κεραυνοὶ αὐτοῖσι ἐνέπιπτον, ἀπὸ δὲ τοῦ
Παρνησοῦ ἀπορραγεῖσαι δύο κορυφαὶ ἐφέροντο
πολλῷ πατάγῳ ἐς αὐτοὺς καὶ κατέβαλον συχνούς
σφεων, ἐκ δὲ τοῦ ἱροῦ τῆς Προναίης βοή τε καὶ
ἀλαλαγμὸς ἐγίνετο.

38. Συμμιγέντων δὲ τούτων πάντων, φόβος
τοῖσι βαρβάροισι ἐνεπεπτώκεε. μαθόντες δὲ οἱ
Δελφοὶ φεύγοντας σφέας, ἐπικαταβάντες ἀπέ-
κτειναν πλῆθός τι αὐτῶν. οἱ δὲ περιεόντες ἰθὺ
Βοιωτῶν ἔφευγον. ἔλεγον δὲ οἱ ἀπονοστήσαντες
οὗτοι τῶν βαρβάρων, ὡς ἐγὼ πυνθάνομαι, ὡς
πρὸς τούτοισι καὶ ἄλλα ὥρων θεῖα· δύο γὰρ
ὁπλίτας μέζονας ἢ κατ' ἀνθρώπων φύσιν ἔχοντας
ἔπεσθαί σφι κτείνοντας καὶ διώκοντας.

39. Τούτους δὲ τοὺς δύο Δελφοὶ λέγουσι εἶναι
ἐπιχωρίους ἥρωας, Φύλακόν τε καὶ Αὐτόνοον,
τῶν τὰ τεμένεα ἐστὶ περὶ τὸ ἱρόν, Φυλάκου μὲν
παρ' αὐτὴν τὴν ὁδὸν κατύπερθε τοῦ ἱροῦ τῆς
Προναίης, Αὐτονόου δὲ πέλας τῆς Κασταλίης
ὑπὸ τῇ Ὑαμπείῃ κορυφῇ. οἱ δὲ πεσόντες ἀπὸ
τοῦ Παρνησοῦ λίθοι ἔτι καὶ ἐς ἡμέας ἦσαν σόοι,

he went to tell the Delphians of this miracle; but when the foreigners came with all speed near to the temple of Athene Pronaea, they were visited by miracles yet greater than the aforesaid. Marvellous indeed it is, that weapons of war should of their own motion appear lying outside before the shrine; but the visitation which followed upon that was more wondrous than aught else ever seen. For when the foreigners were near in their coming to the temple of Athene Pronaea, there were they smitten by thunderbolts from heaven, and two peaks brake off from Parnassus and came rushing among them with a mighty noise and overwhelmed many of them; and from the temple of Athene there was heard a shout and a cry of triumph.

38. All this joining together struck panic into the foreigners; and the Delphians, perceiving that they fled, descended upon them and slew a great number. The survivors fled straight to Boeotia. Those of the foreigners who returned said (as I have been told) that they had seen other signs of heaven's working besides the aforesaid: two men-at-arms of stature greater than human (they said) had followed hard after them, slaying and pursuing.

39. These two, say the Delphians, were the native heroes Phylacus and Autonous, whose precincts are near the temple, Phylacus' by the road itself above the shrine of Athene Pronaea, and Autonous' near the Castalian spring, under the Hyampean peak. The rocks that fell[1] from Parnassus were yet to be

---

[1] "Among the olives in the glen below" the remains of the temple of Athene Pronaea "are some large masses of reddish-grey rock, which might be those said to have come hurtling from the cliffs above" (How and Wells).

ἐν τῷ τεμένεϊ τῆς Προναίης Ἀθηναίης κείμενοι,
ἐς τὸ ἐνέσκηψαν διὰ τῶν βαρβάρων φερόμενοι.
τούτων μέν νυν τῶν ἀνδρῶν αὕτη ἀπὸ τοῦ ἱροῦ
ἀπαλλαγὴ γίνεται.

40. Ὁ δὲ Ἑλλήνων ναυτικὸς στρατὸς ἀπὸ τοῦ
Ἀρτεμισίου Ἀθηναίων δεηθέντων ἐς Σαλαμῖνα
κατίσχει τὰς νέας. τῶνδε δὲ εἵνεκα προσεδεήθησαν
αὐτῶν σχεῖν πρὸς Σαλαμῖνα Ἀθηναῖοι, ἵνα αὐτοὶ
παῖδάς τε καὶ γυναῖκας ὑπεξαγάγωνται ἐκ τῆς
Ἀττικῆς, πρὸς δὲ καὶ βουλεύσωνται τὸ ποιητέον
αὐτοῖσι ἔσται. ἐπὶ γὰρ τοῖσι κατήκουσι πρήγμασι βουλὴν ἔμελλον ποιήσασθαι ὡς ἐψευσμένοι
γνώμης. δοκέοντες γὰρ εὑρήσειν Πελοποννησίους
πανδημεὶ ἐν τῇ Βοιωτίῃ ὑποκατημένους τὸν βάρβαρον, τῶν μὲν εὗρον οὐδὲν ἐόν, οἱ δὲ ἐπυνθάνοντο
τὸν Ἰσθμὸν αὐτοὺς τειχέοντας, ὡς τὴν Πελοπόννησον περὶ πλείστου τε ποιευμένους περιεῖναι
καὶ ταύτην ἔχοντας ἐν φυλακῇ, τὰ ἄλλα δὲ ἀπι-
έναι. ταῦτα πυνθανόμενοι οὕτω δὴ προσεδεήθησαν
σφέων σχεῖν πρὸς τὴν Σαλαμῖνα.

41. Οἱ μὲν δὴ ἄλλοι κατέσχον ἐς τὴν Σαλαμῖνα,
Ἀθηναῖοι δὲ ἐς τὴν ἑωυτῶν. μετὰ δὲ τὴν ἄπιξιν
κήρυγμα ἐποιήσαντο, Ἀθηναίων τῇ τις δύναται
σώζειν τέκνα τε καὶ τοὺς οἰκέτας. ἐνθαῦτα οἱ
μὲν πλεῖστοι ἐς Τροίζηνα ἀπέστειλαν, οἱ δὲ ἐς
Αἴγιναν, οἱ δὲ ἐς Σαλαμῖνα. ἔσπευσαν δὲ ταῦτα
ὑπεκθέσθαι τῷ χρηστηρίῳ τε βουλόμενοι ὑπηρε-
τέειν καὶ δὴ καὶ τοῦδε εἵνεκα οὐκ ἥκιστα. λέγουσι
Ἀθηναῖοι ὄφιν μέγαν φύλακα τῆς ἀκροπόλιος
ἐνδιαιτᾶσθαι ἐν τῷ ἱρῷ· λέγουσί τε ταῦτα καὶ
δὴ ὡς ἐόντι ἐπιμήνια ἐπιτελέουσι προτιθέντες·
τὰ δ' ἐπιμήνια μελιτόεσσα ἐστί. αὕτη δὴ ἡ

seen in my day, lying in the precinct of Athene
Pronaea, whither their descent through the foreigners' ranks had hurled them. Such, then, was
the manner of those men's departure from the
temple.

40. The Greek fleet, after it had left Artemisium
came by the Athenians' entreaty to land at Salamis ;
the reason why the Athenians entreated them to put
in there being, that they themselves might convey
their children and women safe out of Attica, and
moreover take counsel as to what they should do.
For inasmuch as the present turn of affairs had
disappointed their judgment they were now to hold
a council ; they had thought to find the whole
Peloponnesian force awaiting the foreigners' attack
in Boeotia, but now of that they found no whit,
but learnt contrariwise that the Peloponnesians were
fortifying the Isthmus, and letting all else go, as
deeming the defence of the Peloponnese to be of
greatest moment. Learning this, they therefore
entreated the fleet to put in at Salamis.

41. So the rest made sail thither, and the Athenians
to their own country. Being there arrived they made
a proclamation that every Athenian should save his
children and servants as he best could. Thereat
most of them sent their households to Troezen, and
some to Aegina and Salamis. They made haste to
convey all out of harm because they desired to be
guided by the oracle, and for another reason, too,
which was this : it is said by the Athenians that
a great snake lives in their temple, to guard the
acropolis ; in proof whereof they do ever duly set
out a honey-cake as a monthly offering for it ; this

μελιτόεσσα ἐν τῷ πρόσθε αἰεὶ χρόνῳ ἀναισιμου-
μένη τότε ἦν ἄψαυστος. σημηνάσης δὲ ταῦτα
τῆς ἱρείης, μᾶλλόν τι οἱ Ἀθηναῖοι καὶ προθυμότερον ἐξέλιπον τὴν πόλιν, ὡς καὶ τῆς θεοῦ
ἀπολελοιπυίης τὴν ἀκρόπολιν. ὡς δέ σφι πάντα
ὑπεξέκειτο, ἔπλεον ἐς τὸ στρατόπεδον.

42. Ἐπεὶ δὲ οἱ ἀπ᾽ Ἀρτεμισίου ἐς Σαλαμῖνα
κατέσχον τὰς νέας, συνέρρεε καὶ ὁ λοιπὸς πυνθανόμενος ὁ τῶν Ἑλλήνων ναυτικὸς στρατὸς ἐκ
Τροίζηνος· ἐς γὰρ Πώγωνα τὸν Τροιζηνίων λιμένα
προείρητο συλλέγεσθαι. συνελέχθησάν τε δὴ
πολλῷ πλεῦνες νέες ἢ ἐπ᾽ Ἀρτεμισίῳ ἐναυμάχεον
καὶ ἀπὸ πολίων πλεύνων. ναύαρχος μέν νυν
ἐπῆν ωὑτὸς ὅς περ ἐπ᾽ Ἀρτεμισίῳ, Εὐρυβιάδης
ὁ Εὐρυκλείδεω ἀνὴρ Σπαρτιήτης, οὐ μέντοι γένεος
τοῦ βασιληίου ἐών· νέας δὲ πολλῷ πλείστας τε
καὶ ἄριστα πλεούσας παρείχοντο Ἀθηναῖοι.

43. Ἐστρατεύοντο δὲ οἵδε· ἐκ μὲν Πελοποννήσου Λακεδαιμόνιοι ἑκκαίδεκα νέας παρεχόμενοι,
Κορίνθιοι δὲ τὸ αὐτὸ πλήρωμα παρεχόμενοι καὶ
ἐπ᾽ Ἀρτεμισίῳ· Σικυώνιοι δὲ πεντεκαίδεκα παρείχοντο νέας, Ἐπιδαύριοι δὲ δέκα, Τροιζήνιοι δὲ
πέντε, Ἑρμιονέες δὲ τρεῖς, ἐόντες οὗτοι πλὴν
Ἑρμιονέων Δωρικόν τε καὶ Μακεδνὸν ἔθνος, ἐξ
Ἐρινεοῦ τε καὶ Πίνδου καὶ τῆς Δρυοπίδος ὕστατα
ὁρμηθέντες. οἱ δὲ Ἑρμιονέες εἰσὶ Δρύοπες, ὑπὸ
Ἡρακλέος τε καὶ Μηλιέων ἐκ τῆς νῦν Δωρίδος
καλεομένης χώρης ἐξαναστάντες.

44. Οὗτοι μέν νυν Πελοποννησίων ἐστρατεύοντο, οἱ δὲ ἐκ τῆς ἔξω ἠπείρου, Ἀθηναῖοι μὲν
πρὸς πάντας τοὺς ἄλλους παρεχόμενοι νέας ὀγδώκοντα καὶ ἑκατόν, μοῦνοι· ἐν Σαλαμῖνι γὰρ οὐ

cake had ever before been consumed, but was now left untouched. When the priestess made that known, the Athenians were the readier to leave their city, deeming their goddess, too, to have deserted the acropolis. When they had conveyed all away, they returned to the fleet.

42. When the Greeks from Artemisium had put in at Salamis, the rest of their fleet also heard of it and gathered in from Troezen, the port of which, Pogon, had been named for their place of mustering; and the ships that mustered there were more by far than had fought at Artemisium, and came from more cities. Their admiral-in-chief was the same as at Artemisium, Eurybiades son of Euryclides, a Spartan, yet not of the royal blood; but it was the Athenians who furnished by far the most and the sea-worthiest ships.

43. The Peloponnesians that were with the fleet were, firstly, the Lacedaemonians, with sixteen ships, and the Corinthians with the same number of ships as at Artemisium; the Sicyonians furnished fifteen, the Epidaurians ten, the Troezenians five, the people of Hermione three; all these, except the people of Hermione, were of Dorian and Macedonian stock, and had last come from Erineus and Pindus and the Dryopian region. The people of Hermione are Dryopians, driven by Heracles and the Malians from the country now called Doris.

44. These were the Peloponnesians in the fleet. Of those that came from the mainland outside the Peloponnese, the Athenians furnished more ships than any of the rest, namely, a hundred and eighty, of their own sending; for the Plataeans did not

συνεναυμάχησαν Πλαταιέες Ἀθηναίοισι διὰ τοιόνδε τι πρῆγμα· ἀπαλλασσομένων τῶν Ἑλλήνων
ἀπὸ τοῦ Ἀρτεμισίου, ὡς ἐγίνοντο κατὰ Χαλκίδα,
οἱ Πλαταιέες ἀποβάντες ἐς τὴν περαίην τῆς
Βοιωτίης χώρης πρὸς ἐκκομιδὴν ἐτράποντο τῶν
οἰκετέων. οὗτοι μέν νυν τούτους σώζοντες ἐλεί-
φθησαν. Ἀθηναῖοι δὲ ἐπὶ μὲν Πελασγῶν ἐχόντων
τὴν νῦν Ἑλλάδα καλεομένην ἦσαν Πελασγοί,
ὀνομαζόμενοι Κραναοί, ἐπὶ δὲ Κέκροπος βασιλέος
ἐκλήθησαν Κεκροπίδαι, ἐκδεξαμένου δὲ Ἐρεχθέος
τὴν ἀρχὴν Ἀθηναῖοι μετωνομάσθησαν, Ἴωνος δὲ
τοῦ Ξούθου στρατάρχεω γενομένου Ἀθηναίοισι
ἐκλήθησαν ἀπὸ τούτου Ἴωνες.

45. Μεγαρέες δὲ τὠυτὸ πλήρωμα παρείχοντο
καὶ ἐπ' Ἀρτεμισίῳ, Ἀμπρακιῶται δὲ ἑπτὰ νέας
ἔχοντες ἐπεβοήθησαν, Λευκάδιοι δὲ τρεῖς, ἔθνος
ἐόντες οὗτοι Δωρικὸν ἀπὸ Κορίνθου.

46. Νησιωτέων δὲ Αἰγινῆται τριήκοντα παρείχοντο. ἦσαν μέν σφι καὶ ἄλλαι πεπληρωμέναι
νέες, ἀλλὰ τῇσι μὲν τὴν ἑωυτῶν ἐφύλασσον,
τριήκοντα δὲ τῇσι ἄριστα πλεούσῃσι ἐν Σαλαμῖνι
ἐναυμάχησαν. Αἰγινῆται δὲ εἰσὶ Δωριέες ἀπὸ
Ἐπιδαύρου· τῇ δὲ νήσῳ πρότερον οὔνομα ἦν
Οἰνώνη. μετὰ δὲ Αἰγινήτας Χαλκιδέες τὰς ἐπ'
Ἀρτεμισίῳ εἴκοσι παρεχόμενοι καὶ Ἐρετριέες τὰς
ἑπτά· οὗτοι δὲ Ἴωνες εἰσί. μετὰ δὲ Κήιοι τὰς
αὐτὰς παρεχόμενοι, ἔθνος ἐὸν Ἰωνικὸν ἀπὸ
Ἀθηνέων. Νάξιοι δὲ παρείχοντο τέσσερας, ἀποπεμφθέντες μὲν ἐς τοὺς Μήδους ὑπὸ τῶν πολιη-

fight beside the Athenians at Salamis, whereof the
reason was that when the Greeks sailed from Artemisium, and had arrived off Chalcis, the Plataeans
landed on the opposite Boeotian shore and set about
conveying their households away. So they were
left behind bringing these to safety. The Athenians,
while the Pelasgians ruled what is now called Hellas,
were Pelasgians, bearing the name of Cranai[1]; in
the time of their king Cecrops they came to be
called Cecropidae, and when the kingship fell to
Erechtheus they changed their name and became
Athenians, but when Ion son of Xuthus was made
leader of their armies they were called after him
Ionians.

45. The Megarians furnished the same complement
as at Artemisium; the Ampraciots brought seven
ships to the fleet, and the Leucadians (who are of
Dorian stock from Corinth) brought three.

46. Of the islanders, the Aeginetans furnished
thirty. They had other ships, too, manned; but
they used them to guard their own coasts, and
fought at Salamis with the thirty that were most
seaworthy. The Aeginetans are Dorians from Epidaurus; their island was formerly called Oenone.
After the Aeginetans came the Chalcidians with
the twenty, and the Eretrians with the seven which
had fought at Artemisium; they are Ionians; and
next the Ceans, furnishing the same ships as before;
they are of Ionian stock, from Athens. The Naxians
furnished four ships; they had been sent by their
townsmen to the Persians, like the rest of the

[1] That is, probably, "dwellers on the heights." All
pre-Dorian inhabitants of Hellas are "Pelasgian" to
Herodotus.

τέων κατά περ οἱ ἄλλοι νησιῶται, ἀλογήσαντες
δὲ τῶν ἐντολέων ἀπίκατο ἐς τοὺς Ἕλληνας
Δημοκρίτου σπεύσαντος, ἀνδρὸς τῶν ἀστῶν δοκί-
μου καὶ τότε τριηραρχέοντος. Νάξιοι δὲ εἰσὶ
Ἴωνες ἀπὸ Ἀθηνέων γεγονότες. Στυρέες δὲ τὰς
αὐτὰς παρείχοντο νέας τάς περ ἐπ᾽ Ἀρτεμισίῳ,
Κύθνιοι δὲ μίαν καὶ πεντηκόντερον, ἐόντες συναμ-
φότεροι οὗτοι Δρύοπες. καὶ Σερίφιοί τε καὶ
Σίφνιοι καὶ Μήλιοι ἐστρατεύοντο· οὗτοι γὰρ οὐκ
ἔδοσαν μοῦνοι νησιωτέων τῷ βαρβάρῳ γῆν τε καὶ
ὕδωρ.

47. Οὗτοι μὲν ἅπαντες ἐντὸς οἰκημένοι Θεσ-
πρωτῶν καὶ Ἀχέροντος ποταμοῦ ἐστρατεύοντο·
Θεσπρωτοὶ γὰρ εἰσὶ ὁμουρέοντες Ἀμπρακιώτῃσι
καὶ Λευκαδίοισι, οἳ ἐξ ἐσχατέων χωρέων ἐστρατεύοντο. τῶν δὲ ἐκτὸς τούτων οἰκημένων Κροτωνιῆται μοῦνοι ἦσαν οἳ ἐβοήθησαν τῇ Ἑλλάδι
κινδυνευούσῃ μιῇ νηΐ, τῆς ἦρχε ἀνὴρ τρὶς πυ-
θιονίκης Φάυλλος· Κροτωνιῆται δὲ γένος εἰσὶ
Ἀχαιοί.

48. Οἱ μέν νυν ἄλλοι τριήρεας παρεχόμενοι
ἐστρατεύοντο, Μήλιοι δὲ καὶ Σίφνιοι καὶ Σερίφιοι
πεντηκοντέρους· Μήλιοι μὲν γένος ἐόντες ἀπὸ
Λακεδαίμονος δύο παρείχοντο, Σίφνιοι δὲ καὶ
Σερίφιοι Ἴωνες ἐόντες ἀπ᾽ Ἀθηνέων μίαν ἑκάτεροι.
ἀριθμὸς δὲ ἐγένετο ὁ πᾶς τῶν νεῶν, πάρεξ τῶν
πεντηκοντέρων, τριηκόσιαι καὶ ἑβδομήκοντα καὶ
ὀκτώ.

49. Ὡς δὲ ἐς τὴν Σαλαμῖνα συνῆλθον οἱ στρατηγοὶ ἀπὸ τῶν εἰρημενέων πολίων, ἐβουλεύοντο,
προθέντος Εὐρυβιάδεω γνώμην ἀποφαίνεσθαι τὸν
βουλόμενον, ὅκου δοκέοι ἐπιτηδεότατον εἶναι ναυ-

islanders; but they paid no heed to the command and joined themselves to the Greeks, being invited thereto by Democritus, a man of note in their town, who was then captain of a trireme. The Naxians are Ionians, of Athenian lineage. The Styrians furnished the same number as at Artemisium, and the Cythnians one trireme and a fifty-oared bark; both these peoples are Dryopians. There were also in the fleet men of Seriphos and Siphnos and Melos, these being the only islanders who had not given the foreigner earth and water.

47. All these aforesaid came to the war from countries nearer than Thesprotia and the river Acheron; for Thesprotia marches with the Ampraciots and Leucadians, who came from the lands farthest distant. Of those that dwell farther off than these, the men of Croton alone came to aid Hellas in its peril, and they with one ship, whereof the captain was Phaÿllus, a victor in the Pythian games. These Crotoniats are of Achaean blood.

48. All these furnished triremes for the fleet save the Melians and Siphnians and Seriphians, who brought fifty-oared barks, the Melians (who are of Lacedaemonian stock) two, and the Siphnians and Seriphians (who are Ionians of Athenian lineage) one each. The whole number of the ships, besides the fifty-oared barks, was three hundred and seventy eight.

49. When the leaders from the cities aforenamed met at Salamis, they held a council; Eurybiades laid the matter before them, bidding whosoever would to declare what waters in his judgment were fittest for a sea-fight, among all places whereof the Greeks

μαχίην ποιέεσθαι τῶν αὐτοὶ χωρέων ἐγκρατέες
εἰσί· ἡ γὰρ Ἀττικὴ ἀπεῖτο ἤδη, τῶν δὲ λοιπέων
πέρι προετίθεε. αἱ γνῶμαι δὲ τῶν λεγόντων αἱ
πλεῖσται συνεξέπιπτον πρὸς τὸν Ἰσθμὸν πλώ-
σαντας ναυμαχέειν πρὸ τῆς Πελοποννήσου, ἐπι-
λέγοντες τὸν λόγον τόνδε, ὡς εἰ νικηθέωσι τῇ
ναυμαχίῃ, ἐν Σαλαμῖνι μὲν ἐόντες πολιορκήσονται
ἐν νήσῳ, ἵνα σφι τιμωρίη οὐδεμία ἐπιφανήσεται,
πρὸς δὲ τῷ Ἰσθμῷ ἐς τοὺς ἑωυτῶν ἐξοίσονται.

50. Ταῦτα τῶν ἀπὸ Πελοποννήσου στρατηγῶν
ἐπιλεγομένων, ἐληλύθεε ἀνὴρ Ἀθηναῖος ἀγγέλλων
ἥκειν τὸν βάρβαρον ἐς τὴν Ἀττικὴν καὶ πᾶσαν
αὐτὴν πυρπολέεσθαι. ὁ γὰρ διὰ Βοιωτῶν τραπόμενος στρατὸς ἅμα Ξέρξῃ, ἐμπρήσας Θεσπιέων
τὴν πόλιν, αὐτῶν ἐκλελοιπότων ἐς Πελοπόννησον,
καὶ τὴν Πλαταιέων ὡσαύτως, ἧκέ τε ἐς τὰς
Ἀθήνας καὶ πάντα ἐκεῖνα ἐδηίου. ἐνέπρησε δὲ
Θέσπειάν τε καὶ Πλάταιαν πυθόμενος Θηβαίων
ὅτι οὐκ ἐμήδιζον.

51. Ἀπὸ δὲ τῆς διαβάσιος τοῦ Ἑλλησπόντου,
ἔνθεν πορεύεσθαι ἤρξαντο οἱ βάρβαροι, ἕνα αὐτοῦ
διατρίψαντες μῆνα ἐν τῷ διέβαινον ἐς τὴν
Εὐρώπην, ἐν τρισὶ ἑτέροισι μησὶ ἐγένοντο ἐν
τῇ Ἀττικῇ, Καλλιάδεω ἄρχοντος Ἀθηναίοισι.
καὶ αἱρέουσι ἔρημον τὸ ἄστυ, καί τινας ὀλίγους
εὑρίσκουσι τῶν Ἀθηναίων ἐν τῷ ἱρῷ ἐόντας,
ταμίας τε τοῦ ἱροῦ καὶ πένητας ἀνθρώπους, οἳ
φραξάμενοι τὴν ἀκρόπολιν θύρῃσί τε καὶ ξύλοισι
ἠμύνοντο τοὺς ἐπιόντας, ἅμα μὲν ὑπ᾽ ἀσθενείης
βίου οὐκ ἐκχωρήσαντες ἐς Σαλαμῖνα, πρὸς δὲ
αὐτοὶ δοκέοντες ἐξευρηκέναι τὸ μαντήιον τὸ ἡ
Πυθίη σφι ἔχρησε, τὸ ξύλινον τεῖχος ἀνάλωτον

were masters; of Attica they had no more hope; it
was among other places that he bade them judge.
Then the opinion of most of the speakers tended to
the same conclusion, that they should sail to the
Isthmus and do battle by sea for the safety of the
Peloponnese, the reason which they alleged being
this, that if they were defeated in the fight at
Salamis they would be beleaguered in an island,
where no help could come to them; but off the
Isthmus they could win to their own coasts.

50. While the Peloponnesian captains held this
argument, there came a man of Athens, bringing
news that the foreigner was arrived in Attica, and
was wasting it all with fire. For the army which
followed Xerxes through Boeotia had burnt the
town of the Thespians (who had themselves left
it and gone to the Peloponnese) and Plataea likewise,
and was arrived at Athens, laying waste all the
country round. They burnt Thespia and Plataea
because they learnt from the Thebans that those
towns had not taken the Persian part.

51. Now after the crossing of the Hellespont
whence they began their march, the foreigners had
spent one month in their passage into Europe,
and in three more months they arrived in Attica,
Calliades being then archon at Athens. There they
took the city, then left desolate; but they found in
the temple some few Athenians, temple-stewards
and needy men, who defended themselves against
the assault by fencing the acropolis with doors and
logs; these had not withdrawn to Salamis, partly
by reason of poverty, and also because they supposed
themselves to have found out the meaning of the
Delphic oracle that the wooden wall should be

ἔσεσθαι· αὐτὸ δὴ τοῦτο εἶναι τὸ κρησφύγετον
κατὰ τὸ μαντήιον καὶ οὐ τὰς νέας.

52. Οἱ δὲ Πέρσαι ἱζόμενοι ἐπὶ τὸν καταντίον
τῆς ἀκροπόλιος ὄχθον, τὸν Ἀθηναῖοι καλέουσι
Ἀρήιον πάγον, ἐπολιόρκεον τρόπον τοιόνδε· ὅκως
στυππεῖον περὶ τοὺς ὀιστοὺς περιθέντες ἅψειαν,
ἐτόξευον ἐς τὸ φράγμα. ἐνθαῦτα Ἀθηναίων οἱ
πολιορκεόμενοι ὅμως ἠμύνοντο, καίπερ ἐς τὸ
ἔσχατον κακοῦ ἀπιγμένοι καὶ τοῦ φράγματος
προδεδωκότος· οὐδὲ λόγους τῶν Πεισιστρατιδέων
προσφερόντων περὶ ὁμολογίης ἐνεδέκοντο, ἀμυνόμενοι δὲ ἄλλα τε ἀντεμηχανῶντο καὶ δὴ καὶ
προσιόντων τῶν βαρβάρων πρὸς τὰς πύλας ὀλοι-
τρόχους ἀπίεσαν, ὥστε Ξέρξην ἐπὶ χρόνον συχνὸν
ἀπορίῃσι ἐνέχεσθαι οὐ δυνάμενον σφέας ἑλεῖν.

53. Χρόνῳ δ᾽ ἐκ τῶν ἀπόρων ἐφάνη δή τις
ἔξοδος τοῖσι βαρβάροισι· ἔδεε γὰρ κατὰ τὸ θεοπρόπιον πᾶσαν τὴν Ἀττικὴν τὴν ἐν τῇ ἠπείρῳ
γενέσθαι ὑπὸ Πέρσῃσι. ἔμπροσθε ὢν πρὸ τῆς
ἀκροπόλιος, ὄπισθε δὲ τῶν πυλέων καὶ τῆς
ἀνόδου, τῇ δὴ οὔτε τις ἐφύλασσε οὔτ᾽ ἂν ἤλπισε
μή κοτέ τις κατὰ ταῦτα ἀναβαίη ἀνθρώπων,
ταύτῃ ἀνέβησαν τινὲς κατὰ τὸ ἱρὸν τῆς Κέκροπος
θυγατρὸς Ἀγλαύρου, καίτοι περ ἀποκρήμνου
ἐόντος τοῦ χώρου. ὡς δὲ εἶδον αὐτοὺς ἀναβε-
βηκότας οἱ Ἀθηναῖοι ἐπὶ τὴν ἀκρόπολιν, οἱ μὲν
ἐρρίπτεον ἑωυτοὺς κατὰ τοῦ τείχεος κάτω καὶ
διεφθείροντο, οἱ δὲ ἐς τὸ μέγαρον κατέφευγον.
τῶν δὲ Περσέων οἱ ἀναβεβηκότες πρῶτον μὲν

---

[1] In vii. 142.

impregnable, and believed that this, and not the ships, was the refuge signified by the prophecy.[1]

52. The Persians sat down on the hill over against the acropolis, which is called by the Athenians the Hill of Ares, and besieged them by shooting arrows wrapped in lighted tow at the barricade. There the Athenians defended themselves against their besiegers, albeit they were in extremity and their barricade had failed them; nor would they listen to the terms of surrender proposed to them by the Pisistratids, but defended themselves by counter-devices, chiefly by rolling great stones down on the foreigners when they assaulted the gates; insomuch that for a long while Xerxes could not take the place, and knew not what to do.

53. But at the last in their quandary the foreigners found an entrance; for the oracle must needs be fulfilled, and all the mainland of Attica be made subject to the Persians. In front of the acropolis, and behind the gates and the ascent thereto, there was a place where none was on guard and none would have thought that any man would ascend that way; here certain men mounted near the shrine of Cecrops' daughter Aglaurus, though the way led up a sheer cliff.[2] When the Athenians saw that they had ascended to the acropolis, some of them cast themselves down from the wall and so perished, and others fled into the inner chamber. Those Persians who had come up first betook themselves

[2] Hdt.'s description (say How and Wells) is accurate and obvious. The ascent was probably made by a steep cleft running under or within the N. wall of the Acropolis; the western entrance of this cleft is 'in front,' facing the same way as the main entrance of the Acropolis. μέγαρον here = ἱρόν.

ἐτράποντο πρὸς τὰς πύλας, ταύτας δὲ ἀνοίξαντες
τοὺς ἱκέτας ἐφόνευον· ἐπεὶ δέ σφι πάντες κατέστρωντο, τὸ ἱρὸν συλήσαντες ἐνέπρησαν πᾶσαν
τὴν ἀκρόπολιν.

54. Σχὼν δὲ παντελέως τὰς Ἀθήνας Ξέρξης
ἀπέπεμψε ἐς Σοῦσα ἄγγελον ἱππέα Ἀρταβάνῳ
ἀγγελέοντα τὴν παρεοῦσάν σφι εὐπρηξίην. ἀπὸ
δὲ τῆς πέμψιος τοῦ κήρυκος δευτέρῃ ἡμέρῃ
συγκαλέσας Ἀθηναίων τοὺς φυγάδας, ἑωυτῷ δὲ
ἑπομένους, ἐκέλευε τρόπῳ τῷ σφετέρῳ θῦσαι τὰ
ἱρὰ ἀναβάντας ἐς τὴν ἀκρόπολιν, εἴτε δὴ ὦν ὄψιν
τινὰ ἰδὼν ἐνυπνίου ἐνετέλλετο ταῦτα, εἴτε καὶ
ἐνθύμιόν οἱ ἐγένετο ἐμπρήσαντι τὸ ἱρόν. οἱ δὲ
φυγάδες τῶν Ἀθηναίων ἐποίησαν τὰ ἐντεταλμένα.

55. Τοῦ δὲ εἵνεκεν τούτων ἐπεμνήσθην, φράσω.
ἔστι ἐν τῇ ἀκροπόλι ταύτῃ Ἐρεχθέος τοῦ γηγε-
νέος λεγομένου εἶναι νηός, ἐν τῷ ἐλαίη τε καὶ
θάλασσα ἔνι, τὰ λόγος παρὰ Ἀθηναίων Ποσει-
δέωνά τε καὶ Ἀθηναίην ἐρίσαντας περὶ τῆς χώρης
μαρτύρια θέσθαι. ταύτην ὦν τὴν ἐλαίην ἅμα τῷ
ἄλλῳ ἱρῷ κατέλαβε ἐμπρησθῆναι ὑπὸ τῶν βαρ-
βάρων· δευτέρῃ δὲ ἡμέρῃ ἀπὸ τῆς ἐμπρήσιος
Ἀθηναίων οἱ θύειν ὑπὸ βασιλέος κελευόμενοι
ὡς ἀνέβησαν ἐς τὸ ἱρόν, ὥρων βλαστὸν ἐκ τοῦ
στελέχεος ὅσον τε πηχυαῖον ἀναδεδραμηκότα.
οὗτοι μέν νυν ταῦτα ἔφρασαν.

56. Οἱ δὲ ἐν Σαλαμῖνι Ἕλληνες, ὥς σφι ἐξηγ-
γέλθη ὡς ἔσχε τὰ περὶ τὴν Ἀθηναίων ἀκρόπολιν,
ἐς τοσοῦτον θόρυβον ἀπίκοντο ὡς ἔνιοι τῶν στρατηγῶν οὐδὲ κυρωθῆναι ἔμενον τὸ προκείμενον
πρῆγμα, ἀλλ' ἔς τε τὰς νέας ἐσέπιπτον καὶ ἱστία
ἀείροντο ὡς ἀποθευσόμενοι· τοῖσί τε ὑπολειπο-

to the gates, which they opened, and slew the
suppliants; and when they had laid all the Athenians low, they plundered the temple and burnt the
whole of the acropolis.

54. Being now wholly master of Athens, Xerxes
sent a horseman to Susa to announce his present
success to Artabanus. On the next day after the
messenger was sent he called·together the Athenian
exiles who followed in his train, and bade them go
up to the acropolis and offer sacrifice after their
manner, whether it was some vision seen of him
in sleep that led him to give this charge, or that
he repented of his burning of the temple. The
Athenian exiles did as they were bidden.

55. I will now show wherefore I make mention of
this: on that acropolis there is a shrine of Erechtheus the Earthborn (as he is called), wherein is an
olive tree, and a salt-pool, which (as the Athenians
say) were set there by Poseidon and Athene as
tokens of their contention for the land.[1] Now it
was so, that the olive tree was burnt with the
temple by the foreigners; but on the day after its
burning, when the Athenians bidden by the king
to sacrifice went up to the temple, they saw a shoot
of about a cubit's length sprung from the trunk;
which thing they reported.

56. When it was told to the Greeks at Salamis
what had befallen the Athenian acropolis, they were
so panic-struck that some of their captains would not
wait till the matter whereon they debated should be
resolved, but threw themselves aboard their ships
and hoisted their sails for flight. Those that were

[1] Athene created the olive, Poseidon the salt pool; Cecrops
adjudged the land to Athene.

μένοισι αὐτῶν ἐκυρώθη πρὸ τοῦ Ἰσθμοῦ ναυμαχέειν. νύξ τε ἐγίνετο καὶ οἳ διαλυθέντες ἐκ τοῦ συνεδρίου ἐσέβαινον ἐς τὰς νέας.

57. Ἐνθαῦτα δὴ Θεμιστοκλέα ἀπικόμενον ἐπὶ τὴν νέα εἴρετο Μνησίφιλος ἀνὴρ Ἀθηναῖος ὅ τι σφι εἴη βεβουλευμένον. πυθόμενος δὲ πρὸς αὐτοῦ ὡς εἴη δεδογμένον ἀνάγειν τὰς νέας πρὸς τὸν Ἰσθμὸν καὶ πρὸ τῆς Πελοποννήσου ναυμαχέειν, εἶπε "Οὔτ' ἄρα, ἢν ἀπαείρωσι τὰς νέας ἀπὸ Σαλαμῖνος, περὶ οὐδεμιῆς ἔτι πατρίδος ναυμαχήσεις· κατὰ γὰρ πόλις ἕκαστοι τρέψονται, καὶ οὔτε σφέας Εὐρυβιάδης κατέχειν δυνήσεται οὔτε τις ἀνθρώπων ἄλλος ὥστε μὴ οὐ διασκεδασθῆναι τὴν στρατιήν· ἀπολέεταί τε ἡ Ἑλλὰς ἀβουλίῃσι. ἀλλ' εἴ τις ἐστὶ μηχανή,. ἴθι καὶ πειρῶ διαχέαι τὰ βεβουλευμένα, ἤν κως δύνῃ ἀναγνῶσαι Εὐρυβιάδην μεταβουλεύσασθαι ὥστε αὐτοῦ μένειν."

58. Κάρτα τε τῷ Θεμιστοκλέι ἤρεσε ἡ ὑποθήκη, καὶ οὐδὲν πρὸς ταῦτα ἀμειψάμενος ἤιε ἐπὶ τὴν νέα τὴν Εὐρυβιάδεω. ἀπικόμενος δὲ ἔφη ἐθέλειν οἱ κοινόν τι πρῆγμα συμμῖξαι· ὃ δ' αὐτὸν ἐς τὴν νέα ἐκέλευε ἐσβάντα λέγειν, εἴ τι θέλει. ἐνθαῦτα ὁ Θεμιστοκλέης παριζόμενός οἱ καταλέγει ἐκεῖνά τε πάντα τὰ ἤκουσε Μνησιφίλου, ἑωυτοῦ ποιεύμενος, καὶ ἄλλα πολλὰ προστιθείς, ἐς ὃ ἀνέγνωσε χρηίζων ἔκ τε τῆς νεὸς ἐκβῆναι συλλέξαι τε τοὺς στρατηγοὺς ἐς τὸ συνέδριον.

59. Ὡς δὲ ἄρα συνελέχθησαν, πρὶν ἢ τὸν Εὐρυβιάδην προθεῖναι τὸν λόγον τῶν εἵνεκα συνήγαγε τοὺς στρατηγούς, πολλὸς ἦν ὁ Θεμιστοκλέης ἐν τοῖσι λόγοισι οἷα κάρτα δεόμενος·

left behind resolved that the fleet should fight to
guard the Isthmus; and at nightfall they broke up
from the assembly and embarked.

57. Themistocles then being returned to his ship,
Mnesiphilus, an Athenian, asked him what was the
issue of their counsels. Learning from him that their
plan was to sail to the Isthmus and fight in defence
of the Peloponnese, "Then," said Mnesiphilus, "if
they put out to sea from Salamis, your ships will
have no country left wherefor to fight; for everyone will betake himself to his own city, and neither
Eurybiades, nor any other man, will be able to
hold them, but the armament will be scattered
abroad; and Hellas will perish. by unwisdom. Nay,
if there be any means thereto, go now and strive to
undo this plan, if haply you may be able to persuade
Eurybiades to change his purpose and so abide
here."

58. This advice pleased Themistocles well; making
no answer to Mnesiphilus, he went to Eurybiades'
ship, and said that he would confer with him on a
matter of their common interest. Eurybiades bidding him come aboard and say what he would,
Themistocles sat by him and told him all that he
had heard from Mnesiphilus, as it were of his own
devising, and added much thereto, till he prevailed
with the Spartan by entreaty to come out of his
ship and assemble the admirals in their place of
meeting.

59. They being assembled (so it is said), before
Eurybiades had laid before them the matter wherefor
the generals were brought together, Themistocles
spoke long and vehemently in the earnestness of his
entreaty; and while he yet spoke, Adimantus son

λέγοντος δὲ αὐτοῦ, ὁ Κορίνθιος στρατηγὸς Ἀδείμαντος ὁ Ὠκύτου εἶπε "Ὦ Θεμιστόκλεες, ἐν τοῖσι
ἀγῶσι οἱ προεξανιστάμενοι ῥαπίζονται." ὁ δὲ
ἀπολυόμενος ἔφη "Οἱ δέ γε ἐγκαταλειπόμενοι οὐ
στεφανοῦνται."

60. Τότε μὲν ἠπίως πρὸς τὸν Κορίνθιον ἀμεί-
ψατο, πρὸς δὲ τὸν Εὐρυβιάδην ἔλεγε ἐκείνων μὲν
ἔτι οὐδὲν τῶν πρότερον λεχθέντων, ὡς ἐπεὰν
ἀπαείρωσι ἀπὸ Σαλαμῖνος διαδρήσονται· παρεόντων γὰρ τῶν συμμάχων οὐκ ἔφερέ οἱ κόσμον
οὐδένα κατηγορέειν· ὁ δὲ ἄλλου λόγου εἴχετο,
λέγων τάδε. "Ἐν σοὶ νῦν ἐστὶ σῶσαι τὴν Ἑλλάδα,
ἢν ἐμοὶ πείθῃ ναυμαχίην αὐτοῦ μένων ποιέεσθαι,
μηδὲ πειθόμενος τούτων τοῖσι λόγοισι ἀναζεύξῃς
πρὸς τὸν Ἰσθμὸν τὰς νέας. · ἀντίθες γὰρ ἑκάτερον
ἀκούσας. πρὸς μὲν τῷ Ἰσθμῷ συμβάλλων ἐν
πελάγεϊ ἀναπεπταμένῳ ναυμαχήσεις, ἐς τὸ ἥκιστα
ἡμῖν σύμφορον ἐστὶ νέας ἔχουσι βαρυτέρας καὶ
ἀριθμὸν ἐλάσσονας· τοῦτο δὲ ἀπολέεις Σαλαμῖνά
τε καὶ Μέγαρα καὶ Αἴγιναν, ἤν περ καὶ τὰ ἄλλα
εὐτυχήσωμεν. ἅμα δὲ τῷ ναυτικῷ αὐτῶν ἕψεται
καὶ ὁ πεζὸς στρατός, καὶ οὕτω σφέας αὐτὸς ἄξεις
ἐπὶ τὴν Πελοπόννησον, κινδυνεύσεις τε ἁπάσῃ τῇ
Ἑλλάδι. ἢν δὲ τὰ ἐγὼ λέγω ποιήσῃς, τοσάδε ἐν
αὐτοῖσι χρηστὰ εὑρήσεις· πρῶτα μὲν ἐν στεινῷ
συμβάλλοντες νηυσὶ ὀλίγῃσι πρὸς πολλάς, ἢν τὰ
οἰκότα ἐκ τοῦ πολέμου ἐκβαίνῃ, πολλὸν κρατή-
σομεν· τὸ γὰρ ἐν στεινῷ ναυμαχέειν πρὸς ἡμέων
ἐστί, ἐν εὐρυχωρίῃ δὲ πρὸς ἐκείνων. αὖτις δὲ
Σαλαμὶς περιγίνεται, ἐς τὴν ἡμῖν ὑπέκκειται
τέκνα τε καὶ γυναῖκες. καὶ μὲν καὶ τόδε ἐν
αὐτοῖσι ἔνεστι, τοῦ καὶ περιέχεσθε μάλιστα·

54

of Ocytus, the Corinthian admiral, said, " At the games, Themistocles, they that come forward before their time are beaten with rods." " Ay," said Themistocles, justifying himself, " but they that wait too long win no crown."

60. Thus for the nonce he made the Corinthian a soft answer ; then turning to Eurybiades, he said now nought of what he had said before, how that if they set sail from Salamis they would scatter and flee ; for it would have ill become him to bring railing accusations against the allies in their presence ; he trusted to another plea instead. " It lies in your hand," said he, " to save Hellas, if you will be guided by me and fight here at sea, and not be won by the words of these others to remove your ships over to the Isthmus. Hear me now, and judge between two plans. If you engage off the Isthmus you will fight in open waters, where it is least for our advantage, our ships being the heavier and the fewer in number ; and moreover you will lose Salamis and Megara and Aegina, even if victory attend us otherwise ; and their land army will follow with their fleet, and so you will lead them to the Peloponnese, and imperil all Hellas. But if you do as I counsel you, you will thereby profit as I shall show : firstly, by engaging their many ships with our few in narrow seas, we shall win a great victory, if the war have its rightful issue ; for it is for our advantage to fight in a strait as it is theirs to have wide sea-room. Secondly, we save Salamis, whither we have conveyed away our children and our women. Moreover, there is this, too, in my plan, and it is your chiefest desire : you will be defending the

ὁμοίως αὐτοῦ τε μένων προναυμαχήσεις Πελοποννήσου καὶ πρὸς τῷ Ἰσθμῷ, οὐδὲ σφέας, εἴ
περ εὖ φρονέεις, ἄξεις ἐπὶ τὴν Πελοπόννησον.
ἢν δέ γε καὶ τὰ ἐγὼ ἐλπίζω γένηται καὶ νικήσωμεν
τῇσι νηυσί, οὔτε ὑμῖν ἐς τὸν Ἰσθμὸν παρέσονται
οἱ βάρβαροι οὔτε προβήσονται ἑκαστέρω τῆς
Ἀττικῆς, ἀπίασί τε οὐδενὶ κόσμῳ, Μεγάροισί τε
κερδανέομεν περιεοῦσι καὶ Αἰγίνῃ καὶ Σαλαμῖνι,
ἐν τῇ ἡμῖν καὶ λόγιον ἐστὶ τῶν ἐχθρῶν κατύπερθε
γενέσθαι. οἰκότα μέν νυν βουλευομένοισι ἀνθρώποισι ὡς τὸ ἐπίπαν ἐθέλει γίνεσθαι· μὴ δὲ οἰκότα
βουλευομένοισι οὐκ ἐθέλει οὐδὲ ὁ θεὸς προσχωρέειν
πρὸς τὰς ἀνθρωπηίας γνώμας."

61. Ταῦτα λέγοντος Θεμιστοκλέος αὖτις ὁ
Κορίνθιος Ἀδείμαντος ἐπεφέρετο, σιγᾶν τε
κελεύων τῷ μὴ ἐστὶ πατρὶς καὶ Εὐρυβιάδην οὐκ
ἐῶν ἐπιψηφίζειν ἀπόλι ἀνδρί· πόλιν γὰρ τὸν
Θεμιστοκλέα παρεχόμενον οὕτω ἐκέλευε γνώμας
συμβάλλεσθαι. ταῦτα δέ οἱ προέφερε ὅτι ἡλώ-
κεσάν τε καὶ κατείχοντο αἱ Ἀθῆναι. τότε δὴ ὁ
Θεμιστοκλέης κεῖνόν τε καὶ τοὺς Κορινθίους
πολλά τε καὶ κακὰ ἔλεγε, ἑωυτοῖσί τε ἐδήλου
λόγῳ ὡς εἴη καὶ πόλις καὶ γῆ μέζων ἤ περ
ἐκείνοισι, ἔστ' ἂν διηκόσιαι νέες σφι ἔωσι
πεπληρωμέναι· οὐδαμοὺς γὰρ Ἑλλήνων αὐτοὺς
ἐπιόντας ἀποκρούσεσθαι.

62. Σημαίνων δὲ ταῦτα τῷ λόγῳ διέβαινε ἐς
Εὐρυβιάδην, λέγων μᾶλλον ἐπεστραμμένα. "Σὺ
εἰ μενέεις αὐτοῦ καὶ μένων ἔσεαι ἀνὴρ ἀγαθός·
εἰ δὲ μή, ἀνατρέψεις τὴν Ἑλλάδα· τὸ πᾶν γὰρ
ἡμῖν τοῦ πολέμου φέρουσι αἱ νέες. ἀλλ' ἐμοὶ
πείθεο. εἰ δὲ ταῦτα μὴ ποιήσῃς, ἡμεῖς μὲν ὡς

Peloponnese as well by abiding here as you would by fighting off the Isthmus, and you will not lead our enemies (if you be wise) to the Isthmus. And if that happen which I expect, you will never have the foreigners upon you at the Isthmus; they will advance no further than Attica, but depart in disorderly fashion; and we shall gain by the saving of Megara and Aegina and Salamis, where it is told us by an oracle that we shall have the upper hand of our enemies. Success comes oftenest to men when they make reasonable designs; but if they do not so, neither will heaven for its part side with human devices."

61. Thus said Themistocles; but Adimantus the Corinthian attacked him again, saying that a landless man should hold his peace, and that Eurybiades must not suffer one that had no city to vote; let Themistocles (said he) have a city at his back ere he took part in council,—taunting him thus because Athens was taken and held by the enemy. Thereupon Themistocles spoke long and bitterly against Adimantus and the Corinthians, giving them plainly to understand that the Athenians had a city and country greater than theirs, as long as they had two hundred ships fully manned; for there were no Greeks that could beat them off.

62. Thus declaring, he passed over to Eurybiades, and spoke more vehemently than before. "If you abide here, by so abiding you will be a right good man; but if you will not, you will overthrow Hellas; for all our strength for war is in our ships. Nay, be guided by me. But if you do not so, we then

ἔχομεν ἀναλαβόντες τοὺς οἰκέτας κομιεύμεθα ἐς
Σῖριν τὴν ἐν Ἰταλίῃ, ἥ περ ἡμετέρη τε ἐστὶ ἐκ
παλαιοῦ ἔτι, καὶ τὰ λόγια λέγει ὑπ᾽ ἡμέων αὐτὴν
δέειν κτισθῆναι· ὑμεῖς δὲ συμμάχων τοιῶνδε
μουνωθέντες μεμνήσεσθε τῶν ἐμῶν λόγων."

63. Ταῦτα δὲ Θεμιστοκλέος λέγοντος ἀνεδιδάσκετο Εὐρυβιάδης· δοκέειν δέ μοι, ἀρρωδήσας
μάλιστα τοὺς Ἀθηναίους ἀνεδιδάσκετο, μή σφεας
ἀπολίπωσι, ἢν πρὸς τὸν Ἰσθμὸν ἀγάγῃ τὰς νέας·
ἀπολιπόντων γὰρ Ἀθηναίων οὐκέτι ἐγίνοντο
ἀξιόμαχοι οἱ λοιποί. ταύτην δὲ αἱρέεται τὴν
γνώμην, αὐτοῦ μένοντας διαναυμαχέειν.

64. Οὕτω μὲν οἱ περὶ Σαλαμῖνα ἔπεσι ἀκρο-
βολισάμενοι, ἐπείτε Εὐρυβιάδῃ ἔδοξε, αὐτοῦ
παρεσκευάζοντο ὡς ναυμαχήσοντες. ἡμέρη τε
ἐγίνετο καὶ ἅμα τῷ ἡλίῳ ἀνιόντι σεισμὸς ἐγένετο
ἔν τε τῇ γῇ καὶ τῇ θαλάσσῃ. ἔδοξε δέ σφι
εὔξασθαι τοῖσι θεοῖσι καὶ ἐπικαλέσασθαι τοὺς
Αἰακίδας συμμάχους. ὡς δέ σφι ἔδοξε, καὶ
ἐποίευν ταῦτα· εὐξάμενοι γὰρ πᾶσι τοῖσι θεοῖσι,
αὐτόθεν μὲν ἐκ Σαλαμῖνος Αἴαντά τε καὶ Τελα-
μῶνα ἐπεκαλέοντο, ἐπὶ δὲ Αἰακὸν καὶ τοὺς ἄλλους
Αἰακίδας νέα ἀπέστελλον ἐς Αἴγιναν.

65. Ἔφη δὲ Δίκαιος ὁ Θεοκύδεος, ἀνὴρ Ἀθηναῖος
φυγάς τε καὶ παρὰ Μήδοισι λόγιμος γενόμενος
τοῦτον τὸν χρόνον, ἐπείτε ἐκείρετο ἡ Ἀττικὴ
χώρη ὑπὸ τοῦ πεζοῦ στρατοῦ τοῦ Ξέρξεω ἐοῦσα
ἔρημος Ἀθηναίων, τυχεῖν τότε ἐὼν ἅμα Δημαρήτῳ
τῷ Λακεδαιμονίῳ ἐν τῷ Θριασίῳ πεδίῳ, ἰδεῖν δὲ

---

[1] The images of Aeacus and his sons; *cp.* v. 80.

[2] N.W. of Athens, from which Eleusis is about 15 miles
distant. Plutarch says that the vision was seen on the day

without more ado will take our households and voyage
to Siris in Italy, which has been ours from old time,
and the oracles tell that we must there plant a
colony ; and you, left without allies such as we are,
will have cause to remember what I have said."

63. These words of Themistocles moved Eurybiades
to change his purpose ; which to my thinking he did
chiefly because he feared lest the Athenians should
leave him if he took his ships to the Isthmus ; for
if the Athenians should leave the fleet the rest
would be no match for the enemy. He chose then
the plan aforesaid, namely, to abide and fight on the
seas where they were.

64. Thus after this wordy skirmish the Greeks at
Salamis prepared, since Eurybiades so willed, to
fight their battle where they were. At sunrise on
the next day there was an earthquake on land and
sea ; and they resolved to pray to the gods, and to
call the sons of Aeacus to be their helpers. As they
resolved, so they did ; they prayed to all the gods,
and called Aias and Telamon to come to them from
Salamis, where the Greeks were; and they sent a
ship to Aegina for Aeacus and the rest that were of
his House.[1]

65. There was one Dicaeus, son of Theocydes, an
exile from Athens who had attained to estimation
among the Medes. This was the tale that he told :
At the time when the land of Attica was being laid
waste by Xerxes' army, and no Athenians were
therein, he, being with Demaratus the Lacedaemonian on the Thriasian [2] plain, saw dust coming

of the battle of Salamis, which would thus have been fought
on September 22 (20th of Boedromion) ; for it is assumed that
the vision coincided in date with the standing date of the
Eleusinian festival.

κονιορτὸν χωρέοντα ἀπ' Ἐλευσῖνος ὡς ἀνδρῶν
μάλιστά κῃ τρισμυρίων, ἀποθωμάζειν τε σφέας
τὸν κονιορτὸν ὅτεων κοτὲ εἴη ἀνθρώπων, καὶ
πρόκατε φωνῆς ἀκούειν, καί οἱ φαίνεσθαι τὴν
φωνὴν εἶναι τὸν μυστικὸν ἴακχον. εἶναι δ'
ἀδαήμονα τῶν ἱρῶν τῶν ἐν Ἐλευσῖνι γινομένων
τὸν Δημάρητον, εἰρέσθαί τε αὐτὸν ὅ τι τὸ φθεγγόμενον εἴη τοῦτο. αὐτὸς δὲ εἰπεῖν "Δημάρητε,
οὐκ ἔστι ὅκως οὐ μέγα τι σίνος ἔσται τῇ βασιλέος
στρατιῇ· τάδε γὰρ ἀρίδηλα, ἐρήμου ἐούσης τῆς
Ἀττικῆς, ὅτι θεῖον τὸ φθεγγόμενον, ἀπ' Ἐλευσῖνος
ἰὸν ἐς τιμωρίην Ἀθηναίοισί τε καὶ τοῖσι συμμάχοισι. καὶ ἢν μέν γε κατασκήψῃ ἐς τὴν
Πελοπόννησον, κίνδυνος αὐτῷ τε βασιλέι καὶ
τῇ στρατιῇ τῇ ἐν τῇ ἠπείρῳ ἔσται, ἢν δὲ ἐπὶ
τὰς νέας τράπηται τὰς ἐν Σαλαμῖνι, τὸν ναυτικὸν
στρατὸν κινδυνεύσει βασιλεὺς ἀποβαλεῖν. τὴν
δὲ ὁρτὴν ταύτην ἄγουσι Ἀθηναῖοι ἀνὰ πάντα
ἔτεα τῇ Μητρὶ καὶ τῇ Κούρῃ, καὶ αὐτῶν τε ὁ
βουλόμενος καὶ τῶν ἄλλων Ἑλλήνων μυεῖται·
καὶ τὴν φωνὴν τῆς ἀκούεις ἐν ταύτῃ τῇ ὁρτῇ
ἰακχάζουσι." πρὸς ταῦτα εἰπεῖν Δημάρητον
"Σίγα τε καὶ μηδενὶ ἄλλῳ τὸν λόγον τοῦτον
εἴπῃς· ἢν γάρ τοι ἐς βασιλέα ἀνενειχθῇ τὰ ἔπεα
ταῦτα, ἀποβαλέεις τὴν κεφαλήν, καί σε οὔτε ἐγὼ
δυνήσομαι ῥύσασθαι οὔτ' ἄλλος ἀνθρώπων οὐδὲ
εἷς. ἀλλ' ἔχ' ἥσυχος, περὶ δὲ στρατιῆς τῆσδε
θεοῖσι μελήσει." τὸν μὲν δὴ ταῦτα παραινέειν,
ἐκ δὲ τοῦ κονιορτοῦ καὶ τῆς φωνῆς γενέσθαι
νέφος καὶ μεταρσιωθὲν φέρεσθαι ἐπὶ Σαλαμῖνος
ἐπὶ τὸ στρατόπεδον τὸ τῶν Ἑλλήνων. οὕτω δὴ
αὐτοὺς μαθεῖν ὅτι τὸ ναυτικὸν τὸ Ξέρξεω ἀπο-

from Eleusis as it were raised by the feet of about thirty thousand men; and as they marvelled greatly what men they should be whence the dust came, immediately they heard a cry, which cry seemed to him to be the Iacchus-song of the mysteries. Demaratus, not being conversant with the rites of Eleusis, asked him what this voice might be; and Dicaeus said, "Without doubt, Demaratus, some great harm will befall the king's host; for Attica being unpeopled, it is plain hereby that the voice we hear is of heaven's sending, and comes from Eleusis to the aid of the Athenians and their allies. And if the vision descend upon the Peloponnese, the king himself and his army on land will be endangered; but if it turn towards the ships at Salamis, the king will be in peril of losing his fleet. As for this feast, it is kept by the Athenians every year for the honour of the Mother and the Maid,[1] and whatever Greek will, be he Athenian or other, is then initiated; and the cry which you hear is the 'Iacchus' which is uttered at this feast." Demaratus replied thereto, "Keep silence, and speak to none other thus; for if these words of yours be reported to the king, you will lose your head, and neither I nor any other man will avail to save you. Hold your peace; and for this host, the gods shall look to it." Such was Demaratus' counsel; and after the dust and the cry came a cloud, which rose aloft and floated away towards Salamis, to the Greek fleet. By this they understood, that Xerxes' ships must perish.—This was

---

[1] Demeter and Persephone.

λέεσθαι μέλλοι. ταῦτα μὲν Δίκαιος ὁ Θεοκύδεος
ἔλεγε, Δημαρήτου τε καὶ ἄλλων μαρτύρων
καταπτόμενος.

66. Οἱ δὲ ἐς τὸν Ξέρξεω ναυτικὸν στρατὸν
ταχθέντες, ἐπειδὴ ἐκ Τρηχῖνος θεησάμενοι τὸ
τρῶμα τὸ Λακωνικὸν διέβησαν ἐς τὴν Ἱστιαίην,
ἐπισχόντες ἡμέρας τρεῖς ἔπλεον δι' Εὐρίπου, καὶ
ἐν ἑτέρῃσι τρισὶ ἡμέρῃσι ἐγένοντο ἐν Φαλήρῳ.
ὡς μὲν ἐμοὶ δοκέειν, οὐκ ἐλάσσονες ἐόντες ἀριθμὸν ἐσέβαλον ἐς τὰς Ἀθήνας, κατά τε ἤπειρον
καὶ τῇσι νηυσὶ ἀπικόμενοι, ἢ ἐπί τε Σηπιάδα
ἀπίκοντο καὶ ἐς Θερμοπύλας· ἀντιθήσω γὰρ
τοῖσί τε ὑπὸ τοῦ χειμῶνος αὐτῶν ἀπολομένοισι
καὶ τοῖσι ἐν Θερμοπύλῃσι καὶ τῇσι ἐπ' Ἀρτεμισίῳ
ναυμαχίῃσι τούσδε τοὺς τότε οὔκω ἑπομένους
βασιλέι, Μηλιέας καὶ Δωριέας καὶ Λοκροὺς καὶ
Βοιωτοὺς πανστρατιῇ ἑπομένους πλὴν Θεσπιέων
καὶ Πλαταιέων, καὶ μάλα Καρυστίους τε καὶ
Ἀνδρίους καὶ Τηνίους τε καὶ τοὺς λοιποὺς
νησιώτας πάντας, πλὴν τῶν πέντε πολίων τῶν
ἐπεμνήσθημεν πρότερον τὰ οὐνόματα. ὅσῳ γὰρ
δὴ προέβαινε ἐσωτέρω τῆς Ἑλλάδος ὁ Πέρσης,
τοσούτῳ πλέω ἔθνεά οἱ εἵπετο.

67. Ἐπεὶ ὧν ἀπίκατο ἐς τὰς Ἀθήνας πάντες
οὗτοι πλὴν Παρίων (Πάριοι δὲ ὑπολειφθέντες ἐν
Κύθνῳ ἐκαραδόκεον τὸν πόλεμον κῇ ἀποβήσεται),
οἱ δὲ λοιποὶ ὡς ἀπίκοντο ἐς τὸ Φάληρον, ἐνθαῦτα
κατέβη αὐτὸς Ξέρξης ἐπὶ τὰς νέας, ἐθέλων σφι
συμμῖξαί τε καὶ πυθέσθαι τῶν ἐπιπλεόντων τὰς
γνώμας. ἐπεὶ δὲ ἀπικόμενος προΐζετο, παρῆσαν
μετάπεμπτοι οἱ τῶν ἐθνέων τῶν σφετέρων τύ-
ραννοι καὶ ταξίαρχοι ἀπὸ τῶν νεῶν, καὶ ἵζοντο

the tale told by Dicaeus, son of Theocydes; and Demaratus and others (he said) could prove it true.

66. They that were appointed to serve in Xerxes' fleet, when they had viewed the hurt done to the Laconians and crossed over from Trachis to Histiaea, after three days' waiting sailed through the Euripus, and in three more days they arrived at Phalerum. To my thinking, the forces both of land and sea were no fewer in number when they brake into Athens than when they came to Sepias and Thermopylae; for against those that were lost in the storm, and at Thermopylae, and in the sea-fights off Artemisium, I set these, who at that time were not yet in the king's following—namely, the Melians, the Dorians, the Locrians, and the whole force of Boeotia (save only the Thespians and Plataeans), yea, and the men of Carystus and Andros and Tenos and the rest of the islands, save the five states of which I have before made mention.[1] For the farther the Persian pressed on into Hellas the more were the peoples that followed in his train.

67. So when all these were come to Athens, except the Parians (who had been left behind in Cythnus watching to see which way the war should incline)—the rest, I say, being come to Phalerum, Xerxes then came himself down to the fleet, that he might consort with the shipmen and hear their opinions. When he was come, and sat enthroned, there appeared before him at his summons the despots of their cities and the leaders of companies from the ships, and they sat according to the

---

[1] In ch. 46, where, however, six states are mentioned.

ὥς σφι βασιλεὺς ἑκάστῳ τιμὴν ἐδεδώκεε, πρῶτος
μὲν ὁ Σιδώνιος βασιλεύς, μετὰ δὲ ὁ Τύριος, ἐπὶ
δὲ ὧλλοι. ὡς δὲ κόσμῳ ἐπεξῆς ἵζοντο, πέμψας
Ξέρξης Μαρδόνιον εἰρώτα ἀποπειρώμενος ἑκάστου
εἰ ναυμαχίην ποιέοιτο.

68. Ἐπεὶ δὲ περιιὼν εἰρώτα ὁ Μαρδόνιος ἀρξά-
μενος ἀπὸ τοῦ Σιδωνίου, οἱ μὲν ἄλλοι κατὰ
τὠυτὸ γνώμην ἐξεφέροντο κελεύοντες ναυμαχίην
ποιέεσθαι, Ἀρτεμισίη δὲ τάδε ἔφη. " Εἰπεῖν μοι
πρὸς βασιλέα, Μαρδόνιε, ὡς ἐγὼ τάδε λέγω, οὔτε
κακίστη γενομένη ἐν τῇσι ναυμαχίῃσι τῇσι πρὸς
Εὐβοίῃ οὔτε ἐλάχιστα ἀποδεξαμένη. δέσποτα,
τὴν δὲ ἐοῦσαν γνώμην με δίκαιον ἐστὶ ἀποδεί-
κνυσθαι, τὰ τυγχάνω φρονέουσα ἄριστα ἐς πρήγματα τὰ σά. καί τοι τάδε λέγω, φείδεο τῶν νεῶν
μηδὲ ναυμαχίην ποιέο. οἱ γὰρ ἄνδρες τῶν σῶν
ἀνδρῶν κρέσσονες τοσοῦτο εἰσὶ κατὰ θάλασσαν
ὅσον ἄνδρες γυναικῶν. τί δὲ πάντως δέει σε
ναυμαχίῃσι ἀνακινδυνεύειν; οὐκ ἔχεις μὲν τὰς
Ἀθήνας, τῶν περ εἵνεκα ὁρμήθης στρατεύεσθαι,
ἔχεις δὲ τὴν ἄλλην Ἑλλάδα; ἐμποδὼν δέ τοι
ἵσταται οὐδείς· οἱ δέ τοι ἀντέστησαν, ἀπήλλαξαν
οὕτω ὡς κείνους ἔπρεπε. τῇ δὲ ἐγὼ δοκέω ἀποβήσεσθαι τὰ τῶν ἀντιπολέμων πρήγματα, τοῦτο
φράσω. ἢν μὲν μὴ ἐπειχθῇς ναυμαχίην ποιεύμενος, ἀλλὰ τὰς νέας αὐτοῦ ἔχῃς πρὸς γῇ μένων
ἢ καὶ προβαίνων ἐς τὴν Πελοπόννησον, εὐπετέως
τοι δέσποτα χωρήσει τὰ νοέων ἐλήλυθας. οὐ
γὰρ οἷοί τε πολλὸν χρόνον εἰσί τοι ἀντέχειν οἱ
Ἕλληνες, ἀλλὰ σφέας διασκεδᾷς, κατὰ πόλις δὲ
ἕκαστοι φεύξονται. οὔτε γὰρ σῖτος πάρα σφι ἐν
τῇ νήσῳ ταύτῃ, ὡς ἐγὼ πυνθάνομαι, οὔτε αὐτοὺς

honourable rank which the king had granted them
severally, first in place the king of Sidon, and next
he of Tyre, and then the rest. When they had sat
down in order one after another, Xerxes sent Mardonius and put each to the test by questioning him
if the Persian ships should offer battle.

68. Mardonius went about questioning them, from
the Sidonian onwards; and all the rest gave their
united voice for offering battle at sea; but Artemisia said: "Tell the king, I pray you, Mardonius,
that I who say this have not been the hindmost in
courage or in feats of arms in the fights near Euboea.
Nay, master, but it is right that I should declare my
opinion, even that which I deem best for your cause.
And this I say to you—Spare your ships, and offer
no battle at sea; for their men are as much stronger
by sea than yours, as men are stronger than women.
And why must you at all costs imperil yourself by
fighting battles on the sea? have you not possession
of Athens, for the sake of which you set out on this
march, and of the rest of Hellas? no man stands in
your path; they that resisted you have come off in
such plight as beseemed them. I will show you now
what I think will be the course of your enemies'
doings. If you make no haste to fight at sea, but
keep your ships here and abide near the land, or
even go forward into the Peloponnese, then, my
master, you will easily gain that end wherefor you
have come. For the Greeks are not able to hold
out against you for a long time, but you will scatter
them, and they will flee each to his city; they have
no food in this island, as I am informed, nor, if you

65

οἰκός, ἢν σὺ ἐπὶ τὴν Πελοπόννησον ἐλαύνῃς τὸν πεζὸν στρατόν, ἀτρεμιεῖν τοὺς ἐκεῖθεν αὐτῶν ἥκοντας, οὐδέ σφι μελήσει πρὸ τῶν Ἀθηνέων ναυμαχέειν. ἢν δὲ αὐτίκα ἐπειχθῇς ναυμαχῆσαι, δειμαίνω μὴ ὁ ναυτικὸς στρατὸς κακωθεὶς τὸν πεζὸν προσδηλήσηται. πρὸς δέ, ὦ βασιλεῦ, καὶ τόδε ἐς θυμὸν βάλευ, ὡς τοῖσι μὲν χρηστοῖσι τῶν ἀνθρώπων κακοὶ δοῦλοι φιλέουσι γίνεσθαι, τοῖσι δὲ κακοῖσι χρηστοί. σοὶ δὲ ἐόντι ἀρίστῳ ἀνδρῶν πάντων κακοὶ δοῦλοι εἰσί, οἳ ἐν συμμάχων λόγῳ λέγονται εἶναι ἐόντες Αἰγύπτιοί τε καὶ Κύπριοι καὶ Κίλικες καὶ Πάμφυλοι, τῶν ὄφελος ἐστὶ οὐδέν."

69. Ταῦτα λεγούσης πρὸς Μαρδόνιον, ὅσοι μὲν ἦσαν εὔνοοι τῇ Ἀρτεμισίῃ, συμφορὴν ἐποιεῦντο τοὺς λόγους ὡς κακόν τι πεισομένης πρὸς βασιλέος, ὅτι οὐκ ἔα ναυμαχίην ποιέεσθαι· οἱ δὲ ἀγεόμενοί τε καὶ φθονέοντες αὐτῇ, ἅτε ἐν πρώτοισι τετιμημένης διὰ πάντων τῶν συμμάχων, ἐτέρποντο τῇ ἀνακρίσι ὡς ἀπολεομένης αὐτῆς. ἐπεὶ δὲ ἀνηνείχθησαν αἱ γνῶμαι ἐς Ξέρξην, κάρτα τε ἥσθη τῇ γνώμῃ τῇ Ἀρτεμισίης, καὶ νομίζων ἔτι πρότερον σπουδαίην εἶναι τότε πολλῷ μᾶλλον αἴνεε. ὅμως δὲ τοῖσι πλέοσι πείθεσθαι ἐκέλευε, τάδε καταδόξας, πρὸς μὲν Εὐβοίῃ σφέας ἐθελοκακέειν ὡς οὐ παρεόντος αὐτοῦ, τότε δὲ αὐτὸς παρεσκεύαστο θεήσασθαι ναυμαχέοντας.

70. Ἐπεὶ δὲ παρήγγελλον ἀναπλέειν, ἀνῆγον τὰς νέας ἐπὶ τὴν Σαλαμῖνα καὶ παρεκρίθησαν διαταχθέντες κατ' ἡσυχίην. τότε μέν νυν οὐκ ἐξέχρησέ σφι ἡ ἡμέρη ναυμαχίην ποιήσασθαι· νὺξ γὰρ ἐπεγένετο· οἱ δὲ παρεσκευάζοντο ἐς τὴν

lead your army into the Peloponnese, is it likely
that those of them who have come from thence will
abide unmoved; they will have no mind to fight
sea-battles for Athens. But if you make haste to
fight at once on sea, I fear lest your fleet take some
hurt and thereby harm your army likewise. Moreover, O king, call this to mind—good men's slaves
are wont to be evil and bad men's slaves good; and
you, who are the best of all men, have evil slaves,
that pass for your allies, men of Egypt and Cyprus
and Cilicia and Pamphylia, in whom is no usefulness."

69. When Artemisia spoke thus to Mardonius, all
that were her friends were sorry for her words,
thinking that the king would do her some hurt for
counselling him against a sea-fight; but they that
had ill-will and jealousy against her for the honour
in which she was held above all the allies were glad
at her answer, thinking it would be her undoing.
But when the opinions were reported to Xerxes he
was greatly pleased by the opinion of Artemisia; he
had ever deemed her a woman of worth and now
held her in much higher esteem. Nevertheless he
bade the counsel of the more part to be followed;
for he thought that off Euboea his men had been
slack fighters by reason of his absence, and now he
purposed to watch the battle himself.

70. When the command to set sail was given, they
put out to Salamis and arrayed their line in order
at their ease. That day there was not time enough
left to offer battle, for the night came; and they
made preparation for the next day instead. But the

67

ὑστεραίην. τοὺς δὲ ʺΕλληνας εἶχε δέος τε καὶ
ἀρρωδίη, οὐκ ἥκιστα δὲ τοὺς ἀπὸ Πελοποννήσου·
ἀρρώδεον δὲ ὅτι αὐτοὶ μὲν ἐν Σαλαμῖνι κατήμενοι
ὑπὲρ γῆς τῆς Ἀθηναίων ναυμαχέειν μέλλοιεν,
νικηθέντες τε ἐν νήσῳ ἀπολαμφθέντες πολιορκήσονται, ἀπέντες τὴν ἑωυτῶν ἀφύλακτον· τῶν
δὲ βαρβάρων ὁ πεζὸς ὑπὸ τὴν παρεοῦσαν νύκτα
ἐπορεύετο ἐπὶ τὴν Πελοπόννησον.

71. Καίτοι τὰ δυνατὰ πάντα ἐμεμηχάνητο
ὅκως κατ' ἤπειρον μὴ ἐσβάλοιεν οἱ βάρβαροι.
ὡς γὰρ ἐπύθοντο τάχιστα Πελοποννήσιοι τοὺς
ἀμφὶ Λεωνίδην ἐν Θερμοπύλῃσι τετελευτηκέναι,
συνδραμόντες ἐκ τῶν πολίων ἐς τὸν Ἰσθμὸν ἵζοντο,
καί σφι ἐπῆν στρατηγὸς Κλεόμβροτος ὁ Ἀνα-
ξανδρίδεω, Λεωνίδεω δὲ ἀδελφεός. ἱζόμενοι δὲ
ἐν τῷ Ἰσθμῷ καὶ συγχώσαντες τὴν Σκιρωνίδα
ὁδόν, μετὰ τοῦτο ὥς σφι ἔδοξε βουλευομένοισι,
οἰκοδόμεον διὰ τοῦ Ἰσθμοῦ τεῖχος. ἅτε δὲ
ἐουσέων μυριάδων πολλέων καὶ παντὸς ἀνδρὸς
ἐργαζομένου, ἤνετο τὸ ἔργον· καὶ γὰρ λίθοι καὶ
πλίνθοι καὶ ξύλα καὶ φορμοὶ ψάμμου πλήρεες
ἐσεφέροντο, καὶ ἐλίννυον οὐδένα χρόνον οἱ βοηθήσαντες ἐργαζόμενοι, οὔτε νυκτὸς οὔτε ἡμέρης.

72. Οἱ δὲ βοηθήσαντες ἐς τὸν Ἰσθμὸν πανδημεὶ
οἵδε ἦσαν Ἑλλήνων, Λακεδαιμόνιοί τε καὶ Ἀρκάδες πάντες καὶ Ἠλεῖοι καὶ Κορίνθιοι καὶ Ἐπιδαύριοι καὶ Φλιάσιοι καὶ Τροιζήνιοι καὶ Ἑρμιονέες.
οὗτοι μὲν ἦσαν οἱ βοηθήσαντες καὶ ὑπεραρρω-
δέοντες τῇ Ἑλλάδι κινδυνευούσῃ· τοῖσι δὲ ἄλλοισι

_____

[1] A track (later made into a regular road) leading to the
Isthmus along the face of Geraneia : narrow and even

Greeks were in fear and dread, and especially they that were from the Peloponnese; and the cause of their fear was, that they themselves were about to fight for the Athenians' country where they lay at Salamis, and if they were overcome they must be shut up and beleaguered in an island, leaving their own land unguarded. At the next nightfall, the land army of the foreigners began its march to the Peloponnese.

71. Nathless the Greeks had used every device possible to prevent the foreigners from breaking in upon them by land. For as soon as the Peloponnesians heard that Leonidas' men at Thermopylae were dead, they hasted together from their cities and encamped on the Isthmus, their general being the brother of Leonidas, Cleombrotus son of Anaxandrides. Being there encamped they broke up the Scironian road,[1] and thereafter built a wall across the Isthmus, having resolved in council so to do. As there were many tens of thousands there and all men wrought, the work was brought to accomplishment; for they carried stones to it and bricks and logs and crates full of sand, and they that mustered there never rested from their work by night or by day.

72. Those Greeks that mustered all their people at the Isthmus were the Lacedaemonians and all the Arcadians, the Eleans, Corinthians, Sicyonians, Epidaurians, Phliasians, Troezenians, and men of Hermione. These were they who mustered there, and were moved by great fear for Hellas in her peril; but the rest of the Peloponnesians cared

dangerous for some six miles, and very easily made impassable.

Πελοποννησίοισι ἔμελε οὐδέν. Ὀλύμπια δὲ καὶ
Κάρνεια παροιχώκεε ἤδη.

73. Οἰκέει δὲ τὴν Πελοπόννησον ἔθνεα ἑπτά.
τούτων δὲ τὰ μὲν δύο αὐτόχθονα ἐόντα κατὰ
χώρην ἵδρυται νῦν τε καὶ τὸ πάλαι οἴκεον,
Ἀρκάδες τε καὶ Κυνούριοι· ἓν δὲ ἔθνος τὸ Ἀχαιϊ-
κὸν ἐκ μὲν Πελοποννήσου οὐκ ἐξεχώρησε, ἐκ
μέντοι τῆς ἑωυτῶν, οἰκέει δὲ τὴν ἀλλοτρίην. τὰ
δὲ λοιπὰ ἔθνεα τῶν ἑπτὰ τέσσερα ἐπήλυδα ἐστί,
Δωριέες τε καὶ Αἰτωλοὶ καὶ Δρύοπες καὶ Λήμνιοι.
Δωριέων μὲν πολλαί τε καὶ δόκιμοι πόλιες,
Αἰτωλῶν δὲ Ἦλις μούνη, Δρυόπων δὲ Ἑρμιών
τε καὶ Ἀσίνη ἡ πρὸς Καρδαμύλῃ τῇ Λακωνικῇ,
Λημνίων δὲ Παρωρεῆται πάντες. οἱ δὲ Κυνούριοι
αὐτόχθονες ἐόντες δοκέουσι μοῦνοι εἶναι Ἴωνες,
ἐκδεδωρίευνται δὲ ὑπό τε Ἀργείων ἀρχόμενοι καὶ
τοῦ χρόνου, ἐόντες Ὀρνεῆται καὶ οἱ περίοικοι.
τούτων ὦν τῶν ἑπτὰ ἐθνέων αἱ λοιπαὶ πόλιες,
πάρεξ τῶν κατέλεξα, ἐκ τοῦ μέσου κατέατο· εἰ δὲ
ἐλευθέρως ἔξεστι εἰπεῖν, ἐκ τοῦ μέσου κατήμενοι
ἐμήδιζον.

74. Οἳ μὲν δὴ ἐν τῷ Ἰσθμῷ τοιούτῳ πόνῳ
συνέστασαν, ἅτε περὶ τοῦ παντὸς ἤδη δρόμου
θέοντες καὶ τῇσι νηυσὶ οὐκ ἐλπίζοντες ἐλλάμψε-
σθαι· οἳ δὲ ἐν Σαλαμῖνι ὅμως ταῦτα πυνθανόμενοι
ἀρρώδεον, οὐκ οὕτω περὶ σφίσι αὐτοῖσι δειμαίνοντες ὡς περὶ τῇ Πελοποννήσῳ. τέως μὲν
δὴ αὐτῶν ἀνὴρ ἀνδρὶ παραστὰς σιγῇ λόγον
ἐποιέετο, θῶμα ποιεύμενοι τὴν Εὐρυβιάδεω ἀβου-
λίην· τέλος δὲ ἐξερράγη ἐς τὸ μέσον. σύλλογός
τε δὴ ἐγίνετο καὶ πολλὰ ἐλέγετο περὶ τῶν αὐτῶν,

nothing; and the Olympian and Carnean festivals were now past.[1]

73. Seven nations inhabit the Peloponnese; two of these, the Arcadians and Cynurians, are native to the soil and are now settled where they have ever been; and one nation, the Achaean, has never departed from the Peloponnese, but has left its own country and dwells in another. The four that remain of the seven have come from elsewhere, namely, the Dorians and Aetolians and Dryopians and Lemnians; the Dorians have many notable cities, the Aetolians Elis alone; the Dryopians have Hermione and that Asine which is near Cardamyle of Laconia; and the Lemnians, all the Paroreatae. The Cynurians are held to be Ionians, and the only Ionians native to the soil, but their Argive masters and time have made Dorians of them; they are the people of Orneae and the country round. Now of these seven nations all the cities, save those aforesaid, sat apart from the war; and if I may speak freely, by so doing they took the part of the enemy.

74. So the Greeks on the Isthmus had such labour to cope withal, seeing that now all they had was at stake, and they had no hope of winning renown with their ships; but they that were at Salamis, although they heard of the work, were affrighted, and their dread was less for themselves than for the Peloponnese. For a while there was but murmuring between man and man, and wonder at Eurybiades' unwisdom, but at the last came an open outbreak; and an assembly was held, where there was much speaking of the same matters as before, some saying

---

[1] That is, there was no longer any excuse for their not coming. *Cp.* vii. 205.

οἳ μὲν ὡς ἐς τὴν Πελοπόννησον χρεὸν εἴη ἀποπλέειν καὶ περὶ ἐκείνης κινδυνεύειν μηδὲ πρὸ
χώρης δοριαλώτου μένοντας μάχεσθαι, Ἀθηναῖοι
δὲ καὶ Αἰγινῆται καὶ Μεγαρέες αὐτοῦ μένοντας
ἀμύνεσθαι.

75. Ἐνθαῦτα Θεμιστοκλέης ὡς ἑσσοῦτο τῇ
γνώμῃ ὑπὸ τῶν Πελοποννησίων, λαθὼν ἐξέρχεται
ἐκ τοῦ συνεδρίου, ἐξελθὼν δὲ πέμπει ἐς τὸ στρατόπεδον τὸ Μήδων ἄνδρα πλοίῳ ἐντειλάμενος τὰ
λέγειν χρεόν, τῷ οὔνομα μὲν ἦν Σίκιννος, οἰκέτης
δὲ καὶ παιδαγωγὸς ἦν τῶν Θεμιστοκλέος παίδων·
τὸν δὴ ὕστερον τούτων τῶν πρηγμάτων Θεμιστοκλέης Θεσπιέα τε ἐποίησε, ὡς ἐπεδέκοντο οἱ
Θεσπιέες πολιήτας, καὶ χρήμασι ὄλβιον. ὃς τότε
πλοίῳ ἀπικόμενος ἔλεγε πρὸς τοὺς στρατηγοὺς
τῶν βαρβάρων τάδε. "Ἔπεμψέ με στρατηγὸς ὁ
Ἀθηναίων λάθρῃ τῶν ἄλλων Ἑλλήνων (τυγχάνει
γὰρ φρονέων τὰ βασιλέος καὶ βουλόμενος μᾶλλον
τὰ ὑμέτερα κατύπερθε γίνεσθαι ἢ τὰ τῶν Ἑλλήνων
πρήγματα) φράσοντα ὅτι οἱ Ἕλληνες δρησμὸν
βουλεύονται καταρρωδηκότες, καὶ νῦν παρέχει
κάλλιστον ὑμέας ἔργων ἁπάντων ἐξεργάσασθαι,
ἢν μὴ περιίδητε διαδράντας αὐτούς. οὔτε γὰρ
ἀλλήλοισι ὁμοφρονέουσι οὔτε ἀντιστήσονται ὑμῖν,
πρὸς ἑωυτούς τε σφέας ὄψεσθε ναυμαχέοντας τοὺς
τὰ ὑμέτερα φρονέοντας καὶ τοὺς μή."

76. Ὁ μὲν ταῦτά σφι σημήνας ἐκποδὼν ἀπαλ-
λάσσετο· τοῖσι δὲ ὡς πιστὰ ἐγίνετο τὰ ἀγγελ-
θέντα, τοῦτο μὲν ἐς τὴν νησῖδα τὴν Ψυττάλειαν,
μεταξὺ Σαλαμῖνός τε κειμένην καὶ τῆς ἠπείρου,
πολλοὺς τῶν Περσέων ἀπεβίβασαν· τοῦτο δέ,
ἐπειδὴ ἐγίνοντο μέσαι νύκτες, ἀνῆγον μὲν τὸ ἀπ᾽

that they must sail away to the Peloponnese and face
danger for that country, rather than abide and fight
for a land won from them by the spear; but the
Athenians and Aeginetans and Megarians pleading
that they should remain and defend themselves
where they were.

75. Then Themistocles, when the Peloponnesians
were outvoting him, went privily out of the assembly,
and sent to the Median fleet a man in a boat, charged
with a message that he must deliver. This man's
name was Sicinnus, and he was of Themistocles'
household and attendant on his children; at a later
day, when the Thespians were receiving men to be
their citizens, Themistocles made him a Thespian,
and a wealthy man withal. He now came in a boat
and spoke thus to the foreigners' admirals: "I am
sent by the admiral of the Athenians without the
knowledge of the other Greeks (he being a friend
to the king's cause and desiring that you rather than
the Greeks should have the mastery) to tell you that
the Greeks have lost heart and are planning flight,
and that now is the hour for you to achieve an
incomparable feat of arms, if you suffer them not to
escape. For there is no union in their counsels, nor
will they withstand you any more, and you will see
them battling against each other, your friends against
your foes."

76. With that declaration he departed away. The
Persians put faith in the message; and first they
landed many of their men on the islet Psyttalea,
which lies between Salamis and the mainland; then,
at midnight, they advanced their western wing

ἑσπέρης κέρας κυκλούμενοι πρὸς τὴν Σαλαμῖνα,
ἀνῆγον δὲ οἱ ἀμφὶ τὴν Κέον τε καὶ τὴν Κυνόσουραν
τεταγμένοι, κατεῖχόν τε μέχρι Μουνυχίης πάντα
τὸν πορθμὸν τῆσι νηυσί. τῶνδε δὲ εἵνεκα ἀνῆγον
τὰς νέας, ἵνα δὴ τοῖσι Ἕλλησι μηδὲ φυγεῖν ἐξῇ,
ἀλλ' ἀπολαμφθέντες ἐν τῇ Σαλαμῖνι δοῖεν τίσιν
τῶν ἐπ' Ἀρτεμισίῳ ἀγωνισμάτων. ἐς δὲ τὴν
νησῖδα τὴν Ψυττάλειαν καλεομένην ἀπεβίβαζον
τῶν Περσέων τῶνδε εἵνεκεν, ὡς ἐπεὰν γίνηται
ναυμαχίη, ἐνθαῦτα μάλιστα ἐξοισομένων τῶν τε
ἀνδρῶν καὶ τῶν ναυηγίων (ἐν γὰρ δὴ πόρῳ τῆς
ναυμαχίης τῆς μελλούσης ἔσεσθαι ἔκειτο ἡ
νῆσος), ἵνα τοὺς μὲν περιποιέωσι τοὺς δὲ δια-
φθείρωσι. ἐποίευν δὲ σιγῇ ταῦτα, ὡς μὴ πυνθα-
νοίατο οἱ ἐναντίοι. οἱ μὲν δὴ ταῦτα τῆς νυκτὸς
οὐδὲν ἀποκοιμηθέντες παραρτέοντο.

77. Χρησμοῖσι δὲ οὐκ ἔχω ἀντιλέγειν ὡς οὐκ
εἰσὶ ἀληθέες, οὐ βουλόμενος ἐναργέως λέγοντας
πειρᾶσθαι καταβάλλειν, ἐς τοιάδε πρήγματα [1]
ἐσβλέψας.

ἀλλ' ὅταν Ἀρτέμιδος χρυσαόρου ἱερὸν ἀκτὴν
νηυσὶ γεφυρώσωσι καὶ εἰναλίην Κυνόσουραν
ἐλπίδι μαινομένῃ, λιπαρὰς πέρσαντες Ἀθήνας,
δῖα δίκη σβέσσει κρατερὸν κόρον, ὕβριος υἱόν,
δεινὸν μαιμώοντα, δοκεῦντ' ἀνὰ πάντα πίεσθαι.

---

[1] ῥήματα is suggested, and would certainly be more natural.

---

[1] For a brief notice of controversy respecting the operations
off Salamis, see the Introduction to this volume. The locality
of Ceos and Cynosura is conjectural.

towards Salamis for encirclement, and they too put
out to sea that were stationed off Ceos and Cynosura ;
and they held all the passage with their ships as far
as Munychia.[1] The purpose of their putting out to
sea was, that the Greeks might have no liberty even
to flee, but should be hemmed in at Salamis and
punished for their fighting off Artemisium. And
the purpose of their landing Persians on the islet
called Psyttalea was this, that as it was here in
especial that in the sea fight men and wrecks would
be washed ashore (for the island lay in the very path
of the battle that was to be), they might thus save
their friends and slay their foes. All this they did in
silence, lest their enemies should know of it. So they
made these preparations in the night, taking no rest.

77. But, for oracles, I have no way of gainsaying
their truth ; for they speak clearly, and I would
not essay to overthrow them, when I look into such
matter as this :

" When that with lines of ships thy sacred coasts
they have fencèd,
Artemis [2] golden-sworded, and thine, sea-washed
Cynosura,
All in the madness of hope, having ravished the
glory of Athens,
Then shall desire full fed, by pride o'erweening
engendered,
Raging in dreadful wrath and athirst for the
nations' destruction,
Utterly perish and fall ; for the justice of heaven
shall quench it ;

[2] There were temples of Artemis both at Salamis and at
Munychia on the Attic shore.

χαλκὸς γὰρ χαλκῷ συμμίξεται, αἵματι δ᾽ Ἄρης
πόντον φοινίξει. τότ᾽ ἐλεύθερον Ἑλλάδος ἦμαρ
εὐρύοπα Κρονίδης ἐπάγει καὶ πότνια Νίκη.

ἐς τοιαῦτα μὲν καὶ οὕτω ἐναργέως λέγοντι Βάκιδι
ἀντιλογίης χρησμῶν πέρι οὔτε αὐτὸς λέγειν
τολμέω οὔτε παρ᾽ ἄλλων ἐνδέκομαι.

78. Τῶν δὲ ἐν Σαλαμῖνι στρατηγῶν ἐγίνετο
ὠθισμὸς λόγων πολλός· ᾔδεσαν δὲ οὔκω ὅτι
σφέας περιεκυκλοῦντο τῇσι νηυσὶ οἱ βάρβαροι,
ἀλλ᾽ ὥσπερ τῆς ἡμέρης ὥρων αὐτοὺς τεταγμένους,
ἐδόκεον κατὰ χώρην εἶναι.

79. Συνεστηκότων δὲ τῶν στρατηγῶν, ἐξ Αἰγίνης
διέβη Ἀριστείδης ὁ Λυσιμάχου, ἀνὴρ Ἀθηναῖος
μὲν ἐξωστρακισμένος δὲ ὑπὸ τοῦ δήμου· τὸν ἐγὼ
νενόμικα, πυνθανόμενος αὐτοῦ τὸν τρόπον, ἄριστον
ἄνδρα γενέσθαι ἐν Ἀθήνῃσι καὶ δικαιότατον.
οὗτος ὡνὴρ στὰς ἐπὶ τὸ συνέδριον ἐξεκαλέετο
Θεμιστοκλέα, ἐόντα μὲν ἑωυτῷ οὐ φίλον ἐχθρὸν
δὲ τὰ μάλιστα· ὑπὸ δὲ μεγάθεος τῶν παρεόντων
κακῶν λήθην ἐκείνων ποιεύμενος ἐξεκαλέετο, θέλων
αὐτῷ συμμῖξαι· προακηκόεε δὲ ὅτι σπεύδοιεν οἱ
ἀπὸ Πελοποννήσου ἀνάγειν τὰς νέας πρὸς τὸν
Ἰσθμόν. ὡς δὲ ἐξῆλθέ οἱ Θεμιστοκλῆς, ἔλεγε
Ἀριστείδης τάδε. "Ἡμέας στασιάζειν χρεόν ἐστι
ἔν τε τῷ ἄλλῳ καιρῷ καὶ δὴ καὶ ἐν τῷδε περὶ τοῦ
ὁκότερος ἡμέων πλέω ἀγαθὰ τὴν πατρίδα ἐργά-
σεται. λέγω δέ τοι ὅτι ἴσον ἐστὶ πολλά τε καὶ
ὀλίγα λέγειν περὶ ἀποπλόου τοῦ ἐνθεῦτεν Πελο-

Bronze upon bronze shall clash, and the terrible
    bidding of Ares
Redden the seas with blood. But Zeus far-seeing,
    and hallowed
Victory then shall grant that Freedom dawn upon
    Hellas."

Looking at such matters and seeing how clear is
the utterance of Bacis, I neither venture myself to
gainsay him as touching oracles nor suffer such
gainsaying by others.

78. But among the admirals at Salamis there was
a hot bout of argument ; and they knew not as yet
that the foreigners had drawn their ships round
them, but supposed the enemy to be still where they
had seen him stationed in the daylight.

79. But as they contended, there crossed over from
Aegina Aristides son of Lysimachus, an Athenian,
but one that had been ostracised by the commonalty ;
from that which I have learnt of his way of life I am
myself well persuaded that he was the best and the
justest man at Athens. He then came and stood in
the place of council and called Themistocles out of
it, albeit Themistocles was no friend of his but his
chiefest enemy ; but in the stress of the present
danger he put that old feud from his mind, and so
called Themistocles out, that he might converse
with him. Now he had heard already, that the
Peloponnesians desired to sail to the Isthmus. So
when Themistocles came out, Aristides said, " Let
the rivalry between us be now as it has been before,
to see which of us two shall do his country more
good. I tell you now, that it is all one for the
Peloponnesians to talk much or little about sailing

πονννησίοισι. ἐγὼ γὰρ αὐτόπτης τοι λέγω γενόμενος ὅτι νῦν οὐδ᾽ ἢν θέλωσι Κορίνθιοί τε καὶ
αὐτὸς Εὐρυβιάδης οἷοί τε ἔσονται ἐκπλῶσαι·
περιεχόμεθα γὰρ ὑπὸ τῶν πολεμίων κύκλῳ. ἀλλ᾽
ἐσελθὼν σφι ταῦτα σήμηνον." ὃ δ᾽ ἀμείβετο
τοῖσιδε.

80. "Κάρτα τε χρηστὰ διακελεύεαι καὶ εὖ
ἤγγειλας· τὰ γὰρ ἐγὼ ἐδεόμην γενέσθαι, αὐτὸς
αὐτόπτης γενόμενος ἥκεις. ἴσθι γὰρ ἐξ ἐμέο τὰ
ποιεύμενα ὑπὸ Μήδων· ἔδεε γάρ, ὅτε οὐκ ἑκόντες
ἤθελον ἐς μάχην κατίστασθαι οἱ Ἕλληνες,
ἀέκοντας παραστήσασθαι. σὺ δὲ ἐπεί περ ἥκεις
χρηστὰ ἀπαγγέλλων, αὐτός σφι ἄγγειλον. ἢν
γὰρ ἐγὼ αὐτὰ λέγω, δόξω πλάσας λέγειν καὶ οὐ
πείσω, ὡς οὐ ποιεύντων τῶν βαρβάρων ταῦτα.
ἀλλά σφι σήμηνον αὐτὸς παρελθὼν ὡς ἔχει.
ἐπεὰν δὲ σημήνῃς, ἢν μὲν πείθωνται, ταῦτα δὴ
τὰ κάλλιστα, ἢν δὲ αὐτοῖσι μὴ πιστὰ γένηται,
ὅμοιον ἡμῖν ἔσται· οὐ γὰρ ἔτι διαδρήσονται, εἴ
περ περιεχόμεθα πανταχόθεν, ὡς σὺ λέγεις."

81. Ἐνθαῦτα ἔλεγε παρελθὼν ὁ Ἀριστείδης,
φάμενος ἐξ Αἰγίνης τε ἥκειν καὶ μόγις ἐκπλῶσαι
λαθὼν τοὺς ἐπορμέοντας· περιέχεσθαι γὰρ πᾶν
τὸ στρατόπεδον τὸ Ἑλληνικὸν ὑπὸ τῶν νεῶν τῶν
Ξέρξεω· παραρτέεσθαί τε συνεβούλευε ὡς ἀλε-
ξησομένους. καὶ ὃ μὲν ταῦτα εἴπας μετεστήκεε,
τῶν δὲ αὖτις ἐγίνετο λόγων ἀμφισβασίη· οἱ γὰρ
πλεῦνες τῶν στρατηγῶν οὐκ ἐπείθοντο τὰ
ἐσαγγελθέντα.

82. Ἀπιστεόντων δὲ τούτων ἧκε τριήρης ἀνδρῶν
Τηνίων αὐτομολέουσα, τῆς ἦρχε ἀνὴρ Παναίτιος
ὁ Σωσιμένεος, ἥ περ δὴ ἔφερε τὴν ἀληθείην πᾶσαν.

away from hence; for I say from that which my eyes have seen that now even if the Corinthians and Eurybiades himself desire to sail out, they cannot; we are hemmed in on all sides by our enemies. Do you go in now, and tell them this."

80. "Your exhortation is right useful," Themistocles answered, "and your news is good; for you have come with your own eyes for witnesses of that which I desired might happen. Know that what the Medes do is of my contriving; for when the Greeks would not of their own accord prepare for battle, it was needful to force them to it willy-nilly. But now since you have come with this good news, give your message to them yourself. If I tell it, they will think it is of my own devising, and they will never take my word for it that the foreigners are doing as you say; nay, go before them yourself and tell them how it stands. When you have told them, if they believe you, that is best; but if they will not believe you, it will be the same thing to us; for if we are hemmed in on every side, as you say, they will no longer be able to take to flight."

81. Aristides then came forward and told them; he was come, he said, from Aegina, and had been hard put to it to slip unseen through the blockade; for all the Greek fleet was compassed round by Xerxes' ships, and they had best (he said) prepare to defend themselves. Thus he spoke, and took his departure. They fell a-wrangling again; for the more part of the admirals would not believe that the news was true.

82. But while they yet disbelieved, there came a trireme with Tenian deserters, whose captain was one Panaetius son of Sosimenes, and this brought

διὰ δὲ τοῦτο τὸ ἔργον ἐνεγράφησαν Τήνιοι ἐν
Δελφοῖσι ἐς τὸν τρίποδα ἐν τοῖσι τὸν βάρβαρον
κατελοῦσι. σὺν δὲ ὦν ταύτῃ τῇ νηὶ τῇ αὐτο-
μολησάσῃ ἐς Σαλαμῖνα καὶ τῇ πρότερον ἐπ᾽
Ἀρτεμίσιον τῇ Λημνίῃ ἐξεπληροῦτο τὸ ναυτικὸν
τοῖσι Ἕλλησι ἐς τὰς ὀγδώκοντα καὶ τριηκοσίας
νέας· δύο γὰρ δὴ νεῶν τότε κατέδεε ἐς τὸν
ἀριθμόν.

83. Τοῖσι δὲ Ἕλλησι ὡς πιστὰ δὴ τὰ λεγόμενα
ἦν τῶν Τηνίων ῥήματα, παρεσκευάζοντο ὡς ναυμαχήσοντες. ἠώς τε διέφαινε καὶ οἳ σύλλογον
τῶν ἐπιβατέων ποιησάμενοι, προηγόρευε εὖ ἔχοντα
μὲν ἐκ πάντων Θεμιστοκλέης, τὰ δὲ ἔπεα ἦν
πάντα κρέσσω τοῖσι ἥσσοσι ἀντιτιθέμενα, ὅσα
δὴ ἐν ἀνθρώπου φύσι καὶ καταστάσι ἐγγίνεται·
παραινέσας δὲ τούτων τὰ κρέσσω αἱρέεσθαι καὶ
καταπλέξας τὴν ῥῆσιν, ἐσβαίνειν ἐκέλευε ἐς τὰς
νέας. καὶ οὗτοι μὲν δὴ ἐσέβαινον, καὶ ἧκε ἡ
ἀπ᾽ Αἰγίνης τριήρης, ἣ κατὰ τοὺς Αἰακίδας
ἀπεδήμησε.

84. Ἐνθαῦτα ἀνῆγον τὰς νέας ἁπάσας Ἕλληνες,
ἀναγομένοισι δέ σφι αὐτίκα ἐπεκέατο οἱ βάρβαροι. οἱ μὲν δὴ ἄλλοι Ἕλληνες ἐπὶ πρύμνην
ἀνεκρούοντο καὶ ὤκελλον τὰς νέας, Ἀμεινίης δὲ
Παλληνεὺς ἀνὴρ Ἀθηναῖος ἐξαναχθεὶς νηὶ ἐμβάλ-
λει· συμπλακείσης δὲ τῆς νεὸς καὶ οὐ δυναμένων
ἀπαλλαγῆναι, οὕτω δὴ οἱ ἄλλοι Ἀμεινίῃ βοη-
θέοντες συνέμισγον. Ἀθηναῖοι μὲν οὕτω λέγουσι
τῆς ναυμαχίης γενέσθαι τὴν ἀρχήν, Αἰγινῆται δὲ
τὴν κατὰ τοὺς Αἰακίδας ἀποδημήσασαν ἐς Αἴγιναν,
ταύτην εἶναι τὴν ἄρξασαν. λέγεται δὲ καὶ τάδε,
ὡς φάσμα σφι γυναικὸς ἐφάνη, φανεῖσαν δὲ διακε-

them the whole truth. For that deed the men of Tenos were engraved on the tripod at Delphi among those that had vanquished the foreigner. With this ship that deserted to Salamis and the Lemnian which had already deserted to Artemisium, the Greek fleet, which had fallen short by two of three hundred and eighty, now attained to that full number.

83. The Greeks, believing at last the tale of the Tenians, made ready for battle. It was now earliest dawn, and they called the fighting men to an assembly, wherein Themistocles made an harangue in which he excelled all others; the tenor of his words was to array all the good in man's nature and estate against the evil; and having exhorted them to choose the better, he made an end of speaking and bade them embark. Even as they so did, came the trireme from Aegina which had been sent away for the Sons of Aeacus.[1]

84. With that the Greeks stood out to sea in full force, and as they stood out the foreigners straightway fell upon them. The rest of the Greeks began to back water and beach their ships; but Aminias of Pallene, an Athenian, pushed out to the front and charged a ship; which being entangled with his, and the two not able to be parted, the others did now come to Aminias' aid and joined battle. This is the Athenian story of the beginning of the fight; but the Aeginetans say that the ship which began it was that one which had been sent away to Aegina for the Sons of Aeacus. This story also is told,—that they saw the vision of a woman, who

[1] *cp.* 64.

λεύσασθαι ὥστε καὶ ἄπαν ἀκοῦσαι τὸ τῶν
Ἑλλήνων στρατόπεδον, ὀνειδίσασαν πρότερον
τάδε, "Ὦ δαιμόνιοι, μέχρι κόσου ἔτι πρύμνην
ἀνακρούεσθε; "

85. Κατὰ μὲν δὴ Ἀθηναίους ἐτετάχατο Φοίνικες
(οὗτοι γὰρ εἶχον τὸ πρὸς Ἐλευσῖνός τε καὶ
ἑσπέρης κέρας), κατὰ δὲ Λακεδαιμονίους Ἴωνες·
οὗτοι δ' εἶχον τὸ πρὸς τὴν ἠῶ τε καὶ τὸν Πειραιέα.
ἐθελοκάκεον μέντοι αὐτῶν κατὰ τὰς Θεμιστοκλέος
ἐντολὰς ὀλίγοι, οἱ δὲ πλεῦνες οὔ. ἔχω μέν νυν
συχνῶν οὐνόματα τριηράρχων καταλέξαι τῶν
νέας Ἑλληνίδας ἑλόντων, χρήσομαι δὲ αὐτοῖσι
οὐδὲν πλὴν Θεομήστορός τε τοῦ Ἀνδροδάμαντος
καὶ Φυλάκου τοῦ Ἱστιαίου, Σαμίων ἀμφοτέρων.
τοῦδε δὲ εἵνεκα μέμνημαι τούτων μούνων, ὅτι
Θεομήστωρ μὲν διὰ τοῦτο τὸ ἔργον Σάμου ἐτυ-
ράννευσε καταστησάντων τῶν Περσέων, Φύλακος
δὲ εὐεργέτης βασιλέος ἀνεγράφη καὶ χώρῃ ἐδω-
ρήθη πολλῇ. οἱ δ' εὐεργέται βασιλέος ὀροσάγγαι
καλέονται περσιστί.

86. Περὶ μὲν νυν τούτους οὕτω εἶχε· τὸ δὲ
πλῆθος τῶν νεῶν ἐν τῇ Σαλαμῖνι ἐκεραΐζετο,
αἱ μὲν ὑπ' Ἀθηναίων διαφθειρόμεναι αἱ δὲ ὑπ'
Αἰγινητέων. ἅτε γὰρ τῶν μὲν Ἑλλήνων σὺν
κόσμῳ ναυμαχεόντων καὶ κατὰ τάξιν, τῶν δὲ
βαρβάρων οὔτε τεταγμένων ἔτι οὔτε σὺν νόῳ
ποιεόντων οὐδέν, ἔμελλε τοιοῦτό σφι συνοίσεσθαι
οἷόν περ ἀπέβη. καίτοι ἦσάν γε καὶ ἐγένοντο
ταύτην τὴν ἡμέρην μακρῷ ἀμείνονες αὐτοὶ ἑωυτῶν
ἢ πρὸς Εὐβοίῃ, πᾶς τις προθυμεόμενος καὶ
δειμαίνων Ξέρξην, ἐδόκεέ τε ἕκαστος ἑωυτὸν
θεήσασθαι βασιλέα.

cried commands loud enough for all the Greek fleet to hear, uttering first this reproach, "Sirs, what madness is this? how long will you still be backing water?"

85. The Phoenicians (for they had the western wing, towards Eleusis) were arrayed opposite to the Athenians, and to the Lacedaemonians the Ionians, on the eastern wing, nearest to Piraeus. Yet but few of them fought slackly, as Themistocles had bidden them, and the more part did not so. Many names I could record of ships' captains that took Greek ships; but I will speak of none save Theomestor son of Androdamas and Phylacus son of Histiaeus, Samians both; and I make mention of these alone, because Theomestor was for this feat of arms made by the Persians despot of Samos, and Phylacus was recorded among the king's benefactors and given much land. These benefactors of the king are called in the Persian language, orosangae.[1]

86. Thus it was with these two; but the great multitude of the ships were shattered at Salamis, some destroyed by the Athenians and some by the Aeginetans. For since the Greeks fought orderly and in array, but the foreigners were by now disordered and did nought of set purpose, it was but reason that they should come to such an end as befel them. Yet on that day they were and approved themselves by far better men than off Euboea; all were zealous, and feared Xerxes, each man thinking that the king's eye was on him.

---

[1] Perhaps from old Persian *var*, to guard, and *Kshayata*, king; or, as Rawlinson suggests, from *Khur sangha* (Zend) = worthy of praise or record. (How and Wells' note.)

87. Κατὰ μὲν δὴ τοὺς ἄλλους οὐκ ἔχω μετεξετέρους εἰπεῖν ἀτρεκέως ὡς ἕκαστοι τῶν βαρβάρων ἢ τῶν Ἑλλήνων ἠγωνίζοντο· κατὰ δὲ Ἀρτεμισίην τάδε ἐγένετο, ἀπ' ὧν εὐδοκίμησε μᾶλλον ἔτι παρὰ βασιλέι. ἐπειδὴ γὰρ ἐς θόρυβον πολλὸν ἀπίκετο τὰ βασιλέος πρήγματα, ἐν τούτῳ τῷ καιρῷ ἡ νηῦς ἡ Ἀρτεμισίης ἐδιώκετο ὑπὸ νεὸς Ἀττικῆς· καὶ ἣ οὐκ ἔχουσα διαφυγεῖν, ἔμπροσθε γὰρ αὐτῆς ἦσαν ἄλλαι νέες φίλιαι, ἡ δὲ αὐτῆς πρὸς τῶν πολεμίων μάλιστα ἐτύγχανε ἐοῦσα, ἔδοξέ οἱ τόδε ποιῆσαι, τὸ καὶ συνήνεικε ποιησάσῃ. διωκομένη γὰρ ὑπὸ τῆς Ἀττικῆς φέρουσα ἐνέβαλε νηὶ φιλίῃ ἀνδρῶν τε Καλυνδέων καὶ αὐτοῦ ἐπιπλέοντος τοῦ Καλυνδέων βασιλέος Δαμασιθύμου. εἰ μὲν καί τι νεῖκος πρὸς αὐτὸν ἐγεγόνεε ἔτι περὶ Ἑλλήσποντον ἐόντων, οὐ μέντοι ἔχω γε εἰπεῖν οὔτε εἰ ἐκ προνοίης αὐτὰ ἐποίησε, οὔτε εἰ συνεκύρησε ἡ τῶν Καλυνδέων κατὰ τύχην παραπεσοῦσα νηῦς. ὡς δὲ ἐνέβαλέ τε καὶ κατέδυσε, εὐτυχίῃ χρησαμένη διπλᾶ ἑωυτὴν ἀγαθὰ ἐργάσατο. ὅ τε γὰρ τῆς Ἀττικῆς νεὸς τριήραρχος ὡς εἶδέ μιν ἐμβάλλουσαν νηὶ ἀνδρῶν βαρβάρων, νομίσας τὴν νέα τὴν Ἀρτεμισίης ἢ Ἑλληνίδα εἶναι ἢ αὐτομολέειν ἐκ τῶν βαρβάρων καὶ αὐτοῖσι ἀμύνειν, ἀποστρέψας πρὸς ἄλλας ἐτράπετο.

88. Τοῦτο μὲν τοιοῦτο αὐτῇ συνήνεικε γενέσθαι διαφυγεῖν τε καὶ μὴ ἀπολέσθαι, τοῦτο δὲ συνέβη ὥστε κακὸν ἐργασαμένην ἀπὸ τούτων αὐτὴν μάλιστα εὐδοκιμῆσαι παρὰ Ξέρξῃ. λέγεται γὰρ βασιλέα θηεύμενον μαθεῖν τὴν νέα ἐμβαλοῦσαν, καὶ δή τινα εἰπεῖν τῶν παρεόντων " Δέσποτα, ὁρᾷς Ἀρτεμισίην ὡς εὖ ἀγωνίζεται καὶ νέα τῶν πολε-

84

87. Now as touching some of the others I cannot with exactness say how they fought severally, foreigners or Greeks; but what befel Artemisia made her to be esteemed by the king even more than before. The king's side being now in dire confusion, Artemisia's ship was at this time being pursued by a ship of Attica; and she could not escape, for other friendly ships were in her way, and it chanced that she was the nearest to the enemy; wherefore she resolved that she would do that which afterwards tended to her advantage, and as she fled pursued by the Athenian she charged a friendly ship that bore men of Calyndus and the king himself of that place, Damasithymus. It may be that she had had some quarrel with him while they were still at the Hellespont, but if her deed was done of set purpose, or if the Calyndian met her by crossing her path at haphazard, I cannot say. But having charged and sunk the ship, she had the good luck to work for herself a double advantage. For when the Attic captain saw her charge a ship of foreigners, he supposed that Artemisia's ship was Greek or a deserter from the foreigners fighting for the Greeks, and he turned aside to deal with others.

88. By this happy chance it came about that she escaped and avoided destruction; and moreover the upshot was that the very harm which she had done won her great favour in Xerxes' eyes. For the king (it is said) saw her charge the ship as he viewed the battle, and one of the bystanders said, "Sire, see you Artemisia, how well she fights, and

85

HERODOTUS

μίων κατέδυσε;" καὶ τὸν ἐπειρέσθαι εἰ ἀληθέως
ἐστὶ Ἀρτεμισίης τὸ ἔργον, καὶ τοὺς φάναι, σαφέως
τὸ ἐπίσημον τῆς νεὸς ἐπισταμένους· τὴν δὲ δια-
φθαρεῖσαν ἠπιστέατο εἶναι πολεμίην. τά τε γὰρ
ἄλλα, ὡς εἴρηται, αὐτὴ συνήνεικε ἐς εὐτυχίην
γενόμενα, καὶ τὸ τῶν ἐκ τῆς Καλυνδικῆς νεὸς
μηδένα ἀποσωθέντα κατήγορον γενέσθαι. Ξέρξην
δὲ εἰπεῖν λέγεται πρὸς τὰ φραζόμενα "Οἱ μὲν
ἄνδρες γεγόνασί μοι γυναῖκες, αἱ δὲ γυναῖκες
ἄνδρες." ταῦτα μὲν Ξέρξην φασὶ εἰπεῖν.

89. Ἐν δὲ τῷ πόνῳ τούτῳ ἀπὸ μὲν ἔθανε ὁ
στρατηγὸς Ἀριαβίγνης ὁ Δαρείου, Ξέρξεω ἐὼν
ἀδελφεός, ἀπὸ δὲ ἄλλοι πολλοί τε καὶ ὀνομαστοὶ
Περσέων καὶ Μήδων καὶ τῶν ἄλλων συμμάχων,
ὀλίγοι δὲ τινὲς καὶ Ἑλλήνων· ἅτε γὰρ νέειν
ἐπιστάμενοι, τοῖσι αἱ νέες διεφθείροντο, καὶ μὴ
ἐν χειρῶν νόμῳ ἀπολλύμενοι, ἐς τὴν Σαλαμῖνα
διένεον. τῶν δὲ βαρβάρων οἱ πολλοὶ ἐν τῇ
θαλάσσῃ διεφθάρησαν νέειν οὐκ ἐπιστάμενοι.
ἐπεὶ δὲ αἱ πρῶται ἐς φυγὴν ἐτράποντο, ἐνθαῦτα
αἱ πλεῖσται διεφθείροντο· οἱ γὰρ ὄπισθε τεταγμένοι, ἐς τὸ πρόσθε τῇσι νηυσὶ παριέναι πειρώμενοι ὡς ἀποδεξόμενοί τι καὶ αὐτοὶ ἔργον βασιλέι,
τῇσι σφετέρῃσι νηυσὶ φευγούσῃσι περιέπιπτον.

90. Ἐγένετο δὲ καὶ τόδε ἐν τῷ θορύβῳ τούτῳ.
τῶν τινες Φοινίκων, τῶν αἱ νέες διεφθάρατο,
ἐλθόντες παρὰ βασιλέα διέβαλλον τοὺς Ἴωνας,
ὡς δι' ἐκείνους ἀπολοίατο αἱ νέες, ὡς προδόντων.
συνήνεικε ὦν οὕτω ὥστε Ἰώνων τε τοὺς στρατηγοὺς μὴ ἀπολέσθαι Φοινίκων τε τοὺς δια-
βάλλοντας λαβεῖν τοιόνδε μισθόν. ἔτι τούτων
ταῦτα λεγόντων ἐνέβαλε νηὶ Ἀττικῇ Σαμοθρηικίη
86

how she has sunk an enemy ship?" Xerxes then asking if it were truly Artemisia that had done the deed, they affirmed it, knowing well the ensign of her ship ; and they supposed that the ship she had sunk was an enemy ; for the luckiest chance of all which had (as I have said) befallen her was, that not one from the Calyndian ship was saved alive to be her accuser. Hearing what they told him, Xerxes is reported to have said, "My men have become women, and my women men "; such, they say, were his words.

89. In that hard fighting Xerxes' brother the admiral Ariabignes, son of Darius, was slain, and withal many other Persians and Medes and allies of renown, and some Greeks, but few ; for since they could swim, they who lost their ships, yet were not slain in hand-to-hand fight, swam across to Salamis ; but the greater part of the foreigners were drowned in the sea, not being able to swim. When the foremost ships were turned to flight, it was then that the most of them were destroyed ; for the men of the rearmost ranks, pressing forward in their ships that they too might display their valour to the king, ran foul of their friends' ships that were in flight.

90. It happened also amid this disorder that certain Phoenicians whose ships had been destroyed came to the king and accused the Ionians of treason, saying that it was by their doing that the ships had been lost ; the end of which matter was, that the Ionian captains were not put to death, and those Phoenicians who accused them were rewarded as I will show. While they yet spoke as aforesaid, a Samothracian ship charged an Attic ; and while

νηῦς. ἥ τε δὴ Ἀττικὴ κατεδύετο καὶ ἐπιφερομένη
Αἰγιναίη νηῦς κατέδυσε τῶν Σαμοθρηίκων τὴν
νέα. ἅτε δὲ ἐόντες ἀκοντισταὶ οἱ Σαμοθρήικες
τοὺς ἐπιβάτας ἀπὸ τῆς καταδυσάσης νεὸς βάλλοντες ἀπήραξαν καὶ ἐπέβησάν τε καὶ ἔσχον
αὐτήν. ταῦτα γενόμενα τοὺς Ἴωνας ἐρρύσατο·
ὡς γὰρ εἶδε σφέας Ξέρξης ἔργον μέγα ἐργασα-
μένους, ἐτράπετο πρὸς τοὺς Φοίνικας οἷα ὑπερλυ-
πεόμενός τε καὶ πάντας αἰτιώμενος, καί σφεων
ἐκέλευσε τὰς κεφαλὰς ἀποταμεῖν, ἵνα μὴ αὐτοὶ
κακοὶ γενόμενοι τοὺς ἀμείνονας διαβάλλωσι.
ὅκως γάρ τινα ἴδοι Ξέρξης τῶν ἑωυτοῦ ἔργον
τι ἀποδεικνύμενον ἐν τῇ ναυμαχίῃ, κατήμενος
ὑπὸ τῷ ὄρεϊ τῷ ἀντίον Σαλαμῖνος τὸ καλέεται
Αἰγάλεως, ἀνεπυνθάνετο τὸν ποιήσαντα, καὶ οἱ
γραμματισταὶ ἀνέγραφον πατρόθεν τὸν τριήραρχον
καὶ τὴν πόλιν. πρὸς δέ τι καὶ προσεβάλετο
φίλος ἐὼν Ἀριαράμνης ἀνὴρ Πέρσης παρεὼν
τούτου τοῦ Φοινικηίου πάθεος. οἱ μὲν δὴ πρὸς
τοὺς Φοίνικας ἐτράποντο.

91. Τῶν δὲ βαρβάρων ἐς φυγὴν τραπομένων
καὶ ἐκπλεόντων πρὸς τὸ Φάληρον, Αἰγινῆται
ὑποστάντες ἐν τῷ πορθμῷ ἔργα ἀπεδέξαντο λόγου
ἄξια. οἱ μὲν γὰρ Ἀθηναῖοι ἐν τῷ θορύβῳ ἐκε-
ράιζον τάς τε ἀντισταμένας καὶ τὰς φευγούσας
τῶν νεῶν, οἱ δὲ Αἰγινῆται τὰς ἐκπλεούσας· ὅκως
δέ τινες τοὺς Ἀθηναίους διαφύγοιεν, φερόμενοι
ἐσέπιπτον ἐς τοὺς Αἰγινήτας.

92. Ἐνθαῦτα συνεκύρεον νέες ἥ τε Θεμιστοκλέος
διώκουσα νέα καὶ ἡ Πολυκρίτου τοῦ Κριοῦ ἀνδρὸς
Αἰγινήτεω νηὶ ἐμβαλοῦσα Σιδωνίη, ἥ περ εἷλε
τὴν προφυλάσσουσαν ἐπὶ Σκιάθῳ τὴν Αἰγιναίην,

the Attic ship was sinking, a ship of **Aegina** bore
down and sank the Samothracian; but the Samo-
thracians, being javelin throwers, swept the fighting
men with a shower of javelins off from the ship that
had sunk theirs, and boarded and seized her themselves. Thereby the Ionians were saved; for when
Xerxes saw this great feat of their arms, he turned
on the Phoenicians (being moved to blame all in the
bitterness of his heart) and commanded that their
heads be cut off, that so they might not accuse
better men, being themselves cowards. For whenever Xerxes, from his seat under the hill over against
Salamis called Aegaleos, saw any feat achieved by
his own men in the battle, he inquired who was
the doer of it, and his scribes wrote down the names
of the ship's captain and his father and his city.
Moreover it tended somewhat to the doom of the
Phoenicians that Ariaramnes, a Persian, was there,
who was a friend of the Ionians. So Xerxes' men
dealt with the Phoenicians.

91. The foreigners being routed and striving to
win out to Phalerum, the Aeginetans lay in wait
for them in the passage and then achieved notable
deeds; for the Athenians amid the disorder made
havoc of all ships that would resist or fly, and so did
the Aeginetans with those that were sailing out of
the strait; and all that escaped from the Athenians
fell in their course among the Aeginetans.

92. Two ships met there, Themistocles' ship
pursuing another, and one that bore Polycritus
son of Crius of Aegina; this latter had charged a
Sidonian, the same which had taken the Aeginetan

ἐπ' ἧς ἔπλεε Πυθέης ὁ Ἰσχενόου, τὸν οἱ Πέρσαι
κατακοπέντα ἀρετῆς εἵνεκα εἶχον ἐν τῇ νηὶ ἐκπα-
γλεόμενοι· τὸν δὴ περιάγουσα ἅμα τοῖσι Πέρσῃσι
ἥλω ἡ νηῦς ἡ Σιδωνίη, ὥστε Πυθέην οὕτω
σωθῆναι ἐς Αἴγιναν. ὡς δὲ ἐσεῖδε τὴν νέα τὴν
Ἀττικὴν ὁ Πολύκριτος, ἔγνω τὸ σημήιον ἰδὼν
τῆς στρατηγίδος, καὶ βώσας τὸν Θεμιστοκλέα
ἐπεκερτόμησε ἐς τῶν Αἰγινητέων τὸν μηδισμὸν
ὀνειδίζων. ταῦτα μέν νυν νηὶ ἐμβαλὼν ὁ Πολύκριτος ἀπέρριψε ἐς Θεμιστοκλέα· οἱ δὲ βάρβαροι
τῶν αἱ νέες περιεγένοντο, φεύγοντες ἀπίκοντο ἐς
Φάληρον ὑπὸ τὸν πεζὸν στρατόν.

93. Ἐν δὲ τῇ ναυμαχίῃ ταύτῃ ἤκουσαν Ἑλλήνων ἄριστα Αἰγινῆται, ἐπὶ δὲ Ἀθηναῖοι,
ἀνδρῶν δὲ Πολύκριτός τε ὁ Αἰγινήτης καὶ
Ἀθηναῖοι Εὐμένης τε ὁ Ἀναγυράσιος καὶ Ἀμεινίης
Παλληνεύς, ὃς καὶ Ἀρτεμισίην ἐπεδίωξε. εἰ μέν
νυν ἔμαθε ὅτι ἐν ταύτῃ πλέοι Ἀρτεμισίη, οὐκ
ἂν ἐπαύσατο πρότερον ἢ εἷλέ μιν ἢ καὶ αὐτὸς
ἥλω. τοῖσι γὰρ Ἀθηναίων τριηράρχοισι παρε-
κεκέλευστο, πρὸς δὲ καὶ ἄεθλον ἔκειτο μύριαι
δραχμαί, ὃς ἄν μιν ζωὴν ἕλῃ· δεινὸν γάρ τι
ἐποιεῦντο γυναῖκα ἐπὶ τὰς Ἀθήνας στρατεύεσθαι.
αὕτη μὲν δή, ὡς πρότερον εἴρηται, διέφυγε· ἦσαν
δὲ καὶ οἱ ἄλλοι, τῶν αἱ νέες περιεγεγόνεσαν, ἐν
τῷ Φαλήρῳ.

94. Ἀδείμαντον δὲ τὸν Κορίνθιον στρατηγὸν
λέγουσι Ἀθηναῖοι αὐτίκα κατ' ἀρχάς, ὡς συνέμισγον αἱ νέες, ἐκπλαγέντα τε καὶ ὑπερδείσαντα,

---

[1] Polycritus cries to Themistocles, "See how friendly we
are to the Persians!" Polycritus and his father had been

ship that watched off Sciathus, wherein was Pytheas son of Ischenous, that Pytheas whom when gashed with wounds the Persians kept aboard their ship and made much of for his valour; this Sidonian ship was carrying Pytheas among the Persians when she was now taken, so that thereby he came safe back to Aegina. When Polycritus saw the Attic ship, he knew it by seeing the admiral's ship's ensign, and cried out to Themistocles with bitter taunt and reproach as to the friendship of Aegina with the Persians.[1] Such taunts did Polycritus hurl at Themistocles, after that he had charged an enemy ship. As for the foreigners whose ships were yet undestroyed, they fled to Phalerum and took refuge with the land army.

93. In that sea-fight the nations that won most renown were the Aeginetans, and next to them the Athenians; among men the most renowned were Polycritus of Aegina and two Athenians, Eumenes of Anagyrus and Aminias of Pallene, he who pursued after Artemisia. Had he known that she was in that ship, he had never been stayed ere he took hers or lost his own; such was the bidding given to the Athenian captain, and there was a prize withal of ten thousand drachmae for whoever should take her alive; for there was great wrath that a woman should come to attack Athens. She, then, escaped as I have already said; and the rest also whose ships were undestroyed were at Phalerum.

94. As for the Corinthian admiral Adimantus, the Athenians say that at the very moment when the ships joined battle he was struck with terror and

taken as hostages by the Athenians when Aegina was charged with favouring the Persians (vi. 49, 73).

τὰ ἱστία ἀειράμενον οἴχεσθαι φεύγοντα, ἰδόντας
δὲ τοὺς Κορινθίους τὴν στρατηγίδα φεύγουσαν
ὡσαύτως οἴχεσθαι. ὡς δὲ ἄρα φεύγοντας γίνεσθαι
τῆς Σαλαμινίης κατὰ ἱρὸν Ἀθηναίης Σκιράδος,
περιπίπτειν σφι κέλητα θείῃ πομπῇ, τὸν οὔτε
πέμψαντα φανῆναι οὐδένα, οὔτε τι τῶν ἀπὸ τῆς
στρατιῆς εἰδόσι προσφέρεσθαι τοῖσι Κορινθίοισι.
τῇδε δὲ συμβάλλονται εἶναι θεῖον τὸ πρῆγμα.
ὡς γὰρ ἀγχοῦ γενέσθαι τῶν νεῶν, τοὺς ἀπὸ τοῦ
κέλητος λέγειν τάδε. "Ἀδείμαντε, σὺ μὲν ἀποστρέψας τὰς νέας ἐς φυγὴν ὅρμησαι καταπροδοὺς
τοὺς Ἕλληνας· οἱ δὲ καὶ δὴ νικῶσι ὅσον αὐτοὶ
ἠρῶντο ἐπικρατήσαντες τῶν ἐχθρῶν." ταῦτα
λεγόντων ἀπιστέειν γὰρ τὸν Ἀδείμαντον, αὖτις
τάδε λέγειν, ὡς αὐτοὶ οἷοί τε εἶεν ἀγόμενοι ὅμηροι
ἀποθνήσκειν, ἢν μὴ νικῶντες φαίνωνται οἱ Ἕλληνες. οὕτω δὴ ἀποστρέψαντα τὴν νέα αὐτόν
τε καὶ τοὺς ἄλλους ἐπ᾽ ἐξεργασμένοισι ἐλθεῖν ἐς
τὸ στρατόπεδον. τούτους μὲν τοιαύτη φάτις ἔχει
ὑπὸ Ἀθηναίων, οὐ μέντοι αὐτοί γε Κορίνθιοι
ὁμολογέουσι, ἀλλ᾽ ἐν πρώτοισι σφέας αὐτοὺς τῆς
ναυμαχίης νομίζουσι γενέσθαι· μαρτυρέει δέ σφι
καὶ ἡ ἄλλη Ἑλλάς.

95. Ἀριστείδης δὲ ὁ Λυσιμάχου ἀνὴρ Ἀθηναῖος,
τοῦ καὶ ὀλίγῳ τι πρότερον τούτων ἐπεμνήσθην ὡς
ἀνδρὸς ἀρίστου, οὗτος ἐν τῷ θορύβῳ τούτῳ τῷ
περὶ Σαλαμῖνα γενομένῳ τάδε ἐποίεε· παραλαβὼν
πολλοὺς τῶν ὁπλιτέων οἳ παρατετάχατο παρὰ
τὴν ἀκτὴν τῆς Σαλαμινίης χώρης, γένος ἐόντες

panic, and hoisting his sails fled away ; and when
the Corinthians saw their admiral's ship fleeing they
were off and away likewise. But when (so the story
goes) they came in their flight near that part of
Salamis where is the temple of Athene Sciras,[1]
there by heaven's providence a boat met them
which none was known to have sent, nor had the
Corinthians, ere it drew nigh to them, known aught
of the doings of the fleet ; and this is how they infer
heaven's hand in the matter : when the boat came
nigh the ships, those that were in it cried, " Adimantus, you have turned back with your ships in
flight, and betrayed the Greeks ; but even now
they are winning the day as fully as they ever
prayed that they might vanquish their enemies."
Thus they spoke, and when Adimantus would not
believe they said further that they were ready to
be taken for hostages and slain if the Greeks were
not victorious for all to see. Thereupon Adimantus
and the rest did turn their ships about and came
to the fleet when all was now over and done.
Thus the Athenians report of the Corinthians ; but
the Corinthians deny it, and hold that they were
among the foremost in the battle ; and all Hellas
bears them witness likewise.

95. But Aristides son of Lysimachus, that Athenian
of whose great merit I have lately made mention, did
in this rout at Salamis as I will show : taking many
of the Athenian men-at-arms who stood arrayed on
the shores of Salamis, he carried them across to

[1] The temple stood on the southern extremity of Salamis.
If the Persians at the outset of the battle were occupying the
ends of the whole strait between Salamis and the mainland,
it is not clear how the Corinthians could get to this point.

Ἀθηναῖοι, ἐς τὴν Ψυττάλειαν νῆσον ἀπέβησε
ἄγων, οἳ τοὺς Πέρσας τοὺς ἐν τῇ νησῖδι ταύτῃ
κατεφόνευσαν πάντας.

96. Ὡς δὲ ἡ ναυμαχίη διελέλυτο, κατειρύσαντες
ἐς τὴν Σαλαμῖνα οἱ Ἕλληνες τῶν ναυηγίων ὅσα
ταύτῃ ἐτύγχανε ἔτι ἐόντα, ἕτοιμοι ἦσαν ἐς ἄλλην
ναυμαχίην, ἐλπίζοντες τῇσι περιεούσῃσι νηυσὶ
ἔτι χρήσεσθαι βασιλέα. τῶν δὲ ναυηγίων πολλὰ
ὑπολαβὼν ἄνεμος ζέφυρος ἔφερε τῆς Ἀττικῆς ἐπὶ
τὴν ἠιόνα τὴν καλεομένην Κωλιάδα· ὥστε ἀπο-
πλησθῆναι τὸν χρησμὸν τόν τε ἄλλον πάντα τὸν
περὶ τῆς ναυμαχίης ταύτης εἰρημένον Βάκιδι καὶ
Μουσαίῳ, καὶ δὴ καὶ κατὰ τὰ ναυήγια τὰ ταύτῃ
ἐξενειχθέντα τὸ εἰρημένον πολλοῖσι ἔτεσι πρότερον
τούτων ἐν χρησμῷ Λυσιστράτῳ Ἀθηναίῳ ἀνδρὶ
χρησμολόγῳ, τὸ ἐλελήθεε πάντας τοὺς Ἕλληνας,

Κωλιάδες δὲ γυναῖκες ἐρετμοῖσι φρύξουσι

τοῦτο δὲ ἔμελλε ἀπελάσαντος βασιλέος ἔσεσθαι.

97. Ξέρξης δὲ ὡς ἔμαθε τὸ γεγονὸς πάθος,
δείσας μή τις τῶν Ἰώνων ὑποθῆται τοῖσι Ἕλλησι
ἢ αὐτοὶ νοήσωσι πλέειν ἐς τὸν Ἑλλήσποντον
λύσοντες τὰς γεφύρας, καὶ ἀπολαμφθεὶς ἐν τῇ
Εὐρώπῃ κινδυνεύσῃ ἀπολέσθαι, δρησμὸν ἐβούλευε.
θέλων δὲ μὴ ἐπίδηλος εἶναι μήτε τοῖσι Ἕλλησι
μήτε τοῖσι ἑωυτοῦ, ἐς τὴν Σαλαμῖνα χῶμα ἐπειρᾶτο διαχοῦν, γαύλους τε Φοινικηίους συνέδεε,
ἵνα ἀντί τε σχεδίης ἔωσι καὶ τείχεος, ἀρτέετό τε
ἐς πόλεμον ὡς ναυμαχίην ἄλλην ποιησόμενος.

---

[1] A narrow headland 2½ miles south of Phalerum; just
where ships would be driven from the battle by a west wind.

the island Psyttalea, and they slaughtered all the Persians who were on that islet.

96. The sea-fight being broken off, the Greeks towed to Salamis all the wrecks that were still afloat in those waters, and held themselves ready for another battle, thinking that the king would yet again use his ships that were left. But many of the wrecks were caught by a west wind and carried to the strand in Attica called Colias;[1] so that not only was the rest of the prophecy fulfilled which had been uttered by Bacis and Musaeus concerning that sea-fight, but also that which had been prophesied many years ago by an Athenian oracle-monger named Lysistratus, about the wrecks that were here cast ashore (the import of which prophecy no Greek had noted):

"Also the Colian dames shall roast their barley
    with oar-blades."

But this was to happen after the king's departure.

97. When Xerxes was aware of the calamity that had befallen him, he feared lest the Greeks (by Ionian counsel or their own devising) might sail to the Hellespont to break his bridges, and he might be cut off in Europe and in peril of his life; and so he planned flight. But that neither the Greeks nor his own men might discover his intent, he essayed to build a mole across to Salamis,[2] and made fast a line of Phoenician barges to be a floating bridge and a wall; and he made preparation for war, as though he would fight at sea again. The rest who saw him

[2] Ctesias and Strabo place this project before and not after the battle; plainly it would have been useless (and indeed impossible) to the Persians after their defeat.

ὁρῶντες δέ μιν πάντες οἱ ἄλλοι ταῦτα πρήσσοντα
εὖ ἠπιστέατο ὡς ἐκ παντὸς νόου παρεσκεύασται
μένων πολεμήσειν· Μαρδόνιον δ᾽ οὐδὲν τούτων
ἐλάνθανε ὡς μάλιστα ἔμπειρον ἐόντα τῆς ἐκείνου
διανοίης.

98. Ταῦτά τε ἅμα Ξέρξης ἐποίεε καὶ ἔπεμπε ἐς
Πέρσας ἀγγελέοντα τὴν παρεοῦσάν σφι συμφορήν.
τούτων δὲ τῶν ἀγγέλων ἐστὶ οὐδὲν ὅ τι θᾶσσον
παραγίνεται θνητὸν ἐόν· οὕτω τοῖσι Πέρσῃσι
ἐξεύρηται τοῦτο. λέγουσι γὰρ ὡς ὁσέων ἂν
ἡμερέων ᾖ ἡ πᾶσα ὁδός, τοσοῦτοι ἵπποι τε καὶ
ἄνδρες διεστᾶσι κατὰ ἡμερησίην ὁδὸν ἑκάστην
ἵππος τε καὶ ἀνὴρ τεταγμένος· τοὺς οὔτε νιφετός,
οὐκ ὄμβρος, οὐ καῦμα, οὐ νὺξ ἔργει μὴ οὐ κατα-
νύσαι τὸν προκείμενον αὐτῷ δρόμον τὴν ταχίστην.
ὁ μὲν δὴ πρῶτος δραμὼν παραδιδοῖ τὰ ἐντεταλμένα
τῷ δευτέρῳ, ὁ δὲ δεύτερος τῷ τρίτῳ· τὸ δὲ ἐνθεῦτεν
ἤδη κατ᾽ ἄλλον καὶ ἄλλον διεξέρχεται παραδιδό-
μενα, κατά περ ἐν Ἕλλησι ἡ λαμπαδηφορίη τὴν
τῷ Ἡφαίστῳ ἐπιτελέουσι. τοῦτο τὸ δράμημα
τῶν ἵππων καλέουσι Πέρσαι ἀγγαρήιον.

99. Ἡ μὲν δὴ πρώτη ἐς Σοῦσα ἀγγελίη ἀπι-
κομένη, ὡς ἔχοι Ἀθήνας Ξέρξης, ἔτερψε οὕτω
δή τι Περσέων τοὺς ὑπολειφθέντας ὡς τάς τε
ὁδοὺς μυρσίνῃ πάσας ἐστόρεσαν καὶ ἐθυμίων
θυμιήματα καὶ αὐτοὶ ἦσαν ἐν θυσίῃσί τε καὶ
εὐπαθείῃσι. ἡ δὲ δευτέρη σφι ἀγγελίη ἐπεσελ-
θοῦσα συνέχεε οὕτω ὥστε τοὺς κιθῶνας κατερρή-

---

[1] Torch-races were run at certain Athenian festivals.
They were of various kinds. One was "a relay or team race.
There were several lines of runners; the first man in each

so doing were fully persuaded that he was in all
earnestness prepared to remain there and carry on
the war; but none of this deceived Mardonius, who
had best experience of Xerxes' purposes.

98. While Xerxes did thus, he sent a messenger
to Persia with news of his present misfortune. Now
there is nothing mortal that accomplishes a course
more swiftly than do these messengers, by the
Persians' skilful contrivance. It is said that as many
days as there are in the whole journey, so many are
the men and horses that stand along the road, each
horse and man at the interval of a day's journey;
and these are stayed neither by snow nor rain nor
heat nor darkness from accomplishing their appointed
course with all speed. The first rider delivers his
charge to the second, the second to the third, and
thence it passes on from hand to hand, even as in the
Greek torch-bearers' race [1] in honour of Hephaestus.
This riding-post is called in Persia, angareïon. [2]

99. When the first message came to Susa, telling
that Xerxes had taken Athens, it gave such delight
to the Persians who were left at home that they
strewed all the roads with myrtle boughs and burnt
incense and gave themselves up to sacrificial feasts
and jollity; but the second, coming on the heels
of the first, so confounded them that they all rent

line had his torch lighted at the altar and ran with it at full
speed to the second, to whom he passed it on, the second to
the third, and so on till the last man carried it to the goal.
The line of runners which first passed its torch alight to the
goal was the winning team " (How and Wells).

[2] ἄγγαρος is apparently a Babylonian word, the Persian
word for a post-rider being in Greek ἀστάνδης (How and
Wells). ἄγγαρος passed into Greek usage; cp. Aesch. Ag.
282.

ξαντο πάντες, βοῇ τε καὶ οἰμωγῇ ἐχρέωντο
ἀπλέτῳ, Μαρδόνιον ἐν αἰτίῃ τιθέντες. οὐκ οὕτω
δὲ περὶ τῶν νεῶν ἀχθόμενοι ταῦτα οἱ Πέρσαι
ἐποίευν ὡς περὶ αὐτῷ Ξέρξῃ δειμαίνοντες.

100. Καὶ περὶ Πέρσας μὲν ἦν ταῦτα τὸν πάντα
μεταξὺ χρόνον γενόμενον, μέχρι οὗ Ξέρξης αὐτός
σφεας ἀπικόμενος ἔπαυσε. Μαρδόνιος δὲ ὁρῶν
μὲν Ξέρξην συμφορὴν μεγάλην ἐκ τῆς ναυμαχίης
ποιεύμενον, ὑποπτεύων δὲ αὐτὸν δρησμὸν βου-
λεύειν ἐκ τῶν Ἀθηνέων, φροντίσας πρὸς ἑωυτὸν
ὡς δώσει δίκην ἀναγνώσας βασιλέα στρατεύεσθαι
ἐπὶ τὴν Ἑλλάδα, καί οἱ κρέσσον εἴη ἀνακινδυνεῦ-
σαι ἢ κατεργάσασθαι τὴν Ἑλλάδα ἢ αὐτὸν καλῶς
τελευτῆσαι τὸν βίον ὑπὲρ μεγάλων αἰωρηθέντα·
πλέον μέντοι ἔφερέ οἱ ἡ γνώμη κατεργάσασθαι
τὴν Ἑλλάδα· λογισάμενος ὦν ταῦτα προσέφερε
τὸν λόγον τόνδε. "Δέσποτα, μήτε λυπέο μήτε
συμφορὴν μηδεμίαν μεγάλην ποιεῦ τοῦδε τοῦ
γεγονότος εἵνεκα πρήγματος. οὐ γὰρ ξύλων ἀγὼν
ὁ τὸ πᾶν φέρων ἐστὶ ἡμῖν, ἀλλ᾽ ἀνδρῶν τε καὶ
ἵππων. σοὶ δὲ οὔτε τις τούτων τῶν τὸ πᾶν
σφίσι ἤδη δοκεόντων κατεργάσθαι ἀποβὰς ἀπὸ
τῶν νεῶν πειρήσεται ἀντιωθῆναι οὔτ᾽ ἐκ τῆς
ἠπείρου τῆσδε· οἵ τε ἡμῖν ἠντιώθησαν, ἔδοσαν
δίκας. εἰ μέν νυν δοκέει, αὐτίκα πειρώμεθα τῆς
Πελοποννήσου· εἰ δὲ καὶ δοκέει ἐπισχεῖν, παρέχει
ποιέειν ταῦτα. μηδὲ δυσθύμεε· οὐ γὰρ ἔστι
Ἕλλησι οὐδεμία ἔκδυσις μὴ οὐ δόντας λόγον τῶν
ἐποίησαν νῦν τε καὶ πρότερον εἶναι σοὺς δούλους.
μάλιστα μέν νυν ταῦτα ποίεε· εἰ δ᾽ ἄρα τοι
βεβούλευται αὐτὸν ἀπελαύνοντα ἀπάγειν τὴν
στρατιήν, ἄλλην ἔχω καὶ ἐκ τῶνδε βουλήν. σὺ

their tunics, and cried and lamented without ceasing,
holding Mardonius to blame ; and it was not so much
in grief for their ships that they did this as because
they feared for Xerxes himself.

100. Such was the plight of the Persians for all
the time until the coming of Xerxes himself ended
it. But Mardonius, seeing that Xerxes was greatly
distressed by reason of the sea-fight, and suspecting
that he planned flight from Athens, considered
with himself that he would be punished for over-
persuading the king to march against Hellas, and
that it was better for him to risk the chance of
either subduing Hellas or dying honourably by flying
at a noble quarry ; yet his hope rather inclined
to the subduing of Hellas ; wherefore taking all
this into account he made this proposal : " Sire, be
not grieved nor greatly distressed by reason of this
that has befallen us. It is not on things of wood
that all the issue hangs for us, but on men and
horses ; and there is not one of these men, who
think that they have now won a crowning victory,
that will disembark from his ship and essay to
withstand you, no, nor anyone from this mainland ;
they that have withstood us have paid the penalty.
If then it so please you, let us straightway attack
the Peloponnese ; or if it please you to wait, that
also we can do. Be not cast down ; for the Greeks
have no way of escape from being accountable for
their former and their latter deeds, and becoming
your slaves. It is best then that you should do as
I have said ; but if you are resolved that you will
lead your army away, even then I have another

Πέρσας, βασιλεῦ, μὴ ποιήσῃς καταγελάστους
γενέσθαι "Ελλησι· οὐδὲ γὰρ ἐν Πέρσῃσί τοί τι
δεδήληται τῶν πρηγμάτων, οὐδ' ἐρέεις ὅκου ἐγε-
νόμεθα ἄνδρες κακοί. εἰ δὲ Φοίνικές τε καὶ
Αἰγύπτιοι καὶ Κύπριοί τε καὶ Κίλικες κακοὶ
ἐγένοντο, οὐδὲν πρὸς Πέρσας τοῦτο προσήκει τὸ
πάθος. ἤδη ὧν, ἐπειδὴ οὐ Πέρσαι τοι αἴτιοί εἰσί,
ἐμοὶ πείθεο· εἴ τοι δέδοκται μὴ παραμένειν, σὺ
μὲν ἐς ἤθεα τὰ σεωυτοῦ ἀπέλαυνε τῆς στρατιῆς
ἀπάγων τὸ πολλόν, ἐμὲ δὲ σοὶ χρὴ τὴν Ἑλλάδα
παρασχεῖν δεδουλωμένην, τριήκοντα μυριάδας τοῦ
στρατοῦ ἀπολεξάμενον."

101. Ταῦτα ἀκούσας Ξέρξης ὡς ἐκ κακῶν
ἐχάρη τε καὶ ἥσθη, πρὸς Μαρδόνιόν τε βουλευσάμενος ἔφη ὑποκρινέεσθαι ὁκότερον ποιήσει
τούτων. ὡς δὲ ἐβουλεύετο ἅμα Περσέων τοῖσι
ἐπικλήτοισι, ἔδοξέ οἱ καὶ Ἀρτεμισίην ἐς συμβου-
λίην μεταπέμψασθαι, ὅτι πρότερον ἐφαίνετο
μούνη νοέουσα τὰ ποιητέα ἦν. ὡς δὲ ἀπίκετο
ἡ Ἀρτεμισίη, μεταστησάμενος τοὺς ἄλλους τούς
τε συμβούλους Περσέων καὶ τοὺς δορυφόρους,
ἔλεξε Ξέρξης τάδε. "Κελεύει με Μαρδόνιος
μένοντα αὐτοῦ πειρᾶσθαι τῆς Πελοποννήσου,
λέγων ὥς μοι Πέρσαι τε καὶ ὁ πεζὸς στρατὸς
οὐδενὸς μεταίτιοι πάθεος εἰσί, ἀλλὰ βουλομένοισί
σφι γένοιτ' ἂν ἀπόδεξις. ἐμὲ ὧν ἢ ταῦτα κελεύει
ποιέειν, ἢ αὐτὸς ἐθέλει τριήκοντα μυριάδας ἀπολε-
ξάμενος τοῦ στρατοῦ παρασχεῖν μοι τὴν Ἑλλάδα
δεδουλωμένην, αὐτὸν δέ με κελεύει ἀπελαύνειν
σὺν τῷ λοιπῷ στρατῷ ἐς ἤθεα τὰ ἐμά. σὺ ὧν
ἐμοί, καὶ γὰρ περὶ τῆς ναυμαχίης εὖ συνεβού-

plan. Do not, O king, make the Persians a laughing-stock to the Greeks; for if you have suffered harm, it is by no fault of the Persians, nor can you say that we have anywhere done less than brave men should; and if Phoenicians and Egyptians and Cyprians and Cilicians have so done, it is not the Persians who have any part in this disaster. Wherefore since the Persians are nowise to blame, be guided by me; if you are resolved that you will not remain, do you march away homewards with the greater part of your army; but it is for me to enslave and deliver Hellas to you, with three hundred thousand of your host whom I will choose."

101. When Xerxes heard that, he was as glad and joyful as a man in his evil case might be, and said to Mardonius that he would answer him when he had first taken counsel which of the two plans he would follow; and as he consulted with those Persians whom he summoned, he was fain to bid Artemisia too to the council, because he saw that she alone at the former sitting had discerned what was best to do. When Artemisia came, Xerxes bade all others withdraw, both Persian councillors and guards, and said to her: " It is Mardonius' counsel that I should abide here and attack the Peloponnese; for the Persians, he says, and the land army are nowise to blame for our disaster, and of that they would willingly give proof. Wherefore it is his counsel that I should do this; else he offers to choose out three hundred thousand men of the army and deliver Hellas to me enslaved, while I myself by his counsel march away homeward with the rest of the host. Now therefore I ask of you:

λεύσας τῆς γενομένης οὐκ ἐῶσα ποιέεσθαι, νῦν
τε συμβούλευσον ὁκότερα ποιέων ἐπιτύχω εὖ
βουλευσάμενος."

102. Ὁ μὲν ταῦτα συνεβουλεύετο, ἦ δὲ λέγει
τάδε. "Βασιλεῦ, χαλεπὸν μὲν ἐστὶ συμβου-
λευομένῳ τυχεῖν τὰ ἄριστα εἴπασαν, ἐπὶ μέντοι
τοῖσι κατήκουσι πρήγμασι δοκέει μοι αὐτὸν μέν
σε ἀπελαύνειν ὀπίσω, Μαρδόνιον δέ, εἰ ἐθέλει
τε καὶ ὑποδέκεται ταῦτα ποιήσειν, αὐτοῦ κατα-
λιπεῖν σὺν τοῖσι ἐθέλει. τοῦτο μὲν γὰρ ἦν
καταστρέψηται τὰ φησὶ θέλειν καί οἱ προχωρήσῃ
τὰ νοέων λέγει, σὸν τὸ ἔργον ὦ δέσποτα γίνεται·
οἱ γὰρ σοὶ δοῦλοι κατεργάσαντο. τοῦτο δὲ ἦν
τὰ ἐναντία τῆς Μαρδονίου γνώμης γένηται, οὐδεμία
συμφορὴ μεγάλη ἔσται σέο τε περιεόντος καὶ
ἐκείνων τῶν πρηγμάτων περὶ οἶκον τὸν σόν· ἢν
γὰρ σύ τε περιῇς καὶ οἶκος ὁ σός, πολλοὺς
πολλάκις ἀγῶνας δραμέονται περὶ σφέων αὐτῶν
οἱ Ἕλληνες. Μαρδονίου δέ, ἤν τι πάθῃ, λόγος
οὐδεὶς γίνεται, οὐδέ τι νικῶντες οἱ Ἕλληνες
νικῶσι, δοῦλον σὸν ἀπολέσαντες· σὺ δέ, τῶν
εἵνεκα τὸν στόλον ἐποιήσαο, πυρώσας τὰς
Ἀθήνας ἀπελᾷς."

103. Ἥσθη τε δὴ τῇ συμβουλίῃ Ξέρξης·
λέγουσα γὰρ ἐπετύγχανε τά περ αὐτὸς ἐνόεε.
οὐδὲ γὰρ εἰ πάντες καὶ πᾶσαι συνεβούλευον
αὐτῷ μένειν, ἔμενε ἂν δοκέειν ἐμοί· οὕτω καταρρω-
δήκεε. ἐπαινέσας δὲ τὴν Ἀρτεμισίην, ταύτην μὲν
ἀποστέλλει ἄγουσαν αὐτοῦ παῖδας ἐς Ἔφεσον·
νόθοι γὰρ τινὲς παῖδές οἱ συνέσποντο.

104. Συνέπεμπε δὲ τοῖσι παισὶ φύλακον Ἑρμό-
τιμον, γένος μὲν ἐόντα Πηδασέα, φερόμενον δὲ

as you did rightly in counselling me against the
late sea-fight, so now counsel me as to which of
these two things I shall be best advised to do."

102. Being thus asked for advice she replied:
"It is difficult, O king, to answer your asking for
advice by saying that which is best; but in the
present turn of affairs I think it best that you
march away back, and that Mardonius, if he wills
and promises to do as he says, be left here with
those whom he desires. For if he subdue all that
he offers to subdue, and prosper in the purpose
wherewith he speaks, the achievement, Sire, is yours;
for it will be your servants that have wrought it.
But if again the issue be contrary to Mardonius'
opinion, it is no great misfortune so long as you
and all that household of yours be safe; for while
you and they of your house are safe, many a time
and oft will the Greeks have to fight for their lives.
As for Mardonius, if aught ill befall him, it is no
matter for that; nor will any victory of the Greeks
be a victory in truth, when they have but slain your
servant; but as for you, you will be marching home
after the burning of Athens, which thing was the
whole purpose of your expedition."

103. Artemisia's counsel pleased Xerxes; for it
happened that she spoke his own purpose; in truth
I think that he would not have remained, though all
men and women had counselled him so to do; so
panic-stricken was he. Having then thanked Artemisia, he sent her away to carry his sons to Ephesus;
for he had some bastard sons with him.

104. With these sons he sent Hermotimus as
guardian; this man was by birth of Pedasa, and the

οὐ τὰ δεύτερα τῶν εὐνούχων παρὰ βασιλέι·[1] [οἱ
δὲ Πηδασέες οἰκέουσι ὑπὲρ Ἁλικαρνησσοῦ· ἐν
δὲ τοῖσι Πηδάσοισι τουτέοισι τοιόνδε συμφέρεται
πρῆγμα γίνεσθαι· ἐπεὰν τοῖσι ἀμφικτυόσι πᾶσι
τοῖσι ἀμφὶ ταύτης οἰκέουσι τῆς πόλιος μέλλῃ
τι ἐντὸς χρόνου ἔσεσθαι χαλεπόν, τότε ἡ ἱερείη
αὐτόθι τῆς Ἀθηναίης φύει πώγωνα μέγαν. τοῦτο
δέ σφι δὶς ἤδη ἐγένετο.

105. Ἐκ τούτων δὴ τῶν Πηδασέων ὁ Ἑρμότιμος
ἦν] τῷ μεγίστη τίσις ἤδη ἀδικηθέντι ἐγένετο
πάντων τῶν ἡμεῖς ἴδμεν. ἁλόντα γὰρ αὐτὸν ὑπὸ
πολεμίων καὶ πωλεόμενον ὠνέεται Πανιώνιος ἀνὴρ
Χῖος, ὃς τὴν ζόην κατεστήσατο ἀπ' ἔργων ἀνοσιω-
τάτων· ὅκως γὰρ κτήσαιτο παῖδας εἴδεος ἐπαμ-
μένους, ἐκτάμνων ἀγινέων ἐπώλεε ἐς Σάρδις τε
καὶ Ἔφεσον χρημάτων μεγάλων. παρὰ γὰρ
τοῖσι βαρβάροισι τιμιώτεροι εἰσὶ οἱ εὐνοῦχοι
πίστιος εἵνεκα τῆς πάσης τῶν ἐνορχίων. ἄλλους
τε δὴ ὁ Πανιώνιος ἐξέταμε πολλούς, ἅτε ποιεύμενος ἐκ τούτου τὴν ζόην, καὶ δὴ καὶ τοῦτον. καὶ
οὐ γὰρ τὰ πάντα ἐδυστύχεε ὁ Ἑρμότιμος, ἀπικνέεται ἐκ τῶν Σαρδίων παρὰ βασιλέα μετ'
ἄλλων δώρων, χρόνου δὲ προϊόντος πάντων τῶν
εὐνούχων ἐτιμήθη μάλιστα παρὰ Ξέρξῃ.

106. Ὡς δὲ τὸ στράτευμα τὸ Περσικὸν ὅρμα
βασιλεὺς ἐπὶ τὰς Ἀθήνας ἐὼν ἐν Σάρδισι, ἐνθαῦτα
καταβὰς κατὰ δή τι πρῆγμα ὁ Ἑρμότιμος ἐς γῆν
τὴν Μυσίην, τὴν Χῖοι μὲν νέμονται Ἀταρνεὺς δὲ
καλέεται, εὑρίσκει τὸν Πανιώνιον ἐνθαῦτα. ἐπι-
γνοὺς δὲ ἔλεγε πρὸς αὐτὸν πολλοὺς καὶ φιλίους
λόγους, πρῶτα μέν οἱ καταλέγων ὅσα αὐτὸς δι'
ἐκεῖνον ἔχοι ἀγαθά, δεύτερα δέ οἱ ὑπισχνεύμενος

most honoured by Xerxes of all his eunuchs. The
people of Pedasa dwell above Halicarnassus. This
happens among these people : when aught untoward
is about to befall within a certain time all those
that dwell about their city, the priestess of Athene
then grows a great beard. This had already happened
to them twice.

105. Hermotimus, who came from this place
Pedasa, had achieved a fuller vengeance for wrong
done to him than had any man within my knowledge.
Being taken captive by enemies and exposed for
sale, he was bought by one Panionius of Chios, a
man that had set himself to earn a livelihood out of
most wicked practices; he would procure beautiful
boys and castrate and take them to Sardis and
Ephesus, where he sold them for a great price; for
the foreigners value eunuchs more than perfect men,
by reason of the full trust that they have in them.
Now among the many whom Panionius had castrated
in the way of trade was Hermotimus, who was not in
all things unfortunate; for he was brought from
Sardis among other gifts to the king, and as time
went on he stood higher in Xerxes' favour than any
other eunuch.

106. Now while the king was at Sardis and there
preparing to lead his Persian armament against
Athens, Hermotimus came for some business that he
had in hand down to the part of Mysia which is
inhabited by Chians and called Atarneus, and there
he found Panionius. Perceiving who he was, he
held long and friendly converse with him; "it is
to you," he said, "that I owe all this prosperity of

---

[1] The words in brackets are probably an interpolation,
from i. 175, where they occur more appropriately.

ἀντὶ τούτων ὅσα μιν ἀγαθὰ ποιήσει ἢν κομίσας
τοὺς οἰκέτας οἰκέῃ ἐκείνη, ὥστε ὑποδεξάμενον
ἄσμενον τοὺς λόγους τὸν Πανιώνιον κομίσαι τὰ
τέκνα καὶ τὴν γυναῖκα. ὡς δὲ ἄρα πανοικίῃ μιν
περιέλαβε, ἔλεγε ὁ Ἑρμότιμος τάδε. "Ὦ πάντων
ἀνδρῶν ἤδη μάλιστα ἀπ' ἔργων ἀνοσιωτάτων τὸν
βίον κτησάμενε, τί σε ἐγὼ κακὸν ἢ αὐτὸς ἢ τῶν
ἐμῶν τίς σε προγόνων ἐργάσατο, ἢ σὲ ἢ τῶν σῶν
τινα, ὅτι με ἀντ' ἀνδρὸς ἐποίησας τὸ μηδὲν εἶναι ;
ἐδόκεές τε θεοὺς λήσειν οἷα ἐμηχανῶ τότε· οἵ σε
ποιήσαντα ἀνόσια, νόμῳ δικαίῳ χρεώμενοι, ὑπή-
γαγον ἐς χεῖρας τὰς ἐμάς, ὥστε σε μὴ μέμψασθαι
τὴν ἀπ' ἐμέο τοι ἐσομένην δίκην." ὡς δέ οἱ
ταῦτα ὠνείδισε, ἀχθέντων τῶν παίδων ἐς ὄψιν
ἠναγκάζετο ὁ Πανιώνιος τῶν ἑωυτοῦ παίδων
τεσσέρων ἐόντων τὰ αἰδοῖα ἀποτάμνειν, ἀναγκα-
ζόμενος δὲ ἐποίεε ταῦτα· αὐτοῦ τε, ὡς ταῦτα
ἐργάσατο, οἱ παῖδες ἀναγκαζόμενοι ἀπέταμνον.
Πανιώνιον μέν νυν οὕτω περιῆλθε ἥ τε τίσις καὶ
Ἑρμότιμος.

107. Ξέρξης δὲ ὡς τοὺς παῖδας ἐπέτρεψε
Ἀρτεμισίῃ ἀπάγειν ἐς Ἔφεσον, καλέσας Μαρδόνιον ἐκέλευσέ μιν τῆς στρατιῆς διαλέγειν τοὺς
βούλεται, καὶ ποιέειν τοῖσι λόγοισι τὰ ἔργα
πειρώμενον ὅμοια. ταύτην μὲν τὴν ἡμέρην ἐς
τοσοῦτο ἐγίνετο, τῆς δὲ νυκτὸς κελεύσαντος
βασιλέος τὰς νέας οἱ στρατηγοὶ ἐκ τοῦ Φαλήρου
ἀπῆγον ὀπίσω ἐς τὸν Ἑλλήσποντον ὡς τάχεος
εἶχε ἕκαστος, διαφυλαξούσας τὰς σχεδίας πορευ-
θῆναι βασιλέι. ἐπεὶ δὲ ἀγχοῦ ἦσαν Ζωστῆρος
πλέοντες οἱ βάρβαροι, ἀνατείνουσι γὰρ ἄκραι

mine; now if you will bring your household and
dwell here, I will make you prosperous in return,"—
promising this and that; Panionius accepted his
offer gladly, and brought his children and his wife.
But Hermotimus, having got the man and all his
household in his power, said to him: "Tell me,
you that have made a livelihood out of the wickedest
trade on earth! what harm had I or any of my forefathers done to you, to you or yours, that you made
me to be no man, but a thing of nought? ay, you
thought that the gods would have no knowledge of
your devices of old; but their just law has brought
you for your wicked deeds into my hands, and now
you shall be well content with the fulness of that
justice which I will execute upon you." With these
words of reproach, he brought Panionius' sons before
him and compelled him to castrate all four of them,
his own children; this Panionius was compelled to
do; which done, the sons were compelled to castrate
their father in turn. Thus was Panionius overtaken
by vengeance and by Hermotimus.

107. Having given his sons to Artemisia's charge
to be carried to Ephesus, Xerxes called Mardonius
to him and bade him choose out whom he would
from the army, and make his words good so far as
endeavour availed. For that day matters went thus
far; in the night, the admirals by the king's command put out to sea from Phalerum and made for
the Hellespont again with all speed, to guard the
bridges for the king's passage. When the foreigners
came near to the "Girdle"[1] in their course, they
thought that certain little headlands, which here jut

[1] A promontory on the west coast of Attica, between
Piraeus and Sunium.

λεπταὶ τῆς ἠπείρου ταύτης, ἔδοξάν τε νέας εἶναι
καὶ ἔφευγον ἐπὶ πολλόν· χρόνῳ δὲ μαθόντες ὅτι
οὐ νέες εἶεν ἀλλ᾽ ἄκραι, συλλεχθέντες ἐκομίζοντο.

108. Ὡς δὲ ἡμέρη ἐγίνετο, ὁρῶντες οἱ Ἕλληνες
κατὰ χώρην μένοντα τὸν στρατὸν τὸν πεζὸν
ἤλπιζον καὶ τὰς νέας εἶναι περὶ Φάληρον, ἐδόκεόν
τε ναυμαχήσειν σφέας παραρτέοντό τε ὡς ἀλεξη-
σόμενοι. ἐπεὶ δὲ ἐπύθοντο τὰς νέας οἰχωκυίας,
αὐτίκα μετὰ ταῦτα ἐδόκεε ἐπιδιώκειν. τὸν μέν
νυν ναυτικὸν τὸν Ξέρξεω στρατὸν οὐκ ἐπεῖδον
διώξαντες μέχρι Ἄνδρου, ἐς δὲ τὴν Ἄνδρον ἀπικόμενοι ἐβουλεύοντο. Θεμιστοκλέης μέν νυν
γνώμην ἀπεδείκνυτο διὰ νήσων τραπομένους καὶ
ἐπιδιώξαντας τὰς νέας πλέειν ἰθέως ἐπὶ τὸν
Ἑλλήσποντον λύσοντας τὰς γεφύρας· Εὐρυβιάδης δὲ τὴν ἐναντίην ταύτῃ γνώμην ἐτίθετο,
λέγων ὡς εἰ λύσουσι τὰς σχεδίας, τοῦτ᾽ ἂν μέγιστον πάντων σφι κακῶν τὴν Ἑλλάδα ἐργάσαιτο.
εἰ γὰρ ἀναγκασθείη ὁ Πέρσης μένειν ἐν τῇ
Εὐρώπῃ, πειρῷτο ἂν ἡσυχίην μὴ ἄγειν, ὡς ἄγοντι
μέν οἱ ἡσυχίην οὔτε τι προχωρέειν οἷόν τε ἔσται
τῶν πρηγμάτων οὔτε τις κομιδὴ τὰ ὀπίσω φανήσεται, λιμῷ τέ οἱ ἡ στρατιὴ διαφθερέεται,
ἐπιχειρέοντι δὲ αὐτῷ καὶ ἔργου ἐχομένῳ πάντα
τὰ κατὰ τὴν Εὐρώπην οἷά τε ἔσται προσχωρῆσαι
κατὰ πόλις τε καὶ κατὰ ἔθνεα, ἤτοι ἁλισκομένων
γε ἢ πρὸ τούτου ὁμολογεόντων· τροφήν τε ἕξειν
σφέας τὸν ἐπέτειον αἰεὶ τὸν τῶν Ἑλλήνων καρπόν. ἀλλὰ δοκέειν γὰρ νικηθέντα τῇ ναυμαχίῃ
οὐ μενέειν ἐν τῇ Εὐρώπῃ τὸν Πέρσην· ἐατέον ὦν
εἶναι φεύγειν, ἐς ὃ ἔλθοι φεύγων ἐς τὴν ἑωυτοῦ·
τὸ ἐνθεῦτεν δὲ περὶ τῆς ἐκείνου ποιέεσθαι ἤδη τὸν

out from the mainland, were ships, and they fled for a long way; but learning at last that they were no ships but headlands they drew together and went on their way.

108. When it was day, the Greeks saw the land army abiding where it had been and supposed the ships also to be at Phalerum; and thinking that there would be a sea-fight they prepared to defend themselves. But when they learnt that the ships were gone, they straightway resolved on pursuit; so they pursued Xerxes' fleet as far as Andros, but had no sight of it; and when they came to Andros they held a council there. Themistocles declared his opinion that they should hold their course through the islands, and having pursued after the ships should sail forthwith to the Hellespont to break the bridges; but Eurybiades offered a contrary opinion, saying that to break the bridges would be the greatest harm that they could do to Hellas. "For," said he, "if the Persian be cut off and compelled to remain in Europe, he will essay not to be inactive, seeing that if he be inactive neither can his cause prosper nor can he find any way of return home, but his army will perish of hunger; but if he be adventurous and busy, it may well be that every town and nation in Europe may join itself to him severally, by conquest or ere that by compact; and he will live on whatsoever yearly fruits of the earth Hellas produces. But, as I think that the Persian will not remain in Europe after his defeat in the sea-fight, let us suffer him to flee, till he come in his flight to his own country; and thereafter let it be that country and not ours that is at stake in the war."

ἀγῶνα ἐκέλευε. ταύτης δὲ εἴχοντο τῆς γνώμης
καὶ Πελοποννησίων τῶν ἄλλων οἱ στρατηγοί.

109. Ὡς δὲ ἔμαθε ὅτι οὐ πείσει τούς γε πολλοὺς
πλέειν ἐς τὸν Ἑλλήσποντον ὁ Θεμιστοκλέης,
μεταβαλὼν πρὸς τοὺς Ἀθηναίους (οὗτοι γὰρ
μάλιστα ἐκπεφευγότων περιημέκτεον, ὁρμέατό τε
ἐς τὸν Ἑλλήσποντον πλέειν καὶ ἐπὶ σφέων αὐτῶν
βαλόμενοι, εἰ οἱ ἄλλοι μὴ βουλοίατο) ἔλεγέ σφι
τάδε. "Καὶ αὐτὸς ἤδη πολλοῖσι παρεγενόμην
καὶ πολλῷ πλέω ἀκήκοα τοιάδε γενέσθαι, ἄνδρας
ἐς ἀναγκαίην ἀπειληθέντας νενικημένους ἀναμά-
χεσθαί τε καὶ ἀναλαμβάνειν τὴν προτέρην κακό-
τητα. ἡμεῖς δέ, εὕρημα γὰρ εὑρήκαμεν ἡμέας τε
αὐτοὺς καὶ τὴν Ἑλλάδα, νέφος τοσοῦτο ἀνθρώπων
ἀνωσάμενοι, μὴ διώκωμεν ἄνδρας φεύγοντας. τάδε
γὰρ οὐκ ἡμεῖς κατεργασάμεθα, ἀλλὰ θεοί τε καὶ
ἥρωες, οἳ ἐφθόνησαν ἄνδρα ἕνα τῆς τε Ἀσίης καὶ
τῆς Εὐρώπης βασιλεῦσαι ἐόντα ἀνόσιόν τε καὶ
ἀτάσθαλον· ὃς τά τε ἱρὰ καὶ τὰ ἴδια ἐν ὁμοίῳ
ἐποιέετο, ἐμπιπράς τε καὶ καταβάλλων τῶν θεῶν
τὰ ἀγάλματα· ὃς καὶ τὴν θάλασσαν ἀπεμα-
στίγωσε πέδας τε κατῆκε. ἀλλ᾽ εὖ γὰρ ἔχει ἐς
τὸ παρεὸν ἡμῖν, νῦν μὲν ἐν τῇ Ἑλλάδι καταμεί-
ναντας ἡμέων τε αὐτῶν ἐπιμεληθῆναι καὶ τῶν
οἰκετέων, καί τις οἰκίην τε ἀναπλασάσθω καὶ
σπόρου ἀνακῶς ἐχέτω, παντελέως ἀπελάσας τὸν
βάρβαρον· ἅμα δὲ τῷ ἔαρι καταπλέωμεν ἐπὶ
Ἑλλησπόντου καὶ Ἰωνίης." ταῦτα ἔλεγε ἀπο-
θήκην μέλλων ποιήσασθαι ἐς τὸν Πέρσην, ἵνα
ἢν ἄρα τί μιν καταλαμβάνῃ πρὸς Ἀθηναίων
πάθος ἔχῃ ἀποστροφήν· τά περ ὦν καὶ ἐγένετο.

110. Θεμιστοκλέης μὲν ταῦτα λέγων διέβαλλε,

With that opinion the rest of the Peloponnesian admirals also agreed.

109. When Themistocles perceived that he could not persuade the greater part of them to sail to the Hellespont, he turned to the Athenians (for they were the angriest at the Persians' escape, and they were minded to sail to the Hellespont even by themselves, if the rest would not) and thus addressed them: "This I have often seen with my eyes, and much oftener heard, that beaten men when they be driven to bay will rally and retrieve their former mishap. Wherefore I say to you,—as it is to a fortunate chance that we owe ourselves and Hellas, and have driven away so mighty a cloud of enemies, let us not pursue after men that flee. For it is not we that have won this victory, but the gods and the heroes, who deemed Asia and Europe too great a realm for one man to rule, and that a wicked man and an impious; one that dealt alike with temples and homes, and burnt and overthrew the images of the gods,—yea, that scourged the sea and threw fetters thereinto. But as it is well with us for the nonce, let us abide now in Hellas and take thought for ourselves and our households; let us build our houses again and be diligent in sowing, when we have driven the foreigner wholly away; and when the next spring comes let us set sail for the Hellespont and Ionia." This he said with intent to put somewhat to his credit with the Persian, so that he might have a place of refuge if ever (as might chance) he should suffer aught at the hands of the Athenians; and indeed it did so happen.

110. Thus spoke Themistocles with intent to

Ἀθηναῖοι δὲ ἐπείθοντο· ἐπειδὴ γὰρ καὶ πρότερον
δεδογμένος εἶναι σοφὸς ἐφάνη ἐὼν ἀληθέως σοφός
τε καὶ εὔβουλος, πάντως ἕτοιμοι ἦσαν λέγοντι
πείθεσθαι. ὡς δὲ οὗτοί οἱ ἀνεγνωσμένοι ἦσαν,
αὐτίκα μετὰ ταῦτα ὁ Θεμιστοκλέης ἄνδρας ἀπέ-
πεμπε ἔχοντας πλοῖον, τοῖσι ἐπίστευε σιγᾶν ἐς
πᾶσαν βάσανον ἀπικνεομένοισι τὰ αὐτὸς ἐνετείλατο βασιλέι φράσαι· τῶν καὶ Σίκιννος ὁ οἰκέτης
αὖτις ἐγένετο· οἳ ἐπείτε ἀπίκοντο πρὸς τὴν Ἀττικήν, οἳ μὲν κατέμενον ἐπὶ τῷ πλοίῳ, Σίκιννος δὲ
ἀναβὰς παρὰ Ξέρξην ἔλεγε τάδε. "Ἔπεμψέ με
Θεμιστοκλέης ὁ Νεοκλέος, στρατηγὸς μὲν Ἀθηναίων ἀνὴρ δὲ τῶν συμμάχων πάντων ἄριστος
καὶ σοφώτατος, φράσοντά τοι ὅτι Θεμιστοκλέης
ὁ Ἀθηναῖος, σοὶ βουλόμενος ὑπουργέειν, ἔσχε
τοὺς Ἕλληνας τὰς νέας βουλομένους διώκειν καὶ
τὰς ἐν Ἑλλησπόντῳ γεφύρας λύειν. καὶ νῦν
κατ᾽ ἡσυχίην πολλὴν κομίζεο." οἳ μὲν ταῦτα
σημήναντες ἀπέπλεον ὀπίσω.

111. Οἱ δὲ Ἕλληνες, ἐπείτε σφι ἀπέδοξε μήτ᾽
ἐπιδιώκειν ἔτι προσωτέρω τῶν βαρβάρων τὰς
νέας μήτε πλέειν ἐς τὸν Ἑλλήσποντον λύσοντας
τὸν πόρον, τὴν Ἄνδρον περικατέατο ἐξελεῖν ἐθέλοντες. πρῶτοι γὰρ Ἄνδριοι νησιωτέων αἰτη-
θέντες πρὸς Θεμιστοκλέος χρήματα οὐκ ἔδοσαν,
ἀλλὰ προϊσχομένου Θεμιστοκλέος λόγον τόνδε,
ὡς ἥκοιεν Ἀθηναῖοι περὶ ἑωυτοὺς ἔχοντες δύο
θεοὺς μεγάλους, πειθώ τε καὶ ἀναγκαίην, οὕτω
τέ σφι κάρτα δοτέα εἶναι χρήματα, ὑπεκρίναντο
πρὸς ταῦτα λέγοντες ὡς κατὰ λόγον ἦσαν ἄρα
αἱ Ἀθῆναι μεγάλαι τε καὶ εὐδαίμονες, αἳ καὶ
θεῶν χρηστῶν ἥκοιεν εὖ, ἐπεὶ Ἀνδρίους γε εἶναι

deceive, and the Athenians obeyed him; for since he had ever been esteemed wise and now had shown himself to be both wise and prudent, they were ready to obey whatsoever he said. Having won them over, Themistocles straightway sent men in a boat whom he could trust not to reveal under any question whatsoever the message which he charged them to deliver to the king; of whom one was again his servant Sicinnus. When these men came to Attica, the rest abode with the boat, and Sicinnus went up to Xerxes; "Themistocles son of Neocles," he said, "who is the Athenian general, and of all the allies the worthiest and wisest, has sent me to tell you this: Themistocles the Athenian has out of his desire to do you a service stayed the Greeks when they would pursue your ships and break the bridges of the Hellespont; and now he bids you go your way, none hindering you." With that message, the men returned in their boat.

111. But the Greeks, now that they were no longer minded to pursue the foreigners' ships farther or sail to the Hellespont and break the way of passage, beleaguered Andros that they might take it. For the men of that place, the first islanders of whom Themistocles demanded money, would not give it; but when Themistocles gave them to understand that the Athenians had come with two great gods to aid them, even Persuasion and Necessity, and that therefore the Andrians must assuredly give money, they answered and said, "It is then but reasonable that Athens is great and prosperous, being blest with serviceable gods; as for us Andrians, we are but

γεωπείνας ἐς τὰ μέγιστα ἀνήκοντας, καὶ θεοὺς
δύο ἀχρήστους οὐκ ἐκλείπειν σφέων τὴν νῆσον
ἀλλ' αἰεὶ φιλοχωρέειν, πενίην τε καὶ ἀμηχανίην,
καὶ τούτων τῶν θεῶν ἐπηβόλους ἐόντας Ἀνδρίους
οὐ δώσειν χρήματα· οὐδέκοτε γὰρ τῆς ἑωυτῶν
ἀδυναμίης τὴν Ἀθηναίων δύναμιν εἶναι κρέσσω.

112. Οὗτοι μὲν δὴ ταῦτα ὑποκρινάμενοι καὶ
οὐ δόντες τὰ χρήματα ἐπολιορκέοντο. Θεμιστοκλέης δέ, οὐ γὰρ ἐπαύετο πλεονεκτέων, ἐσπέμπων
ἐς τὰς ἄλλας νήσους ἀπειλητηρίους λόγους αἴτεε
χρήματα διὰ τῶν αὐτῶν ἀγγέλων, χρεώμενος
τοῖσι καὶ πρὸς βασιλέα ἐχρήσατο, λέγων ὡς εἰ
μὴ δώσουσι τὸ αἰτεόμενον, ἐπάξει τὴν στρατιὴν
τῶν Ἑλλήνων καὶ πολιορκέων ἐξαιρήσει. λέγων
ταῦτα συνέλεγε χρήματα μεγάλα παρὰ Καρυστίων
τε καὶ Παρίων, οἳ πυνθανόμενοι τήν τε Ἄνδρον
ὡς πολιορκέοιτο διότι ἐμήδισε, καὶ Θεμιστοκλέα
ὡς εἴη ἐν αἴνῃ μεγίστῃ τῶν στρατηγῶν, δείσαντες
ταῦτα ἔπεμπον χρήματα. εἰ δὲ δὴ τινὲς καὶ
ἄλλοι ἔδοσαν νησιωτέων, οὐκ ἔχω εἰπεῖν, δοκέω
δὲ τινὰς καὶ ἄλλους δοῦναι καὶ οὐ τούτους μούνους.
καίτοι Καρυστίοισί γε οὐδὲν τούτου εἵνεκα τοῦ
κακοῦ ὑπερβολὴ ἐγένετο· Πάριοι δὲ Θεμιστοκλέα
χρήμασι ἱλασάμενοι διέφυγον τὸ στράτευμα.
Θεμιστοκλέης μέν νυν ἐξ Ἄνδρου ὁρμώμενος
χρήματα παρὰ νησιωτέων ἐκτᾶτο λάθρῃ τῶν
ἄλλων στρατηγῶν.

113. Οἱ δ' ἀμφὶ Ξέρξην ἐπισχόντες ὀλίγας
ἡμέρας μετὰ τὴν ναυμαχίην ἐξήλαυνον ἐς Βοιωτοὺς
τὴν αὐτὴν ὁδόν. ἔδοξε γὰρ Μαρδονίῳ ἅμα μὲν
προπέμψαι βασιλέα, ἅμα δὲ ἀνωρίη εἶναι τοῦ
ἔτεος πολεμέειν, χειμερίσαι τε ἄμεινον εἶναι ἐν

blest with a plentiful lack of land, and we have two unserviceable gods who never quit our island but are ever fain to dwell there, even Poverty and Impotence; being possessed of these gods, we of Andros will give no money; for the power of Athens can never be stronger than our inability."

112. So for thus answering and refusing to give they were besieged. There was no end to Themistocles' avarice; using the same agents whom he had used with the king, he sent threatening messages to the other islands, demanding money, and saying that if they would not give what he asked he would bring the Greek armada upon them and besiege and take their islands. Thereby he collected great sums from the Carystians and Parians; for these were informed that Andros was besieged for taking the Persian part, and that Themistocles was of all the generals the most esteemed; which so affrighted them that they sent money; and I suppose that there were other islanders too that gave, and not these alone, but I cannot with certainty say. Nevertheless the Carystians got thereby no respite from misfortune; but the Parians propitiated Themistocles with money and so escaped the armament. So Themistocles issued out from Andros and took monies from the islanders, unknown to the other generals.

113. They that were with Xerxes waited for a few days after the sea-fight and then marched away to Boeotia by the road whereby they had come; for Mardonius was minded to give the king safe conduct, and deemed the time of year unseasonable for war; it was better, he thought, to

Θεσσαλίη, καὶ ἔπειτα ἅμα τῷ ἔαρι πειρᾶσθαι τῆς Πελοποννήσου. ὡς δὲ ἀπίκατο ἐς τὴν Θεσσαλίην, ἐνθαῦτα Μαρδόνιος ἐξελέγετο πρώτους μὲν τοὺς Πέρσας πάντας τοὺς ἀθανάτους καλεομένους, πλὴν Ὑδάρνεος τοῦ στρατηγοῦ (οὗτος γὰρ οὐκ ἔφη λείψεσθαι βασιλέος), μετὰ δὲ τῶν ἄλλων Περσέων τοὺς θωρηκοφόρους καὶ τὴν ἵππον τὴν χιλίην, καὶ Μήδους τε καὶ Σάκας καὶ Βακτρίους τε καὶ Ἰνδούς, καὶ τὸν πεζὸν καὶ τὴν ἄλλην ἵππον. ταῦτα μὲν ἔθνεα ὅλα εἵλετο, ἐκ δὲ τῶν ἄλλων συμμάχων ἐξελέγετο κατ' ὀλίγους, τοῖσι εἰδεά τε ὑπῆρχε διαλέγων καὶ εἰ τεοῖσί τι χρηστὸν συνῄδεε πεποιημένον· ἐν δὲ πλεῖστον ἔθνος Πέρσας αἱρέετο, ἄνδρας στρεπτοφόρους τε καὶ ψελιοφόρους, ἐπὶ δὲ Μήδους· οὗτοι δὲ τὸ πλῆθος μὲν οὐκ ἐλάσσονες ἦσαν τῶν Περσέων, ῥώμῃ δὲ ἥσσονες. ὥστε σύμπαντας τριήκοντα μυριάδας γενέσθαι σὺν ἱππεῦσι.

114. Ἐν δὲ τούτῳ τῷ χρόνῳ, ἐν τῷ Μαρδόνιός τε τὴν στρατιὴν διέκρινε καὶ Ξέρξης ἦν περὶ Θεσσαλίην, χρηστήριον ἐληλύθεε ἐκ Δελφῶν Λακεδαιμονίοισι, Ξέρξην αἰτέειν δίκας τοῦ Λεωνίδεω φόνου καὶ τὸ διδόμενον ἐξ ἐκείνου δέκεσθαι. πέμπουσι δὴ κήρυκα τὴν ταχίστην Σπαρτιῆται, ὃς ἐπειδὴ κατέλαβε ἐοῦσαν ἔτι πᾶσαν τὴν στρατιὴν ἐν Θεσσαλίῃ, ἐλθὼν ἐς ὄψιν τὴν Ξέρξεω ἔλεγε τάδε. "Ὦ βασιλεῦ Μήδων, Λακεδαιμόνιοί τέ σε καὶ Ἡρακλεῖδαι οἱ ἀπὸ Σπάρτης αἰτέουσι φόνου δίκας, ὅτι σφέων τὸν βασιλέα ἀπέκτεινας ῥυόμενον τὴν Ἑλλάδα." ὁ δὲ γελάσας τε καὶ κατασχὼν πολλὸν χρόνον, ὥς οἱ ἐτύγχανε παρε-

winter in Thessaly, and then attack the Peloponnese
in the spring. When they were arrived in Thessaly,
Mardonius there chose out first all the Persians
called Immortals, save only Hydarnes their general,
who said that he would not quit the king's person;
and next, the Persian cuirassiers, and the thousand
horse,[1] and the Medes and Sacae and Bactrians and
Indians, alike their footmen and the rest of the
horsemen. He chose these nations entire; of the
rest of his allies he picked out a few from each
people, the goodliest men and those that he knew
to have done some good service; but the Persians
that he chose (men that wore torques and bracelets)[2]
were more in number than those of any other nation,
and next to them the Medes; these indeed were as
many as the Persians, but not so stout fighters.
Thereby the whole number, with the horsemen,
grew to three hundred thousand men.

114. Now while Mardonius was making choice of
his army and Xerxes was in Thessaly, there came an
oracle from Delphi to the Lacedaemonians, that they
should demand justice of Xerxes for the slaying of
Leonidas, and take what answer he should give
them. The Spartans then sent a herald with all
speed; who finding the army yet undivided in
Thessaly, came into Xerxes' presence and thus
spoke: "The Lacedaemonians and the Heraclidae
of Sparta demand of you, king of the Medes! that
you pay the penalty for the death of their king,
whom you slew while he defended Hellas." At
that Xerxes laughed; and after a long while he

---

[1] Two regiments of a thousand horse are mentioned in
vii. 40 and 55   [2] *cp.* vi. 83.

στεὼς Μαρδόνιος, δεικνὺς ἐς τοῦτον εἶπε "Τοιγὰρ
σφι Μαρδόνιος ὅδε δίκας δώσει τοιαύτας οἵας
ἐκείνοισι πρέπει."

115. Ὁ μὲν δὴ δεξάμενος τὸ ῥηθὲν ἀπαλλάσσετο, Ξέρξης δὲ Μαρδόνιον ἐν Θεσσαλίῃ καταλιπὼν αὐτὸς ἐπορεύετο κατὰ τάχος ἐς τὸν
Ἑλλήσποντον, καὶ ἀπικνέεται ἐς τὸν πόρον τῆς
διαβάσιος ἐν πέντε καὶ τεσσεράκοντα ἡμέρῃσι,
ἀπάγων τῆς στρατιῆς οὐδὲν μέρος ὡς εἰπεῖν.
ὅκου δὲ πορευόμενοι γινοίατο καὶ κατ᾽ οὕστινας
ἀνθρώπους, τὸν τούτων καρπὸν ἁρπάζοντες ἐσι-
τέοντο· εἰ δὲ καρπὸν μηδένα εὕροιεν, οἳ δὲ τὴν
ποίην τὴν ἐκ τῆς γῆς ἀναφυομένην καὶ τῶν
δενδρέων τὸν φλοιὸν περιλέποντες καὶ τὰ φύλλα
καταδρέποντες κατήσθιον, ὁμοίως τῶν τε ἡμέρων
καὶ τῶν ἀγρίων, καὶ ἔλειπον οὐδέν· ταῦτα δ᾽
ἐποίεον ὑπὸ λιμοῦ. ἐπιλαβὼν δὲ λοιμός τε τὸν
στρατὸν καὶ δυσεντερίη κατ᾽ ὁδὸν ἔφθειρε. τοὺς
δὲ καὶ νοσέοντας αὐτῶν κατέλειπε, ἐπιτάσσων
τῇσι πόλισι, ἵνα ἑκάστοτε γίνοιτο ἐλαύνων, μελε-
δαίνειν τε καὶ τρέφειν, ἐν Θεσσαλίῃ τέ τινας καὶ
ἐν Σίρι τῆς Παιονίης καὶ ἐν Μακεδονίῃ. ἔνθα
καὶ τὸ ἱρὸν ἅρμα καταλιπὼν τοῦ Διός, ὅτε ἐπὶ
τὴν Ἑλλάδα ἤλαυνε, ἀπιὼν οὐκ ἀπέλαβε, ἀλλὰ
δόντες οἱ Παίονες τοῖσι Θρήιξι ἀπαιτέοντος
Ξέρξεω ἔφασαν νεμομένας ἁρπασθῆναι ὑπὸ τῶν
ἄνω Θρηίκων τῶν περὶ τὰς πηγὰς τοῦ Στρυμόνος
οἰκημένων.

116. Ἔνθα καὶ ὁ τῶν Βισαλτέων βασιλεὺς γῆς
τε τῆς Κρηστωνικῆς Θρῆιξ ἔργον ὑπερφυὲς ἐργά-
σατο· ὃς οὔτε αὐτὸς ἔφη τῷ Ξέρξῃ ἑκὼν εἶναι
δουλεύσειν, ἀλλ᾽ οἴχετο ἄνω ἐς τὸ ὄρος τὴν

pointed to Mardonius, who chanced to be standing by him, and said, "Then here is Mardonius, who shall pay those you speak of such penalty as befits them."

115. So the herald took that utterance and departed; but Xerxes left Mardonius in Thessaly, and himself journeying with all speed to the Hellespont came in forty-five days to the passage for crossing, bringing back with him as good as none (if one may so say) of his host. Whithersoever and to whatsoever people they came, they seized and devoured its produce; and if they found none, they would take for their eating the grass of the field, and strip the bark and pluck the leaves of the trees, garden and wild alike, leaving nothing; so starved they were for hunger. Moreover a pestilence and a dysentery broke out among them on their way, whereby they died. Some that were sick Xerxes left behind, charging the cities whither he came in his march to care for them and nourish them, some in Thessaly and some in Siris of Paeonia and in Macedonia; in Siris he had left the sacred chariot of Zeus when he was marching to Hellas, but in his return he received it not again; for the Paeonians had given it to the Thracians, and when Xerxes demanded it back they said that the horses had been carried off from pasture by the Thracians of the hills who dwelt about the headwaters of the Strymon.

116. It was then that a monstrous deed was done by the Thracian king of the Bisaltae and the Crestonian country. He had refused to be of his own free will Xerxes' slave, and fled away to the

Ῥοδόπην, τοῖσί τε παισὶ ἀπηγόρευε μὴ στρατεύεσθαι ἐπὶ τὴν Ἑλλάδα. οἱ δὲ ἀλογήσαντες,
ἢ ἄλλως σφι θυμὸς ἐγένετο θεήσασθαι τὸν πόλεμον, ἐστρατεύοντο ἅμα τῷ Πέρσῃ. ἐπεὶ δὲ
ἀνεχώρησαν ἀσινέες πάντες ἐξ ἐόντες, ἐξώρυξε
αὐτῶν ὁ πατὴρ τοὺς ὀφθαλμοὺς διὰ τὴν αἰτίην
ταύτην.

117. Καὶ οὗτοι μὲν τοῦτον τὸν μισθὸν ἔλαβον,
οἱ δὲ Πέρσαι ὡς ἐκ τῆς Θρηίκης πορευόμενοι
ἀπίκοντο ἐπὶ τὸν πόρον, ἐπειγόμενοι τὸν Ἑλλήσποντον τῇσι νηυσὶ διέβησαν ἐς Ἄβυδον· τὰς
γὰρ σχεδίας οὐκ εὗρον ἔτι ἐντεταμένας ἀλλ' ὑπὸ
χειμῶνος διαλελυμένας. ἐνθαῦτα δὲ κατεχόμενοι
σιτία τε πλέω ἢ κατ' ὁδὸν ἐλάγχανον, καὶ οὐδένα
τε κόσμον ἐμπιπλάμενοι καὶ ὕδατα μεταβάλλοντες
ἀπέθνησκον τοῦ στρατοῦ τοῦ περιεόντος πολλοί.
οἱ δὲ λοιποὶ ἅμα Ξέρξῃ ἀπικνέονται ἐς Σάρδις.

118. Ἔστι δὲ καὶ ἄλλος ὅδε λόγος λεγόμενος,
ὡς ἐπειδὴ Ξέρξης ἀπελαύνων ἐξ Ἀθηνέων ἀπίκετο
ἐπ' Ἠιόνα τὴν ἐπὶ Στρυμόνι, ἐνθεῦτεν οὐκέτι
ὁδοιπορίῃσι διεχρᾶτο, ἀλλὰ τὴν μὲν στρατιὴν
Ὑδάρνεϊ ἐπιτράπει ἀπάγειν ἐς τὸν Ἑλλήσποντον,
αὐτὸς δ' ἐπὶ νεὸς Φοινίσσης ἐπιβὰς ἐκομίζετο ἐς
τὴν Ἀσίην. πλέοντα δέ μιν ἄνεμον Στρυμονίην
ὑπολαβεῖν μέγαν καὶ κυματίην. καὶ δὴ μᾶλλον
γάρ τι χειμαίνεσθαι γεμούσης τῆς νεός, ὥστε ἐπὶ
τοῦ καταστρώματος ἐπεόντων συχνῶν Περσέων
τῶν σὺν Ξέρξῃ κομιζομένων, ἐνθαῦτα ἐς δεῖμα
πεσόντα τὸν βασιλέα εἰρέσθαι βώσαντα τὸν
κυβερνήτην εἴ τις ἐστί σφι σωτηρίη, καὶ τὸν
εἶπαι "Δέσποτα, οὐκ ἔστι οὐδεμία, εἰ μὴ τούτων
ἀπαλλαγή τις γένηται τῶν πολλῶν ἐπιβατέων."

mountains called Rhodope; and he forbade his
sons to go with the army to Hellas; but they took
no account of that, for they had ever a desire to see
the war, and they followed the Persians' march; for
which cause, when all the six of them returned back
scatheless, their father tore out their eyes.

117. This was their reward. But the Persians,
journeying through Thrace to the passage, made
haste to cross to Abydos in their ships; for they
found the bridges no longer made fast but broken
by a storm. There their march was stayed, and more
food was given them than on their way; and by reason
of their immoderate gorging and the change of the
water which they drank, many of the army that yet
remained died. The rest came with Xerxes to
Sardis.

118. But there is another tale, which is this:—
When Xerxes came in his march from Athens to
Eïon on the Strymon, he travelled no farther than
that by land, but committed his army to Hydarnes
to be led to the Hellespont, and himself embarked
and set sail for Asia in a Phoenician ship. In which
voyage he was caught by a strong wind called
Strymonian, that lifted up the waves. This storm
bearing the harder upon him by reason of the heavy
lading of the ship (for the Persians of his company
that were on the deck were so many), the king was
affrighted and cried to the ship's pilot asking him if
there were any way of deliverance; whereat the man
said, "Sire, there is none, except there be a riddance
of these many that are on board." Hearing that, it

καὶ Ξέρξην λέγεται ἀκούσαντα ταῦτα εἰπεῖν
‘ "Ἄνδρες Πέρσαι, νῦν τις διαδεξάτω ὑμέων βασιλέος κηδόμενος· ἐν ὑμῖν γὰρ οἶκε εἶναι ἐμοὶ ἡ
σωτηρίη." τὸν μὲν ταῦτα λέγειν, τοὺς δὲ προσκυ-
νέοντας ἐκπηδᾶν ἐς τὴν θάλασσαν, καὶ τὴν νέα
ἐπικουφισθεῖσαν οὕτω δὴ ἀποσωθῆναι ἐς τὴν
Ἀσίην. ὡς δὲ ἐκβῆναι τάχιστα ἐς γῆν τὸν
Ξέρξην, ποιῆσαι τοιόνδε· ὅτι μὲν ἔσωσε βασιλέος
τὴν ψυχήν, δωρήσασθαι χρυσέῃ στεφάνῃ τὸν
κυβερνήτην, ὅτι δὲ Περσέων πολλοὺς ἀπώλεσε,
ἀποταμεῖν τὴν κεφαλὴν αὐτοῦ.

119. Οὗτος δὲ ἄλλος λέγεται λόγος περὶ τοῦ
Ξέρξεω νόστου, οὐδαμῶς ἔμοιγε πιστὸς οὔτε
ἄλλως οὔτε τὸ Περσέων τοῦτο πάθος· εἰ γὰρ
δὴ ταῦτα οὕτω εἰρέθη ἐκ τοῦ κυβερνήτεω πρὸς
Ξέρξην, ἐν μυρίῃσι γνώμῃσι μίαν οὐκ ἔχω
ἀντίξοον μὴ οὐκ ἂν ποιῆσαι βασιλέα τοιόνδε,
τοὺς μὲν ἐπὶ τοῦ καταστρώματος καταβιβάσαι
ἐς κοίλην νέα ἐόντας Πέρσας καὶ Περσέων τοὺς
πρώτους, τῶν δ᾽ ἐρετέων ἐόντων Φοινίκων ὅκως
οὐκ ἂν ἴσον πλῆθος τοῖσι Πέρσῃσι ἐξέβαλε ἐς
τὴν θάλασσαν. ἀλλ᾽ ὁ μέν, ὡς καὶ πρότερόν μοι
εἴρηται, ὁδῷ χρεώμενος ἅμα τῷ ἄλλῳ στρατῷ
ἀπενόστησε ἐς τὴν Ἀσίην.

120. Μέγα δὲ καὶ τόδε μαρτύριον· φαίνεται
γὰρ Ξέρξης ἐν τῇ ὀπίσω κομιδῇ ἀπικόμενος ἐς
Ἄβδηρα καὶ ξεινίην τέ σφι συνθέμενος καὶ
δωρησάμενος αὐτοὺς ἀκινάκῃ τε χρυσέῳ καὶ τιήρῃ
χρυσοπάστῳ. καὶ ὡς αὐτοὶ λέγουσι Ἀβδηρῖται,
λέγοντες ἔμοιγε οὐδαμῶς πιστά, πρῶτον ἐλύσατο
τὴν ζώνην φεύγων ἐξ Ἀθηνέων ὀπίσω, ὡς ἐν
ἀδείῃ ἐών. τὰ δὲ Ἄβδηρα ἵδρυται πρὸς τοῦ

is said, Xerxes said to the Persians, "Now it is for you to prove yourselves careful for your king ; for it seems that my deliverance rests with you " ; whereat they did obeisance and leapt into the sea ; and the ship, being thus lightened, came by these means safe to Asia. No sooner had Xerxes disembarked on land, than he made the pilot a gift of a golden crown for saving the king's life, but cut off his head for being the death of many Persians.

119. This is the other tale of Xerxes' return ; but I for my part believe neither the story of the Persians' fate, nor any other part of it. For if indeed the pilot had spoken to Xerxes as aforesaid, I think that there is not one in ten thousand but would say that the king would have bidden the men on deck (who were Persians and of the best blood of Persia) descend into the ship's hold, and would have taken of the Phoenician rowers a number equal to the number of the Persians and cast them into the sea. Nay, the truth is that Xerxes did as I have already said, and returned to Asia with his army by road.

120. And herein too lies a clear proof of it : it is known that when Xerxes came to Abdera in his return he entered into bonds of friendship with its people, and gave them a golden sword and a gilt tiara ; and as the people of Abdera say (but for my part I wholly disbelieve them), it was here that Xerxes in his flight back from Athens first loosed his girdle,[1] as being here in safety. Now Abdera

---

[1] cp. perhaps v. 106, where Histiaeus swears to Darius that he will not take off his tunic till he reaches Ionia ; or the reference may be to a man's being εὔζωνος (with his 'loins girded up ') for swift travel.

Ἑλλησπόντου μᾶλλον ἢ τοῦ Στρυμόνος καὶ τῆς
Ἠιόνος, ὅθεν δή μιν φασὶ ἐπιβῆναι ἐπὶ τὴν νέα.

121. Οἱ δὲ Ἕλληνες ἐπείτε οὐκ οἷοί τε ἐγίνοντο
ἐξελεῖν τὴν Ἄνδρον, τραπόμενοι ἐς Κάρυστον καὶ
δηιώσαντες αὐτῶν τὴν χώρην ἀπαλλάσσοντο ἐς
Σαλαμῖνα. πρῶτα μέν νυν τοῖσι θεοῖσι ἐξεῖλον
ἀκροθίνια ἄλλα τε καὶ τριήρεας τρεῖς Φοινίσσας,
τὴν μὲν ἐς Ἰσθμὸν ἀναθεῖναι, ἥ περ ἔτι καὶ ἐς
ἐμὲ ἦν, τὴν δὲ ἐπὶ Σούνιον, τὴν δὲ τῷ Αἴαντι
αὐτοῦ ἐς Σαλαμῖνα. μετὰ δὲ τοῦτο διεδάσαντο
τὴν ληίην καὶ τὰ ἀκροθίνια ἀπέπεμψαν ἐς
Δελφούς, ἐκ τῶν ἐγένετο ἀνδριὰς ἔχων ἐν τῇ
χειρὶ ἀκρωτήριον νεός, ἐὼν μέγαθος δυώδεκα
πηχέων· ἕστηκε δὲ οὗτος τῇ περ ὁ Μακεδὼν
Ἀλέξανδρος ὁ χρύσεος.

122. Πέμψαντες δὲ ἀκροθίνια οἱ Ἕλληνες ἐς
Δελφοὺς ἐπειρώτων τὸν θεὸν κοινῇ εἰ λελάβηκε
πλήρεα καὶ ἀρεστὰ τὰ ἀκροθίνια. ὁ δὲ παρ'
Ἑλλήνων μὲν τῶν ἄλλων ἔφησε ἔχειν, παρὰ
Αἰγινητέων δὲ οὔ, ἀλλὰ ἀπαίτεε αὐτοὺς τὰ
ἀριστήια τῆς ἐν Σαλαμῖνι ναυμαχίης. Αἰγινῆται
δὲ πυθόμενοι ἀνέθεσαν ἀστέρας χρυσέους, οἳ ἐπὶ
ἱστοῦ χαλκέου ἑστᾶσι τρεῖς ἐπὶ τῆς γωνίης,
ἀγχοτάτω τοῦ Κροίσου κρητῆρος.

123. Μετὰ δὲ τὴν διαίρεσιν τῆς ληίης ἔπλεον
οἱ Ἕλληνες ἐς τὸν Ἰσθμὸν ἀριστήια δώσοντες
τῷ ἀξιωτάτῳ γενομένῳ Ἑλλήνων ἀνὰ τὸν πόλεμον
τοῦτον. ὡς δὲ ἀπικόμενοι οἱ στρατηγοὶ διένεμον
τὰς ψήφους ἐπὶ τοῦ Ποσειδέωνος τῷ βωμῷ, τὸν
πρῶτον καὶ τὸν δεύτερον κρίνοντες ἐκ πάντων,
ἐνθαῦτα πᾶς τις αὐτῶν ἑωυτῷ ἐτίθετο τὴν ψῆφον,
αὐτὸς ἕκαστος δοκέων ἄριστος γενέσθαι, δεύτερα

lies nearer to the Hellespont than the Strymon and Eïon, where they say that he took ship.

121. As for the Greeks, not being able to take Andros they betook themselves to Carystus, and having laid it waste they returned to Salamis. First of all they set apart for the gods, among other first-fruits, three Phoenician triremes, one to be dedicated at the Isthmus, where it was till my lifetime, the second at Sunium, and the third for Aias at Salamis where they were. After that, they divided the spoil and sent the firstfruits of it to Delphi; whereof was made a man's image twelve cubits high, holding in his hand the figure-head of a ship; this stood in the same place as the golden statue of Alexander the Macedonian.

122. Having sent the firstfruits to Delphi the Greeks inquired in common of the god, if the first-fruits that he had received were of full measure and if he was content therewith; whereat he said that this was so as touching what he received from all other Greeks, but not from the Aeginetans; of these he demanded the victor's prize for the sea-fight of Salamis. When the Aeginetans learnt that, they dedicated three golden stars that are set on a bronze mast, in the angle, nearest to Croesus' bowl.

123. After the division of the spoil, the Greeks sailed to the Isthmus, there to award the prize of excellence to him who had shown himself most worthy of it in that war. But when the admirals came and gave their divers votes at the altar of Poseidon, to judge who was first and who second among them, each of them there voted for himself, supposing himself to have done the best service, but the greater part of them united in giving the second

δὲ οἱ πολλοὶ συνεξέπιπτον Θεμιστοκλέα κρίνοντες.
οἱ μὲν δὴ ἐμουνοῦντο, Θεμιστοκλῆς δὲ δευτερείοισι
ὑπερεβάλλετο πολλόν.

124. Οὐ βουλομένων δὲ ταῦτα κρίνειν τῶν
Ἑλλήνων φθόνῳ, ἀλλ᾽ ἀποπλεόντων ἑκάστων
ἐς τὴν ἑωυτῶν ἀκρίτων, ὅμως Θεμιστοκλῆς
ἐβώσθη τε καὶ ἐδοξώθη εἶναι ἀνὴρ πολλὸν
Ἑλλήνων σοφώτατος ἀνὰ πᾶσαν τὴν Ἑλλάδα.
ὅτι δὲ νικῶν οὐκ ἐτιμήθη πρὸς τῶν ἐν Σαλαμῖνι
ναυμαχησάντων, αὐτίκα μετὰ ταῦτα ἐς Λακεδαίμονα ἀπίκετο θέλων τιμηθῆναι· καί μιν Λακεδαιμόνιοι καλῶς μὲν ὑπεδέξαντο, μεγάλως δὲ
ἐτίμησαν. ἀριστήια μέν νυν ἔδοσαν¹ . . Εὐρυβιάδῃ ἐλαίης στέφανον, σοφίης δὲ καὶ δεξιό-
τητος Θεμιστοκλέι καὶ τούτῳ στέφανον ἐλαίης·
ἐδωρήσαντό τέ μιν ὄχῳ τῷ ἐν Σπάρτῃ καλλι-
στεύσαντι. αἰνέσαντες δὲ πολλά, προέπεμψαν
ἀπιόντα τριηκόσιοι Σπαρτιητέων λογάδες, οὗτοι
οἵ περ ἱππέες καλέονται, μέχρι οὔρων τῶν Τεγεη-
τικῶν. μοῦνον δὴ τοῦτον πάντων ἀνθρώπων τῶν
ἡμεῖς ἴδμεν Σπαρτιῆται προέπεμψαν.

125. Ὡς δὲ ἐκ τῆς Λακεδαίμονος ἀπίκετο ἐς τὰς
Ἀθήνας, ἐνθαῦτα Τιμόδημος Ἀφιδναῖος τῶν
ἐχθρῶν μὲν τῶν Θεμιστοκλέος ἐών, ἄλλως δὲ οὐ
τῶν ἐπιφανέων ἀνδρῶν, φθόνῳ καταμαργέων ἐνεί-
κεε τὸν Θεμιστοκλέα, τὴν ἐς Λακεδαίμονα ἄπιξιν
προφέρων, ὡς διὰ τὰς Ἀθήνας ἔχοι τὰ γέρεα τὰ
παρὰ Λακεδαιμονίων, ἀλλ᾽ οὐ δι᾽ ἑωυτόν. ὁ δέ,
ἐπείτε οὐκ ἐπαύετο λέγων ταῦτα ὁ Τιμόδημος,
εἶπε "Οὕτω ἔχει τοι· οὔτ᾽ ἂν ἐγὼ ἐὼν Βελβινίτης

¹ Stein supposes that something is omitted before Εὐρυβιάδῃ, perhaps ἀνδραγαθίης.

place to Themistocles.   So they each gained but one
vote, but Themistocles far outstripped them in votes
for the second place.

124. The Greeks were too jealous to adjudge the
prize, and sailed away each to his own place, leaving
the matter doubtful; nevertheless, Themistocles was
cried up, and all Hellas glorified him for the wisest
man by far of the Greeks.   But because he had not
received from them that fought at Salamis the honour
due to his pre-eminence, immediately afterwards he
betook himself to Lacedaemon, that he might receive
honour there; and the Lacedaemonians made him
welcome and paid him high honour.   They bestowed
on Eurybiades a crown of olive as the reward of
excellence, and another such crown on Themistocles
for his wisdom and cleverness; and they gave him
the finest chariot in Sparta; and with many words
of praise, they sent him on his homeward way with
the three hundred picked men of Sparta who are
called Knights to escort him as far as the borders
of Tegea.   Themistocles was the only man of whom
I have heard to whom the Spartans gave this escort.

125. But when Themistocles returned to Athens
from Lacedaemon, Timodemus of Aphidnae, who
was one of Themistocles' enemies but a man in nowise notable, was crazed with envy and spoke bitterly
to Themistocles of his visit to Lacedaemon, saying
that the honours he had from the Lacedaemonians
were paid him for Athens' sake and not for his own.
This he would continually be saying; till Themistocles replied, "This is the truth of the matter—
had I been of Belbina[1] I had not been thus honoured

[1] An islet S. of Sunium; a typical instance of an unimportant place.

ἐτιμήθην οὕτω πρὸς Σπαρτιητέων, οὔτ' ἂν σύ,
ὤνθρωπε, ἐὼν Ἀθηναῖος." ταῦτα μέν νυν ἐς τοσοῦτο
ἐγένετο.

126. Ἀρτάβαζος δὲ ὁ Φαρνάκεος ἀνὴρ ἐν Πέρσῃσι λόγιμος καὶ πρόσθε ἐών, ἐκ δὲ τῶν Πλαται-
κῶν καὶ μᾶλλον ἔτι γενόμενος, ἔχων ἐξ μυριάδας
στρατοῦ τοῦ Μαρδόνιος ἐξελέξατο, προέπεμπε
βασιλέα μέχρι τοῦ πόρου. ὡς δὲ ὃ μὲν ἦν ἐν τῇ
Ἀσίῃ, ὃ δὲ ὀπίσω πορευόμενος κατὰ τὴν Παλλήνην ἐγίνετο, ἅτε Μαρδονίου τε χειμερίζοντος περὶ
Θεσσαλίην τε καὶ Μακεδονίην καὶ οὐδέν κω κατε-
πείγοντος ἥκειν ἐς τὸ ἄλλο στρατόπεδον, οὐκ ἐδι-
καίου ἐντυχὼν ἀπεστεῶσι Ποτιδαιήτῃσι μὴ οὐκ
ἐξανδραποδίσασθαι σφέας. οἱ γὰρ Ποτιδαιῆται,
ὡς βασιλεὺς παρεξεληλάκεε καὶ ὁ ναυτικὸς τοῖσι
Πέρσῃσι οἰχώκεε φεύγων ἐκ Σαλαμῖνος, ἐκ τοῦ
φανεροῦ ἀπέστασαν ἀπὸ τῶν βαρβάρων· ὡς δὲ
καὶ οἱ ἄλλοι οἱ τὴν Παλλήνην ἔχοντες.

127. Ἐνθαῦτα δὴ Ἀρτάβαζος ἐπολιόρκεε τὴν
Ποτίδαιαν. ὑποπτεύσας δὲ καὶ τοὺς Ὀλυνθίους
ἀπίστασθαι ἀπὸ βασιλέος, καὶ ταύτην ἐπολιόρκεε·
εἶχον δὲ αὐτὴν Βοττιαῖοι ἐκ τοῦ Θερμαίου κόλπου
ἐξαναστάντες ὑπὸ Μακεδόνων. ἐπεὶ δὲ σφέας
εἷλε πολιορκέων, κατέσφαξε ἐξαγαγὼν ἐς λίμνην,
τὴν δὲ πόλιν παραδιδοῖ Κριτοβούλῳ Τορωναίῳ
ἐπιτροπεύειν καὶ τῷ Χαλκιδικῷ γένεϊ, καὶ οὕτω
Ὄλυνθον Χαλκιδέες ἔσχον.

128. Ἐξελὼν δὲ ταύτην ὁ Ἀρτάβαζος τῇ Ποτι-
δαίῃ ἐντεταμένως προσεῖχε· προσέχοντι δέ οἱ
προθύμως συντίθεται προδοσίην Τιμόξεινος ὁ τῶν
Σκιωναίων στρατηγός, ὅντινα μὲν τρόπον ἀρχήν,
ἔγωγε οὐκ ἔχω εἰπεῖν (οὐ γὰρ ὧν λέγεται), τέλος

by the Spartans; nor had you, sirrah, for all you are of Athens." Such was the end of that business.

126. Artabazus son of Pharnaces, who was already a notable man among the Persians and grew to be yet more so by the Plataean business, escorted the king as far as the passage with sixty thousand men of the army that Mardonius had chosen. Xerxes being now in Asia, when Artabazus came near Pallene in his return (for Mardonius was wintering in Thessaly and Macedonia and making no haste to come to the rest of his army), he thought it right that he should enslave the people of Potidaea, whom he found in revolt. For the king having marched away past the town and the Persian fleet taken flight from Salamis, Potidaea had openly revolted from the foreigners; and so too had the rest of the people of Pallene.

127. Thereupon Artabazus laid siege to Potidaea; and suspecting that Olynthus too was plotting revolt from the king, he laid siege to it also, the town being held by Bottiaeans who had been driven from the Thermaic gulf by the Macedonians. Having besieged and taken Olynthus, he brought these men to a lake and there cut their throats, and delivered their city over to the charge of Critobulus of Torone and the Chalcidian people; and thus the Chalcidians gained possession of Olynthus.

128. Having taken Olynthus, Artabazus was instant in dealing with Potidaea; and his zeal was aided by Timoxenus the general of the Scionaeans, who agreed to betray the place to him; I know not how the agreement was first made, nothing being told thereof; but the end was as I

μέντοι τοιάδε ἐγίνετο· ὅκως βυβλίον γράψειε ἢ
Τιμόξεινος ἐθέλων παρὰ ᾿Αρτάβαζον πέμψαι ἢ
᾿Αρτάβαζος παρὰ Τιμόξεινον, τοξεύματος παρὰ
τὰς γλυφίδας¹ περιειλίξαντες καὶ πτερώσαντες τὸ
βυβλίον ἐτόξευον ἐς συγκείμενον χωρίον. ἐπάιστος δὲ ἐγένετο ὁ Τιμόξεινος προδιδοὺς τὴν Ποτί-
δαιαν· τοξεύων γὰρ ὁ ᾿Αρτάβαζος ἐς τὸ συγκείμενον, ἁμαρτὼν τοῦ χωρίου τούτου βάλλει ἀνδρὸς Ποτιδαιήτεω τὸν ὦμον, τὸν δὲ βληθέντα
περιέδραμε ὅμιλος, οἷα φιλέει γίνεσθαι ἐν πολέμῳ,
οἳ αὐτίκα τὸ τόξευμα λαβόντες ὡς ἔμαθον τὸ
βυβλίον, ἔφερον ἐπὶ τοὺς στρατηγούς· παρῆν δὲ
καὶ τῶν ἄλλων Παλληναίων συμμαχίη. τοῖσι δὲ
στρατηγοῖσι ἐπιλεξαμένοισι τὸ βυβλίον καὶ μα-
θοῦσι τὸν αἴτιον τῆς προδοσίης ἔδοξε μὴ κατα-
πλῆξαι Τιμόξεινον προδοσίῃ τῆς Σκιωναίων
πόλιος εἵνεκα, μὴ νομιζοίατο εἶναι Σκιωναῖοι ἐς
τὸν μετέπειτα χρόνον αἰεὶ προδόται.

129. Ὁ μὲν δὴ τοιούτῳ τρόπῳ ἐπάιστος ἐγε-
γόνεε· ᾿Αρταβάζῳ δὲ ἐπειδὴ πολιορκέοντι ἐγεγόνεσαν τρεῖς μῆνες, γίνεται ἄμπωτις τῆς θαλάσσης
μεγάλη καὶ χρόνον ἐπὶ πολλόν. ἰδόντες δὲ οἱ
βάρβαροι τέναγος γενόμενον παρήισαν ἐς τὴν
Παλλήνην. ὡς δὲ τὰς δύο μὲν μοίρας διοδοιπο-
ρήκεσαν, ἔτι δὲ τρεῖς ὑπόλοιποι ἦσαν, τὰς διελ-
θόντας χρῆν εἶναι ἔσω ἐν τῇ Παλλήνῃ, ἐπῆλθε
πλημμυρὶς τῆς θαλάσσης μεγάλη, ὅση οὐδαμά
κω, ὡς οἱ ἐπιχώριοι λέγουσι, πολλάκις γινομένη.
οἱ μὲν δὴ νέειν αὐτῶν οὐκ ἐπιστάμενοι διεφθεί-

---

¹ Probably points on each side of the notch (where the
arrow lies on the string) to give the fingers better grip.

will now show.   Whenever Timoxenus wrote a
letter for sending to Artabazus, or Artabazus to
Timoxenus, they would wrap it round the shaft of
an arrow at the notches [1] and put feathers to the
letter, and shoot it to a place whereon they had
agreed.   But Timoxenus' plot to betray Potidaea
was discovered; for Artabazus in shooting an arrow
to the place agreed upon, missed it and hit the
shoulder of a man of Potidaea; and a throng
gathering quickly round the man when he was
struck (which is a thing that ever happens in war),
they straightway took the arrow and found the letter
and carried it to their generals, the rest of their
allies of Pallene being also there present.   The
generals read the letter and perceived who was
the traitor, but they resolved for Scione's sake that
they would not smite Timoxenus to the earth with
a charge of treason, lest so the people of Scione
should ever after be called traitors.

129. Thus was Timoxenus' treachery brought to
light.   But when Artabazus had besieged Potidaea
for three months, there was a great ebb-tide in the
sea, lasting for a long while, and when the foreigners
saw that the sea was turned to a marsh they made
to pass over it into Pallene.   But when they had
made their way over two fifths of it and three yet
remained to cross ere they could be in Pallene,
there came a great flood-tide, higher, as the people
of the place say, than any one of the many that had
been before; and some of them that knew not how

"The parchment was rolled round the butt end of the
arrow and then feathers put over it to hide it" (How and
Wells).

ροντο, τοὺς δὲ ἐπισταμένους οἱ Ποτιδαιῆται
ἐπιπλώσαντες πλοίοισι ἀπώλεσαν. αἴτιον δὲ
λέγουσι Ποτιδαιῆται τῆς τε ῥηχίης καὶ τῆς
πλημμυρίδος καὶ τοῦ Περσικοῦ πάθεος γενέσθαι
τόδε, ὅτι τοῦ Ποσειδέωνος ἐς τὸν νηὸν καὶ τὸ
ἄγαλμα τὸ ἐν τῷ προαστείῳ ἠσέβησαν οὗτοι τῶν
Περσέων οἵ περ καὶ διεφθάρησαν ὑπὸ τῆς θαλάσ-
σης· αἴτιον δὲ τοῦτο λέγοντες εὖ λέγειν ἔμοιγε
δοκέουσι. τοὺς δὲ περιγενομένους ἀπῆγε Ἀρτάβαζος ἐς Θεσσαλίην παρὰ Μαρδόνιον. οὗτοι
μὲν οἱ προπέμψαντες βασιλέα οὕτω ἔπρηξαν.

130. Ὁ δὲ ναυτικὸς ὁ Ξέρξεω περιγενόμενος
ὡς προσέμιξε τῇ Ἀσίῃ φεύγων ἐκ Σαλαμῖνος καὶ
βασιλέα τε καὶ τὴν στρατιὴν ἐκ Χερσονήσου
διεπόρθμευσε ἐς Ἄβυδον, ἐχειμέριζε ἐν Κύμῃ.
ἔαρος δὲ ἐπιλάμψαντος πρῶιος συνελέγετο ἐς
Σάμον· αἱ δὲ τῶν νεῶν καὶ ἐχειμέρισαν αὐτοῦ·
Περσέων δὲ καὶ Μήδων οἱ πλεῦνες ἐπεβάτευον.
στρατηγοὶ δέ σφι ἐπῆλθον Μαρδόντης τε ὁ Βα-
γαίου καὶ Ἀρταΰντης ὁ Ἀρταχαίεω· συνῆρχε δὲ
τούτοισι καὶ ἀδελφιδέος αὐτοῦ Ἀρταΰντεω προσ-
ελομένου Ἰθαμίτρης. ἅτε δὲ μεγάλως πλη-
γέντες, οὐ προῆισαν ἀνωτέρω τὸ πρὸς ἑσπέρης,
οὐδ᾽ ἐπηνάγκαζε οὐδείς, ἀλλ᾽ ἐν τῇ Σάμῳ κατήμενοι ἐφύλασσον τὴν Ἰωνίην μὴ ἀποστῇ, νέας
ἔχοντες σὺν τῇσι Ἰάσι τριηκοσίας. οὐ μὲν οὐδὲ
προσεδέκοντο τοὺς Ἕλληνας ἐλεύσεσθαι ἐς τὴν
Ἰωνίην ἀλλ᾽ ἀποχρήσειν σφι τὴν ἑωυτῶν φυλάσσειν, σταθμεύμενοι ὅτι σφέας οὐκ ἐπεδίωξαν
φεύγοντας ἐκ Σαλαμῖνος ἀλλ᾽ ἄσμενοι ἀπαλλάσσοντο. κατὰ μέν νυν τὴν θάλασσαν ἑσσωμένοι
ἦσαν τῷ θυμῷ, πεζῇ δὲ ἐδόκεον πολλῷ κρατήσειν

to swim were drowned, and those that knew were slain by the Potidaeans, who came among them in boats. The Potidaeans say that the cause of the high sea and flood and the Persian disaster lay herein, that those same Persians who now perished in the sea had profaned the temple and the image of Poseidon that was in the suburb of the city; and I think that in saying that this was the cause they say rightly. They that escaped alive were led away by Artabazus to Mardonius in Thessaly. Thus fared these men, who had been the king's escort.

130. All that was left of Xerxes' fleet, having in its flight from Salamis touched the coast of Asia and ferried the king and his army over from the Chersonese to Abydos, wintered at Cyme. Then early in the first dawn of spring they mustered at Samos, where some of the ships had wintered; the most of their fighting men were Persians and Medes. Mardontes son of Bagaeus and Artaÿntes son of Artachaees came to be their admirals, and Artaÿntes chose also his own nephew Ithamitres to have a share in the command. But by reason of the heavy blow dealt them they went no further out to sea westwards, nor was any man instant that they should so do, but they lay off Samos keeping watch against a revolt in Ionia, the whole number of their ships, Ionian and other, being three hundred; nor in truth did they expect that the Greeks would come to Ionia, but rather that they would be content to guard their own country; thus they inferred, because the Greeks had not pursued them when they fled from Salamis, but had been glad to be quit of them. In regard to the sea, the Persians were at heart beaten men, but they supposed that

τὸν Μαρδόνιον. ἐόντες δὲ ἐν Σάμῳ ἅμα μὲν ἐβουλεύοντο εἴ τι δυναίατο κακὸν τοὺς πολεμίους
ποιέειν, ἅμα δὲ καὶ ὠτακούστεον ὅκῃ πεσέεται τὰ
Μαρδονίου πρήγματα.

131. Τοὺς δὲ Ἕλληνας τό τε ἔαρ γινόμενον
ἤγειρε καὶ Μαρδόνιος ἐν Θεσσαλίῃ ἐών. ὁ μὲν δὴ
πεζὸς οὔκω συνελέγετο, ὁ δὲ ναυτικὸς ἀπίκετο ἐς
Αἴγιναν, νέες ἀριθμὸν δέκα καὶ ἑκατόν. στρατηγὸς δὲ καὶ ναύαρχος ἦν Λευτυχίδης ὁ Μενάρεος
τοῦ Ἡγησίλεω τοῦ Ἱπποκρατίδεω τοῦ Λευτυχίδεω τοῦ Ἀναξίλεω τοῦ Ἀρχιδήμου τοῦ Ἀναξαν-
δρίδεω τοῦ Θεοπόμπου τοῦ Νικάνδρου τοῦ Χαρί-
λεω τοῦ Εὐνόμου τοῦ Πολυδέκτεω τοῦ Πρυτάνιος
τοῦ Εὐρυφῶντος τοῦ Προκλέος τοῦ Ἀριστοδήμου
τοῦ Ἀριστομάχου τοῦ Κλεοδαίου τοῦ Ὕλλου τοῦ
Ἡρακλέος, ἐὼν τῆς ἑτέρης οἰκίης τῶν βασιλέων.
οὗτοι πάντες, πλὴν τῶν ἑπτὰ τῶν μετὰ Λευτυ-
χίδεα πρώτων καταλεχθέντων, οἱ ἄλλοι βασιλέες
ἐγένοντο Σπάρτης. Ἀθηναίων δὲ ἐστρατήγεε
Ξάνθιππος ὁ Ἀρίφρονος.

132. Ὡς δὲ παρεγένοντο ἐς τὴν Αἴγιναν πᾶσαι
αἱ νέες, ἀπίκοντο Ἰώνων ἄγγελοι ἐς τὸ στρατόπεδον τῶν Ἑλλήνων, οἳ καὶ ἐς Σπάρτην ὀλίγῳ
πρότερον τούτων ἀπικόμενοι ἐδέοντο Λακεδαιμονίων ἐλευθεροῦν τὴν Ἰωνίην· τῶν καὶ Ἡρόδοτος ὁ
Βασιληίδεω ἦν· οἳ στασιῶται σφίσι γενόμενοι
ἐπεβούλευον θάνατον Στράττι τῷ Χίου τυράννῳ,
ἐόντες ἀρχὴν ἑπτά· ἐπιβουλεύοντες δὲ ὡς φανεροὶ
ἐγένοντο, ἐξενείκαντος τὴν ἐπιχείρησιν ἑνὸς τῶν

---

[1] The first royal house was the line of Agis, from whom
Leonidas was descended (vii. 204). The second was the line
of Euryphon. In the present list "the first king among the

on land Mardonius would easily prevail. So they were at Samos, and there planned to do what harm they could to their enemies, and to listen the while for tidings of how it went with Mardonius.

131. But as for the Greeks, the coming of spring and Mardonius' being in Thessaly moved them to action. They had not yet begun the mustering of their army, but their fleet, an hundred and ten ships, came to Aegina; and their general and admiral was Leutychides son of Menares, tracing his lineage from son to father through Hegesilaus, Hippocratides, Leutychides, Anaxilaus, Archidemus, Anaxandrides, Theopompus, Nicandrus, Charilaus, Eunomus, Polydectes, Prytanis, Euryphon, Procles, Aristodemus, Aristomachus, Cleodaeus, to Hyllus who was the son of Heracles; he was of the second royal house.[1] All the aforesaid had been kings of Sparta, save the seven named first after Leutychides. The general of the Athenians was Xanthippus son of Ariphron.

132. When all the ships were arrived at Aegina, there came to the Greek quarters messengers from the Ionians, the same who a little while before that had gone to Sparta and entreated the Lacedaemonians to free Ionia; of whom one was Herodotus the son of Basileïdes.[2] These, who at first were seven, made a faction and conspired to slay Strattis, the despot of Chios; but when their conspiracy became known, one of the accomplices

ancestors of Leutychides is Theopompus, the seven more immediate ancestors of L. belonging to a younger branch, which gained the throne by the deposition of Demaratus " (How and Wells).

[2] Otherwise unknown.

μετεχόντων, οὕτω δὴ οἱ λοιποὶ ἐξ ἐόντες ὑπεξέ-
σχον ἐκ τῆς Χίου καὶ ἐς Σπάρτην τε ἀπίκοντο καὶ
δὴ καὶ τότε ἐς τὴν Αἴγιναν, τῶν Ἑλλήνων δεόμενοι
καταπλῶσαι ἐς τὴν Ἰωνίην· οἳ προήγαγον αὐτοὺς
μόγις μέχρι Δήλου. τὸ γὰρ προσωτέρω πᾶν δεινὸν ἦν τοῖσι Ἕλλησι οὔτε τῶν χώρων ἐοῦσι ἐμ-
πείροισι, στρατιῆς τε πάντα πλέα ἐδόκεε εἶναι,
τὴν δὲ Σάμον ἐπιστέατο δόξῃ καὶ Ἡρακλέας
στήλας ἴσον ἀπέχειν. συνέπιπτε δὲ τοιοῦτο ὥστε
τοὺς μὲν βαρβάρους τὸ πρὸς ἑσπέρης ἀνωτέρω
Σάμου μὴ τολμᾶν καταπλῶσαι καταρρωδηκότας,
τοὺς δὲ Ἕλληνας, χρηιζόντων Χίων, τὸ πρὸς τὴν
ἠῶ κατωτέρω Δήλου· οὕτω δέος τὸ μέσον ἐφύλασσε σφέων.

133. Οἱ μὲν δὴ Ἕλληνες ἔπλεον ἐς τὴν Δῆλον,
Μαρδόνιος δὲ περὶ τὴν Θεσσαλίην ἐχείμαζε. ἐνθεῦτεν δὲ ὁρμώμενος ἔπεμπε κατὰ τὰ χρηστήρια
ἄνδρα Εὐρωπέα γένος, τῷ οὔνομα ἦν Μῦς, ἐντειλάμενος πανταχῇ μιν χρησόμενον ἐλθεῖν, τῶν οἷά
τε ἦν σφι ἀποπειρήσασθαι. ὅ τι μὲν βουλόμενος
ἐκμαθεῖν πρὸς τῶν χρηστηρίων ταῦτα ἐνετέλλετο,
οὐκ ἔχω φράσαι· οὐ γὰρ ὦν λέγεται· δοκέω δ᾽
ἔγωγε περὶ τῶν παρεόντων πρηγμάτων καὶ οὐκ
ἄλλων πέρι πέμψαι.

134. Οὗτος ὁ Μῦς ἔς τε Λεβάδειαν φαίνεται
ἀπικόμενος καὶ μισθῷ πείσας τῶν ἐπιχωρίων
ἄνδρα καταβῆναι παρὰ Τροφώνιον, καὶ ἐς Ἄβας
τὰς Φωκέων ἀπικόμενος ἐπὶ τὸ χρηστήριον· καὶ
δὴ καὶ ἐς Θήβας πρῶτα ὡς ἀπίκετο, τοῦτο μὲν τῷ
Ἰσμηνίῳ Ἀπόλλωνι ἐχρήσατο· ἔστι δὲ κατά περ

---

[1] "As far off as the Straits of Gibraltar"—a figure of
distance.

having revealed their enterprise, the six that remained got them privily out of Chios, whence they went to Sparta and now to Aegina, entreating the Greeks to sail to Ionia. The Greeks brought them as far as Delos, and that not readily; for they feared all that lay beyond, having no knowledge of those parts, and thinking that armed men were everywhere; and they supposed that Samos was no nearer to them than the Pillars of Heracles.[1] So it fell out that the foreigners were too disheartened to dare to sail farther west than Samos, while at the same time the Greeks dared go at the Chians' request no farther east than Delos; thus fear kept the middle space between them.

133. The Greeks, then, sailed to Delos, and Mardonius wintered in Thessaly. Having here his headquarters he sent thence a man of Europus called Mys to visit the places of divination, charging him to inquire of all the oracles whereof he could make trial. What it was that he desired to learn from the oracles when he gave this charge, I cannot say, for none tells of it; but I suppose that he sent to inquire concerning his present business, and that alone.

134. This man Mys is known to have gone to Lebadea and to have bribed a man of the country to go down into the cave of Trophonius,[2] and to have gone to the place of divination at Abae in Phocis; to Thebes too he first went, where he inquired of Ismenian Apollo (sacrifice is there the

[2] See How and Wells *ad loc.* for a full description of the method of consulting this subterranean deity: also on Amphiaraus and "Ptoan" Apollo. All these shrines are in Boeotia, the home of early Greek superstitions.

ἐν Ὀλυμπίῃ ἱροῖσι αὐτόθι χρηστηριάζεσθαι· τοῦτο δὲ ξεῖνον τινὰ καὶ οὐ Θηβαῖον χρήμασι πείσας
κατεκοίμησε ἐς Ἀμφιάρεω. Θηβαίων δὲ οὐδενὶ
ἔξεστι μαντεύεσθαι αὐτόθι διὰ τόδε· ἐκέλευσε
σφέας ὁ Ἀμφιάρεως διὰ χρηστηρίων ποιεύμενος
ὁκότερα βούλονται ἑλέσθαι τούτων, ἑωυτῷ ἢ ἅτε
μάντι χρᾶσθαι ἢ ἅτε συμμάχῳ, τοῦ ἑτέρου ἀπεχο-
μένους· οἳ δὲ σύμμαχόν μιν εἵλοντο εἶναι. διὰ
τοῦτο μὲν οὐκ ἔξεστι Θηβαίων οὐδενὶ αὐτόθι
ἐγκατακοιμηθῆναι.

135. Τότε δὲ θῶμά μοι μέγιστον γενέσθαι
λέγεται ὑπὸ Θηβαίων· ἐλθεῖν ἄρα τὸν Εὐρωπέα
Μῦν, περιστρωφώμενον πάντα τὰ χρηστήρια, καὶ
ἐς τοῦ Πτῴου Ἀπόλλωνος τὸ τέμενος. τοῦτο δὲ
τὸ ἱρὸν καλέεται μὲν Πτῷον, ἔστι δὲ Θηβαίων,
κεῖται δὲ ὑπὲρ τῆς Κωπαΐδος λίμνης πρὸς ὄρεϊ
ἀγχοτάτω Ἀκραιφίης πόλιος. ἐς τοῦτο τὸ ἱρὸν
ἐπείτε παρελθεῖν τὸν καλεόμενον τοῦτον Μῦν,
ἕπεσθαι δέ οἱ τῶν ἀστῶν αἱρετοὺς ἄνδρας τρεῖς
ἀπὸ τοῦ κοινοῦ ὡς ἀπογραψομένους τὰ θεσπιέειν
ἔμελλε, καὶ πρόκατε τὸν πρόμαντιν βαρβάρῳ
γλώσσῃ χρᾶν. καὶ τοὺς μὲν ἑπομένους τῶν Θηβαίων ἐν θώματι ἔχεσθαι ἀκούοντας βαρβάρου
γλώσσης ἀντὶ Ἑλλάδος, οὐδὲ ἔχειν ὅ τι χρήσων-
ται τῷ παρεόντι πρήγματι· τὸν δὲ Εὐρωπέα Μῦν
ἐξαρπάσαντα παρ᾽ αὐτῶν τὴν ἐφέροντο δέλτον,
τὰ λεγόμενα ὑπὸ τοῦ προφήτεω γράφειν ἐς αὐτήν,
φάναι δὲ Καρίῃ μιν γλώσσῃ χρᾶν, συγγραψά-
μενον δὲ οἴχεσθαι ἀπιόντα ἐς Θεσσαλίην.

136. Μαρδόνιος δὲ ἐπιλεξάμενος ὅ τι δὴ λέγοντα
ἦν τὰ χρηστήρια μετὰ ταῦτα ἔπεμψε ἄγγελον ἐς

way of divination, even as at Olympia), and moreover bribed one that was no Theban but a stranger
to lie down to sleep in the shrine of Amphiaraus.
No Theban may seek a prophecy there; for
Amphiaraus bade them by an oracle to choose
which of the two they would and forgo the other,
and take him either for their prophet or for their ally;
and they chose that he should be their ally; wherefore
no Theban may lay him down to sleep in that place.

135. But at this time there happened, as the
Thebans say, a thing at which I marvel greatly. It
would seem that this man Mys of Europus came in
his wanderings among the places of divination to
the precinct of Ptoan Apollo. This temple is called
Ptoum,[1] and belongs to the Thebans; it lies by a
hill, above the lake Copaïs, very near to the town
Acraephia. When the man called Mys entered into
this temple, three men of the town following him
that were chosen on the state's behalf to write
down the oracles that should be given, straightway
the diviner prophesied in a foreign tongue. The
Thebans that followed him stood astonied to hear a
strange language instead of Greek, and knew not
what this present matter might be; but Mys of
Europus snatched from them the tablet that they
carried and wrote on it that which was spoken by
the prophet, saying that the words of the oracle
were Carian; and having written all down he went
away back to Thessaly.

136. Mardonius read whatever was said in the
oracles; and presently he sent a messenger to Athens,

[1] Called after Ptous, son of Athamas, according to
Apollodorus. The story of Athamas, and his plot with Ino
their stepmother against his children's lives, was localised in
Boeotia as well as Achaea, cp. vii. 197.

Ἀθήνας Ἀλέξανδρον τὸν Ἀμύντεω ἄνδρα Μακε-
δόνα, ἅμα μὲν ὅτι οἱ προσκηδέες οἱ Πέρσαι ἦσαν·
Ἀλεξάνδρου γὰρ ἀδελφεὴν Γυγαίην, Ἀμύντεω δὲ
θυγατέρα, Βουβάρης ἀνὴρ Πέρσης ἔσχε, ἐκ τῆς
οἱ ἐγεγόνεε Ἀμύντης ὁ ἐν τῇ Ἀσίῃ, ἔχων τὸ
οὔνομα τοῦ μητροπάτορος, τῷ δὴ ἐκ βασιλέος τῆς
Φρυγίης ἐδόθη Ἀλάβανδα πόλις μεγάλη νέμεσθαι·
ἅμα δὲ ὁ Μαρδόνιος πυθόμενος ὅτι πρόξεινός τε
εἴη καὶ εὐεργέτης ὁ Ἀλέξανδρος ἔπεμπε. τοὺς
γὰρ Ἀθηναίους οὕτω ἐδόκεε μάλιστα προσκτή-
σεσθαι, λεών τε πολλὸν ἄρα ἀκούων εἶναι καὶ
ἄλκιμον, τά τε κατὰ τὴν θάλασσαν συντυχόντα
σφι παθήματα κατεργασαμένους μάλιστα Ἀθηναίους ἐπίστατο. τούτων δὲ προσγενομένων κατ-
ήλπιζε εὐπετέως τῆς θαλάσσης κρατήσειν, τά
περ ἂν καὶ ἦν, πεζῇ τε ἐδόκεε πολλῷ εἶναι κρέσ-
σων, οὕτω τε ἐλογίζετο κατύπερθέ οἱ τὰ πρήγματα
ἔσεσθαι τῶν Ἑλληνικῶν. τάχα δ᾽ ἂν καὶ τὰ
χρηστήρια ταῦτά οἱ προλέγοι, συμβουλεύοντα
σύμμαχον τὸν Ἀθηναῖον ποιέεσθαι· τοῖσι δὴ
πειθόμενος ἔπεμπε.

137. Τοῦ δὲ Ἀλεξάνδρου τούτου ἕβδομος γενέ-
τωρ Περδίκκης ἐστὶ ὁ κτησάμενος τῶν Μακεδόνων
τὴν τυραννίδα τρόπῳ τοιῷδε. ἐξ Ἄργεος ἔφυγον
ἐς Ἰλλυριοὺς τῶν Τημένου ἀπογόνων τρεῖς ἀδελ-
φεοί, Γαυάνης τε καὶ Ἀέροπος καὶ Περδίκκης, ἐκ
δὲ Ἰλλυριῶν ὑπερβαλόντες ἐς τὴν ἄνω Μακεδονίην ἀπίκοντο ἐς Λεβαίην πόλιν. ἐνθαῦτα δὲ

---

[1] Alabanda was not in Phrygia but in Caria (*cp.* vii. 195);
Stein prefers to read Alabastra, a town which Herodotus,
according to Stephanus of Byzantium, places in Phrygia.

Alexander, a Macedonian, son of Amyntas; him he sent, partly because the Persians were akin to him; for Bubares, a Persian, had taken to wife Gygaea Alexander's sister and Amyntas' daughter, who had borne to him that Amyntas of Asia who was called by the name of his mother's father, and to whom the king gave Alabanda[1] a great city in Phrygia for his dwelling; and partly he sent him because he learnt that Alexander was a protector and benefactor to the Athenians. It was thus that he supposed he could best gain the Athenians for his allies, of whom he heard that they were a numerous and valiant people, and knew that they had been the chief authors of the calamities which had befallen the Persians at sea. If he gained their friendship he looked to be easily master of the seas, as truly he would have been; and on land he supposed himself to be by much the stronger; so he reckoned that thus he would have the upper hand of the Greeks. Peradventure this was the prediction of the oracles, counselling him to make the Athenian his ally, and it was in obedience to this that he sent his messenger.

137. This Alexander was seventh in descent from Perdiccas, who got for himself the despotism of Macedonia in the way that I will show. Three brothers of the lineage of Temenus came as banished men from Argos[2] to Illyria, Gauanes and Aeropus and Perdiccas; and from Illyria they crossed over into the highlands of Macedonia till they came to the town Lebaea. There they served for wages as

[2] The story of an Argive origin of the Macedonian dynasty appears to be mythical. It rests probably on the similarity of the name Argeadae, the tribe to which the dynasty belonged.

ἐθήτευον ἐπὶ μισθῷ παρὰ τῷ βασιλέι, ὃ μὲν
ἵππους νέμων, ὃ δὲ βοῦς, ὁ δὲ νεώτατος αὐτῶν
Περδίκκης τὰ λεπτὰ τῶν προβάτων. ἡ δὲ γυνὴ
τοῦ βασιλέος αὐτὴ τὰ σιτία σφι ἔπεσσε· ἦσαν
γὰρ τὸ πάλαι καὶ αἱ τυραννίδες τῶν ἀνθρώπων
ἀσθενέες χρήμασι, οὐ μοῦνον ὁ δῆμος· ὅκως δὲ
ὀπτῴη, ὁ ἄρτος τοῦ παιδὸς τοῦ θητὸς Περδίκκεω
διπλήσιος ἐγίνετο αὐτὸς ἑωυτοῦ. ἐπεὶ δὲ αἰεὶ
τὠυτὸ τοῦτο ἐγίνετο, εἶπε πρὸς τὸν ἄνδρα τὸν
ἑωυτῆς· τὸν δὲ ἀκούσαντα ἐσῆλθε αὐτίκα ὡς εἴη
τέρας καὶ φέροι μέγα τι. καλέσας δὲ τοὺς θῆτας
προηγόρευέ σφι ἀπαλλάσσεσθαι ἐκ γῆς τῆς ἑωυτοῦ. οἱ δὲ τὸν μισθὸν ἔφασαν δίκαιοι εἶναι ἀπο-
λαβόντες οὕτω ἐξιέναι. ἐνθαῦτα ὁ βασιλεὺς τοῦ
μισθοῦ πέρι ἀκούσας, ἦν γὰρ κατὰ τὴν καπνο-
δόκην ἐς τὸν οἶκον ἐσέχων ὁ ἥλιος, εἶπε θεοβλαβὴς
γενόμενος "Μισθὸν δὲ ὑμῖν ἐγὼ ὑμέων ἄξιον τόνδε
ἀποδίδωμι," δέξας τὸν ἥλιον. ὁ μὲν δὴ Γαυάνης
τε καὶ ὁ Ἀέροπος οἱ πρεσβύτεροι ἕστασαν ἐκ-
πεπληγμένοι, ὡς ἤκουσαν ταῦτα· ὁ δὲ παῖς, ἐτύγχανε γὰρ ἔχων μάχαιραν, εἴπας τάδε "Δεκόμεθα
ὦ βασιλεῦ τὰ διδοῖς," περιγράφει τῇ μαχαίρῃ ἐς
τὸ ἔδαφος τοῦ οἴκου τὸν ἥλιον, περιγράψας δέ, ἐς
τὸν κόλπον τρὶς ἀρυσάμενος τοῦ ἡλίου, ἀπαλλάσσετο αὐτός τε καὶ οἱ μετ' ἐκείνου.

138. Οἱ μὲν δὴ ἀπήισαν, τῷ δὲ βασιλέι σημαί-
νει τις τῶν παρέδρων οἷόν τι χρῆμα ποιήσειε ὁ
παῖς καὶ ὡς σὺν νόῳ κείνων ὁ νεώτατος λάβοι τὰ
διδόμενα. ὃ δὲ ταῦτα ἀκούσας καὶ ὀξυνθεὶς πέμπει ἐπ' αὐτοὺς ἱππέας ἀπολέοντας. ποταμὸς δὲ
ἐστὶ ἐν τῇ χώρῃ ταύτῃ, τῷ θύουσι οἱ τούτων τῶν

thralls in the king's household, one tending horses and another oxen, and Perdiccas, who was the youngest, the lesser flocks. Now the king's wife cooked their food for them; for in old times the ruling houses among men, and not the commonalty alone, were lacking in wealth; and whenever she baked bread, the loaf of the thrall Perdiccas grew double in bigness. Seeing that this ever happened, she told her husband; and it seemed to him when he heard it that this was a portent, signifying some great matter. So he sent for his thralls and bade them depart out of his territory. They said it was but just that they should have their wages ere they departed; whereupon the king, when they spoke of wages, was moved to foolishness, and said, "That is the wage you merit, and it is that I give you," pointing to the sunlight that shone down the smoke-vent into the house. Gauanes and Aeropus, who were the elder, stood astonied when they heard that; but the boy said, "We accept what you give, O king," and with that he took a knife that he had upon him and drew a line with it on the floor of the house round the sunlight[1]; which done, he thrice gathered up the sunlight into the fold of his garment, and went his way with his companions.

138. So they departed; but one of them that sat by declared to the king what this was that the boy had done, and how it was of set purpose that the youngest of them had accepted the gift offered; which when the king heard, he was angered, and sent riders after them to slay them. But there is in that land a river, whereto the descendants from

---

[1] The action is said to symbolise claiming possession of house and land, and also to call the sun to witness the claim. Ancient Germany, apparently, had a similar custom.

ἀνδρῶν ἀπ' Ἄργεος ἀπόγονοι σωτῆρι· οὗτος,
ἐπείτε διέβησαν οἱ Τημενίδαι, μέγας οὕτω ἐρρύη
ὥστε τοὺς ἱππέας μὴ οἵους τε γενέσθαι διαβῆναι.
οἱ δὲ ἀπικόμενοι ἐς ἄλλην γῆν τῆς Μακεδονίης
οἴκησαν πέλας τῶν κήπων τῶν λεγομένων εἶναι
Μίδεω τοῦ Γορδίεω, ἐν τοῖσι φύεται αὐτόματα
ῥόδα, ἓν ἕκαστον ἔχον ἑξήκοντα φύλλα, ὀδμῇ τε
ὑπερφέροντα τῶν ἄλλων. ἐν τούτοισι καὶ ὁ Σιλη-
νὸς τοῖσι κήποισι ἥλω, ὡς λέγεται ὑπὸ Μακεδόνων. ὑπὲρ δὲ τῶν κήπων ὄρος κέεται Βέρμιον
οὔνομα, ἄβατον ὑπὸ χειμῶνος. ἐνθεῦτεν δὲ ὁρμώμενοι, ὡς ταύτην ἔσχον, κατεστρέφοντο καὶ τὴν
ἄλλην Μακεδονίην.

139. Ἀπὸ τούτου δὴ τοῦ Περδίκκεω Ἀλέξανδρος
ὧδε ἐγένετο· Ἀμύντεω παῖς ἦν Ἀλέξανδρος,
Ἀμύντης δὲ Ἀλκέτεω, Ἀλκέτεω δὲ πατὴρ ἦν
Ἀέροπος, τοῦ δὲ Φίλιππος, Φιλίππου δὲ Ἀργαῖος,
τοῦ δὲ Περδίκκης ὁ κτησάμενος τὴν ἀρχήν.

140. Ἐγεγόνεε μὲν δὴ ὧδε ὁ Ἀλέξανδρος ὁ
Ἀμύντεω· ὡς δὲ ἀπίκετο ἐς τὰς Ἀθήνας ἀπο-
πεμφθεὶς ὑπὸ Μαρδονίου, ἔλεγε τάδε. "Ἄνδρες
Ἀθηναῖοι, Μαρδόνιος τάδε λέγει. ἐμοὶ ἀγγελίη
ἥκει παρὰ βασιλέος λέγουσα οὕτω. 'Ἀθηναίοισι
τὰς ἁμαρτάδας τὰς ἐς ἐμὲ ἐξ ἐκείνων γενομένας
πάσας μετίημι. νῦν τε ὧδε Μαρδόνιε ποίεε·
τοῦτο μὲν τὴν γῆν σφι ἀπόδος, τοῦτο δὲ ἄλλην
πρὸς ταύτῃ ἑλέσθων αὐτοί, ἥντινα ἂν ἐθέλωσι,
ἐόντες αὐτόνομοι· ἱρά τε πάντα σφι, ἢν δὴ βού-

---

[1] This was the fertile and beautiful valley in which stood
Aegae or Edessa (modern Vodena), the ancient home of the
Macedonian kings.

Argos of these men offer sacrifice, as their deliverer; this river, when the sons of Temenus had crossed it, rose in such flood that the riders could not cross. So the brothers came to another part of Macedonia and settled near the place called the garden of Midas son of Gordias,[1] wherein roses grow of themselves, each bearing sixty blossoms and of surpassing fragrance; in which garden, by the Macedonian story, Silenus[2] was taken captive; above it rises the mountain called Bermius, which none can ascend for the wintry cold. Thence they issued forth when they had won that country, and presently subdued also the rest of Macedonia.

139. From that Perdiccas Alexander was descended, being the son of Amyntas, who was the son of Alcetes; Alcetes' father was Aeropus, and his was Philippus; Philippus' father was Argaeus, and his again was Perdiccas, who won that lordship.

140. Such was the lineage of Alexander son of Amyntas; who, when he came to Athens from Mardonius who had sent him, spoke on this wise. "This, Athenians, is what Mardonius says to you:— There is a message come to me from the king, saying, 'I forgive the Athenians all the offences which they have committed against me; and now, Mardonius, I bid you do this:—Give them back their territory, and let them choose more for themselves besides, wheresoever they will, and dwell under their own laws; and rebuild all their temples

[2] This is a Phrygian tale, transferred to Macedonia. Silenus was a "nature-deity," inhabiting places of rich vegetation: if captured, he was fabled in the Greek version of the myth to give wise counsel to his captor. One may compare the story of Proteus captured by Menelaus, in the Odyssey.

λωνταί γε ἐμοὶ ὁμολογέειν, ἀνόρθωσον, ὅσα ἐγὼ
ἐνέπρησα.' τούτων δὲ ἀπιγμένων ἀναγκαίως ἔχει
μοι ποιέειν ταῦτα, ἢν μὴ τὸ ὑμέτερον αἴτιον
γένηται. λέγω δὲ ὑμῖν τάδε. νῦν τί μαίνεσθε
πόλεμον βασιλέι ἀειρόμενοι; οὔτε γὰρ ἂν ὑπερ-
βάλοισθε οὔτε οἷοί τε ἐστὲ ἀντέχειν τὸν πάντα
χρόνον. εἴδετε μὲν γὰρ τῆς Ξέρξεω στρατηλασίης τὸ πλῆθος καὶ τὰ ἔργα, πυνθάνεσθε δὲ καὶ
τὴν νῦν παρ' ἐμοὶ ἐοῦσαν δύναμιν· ὥστε καὶ ἢν
ἡμέας ὑπερβάλησθε καὶ νικήσητε, τοῦ περ ὑμῖν
οὐδεμία ἐλπὶς εἴ περ εὖ φρονέετε, ἄλλη παρέσται
πολλαπλησίη. μὴ ὦν βούλεσθε παρισούμενοι
βασιλέι στέρεσθαι μὲν τῆς χώρης, θέειν δὲ αἰεὶ
περὶ ὑμέων αὐτῶν, ἀλλὰ καταλύσασθε· παρέχει
δὲ ὑμῖν κάλλιστα καταλύσασθαι, βασιλέος
ταύτῃ ὁρμημένου. ἔστε ἐλεύθεροι, ἡμῖν ὁμαιχ-
μίην συνθέμενοι ἄνευ τε δόλου καὶ ἀπάτης. Μαρδόνιος μὲν ταῦτα ὦ 'Αθηναῖοι ἐνετείλατό μοι
εἰπεῖν πρὸς ὑμέας· ἐγὼ δὲ περὶ μὲν εὐνοίης τῆς
πρὸς ὑμέας ἐούσης ἐξ ἐμεῦ οὐδὲν λέξω, οὐ γὰρ ἂν
νῦν πρῶτον ἐκμάθοιτε, προσχρηίζω δὲ ὑμέων
πείθεσθαι Μαρδονίῳ. ἐνορῶ γὰρ ὑμῖν οὐκ οἵοισί
τε ἐσομένοισι τὸν πάντα χρόνον πολεμέειν Ξέρξῃ·
εἰ γὰρ ἐνώρων τοῦτο ἐν ὑμῖν, οὐκ ἄν κοτε ἐς ὑμέας
ἦλθον ἔχων λόγους τούσδε· καὶ γὰρ δύναμις ὑπὲρ
ἄνθρωπον ἡ βασιλέος ἐστὶ καὶ χεὶρ ὑπερμήκης.
ἢν ὦν μὴ αὐτίκα ὁμολογήσητε, μεγάλα προτεινόν-
των ἐπ' οἷσι ὁμολογέειν ἐθέλουσι, δειμαίνω ὑπὲρ
ὑμέων ἐν τρίβῳ τε μάλιστα οἰκημένων τῶν συμμάχων πάντων αἰεί τε φθειρομένων μούνων, ἐξαί-
ρετον μεταίχμιόν τε τὴν γῆν ἐκτημένων. ἀλλὰ

that I burnt, if they will make a covenant with me."
This being the message, needs must that I obey it
(says Mardonius), unless you take it upon you to
hinder me. And this I say to you:—Why are you
so mad as to wage war against the king? you
cannot overcome him, nor can you resist him for
ever. For the multitude of Xerxes' host, and what
they did, you have seen, and you have heard of the
power that I now have with me; so that even if you
overcome and conquer us (whereof, if you be in your
right minds, you can have no hope), yet there will
come another host many times as great as this. Be
not then minded to match yourselves against the
king, and thereby lose your land and ever be yourselves in jeopardy, but make peace; which you can
most honourably do, the king being that way
inclined; keep your freedom, and agree to be our
brothers in arms in all faith and honesty.—This,
Athenians, is the message which Mardonius charges
me to give you. For my own part I will say nothing
of the goodwill that I have towards you, for it would
not be the first that you have learnt of that; but I
entreat you to follow Mardonius' counsel. Well I
see that you will not have power to wage war against
Xerxes for ever; did I see such power in you, I had
never come to you with such language as this; for
the king's might is greater than human, and his arm
is long. If therefore you will not straightway agree
with them, when the conditions which they offer
you, whereon they are ready to agree, are so great,
I fear what may befall you; for of all the allies you
dwell most in the very path of the war, and you alone
will never escape destruction, your country being
marked out for a battlefield. Nay, follow his counsel;

πείθεσθε· πολλοῦ γὰρ ὑμῖν ἄξια ταῦτα, εἰ βασιλεύς γε ὁ μέγας μούνοισι ὑμῖν Ἑλλήνων τὰς
ἁμαρτάδας ἀπιεὶς ἐθέλει φίλος γενέσθαι."

141. Ἀλέξανδρος μὲν ταῦτα ἔλεξε. Λακεδαιμόνιοι δὲ πυθόμενοι ἥκειν Ἀλέξανδρον ἐς Ἀθήνας
ἐς ὁμολογίην ἄξοντα τῷ βαρβάρῳ Ἀθηναίους,
ἀναμνησθέντες τῶν λογίων ὥς σφεας χρεόν ἐστι
ἅμα τοῖσι ἄλλοισι Δωριεῦσι ἐκπίπτειν ἐκ Πελοποννήσου ὑπὸ Μήδων τε καὶ Ἀθηναίων, κάρτα
τε ἔδεισαν μὴ ὁμολογήσωσι τῷ Πέρσῃ Ἀθηναῖοι,
αὐτίκα τέ σφι ἔδοξε πέμπειν ἀγγέλους. καὶ δὴ
συνέπιπτε ὥστε ὁμοῦ σφεων γίνεσθαι τὴν κατά-
στασιν· ἐπανέμειναν γὰρ οἱ Ἀθηναῖοι διατρί-
βοντες, εὖ ἐπιστάμενοι ὅτι ἔμελλον Λακεδαιμόνιοι
πεύσεσθαι ἥκοντα παρὰ τοῦ βαρβάρου ἄγγελον
ἐπ' ὁμολογίῃ, πυθόμενοί τε πέμψειν κατὰ τάχος
ἀγγέλους. ἐπίτηδες ὦν ἐποίευν, ἐνδεικνύμενοι
τοῖσι Λακεδαιμονίοισι τὴν ἑωυτῶν γνώμην.

142. Ὡς δὲ ἐπαύσατο λέγων Ἀλέξανδρος, δια-
δεξάμενοι ἔλεγον οἱ ἀπὸ Σπάρτης ἄγγελοι " Ἡμέας
δὲ ἔπεμψαν Λακεδαιμόνιοι δεησομένους ὑμέων
μήτε νεώτερον ποιέειν μηδὲν κατὰ τὴν Ἑλλάδα
μήτε λόγους ἐνδέκεσθαι παρὰ τοῦ βαρβάρου.
οὔτε γὰρ δίκαιον οὐδαμῶς οὔτε κόσμον φέρον οὔτε
γε ἄλλοισι Ἑλλήνων οὐδαμοῖσι, ὑμῖν δὲ δὴ καὶ
διὰ πάντων ἥκιστα πολλῶν εἵνεκα. ἠγείρατε γὰρ
τόνδε τὸν πόλεμον ὑμεῖς οὐδὲν ἡμέων βουλομένων,
καὶ περὶ τῆς ὑμετέρης ἀρχῆθεν ὁ ἀγὼν ἐγένετο,
νῦν δὲ φέρει καὶ ἐς πᾶσαν τὴν Ἑλλάδα· ἄλλως
τε τούτων ἁπάντων αἰτίους γενέσθαι δουλοσύνης

for it is not to be lightly regarded by you that you are the only men in Hellas whose offences the great king is ready to forgive and whose friend he would be."

141. Thus spoke Alexander. But the Lacedaemonians had heard that Alexander was come to Athens to bring the Athenians to an agreement with the foreigner; and remembering the oracles, how that they themselves with the rest of the Dorians must be driven out of the Peloponnese by the Medes and the Athenians, they were greatly afraid lest the Athenians should agree with the Persian, and they straightway resolved that they would send envoys. Moreover it so fell out for both, that they made their entry at one and the same time; for the Athenians delayed, and tarried for them, being well assured that the Lacedaemonians were like to hear that the messenger was come from the Persians for an agreement; and they had heard that the Lacedaemonians would send their envoys with all speed; therefore it was of set purpose that they did it, that they might make their will known to the Lacedaemonians.

142. So when Alexander had made an end of speaking, the envoys from Sparta took up the tale, and said, "We on our part are sent by the Lacedaemonians to entreat you to do nought hurtful to Hellas and accept no offer from the foreigner. That were a thing unjust and dishonourable for any Greek, but for you most of all, on many counts; it was you who stirred up this war, by no desire of ours, and your territory was first the stake of that battle, wherein all Hellas is now engaged; and setting that apart, it is a thing not to be borne that not all this alone but slavery too should be brought

τοῖσι Ἕλλησι Ἀθηναίους οὐδαμῶς ἀνασχετόν,
οἵτινες αἰεὶ καὶ τὸ πάλαι φαίνεσθε πολλοὺς ἐλευ-
θερώσαντες ἀνθρώπων. πιεζευμένοισι μέντοι ὑμῖν
συναχθόμεθα, καὶ ὅτι καρπῶν ἐστερήθητε διξῶν
ἤδη καὶ ὅτι οἰκοφθόρησθε χρόνον ἤδη πολλόν.
ἀντὶ τούτων δὲ ὑμῖν Λακεδαιμόνιοί τε καὶ οἱ σύμμαχοι ἐπαγγέλλονται γυναῖκάς τε καὶ τὰ ἐς
πόλεμον ἄχρηστα οἰκετέων ἐχόμενα πάντα ἐπι-
θρέψειν, ἔστ' ἂν ὁ πόλεμος ὅδε συνεστήκῃ. μηδὲ
ὑμέας Ἀλέξανδρος ὁ Μακεδὼν ἀναγνώσῃ, λεήνας
τὸν Μαρδονίου λόγον. τούτῳ μὲν γὰρ ταῦτα
ποιητέα ἐστί· τύραννος γὰρ ἐὼν τυράννῳ συγ-
κατεργάζεται· ὑμῖν δὲ οὐ ποιητέα, εἴ περ εὖ
τυγχάνετε φρονέοντες, ἐπισταμένοισι ὡς βαρβάροισι ἐστὶ οὔτε πιστὸν οὔτε ἀληθὲς οὐδέν." ταῦτα
ἔλεξαν οἱ ἄγγελοι.

143. Ἀθηναῖοι δὲ πρὸς μὲν Ἀλέξανδρον ὑπεκρίναντο τάδε. "Καὶ αὐτοὶ τοῦτό γε ἐπιστάμεθα
ὅτι πολλαπλησίη ἐστὶ τῷ Μήδῳ δύναμις ἤ περ
ἡμῖν, ὥστε οὐδὲν δέει τοῦτό γε ὀνειδίζειν. ἀλλ'
ὅμως ἐλευθερίης γλιχόμενοι ἀμυνεύμεθα οὕτω
ὅκως ἂν καὶ δυνώμεθα. ὁμολογῆσαι δὲ τῷ βαρβάρῳ μήτε σὺ ἡμέας πειρῶ ἀναπείθειν οὔτε ἡμεῖς
πεισόμεθα. νῦν τε ἀπάγγελλε Μαρδονίῳ ὡς
Ἀθηναῖοι λέγουσι, ἔστ' ἂν ὁ ἥλιος τὴν αὐτὴν ὁδὸν
ἴῃ τῇ περ καὶ νῦν ἔρχεται, μήκοτε ὁμολογήσειν
ἡμέας Ξέρξῃ· ἀλλὰ θεοῖσί τε συμμάχοισι πίσυνοί
μιν ἐπέξιμεν ἀμυνόμενοι καὶ τοῖσι ἥρωσι, τῶν
ἐκεῖνος οὐδεμίαν ὄπιν ἔχων ἐνέπρησε τούς τε
οἴκους καὶ τὰ ἀγάλματα. σύ τε τοῦ λοιποῦ
λόγους ἔχων τοιούσδε μὴ ἐπιφαίνεο Ἀθηναίοισι,
μηδὲ δοκέων χρηστὰ ὑπουργέειν ἀθέμιστα ἔρδειν

upon the Greeks by you Athenians, who have ever of old been known for givers of freedom to many. Nevertheless we grieve with you in your afflictions, for that now you have lost two harvests and your substance has been for a long time wasted; in requital wherefor the Lacedaemonians and their allies declare that they will nourish your women and all of your households that are unserviceable for war, so long as this war shall last. But let not Alexander the Macedonian win you with his smooth-tongued praise of Mardonius' counsel. It is his business to follow that counsel, for as he is a despot so must he be the despot's fellow-worker; but it is not your business, if you be men rightly minded; for you know, that in foreigners there is no faith nor truth." Thus spoke the envoys.

143. But to Alexander the Athenians thus replied : "We know of ourselves that the power of the Mede is many times greater than ours; there is no need to taunt us with that. Nevertheless in our zeal for freedom we will defend ourselves to the best of our ability. But as touching agreements with the foreigner, do not you essay to persuade us thereto, nor will we consent; and now carry this answer back to Mardonius from the Athenians, that as long as the sun holds the course whereby he now goes, we will make no agreement with Xerxes; but we will fight against him without ceasing, trusting in the aid of the gods and the heroes whom he has set at nought and burnt their houses and their adornments. To you we say, come no more to Athenians with such a plea, nor under the semblance of rendering us a service counsel us to do wickedly ;

παραίνεε· οὐ γάρ σε βουλόμεθα οὐδὲν ἄχαρι
πρὸς Ἀθηναίων παθεῖν ἐόντα πρόξεινόν τε καὶ
φίλον."

144. Πρὸς μὲν Ἀλέξανδρον ταῦτα ὑπεκρίναντο,
πρὸς δὲ τοὺς ἀπὸ Σπάρτης ἀγγέλους τάδε. "Τὸ
μὲν δεῖσαι Λακεδαιμονίους μὴ ὁμολογήσωμεν τῷ
βαρβάρῳ, κάρτα ἀνθρωπήιον ἦν· ἀτὰρ αἰσχρῶς
γε οἴκατε ἐξεπιστάμενοι τὸ Ἀθηναίων φρόνημα
ἀρρωδῆσαι, ὅτι οὔτε χρυσός ἐστι γῆς οὐδαμόθι
τοσοῦτος οὔτε χώρη κάλλεϊ καὶ ἀρετῇ μέγα
ὑπερφέρουσα, τὰ ἡμεῖς δεξάμενοι ἐθέλοιμεν ἂν
μηδίσαντες καταδουλῶσαι τὴν Ἑλλάδα. πολλά
τε γὰρ καὶ μεγάλα ἐστὶ τὰ διακωλύοντα ταῦτα
μὴ ποιέειν μηδ' ἢν ἐθέλωμεν, πρῶτα μὲν καὶ
μέγιστα τῶν θεῶν τὰ ἀγάλματα καὶ τὰ οἰκήματα
ἐμπεπρησμένα τε καὶ συγκεχωσμένα, τοῖσι ἡμέας
ἀναγκαίως ἔχει τιμωρέειν ἐς τὰ μέγιστα μᾶλλον
ἤ περ ὁμολογέειν τῷ ταῦτα ἐργασαμένῳ, αὖτις δὲ
τὸ Ἑλληνικὸν ἐὸν ὅμαιμόν τε καὶ ὁμόγλωσσον καὶ
θεῶν ἱδρύματά τε κοινὰ καὶ θυσίαι ἤθεά τε ὁμό-
τροπα, τῶν προδότας γενέσθαι Ἀθηναίους οὐκ
ἂν εὖ ἔχοι. ἐπίστασθέ τε οὕτω, εἰ μὴ πρότερον
ἐτυγχάνετε ἐπιστάμενοι, ἔστ' ἂν καὶ εἷς περιῇ
Ἀθηναίων, μηδαμὰ ὁμολογήσοντας ἡμέας Ξέρξῃ.
ὑμέων μέντοι ἀγάμεθα τὴν προνοίην τὴν πρὸς
ἡμέας ἐοῦσαν, ὅτι προείδετε ἡμέων οἰκοφθορη-
μένων οὕτω ὥστε ἐπιθρέψαι ἐθέλειν ἡμέων τοὺς
οἰκέτας. καὶ ὑμῖν μὲν ἡ χάρις ἐκπεπλήρωται,
ἡμεῖς μέντοι λιπαρήσομεν οὕτω ὅκως ἂν ἔχωμεν,
οὐδὲν λυπέοντες ὑμέας. νῦν δέ, ὡς οὕτω ἐχόντων,
στρατιὴν ὡς τάχιστα ἐκπέμπετε. ὡς γὰρ ἡμεῖς
εἰκάζομεν, οὐκ ἑκὰς χρόνου παρέσται ὁ βάρβαρος

for we would not that you who are our friend and protector should suffer any harm at Athenian hands."

144. Such was their answer to Alexander; but to the Spartan envoys they said, "It was most human that the Lacedaemonians should fear our making an agreement with the foreigner; but we think you do basely to be afraid, knowing the Athenian temper to be such that there is nowhere on earth such store of gold or such territory of surpassing fairness and excellence that the gift of it should win us to take the Persian part and enslave Hellas. For there are many great reasons why we should not do this, even if we so desired; first and chiefest, the burning and destruction of the adornments and temples of our gods, whom we are constrained to avenge to the uttermost rather than make covenants with the doer of these things, and next the kinship of all Greeks in blood and speech, and the shrines of gods and the sacrifices that we have in common, and the likeness of our way of life, to all which it would ill beseem Athenians to be false. Know this now, if you knew it not before, that as long as one Athenian is left alive we will make no agreement with Xerxes. Nevertheless we thank you for your forethought concerning us, in that you have so provided for our wasted state that you offer to nourish our households. For your part, you have given us full measure of kindness; yet for ourselves, we will make shift to endure as best we may, and not be burdensome to you. But now, seeing that this is so, send your army with all speed; for as we guess, the foreigner

ἐσβαλὼν ἐς τὴν ἡμετέρην, ἀλλ᾽ ἐπειδὰν τάχιστα
πύθηται τὴν ἀγγελίην ὅτι οὐδὲν ποιήσομεν τῶν
ἐκεῖνος ἡμέων προσεδέετο. πρὶν ὦν παρεῖναι
ἐκεῖνον ἐς τὴν ᾽Αττικήν, ἡμέας καιρός ἐστι προ-
βοηθῆσαι ἐς τὴν Βοιωτίην." οἱ μὲν ταῦτα ὑπο-
κριναμένων ᾽Αθηναίων ἀπαλλάσσοντο ἐς Σπάρτην.

will be upon us and invading our country in no long time, but as soon as ever the message comes to him that we will do nothing that he requires of us; wherefore, ere he comes into Attica, now is the time for us to march first into Boeotia." At this reply of the Athenians the envoys returned back to Sparta.

BOOK IX

I

1. Μαρδόνιος δέ, ὥς οἱ ἀπονοστήσας Ἀλέξανδρος τὰ παρὰ Ἀθηναίων ἐσήμηνε, ὁρμηθεὶς ἐκ Θεσσαλίης ἦγε τὴν στρατιὴν σπουδῇ ἐπὶ τὰς Ἀθήνας. ὅκου δὲ ἑκάστοτε γίνοιτο, τούτους παρελάμβανε. τοῖσι δὲ Θεσσαλίης ἡγεομένοισι οὔτε τὰ πρὸ τοῦ πεπρηγμένα μετέμελε οὐδὲν πολλῷ τε μᾶλλον ἐπῆγον τὸν Πέρσην, καὶ συμπροέπεμψέ τε Θώρηξ ὁ Ληρισαῖος Ξέρξην φεύγοντα καὶ τότε ἐκ τοῦ φανεροῦ παρῆκε Μαρδόνιον ἐπὶ τὴν Ἑλλάδα.

2. Ἐπεὶ δὲ πορευόμενος γίνεται ὁ στρατὸς ἐν Βοιωτοῖσι, οἱ Θηβαῖοι κατελάμβανον τὸν Μαρδόνιον καὶ συνεβούλευον αὐτῷ λέγοντες ὡς οὐκ εἴη χῶρος ἐπιτηδεότερος ἐνστρατοπεδεύεσθαι ἐκείνου, οὐδὲ ἔων ἰέναι ἑκαστέρω, ἀλλ' αὐτοῦ ἱζόμενον ποιέειν ὅκως ἀμαχητὶ τὴν πᾶσαν Ἑλλάδα καταστρέψεται. κατὰ μὲν γὰρ τὸ ἰσχυρὸν Ἕλληνας ὁμοφρονέοντας, οἵ περ καὶ πάρος ταῦτα ἐγίνωσκον, χαλεπὰ εἶναι περιγίνεσθαι καὶ ἅπασι ἀνθρώποισι· "εἰ δὲ ποιήσεις τὰ ἡμεῖς παραινέομεν," ἔφασαν λέγοντες, "ἕξεις ἀπόνως πάντα τὰ ἐκείνων ἰσχυρὰ βουλεύματα· πέμπε χρήματα ἐς τοὺς δυναστεύοντας ἄνδρας ἐν τῆσι πόλισι, πέμπων δὲ τὴν Ἑλλάδα διαστήσεις· ἐνθεῦτεν δὲ

BOOK IX

1. Mardonius, when Alexander returned and told him what he had heard from the Athenians, set forth from Thessaly and led his army with all zeal against Athens[1]; and to whatsoever country he came he took its people along with him. The rulers of Thessaly repented no whit of what they had already done, and were but readier than before to further his march; and Thorax of Larissa, who had aided to give Xerxes safe-conduct in his flight, did now without disguise open a passage for Mardonius into Hellas.

2. But when the army in its march was come into Boeotia, the Thebans sought to stay Mardonius, advising him that he could find no country better fitted than theirs for encampment; he should not (they pleaded) go further, but rather halt there and so act as to subdue all Hellas without fighting. For as long as the Greeks who before had been of the same way of thinking remained in accord, it would be a hard matter even for the whole world to overcome them by force of arms; "but if you do as we advise," said the Thebans as they spoke, "you will without trouble be master of all their counsels of battle. Send money to the men that have power in their cities, and thereby you will divide Hellas against

[1] In the summer of 479. Mardonius occupied Athens in July.

τοὺς μὴ τὰ σὰ φρονέοντας ῥηιδίως μετὰ τῶν
στασιωτέων καταστρέψαι."

3. Οἱ μὲν ταῦτα συνεβούλευον, ὁ δὲ οὐκ ἐπεί-
θετο, ἀλλά οἱ δεινὸς ἐνέστακτο ἵμερος τὰς Ἀθήνας
δεύτερα ἑλεῖν, ἅμα μὲν ὑπ' ἀγνωμοσύνης, ἅμα δὲ
πυρσοῖσι διὰ νήσων ἐδόκεε βασιλέι δηλώσειν
ἐόντι ἐν Σάρδισι ὅτι ἔχοι Ἀθήνας· ὃς οὐδὲ τότε
ἀπικόμενος ἐς τὴν Ἀττικὴν εὗρε τοὺς Ἀθηναίους,
ἀλλ' ἔν τε Σαλαμῖνι τοὺς πλείστους ἐπυνθάνετο
εἶναι ἔν τε τῆσι νηυσί, αἱρέει τε ἔρημον τὸ ἄστυ.
ἡ δὲ βασιλέος αἵρεσις ἐς τὴν ὑστέρην τὴν Μαρδονίου ἐπιστρατηίην δεκάμηνος ἐγένετο.

4. Ἐπεὶ δὲ ἐν Ἀθήνησι ἐγένετο ὁ Μαρδόνιος,
πέμπει ἐς Σαλαμῖνα Μουρυχίδην ἄνδρα Ἑλλησπόντιον φέροντα τοὺς αὐτοὺς λόγους τοὺς καὶ
Ἀλέξανδρος ὁ Μακεδὼν τοῖσι Ἀθηναίοισι διεπόρθμευσε. ταῦτα δὲ τὸ δεύτερον ἀπέστελλε
προέχων μὲν τῶν Ἀθηναίων οὐ φιλίας γνώμας,
ἐλπίζων δὲ σφέας ὑπήσειν τῆς ἀγνωμοσύνης, ὡς
δοριαλώτου ἐούσης τῆς Ἀττικῆς χώρης καὶ ἐούσης
ὑπ' ἑωυτῷ.

5. Τούτων μὲν εἵνεκα ἀπέπεμψε Μουρυχίδην
ἐς Σαλαμῖνα, ὁ δὲ ἀπικόμενος ἐπὶ τὴν βουλὴν
ἔλεγε τὰ παρὰ Μαρδονίου. τῶν δὲ βουλευτέων
Λυκίδης εἶπε γνώμην ὡς ἐδόκεε ἄμεινον εἶναι δε-
ξαμένους τὸν λόγον, τόν σφι Μουρυχίδης προφέρει,
ἐξενεῖκαι ἐς τὸν δῆμον. ὁ μὲν δὴ ταύτην τὴν
γνώμην ἀπεφαίνετο, εἴτε δὴ δεδεγμένος χρήματα
παρὰ Μαρδονίου, εἴτε καὶ ταῦτά οἱ ἑάνδανε·
Ἀθηναῖοι δὲ αὐτίκα δεινὸν ποιησάμενοι οἵ τε ἐκ
τῆς βουλῆς καὶ οἱ ἔξωθεν ὡς ἐπύθοντο, περι-

itself; and after that, with your partisans to aid, you will easily subdue those who are your adversaries."

3. Such was their counsel, but he would not follow it; rather he was imbued with a wondrous desire to take Athens once more; this was partly of mere perversity, and partly because he thought to signify to the king at Sardis by a line of beacons across the islands that he held Athens. Yet on his coming to Attica he found the Athenians no more there than before, but, as he learnt, the most of them were on shipboard at Salamis; and he took the city, but no men therein. There were ten months between the king's taking of the place and the later invasion of Mardonius.

4. When Mardonius came to Athens, he sent to Salamis one Murychides, a man of the Hellespont, bearing the same offer as Alexander the Macedonian had ferried across to the Athenians. He sent this the second time because, albeit he knew already the Athenians' unfriendly purpose, he expected that they would abate their stiff-neckedness now that Attica was the captive of his spear and lay at his mercy.

5. For this reason he sent Murychides to Salamis, who came before the council and told them Mardonius' message. Then Lycidas, one of the councillors, gave it for his opinion that it seemed to him best to receive the offer brought to them by Murychides and lay it before the people. This was the opinion which he declared, either because he had been bribed by Mardonius, or because the plan pleased him; but the Athenians in the council were very wroth, and so too when they heard of it were they that were outside; and they made a ring

στάντες Λυκίδην κατέλευσαν βάλλοντες, τὸν δὲ
Ἑλλησπόντιον Μουρυχίδην ἀπέπεμψαν ἀσινέα.
γενομένου δὲ θορύβου ἐν τῇ Σαλαμῖνι περὶ τὸν
Λυκίδην, πυνθάνονται τὸ γινόμενον αἱ γυναῖκες
τῶν Ἀθηναίων, διακελευσαμένη δὲ γυνὴ γυναικὶ
καὶ παραλαβοῦσα ἐπὶ τὴν Λυκίδεω οἰκίην ἤισαν
αὐτοκελέες, καὶ κατὰ μὲν ἔλευσαν αὐτοῦ τὴν
γυναῖκα κατὰ δὲ τὰ τέκνα.

6. Ἐς δὲ τὴν Σαλαμῖνα διέβησαν οἱ Ἀθηναῖοι
ὧδε. ἕως μὲν προσεδέκοντο ἐκ τῆς Πελοποννήσου
στρατὸν ἥξειν τιμωρήσοντά σφι, οἱ δὲ ἔμενον ἐν
τῇ Ἀττικῇ· ἐπεὶ δὲ οἱ μὲν μακρότερα καὶ σχολαί-
τερα ἐποίεον, ὁ δὲ ἐπιὼν καὶ δὴ ἐν τῇ Βοιωτίῃ
ἐλέγετο εἶναι, οὕτω δὴ ὑπεξεκομίσαντό τε πάντα
καὶ αὐτοὶ διέβησαν ἐς Σαλαμῖνα, ἐς Λακεδαί-
μονά τε ἔπεμπον ἀγγέλους ἅμα μὲν μεμψομένους
τοῖσι Λακεδαιμονίοισι ὅτι περιεῖδον ἐμβαλόντα
τὸν βάρβαρον ἐς τὴν Ἀττικὴν ἀλλ' οὐ μετὰ
σφέων ἠντίασαν ἐς τὴν Βοιωτίην, ἅμα δὲ ὑπομνή-
σοντας ὅσα σφι ὑπέσχετο ὁ Πέρσης μεταβαλοῦσι
δώσειν, προεῖπαί τε ὅτι εἰ μὴ ἀμυνεῦσι Ἀθηναίοισι, ὡς καὶ αὐτοί τινα ἀλεωρὴν εὑρήσονται.

7. Οἱ γὰρ δὴ Λακεδαιμόνιοι ὅρταζόν τε τοῦτον
τὸν χρόνον καί σφι ἦν Ὑακίνθια, περὶ πλείστου
δ' ἦγον τὰ τοῦ θεοῦ πορσύνειν· ἅμα δὲ τὸ τεῖχός
σφι, τὸ ἐν τῷ Ἰσθμῷ ἐτείχεον, καὶ ἤδη ἐπάλξις
ἐλάμβανε. ὡς δὲ ἀπίκοντο ἐς τὴν Λακεδαίμονα
οἱ ἄγγελοι οἱ ἀπ' Ἀθηνέων, ἅμα ἀγόμενοι ἔκ τε
Μεγάρων ἀγγέλους καὶ ἐκ Πλαταιέων, ἔλεγον

round Lycidas and stoned him to death. But they suffered Murychides the Hellespontian to depart unharmed. There was much noise at Salamis over the business of Lycidas; and when the Athenian women learnt what was afoot, one calling to another and bidding her follow, they went of their own motion to the house of Lycidas, and stoned to death his wife and his children.

6. Now this was how the Athenians had passed over to Salamis. As long as they expected that the Peloponnesian army would come to their aid, so long they abode in Attica. But when the Peloponnesians were ever longer and slower in action, and the invader was said to be already in Boeotia, they did then convey all their goods out of harm's way and themselves crossed over to Salamis; and they sent envoys to Lacedaemon, who should upbraid the Lacedaemonians for suffering the foreigner to invade Attica and not meeting him in Boeotia with the Athenians to aid; and should bid the Lacedaemonians withal remember what promises the Persian had made to Athens if she would change sides, and warn them that the Athenians would devise some succour for themselves if the Lacedaemonians sent them no help.

7. For the Lacedaemonians were at this time holiday-making, keeping the festival of Hyacinthus,[1] and their chiefest care was to give the god his due; moreover, the wall that they were building on the Isthmus was by now even getting its battlements. When the Athenian envoys were arrived at Lacedaemon, bringing with them envoys from Megara

---

[1] A festival said to be of pre-Dorian origin, commemorating the killing of Hyacinthus by Apollo.

τάδε ἐπελθόντες ἐπὶ τοὺς ἐφόρους. "Ἔπεμψαν ἡμέας Ἀθηναῖοι λέγοντες ὅτι ἡμῖν βασιλεὺς ὁ Μῆδων τοῦτο μὲν τὴν χώρην ἀποδιδοῖ, τοῦτο δὲ συμμάχους ἐθέλει ἐπ' ἴσῃ τε καὶ ὁμοίῃ ποιήσασθαι ἄνευ τε δόλου καὶ ἀπάτης, ἐθέλει δὲ καὶ ἄλλην χώρην πρὸς τῇ ἡμετέρῃ διδόναι, τὴν ἂν αὐτοὶ ἑλώμεθα. ἡμεῖς δὲ Δία τε Ἑλλήνιον αἰδεσθέντες καὶ τὴν Ἑλλάδα δεινὸν ποιεύμενοι προδοῦναι οὐ καταινέσαμεν ἀλλ' ἀπειπάμεθα, καίπερ ἀδικεόμενοι ὑπ' Ἑλλήνων καὶ καταπροδιδόμενοι, ἐπιστάμενοί τε ὅτι κερδαλεώτερον ἐστὶ ὁμολογέειν τῷ Πέρσῃ μᾶλλον ἤ περ πολεμέειν· οὐ μὲν οὐδὲ ὁμολογήσομεν ἑκόντες εἶναι. καὶ τὸ μὲν ἀπ' ἡμέων οὕτω ἀκίβδηλον νέμεται ἐπὶ τοὺς Ἕλληνας· ὑμεῖς δὲ ἐς πᾶσαν ἀρρωδίην τότε ἀπικόμενοι μὴ ὁμολογήσωμεν τῷ Πέρσῃ, ἐπείτε ἐξεμάθετε τὸ ἡμέτερον φρόνημα σαφέως, ὅτι οὐδαμὰ προδώσομεν τὴν Ἑλλάδα, καὶ διότι τεῖχος ὑμῖν διὰ τοῦ Ἰσθμοῦ ἐλαυνόμενον ἐν τέλεΐ ἐστί, καὶ δὴ λόγον οὐδένα τῶν Ἀθηναίων ποιέεσθε, συνθέμενοί τε ἡμῖν τὸν Πέρσην ἀντιώσεσθαι ἐς τὴν Βοιωτίην προδεδώκατε, περιείδετέ τε προεσβαλόντα ἐς τὴν Ἀττικὴν τὸν βάρβαρον. ἐς μέν νυν τὸ παρεὸν Ἀθηναῖοι ὑμῖν μηνίουσι· οὐ γὰρ ἐποιήσατε ἐπιτηδέως. νῦν δὲ ὅτι τάχος στρατιὴν ἅμα ἡμῖν ἐκέλευσαν ὑμέας ἐκπέμπειν, ὡς ἂν τὸν βάρβαρον δεκώμεθα ἐν τῇ Ἀττικῇ· ἐπειδὴ γὰρ ἡμάρτομεν τῆς Βοιωτίης, τῆς γε ἡμετέρης ἐπιτηδεότατον ἐστὶ μαχέσασθαι τὸ Θριάσιον πεδίον."

8. Ὡς δὲ ἄρα ἤκουσαν οἱ ἔφοροι ταῦτα, ἀνεβάλλοντο ἐς τὴν ὑστεραίην ὑποκρίνασθαι, τῇ δὲ

and Plataeae, they came before the ephors and said:
"The Athenians have sent us with this message:
The king of the Medes is ready to give us back our
country, and to make us his confederates, equal in
right and standing, in all honour and honesty, and
to give us withal whatever land we ourselves may
choose besides our own. But we, for that we would
not sin against Zeus the god of Hellas, and think
it shame to betray Hellas, have not consented, but
refused, and this though the Greeks are dealing
with us wrongfully and betraying us to our hurt,
and though we know that it is rather for our
advantage to make terms with the Persian than to
wage war with him; yet we will not make terms
with him, of our own free will. Thus for our part
we act honestly by the Greeks; but what of you,
who once were in great dread lest we should make
terms with the Persian? Because now you have clear
knowledge of our temper and are sure that we will
never betray Hellas, and because the wall that you
are building across the Isthmus is well-nigh finished,
to-day you take no account of the Athenians, but
have deserted us for all your promises that you
would withstand the Persian in Boeotia, and have
suffered the foreigner to march into Attica. For
the nonce, then, the Athenians are angry with you;
for that which you have done beseems you ill. But
now they pray you to send with us an army with all
speed, that we may await the foreigner's onset in
Attica; for since we have lost Boeotia, in our own
land the fittest battle-ground is the Thriasian
plain."

8. When the ephors, it would seem, heard that,
they delayed answering till the next day, and again

ὑστεραίη ἐς τὴν ἑτέρην· τοῦτο καὶ ἐπὶ δέκα ἡμέρας
ἐποίεον, ἐξ ἡμέρης ἐς ἡμέρην ἀναβαλλόμενοι. ἐν
δὲ τούτῳ τῷ χρόνῳ τὸν Ἰσθμὸν ἐτείχεον σπουδὴν
ἔχοντες πολλὴν πάντες Πελοποννήσιοι, καί σφι
ἦν πρὸς τέλεϊ. οὐδ' ἔχω εἰπεῖν τὸ αἴτιον διότι
ἀπικομένου μὲν Ἀλεξάνδρου τοῦ Μακεδόνος ἐς
Ἀθήνας σπουδὴν μεγάλην ἐποιήσαντο μὴ μηδίσαι
Ἀθηναίους, τότε δὲ ὤρην ἐποιήσαντο οὐδεμίαν,
ἄλλο γε ἢ ὅτι ὁ Ἰσθμός σφι ἐτετείχιστο καὶ
ἐδόκεον Ἀθηναίων ἔτι δεῖσθαι οὐδέν· ὅτε δὲ
Ἀλέξανδρος ἀπίκετο ἐς τὴν Ἀττικήν, οὔκω ἀπε-
τετείχιστο, ἐργάζοντο δὲ μεγάλως καταρρωδηκότες
τοὺς Πέρσας.

9. Τέλος δὲ τῆς τε ὑποκρίσιος καὶ ἐξόδου τῶν
Σπαρτιητέων ἐγένετο τρόπος τοιόσδε. τῇ προ-
τεραίῃ τῆς ὑστάτης καταστάσιος μελλούσης
ἔσεσθαι Χίλεος ἀνὴρ Τεγεήτης, δυνάμενος ἐν Λα-
κεδαίμονι μέγιστον ξείνων, τῶν ἐφόρων ἐπύθετο
πάντα λόγον τὸν δὴ οἱ Ἀθηναῖοι ἔλεγον· ἀκούσας δὲ ὁ Χίλεος ἔλεγε ἄρα σφι τάδε. "Οὕτω
ἔχει, ἄνδρες ἔφοροι· Ἀθηναίων ἡμῖν ἐόντων μὴ
ἀρθμίων τῷ δὲ βαρβάρῳ συμμάχων, καίπερ
τείχεος διὰ τοῦ Ἰσθμοῦ ἐληλαμένου καρτεροῦ,
μεγάλαι κλισιάδες ἀναπεπτέαται ἐς τὴν Πελοπόννησον τῷ Πέρσῃ. ἀλλ' ἐσακούσατε, πρίν τι
ἄλλο Ἀθηναίοισι δόξαι σφάλμα φέρον τῇ Ἑλλάδι."

10. Ὁ μέν σφι ταῦτα συνεβούλευε· οἱ δὲ
φρενὶ λαβόντες τὸν λόγον αὐτίκα, φράσαντες
οὐδὲν τοῖσι ἀγγέλοισι τοῖσι ἀπιγμένοισι ἀπὸ τῶν
πολίων, νυκτὸς ἔτι ἐκπέμπουσι πεντακισχιλίους
Σπαρτιητέων καὶ ἑπτὰ περὶ ἕκαστον τάξαντες

till the day after; and this they did for ten days, putting off from day to day. In the meantime all the Peloponnesians were fortifying the Isthmus with might and main, and they had the work well-nigh done. Nor can I say why it was that when Alexander the Macedonian came to Athens[1] the Lacedaemonians were urgent that the Athenians should not take the Persian part, yet now made no account of that; except it was that now they had the Isthmus fortified and thought they had no more need of the Athenians, whereas when Alexander came to Attica their wall was not yet built, and they were working thereat in great fear of the Persians.

9. But the manner of their answering at last and sending the Spartan army was this: On the day before that hearing which should have been the last, Chileüs, a man of Tegea, who had more authority with the Lacedaemonians than any other of their guests, learnt from the ephors all that the Athenians had said; and having heard it he said, as the tale goes, to the ephors, "Sirs, this is how the matter stands: if the Athenians be our enemies and the foreigner's allies, then though you drive a strong wall across the Isthmus the Persian has an effectual door opened for passage into the Peloponnese. Nay, hearken to them, ere the Athenians take some new resolve that will bring calamity to Hellas."

10. This was the counsel he gave the ephors, who straightway took it to heart; saying no word to the envoys who were come from the cities, they bade march before dawn of day five thousand Spartans, with seven helots appointed to attend each of them;

[1] cp. viii. 135.

τῶν εἱλώτων, Παυσανίῃ τῷ Κλεομβρότου ἐπιτά-
ξαντες ἐξάγειν. ἐγίνετο μὲν ἡ ἡγεμονίη Πλει-
στάρχου τοῦ Λεωνίδεω· ἀλλ' ὃ μὲν ἦν ἔτι παῖς,
ὃ δὲ τούτου ἐπίτροπός τε καὶ ἀνεψιός. Κλεόμβροτος γὰρ ὁ Παυσανίεω μὲν πατὴρ Ἀναξανδρί-
δεω δὲ παῖς οὐκέτι περιῆν, ἀλλ' ἀπαγαγὼν ἐκ
τοῦ Ἰσθμοῦ τὴν στρατιὴν τὴν τὸ τεῖχος δείμασαν
μετὰ ταῦτα οὐ πολλὸν χρόνον τινὰ βιοὺς ἀπέθανε.
ἀπῆγε δὲ τὴν στρατιὴν ὁ Κλεόμβροτος ἐκ τοῦ
Ἰσθμοῦ διὰ τόδε· θυομένῳ οἱ ἐπὶ τῷ Πέρσῃ ὁ
ἥλιος ἀμαυρώθη ἐν τῷ οὐρανῷ. προσαιρέεται δὲ
ἑωυτῷ Παυσανίης Εὐρυάνακτα τὸν Δωριέος, ἄνδρα
οἰκίης ἐόντα τῆς αὐτῆς.

11. Οἳ μὲν δὴ σὺν Παυσανίῃ ἐξεληλύθεσαν
ἔξω Σπάρτης· οἱ δὲ ἄγγελοι, ὡς ἡμέρη ἐγεγόνεε,
οὐδὲν εἰδότες περὶ τῆς ἐξόδου ἐπῆλθον ἐπὶ τοὺς
ἐφόρους, ἐν νόῳ δὴ ἔχοντες ἀπαλλάσσεσθαι καὶ
αὐτοὶ ἐπὶ τὴν ἑωυτοῦ ἕκαστος· ἐπελθόντες δὲ
ἔλεγον τάδε. "Ὑμεῖς μὲν, ὦ Λακεδαιμόνιοι αὐτοῦ
τῇδε μένοντες Ὑακίνθιά τε ἄγετε καὶ παίζετε,
καταπροδόντες τοὺς συμμάχους· Ἀθηναῖοι δὲ ὡς
ἀδικεόμενοι ὑπὸ ὑμέων χήτεϊ τε συμμάχων κατα-
λύσονται τῷ Πέρσῃ οὕτω ὅκως ἂν δύνωνται·
καταλυσάμενοι δέ, δῆλα γὰρ ὅτι σύμμαχοι βασιλέος γινόμεθα, συστρατευσόμεθα ἐπ' ἣν ἂν ἐκεῖνοι
ἐξηγέωνται. ὑμεῖς δὲ τὸ ἐνθεῦτεν μαθήσεσθε
ὁκοῖον ἄν τι ὑμῖν ἐξ αὐτοῦ ἐκβαίνῃ." ταῦτα λεγόντων τῶν ἀγγέλων, οἱ ἔφοροι εἶπαν ἐπ' ὅρκου
καὶ δὴ δοκέειν εἶναι ἐν Ὀρεσθείῳ στείχοντας ἐπὶ

---

[1] His cousin; Euryanax was son of Dorieus, who was a
brother of Pausanias' father Cleombrotus.

and they gave the command to Pausanias son of
Cleombrotus. The leader's place belonged of right
to Pleistarchus son of Leonidas; but he was yet a
boy, and Pausanias his guardian and cousin. For
Cleombrotus, Pausanias' father and Anaxandrides'
son, was no longer living; after he led away from
the Isthmus the army which had built the wall,
he lived but a little while ere his death. The
reason of Cleombrotus' leading his army away
from the Isthmus was that while he was offering
sacrifice for victory over the Persian the sun was
darkened in the heavens. Pausanias chose as his
colleague a man of the same family,[1] Euryanax son
of Dorieus.

11. So Pausanias' army had marched away from
Sparta; but as soon as it was day, the envoys came
before the ephors, having no knowledge of the
expedition, and being minded themselves too to
depart each one to his own place; and when they
were come, "You Lacedaemonians," they said,
"abide still where you are, keeping your Hyacinthia
and disporting yourselves, leaving your allies deserted; the Athenians, for the wrong that you do
them and for lack of allies, will make their peace
with the Persian as best they can, and thereafter,
seeing that plainly we shall be the king's allies, we
will march with him against whatever land his men
lead us. Then will you learn what the issue of this
matter shall be for you." Thus spoke the envoys;
and the ephors swore to them that they believed
their army to be even now at Orestheum,[2] marching

___

[2] Other references place Orestheum N.W. of Sparta, therefore hardly on the direct route to the Isthmus.

τοὺς ξείνους. ξείνους γὰρ ἐκάλεον τοὺς βαρβάρους. οἳ δὲ ὡς οὐκ εἰδότες ἐπειρώτων τὸ λεγό-
μενον, ἐπειρόμενοι δὲ ἐξέμαθον πᾶν τὸ ἐόν, ὥστε
ἐν θώματι γενόμενοι ἐπορεύοντο τὴν ταχίστην
διώκοντες· σὺν δέ σφι τῶν περιοίκων Λακεδαιμονίων λογάδες πεντακισχίλιοι ὁπλῖται τὠυτὸ τοῦτο
ἐποίεον.

12. Οἳ μὲν δὴ ἐς τὸν Ἰσθμὸν ἠπείγοντο· Ἀργεῖοι
δὲ ἐπείτε τάχιστα ἐπύθοντο τοὺς μετὰ Παυσανίεω
ἐξεληλυθότας ἐκ Σπάρτης, πέμπουσι κήρυκα τῶν
ἡμεροδρόμων ἀνευρόντες τὸν ἄριστον ἐς τὴν
Ἀττικήν, πρότερον αὐτοὶ Μαρδονίῳ ὑποδεξάμενοι
σχήσειν τὸν Σπαρτιήτην μὴ ἐξιέναι· ὃς ἐπείτε
ἀπίκετο ἐς τὰς Ἀθήνας ἔλεγε τάδε. "Μαρδόνιε,
ἔπεμψάν με Ἀργεῖοι φράσοντά τοι ὅτι ἐκ Λακεδαίμονος ἐξελήλυθε ἡ νεότης, καὶ ὡς οὐ δυνατοὶ
αὐτὴν ἔχειν εἰσὶ Ἀργεῖοι μὴ οὐκ ἐξιέναι. πρὸς
ταῦτα τύγχανε εὖ βουλευόμενος."

13. Ὁ μὲν δὴ εἴπας ταῦτα ἀπαλλάσσετο
ὀπίσω, Μαρδόνιος δὲ οὐδαμῶς ἔτι πρόθυμος ἦν
μένειν ἐν τῇ Ἀττικῇ, ὡς ἤκουσε ταῦτα. πρὶν
μέν νυν ἢ πυθέσθαι ἀνεκώχευε, θέλων εἰδέναι τὸ
παρ' Ἀθηναίων, ὁκοῖόν τι ποιήσουσι, καὶ οὔτε
ἐπήμαινε οὔτε ἐσίνετο γῆν τὴν Ἀττικήν, ἐλπίζων
διὰ παντὸς τοῦ χρόνου ὁμολογήσειν σφέας· ἐπεὶ
δὲ οὐκ ἔπειθε, πυθόμενος πάντα λόγον, πρὶν ἢ
τοὺς μετὰ Παυσανίεω ἐς τὸν Ἰσθμὸν ἐσβαλεῖν,
ὑπεξεχώρεε ἐμπρήσας τε τὰς Ἀθήνας, καὶ εἴ κού
τι ὀρθὸν ἦν τῶν τειχέων ἢ τῶν οἰκημάτων ἢ τῶν
ἱρῶν, πάντα καταβαλὼν καὶ συγχώσας. ἐξήλαυνε

---

[1] Inhabitants of the country districts of Laconia, not
enjoying the full privileges of Spartans.

against the "strangers," as they called the foreigners.
Having no knowledge of this, the envoys questioned
them further as to what the tale might mean, and
thereby learnt the whole truth; whereat they marvelled, and took the road with all speed after the
army; and with them went likewise five thousand
chosen men-at-arms of the Lacedaemonian countrymen.[1]

12. So they made haste to reach the Isthmus.
But the Argives had already promised Mardonius
that they would hinder the Spartan from going out
to war; and as soon as they were informed that
Pausanias and his army had departed from Sparta,
they sent as their herald to Attica the swiftest runner
of long distances that they could find; who, when
he came to Athens, spoke on this wise to Mardonius:
"I am sent by the Argives to tell you that the
young men have gone out from Lacedaemon to war,
and that the Argives cannot stay them from so
doing; wherefore, may fortune grant you good
counsel."

13. So spoke the herald, and departed back again;
and when Mardonius heard that, he was no longer
desirous of remaining in Attica. Before he had word
of it, he had held his hand, desiring to know the
Athenians' plan and what they would do, and
neither harmed nor harried the land of Attica,
for he still ever supposed that they would make
terms with him; but when he could not move them,
and learnt all the truth of the matter, he drew off
from before Pausanias' army ere it entered the
Isthmus; but first he burnt Athens, and utterly
overthrew and demolished whatever wall or house
or temple was left standing. The reason of his

δὲ τῶνδε εἵνεκεν, ὅτι οὔτε ἱππασίμη ἡ χώρη ἦν ἡ
Ἀττική, εἴ τε νικῷτο συμβαλών, ἀπάλλαξις οὐκ
ἦν ὅτι μὴ κατὰ στεινόν, ὥστε ὀλίγους σφέας
ἀνθρώπους ἴσχειν. ἐβουλεύετο ὦν ἐπαναχωρήσας
ἐς τὰς Θήβας συμβαλεῖν πρὸς πόλι τε φιλίη καὶ
χώρη ἱππασίμῳ.

14. Μαρδόνιος μὲν δὴ ὑπεξεχώρεε, ἤδη δὲ ἐν
τῇ ὁδῷ ἐόντι αὐτῷ ἦλθε ἀγγελίη πρόδρομον
ἄλλην στρατιὴν ἥκειν ἐς Μέγαρα, Λακεδαιμονίων
χιλίους· πυθόμενος δὲ ταῦτα ἐβουλεύετο θέλων
εἴ κως τούτους πρῶτον ἕλοι. ὑποστρέψας δὲ
τὴν στρατιὴν ἦγε ἐπὶ τὰ Μέγαρα· ἡ δὲ ἵππος
προελθοῦσα κατιππάσατο χώρην τὴν Μεγαρίδα.
ἐς ταύτην δὴ ἑκαστάτω τῆς Εὐρώπης τὸ πρὸς
ἡλίου δύνοντος ἡ Περσικὴ αὕτη στρατιὴ ἀπίκετο.

15. Μετὰ δὲ ταῦτα Μαρδονίῳ ἦλθε ἀγγελίη
ὡς ἁλέες εἴησαν οἱ Ἕλληνες ἐν τῷ Ἰσθμῷ. οὕτω
δὴ ὀπίσω ἐπορεύετο διὰ Δεκελέης· οἱ γὰρ βοιω-
τάρχαι μετεπέμψαντο τοὺς προσχώρους τῶν
Ἀσωπίων, οὗτοι δὲ αὐτῷ τὴν ὁδὸν ἡγέοντο ἐς
Σφενδαλέας, ἐνθεῦτεν δὲ ἐς Τάναγραν· ἐν Τανάγρῃ
δὲ νύκτα ἐναυλισάμενος, καὶ τραπόμενος τῇ ὑστεραίῃ ἐς Σκῶλον ἐν γῇ τῇ Θηβαίων ἦν. ἐνθαῦτα
δὲ τῶν Θηβαίων καίπερ μηδιζόντων ἔκειρε τοὺς
χώρους, οὔτι κατὰ ἔχθος αὐτῶν ἀλλ' ὑπ' ἀναγκαίης
μεγάλης ἐχόμενος ἔρυμά τε τῷ στρατῷ ποιήσασθαι, καὶ ἢν συμβαλόντι οἱ μὴ ἐκβαίνῃ ὁκοῖόν
τι ἐθέλοι, κρησφύγετον τοῦτο ἐποιέετο. παρῆκε
δὲ αὐτοῦ τὸ στρατόπεδον ἀρξάμενον ἀπὸ Ἐρυθρέων

marching away was, that Attica was no country for
horsemen's work, and if he should be worsted in
a battle there was no way of retreat save one so
narrow that a few men could stay his passage.[1]
Wherefore it was his plan to retreat to Thebes and
do battle where he had a friendly city at his back
and ground fitted for horsemen.

14. So Mardonius drew his men off, and when he
had now set forth on his road there came a message
that over and above the rest an advance guard of
a thousand Lacedaemonians was arrived at Megara;
at which hearing he took counsel how he might first
make an end of these; and he turned about and led
his army against Megara, his horse going first and
overrunning the lands of that city. That was the
most westerly place in Europe to which this Persian
armament attained.

15. Presently there came a message to Mardonius
that the Greeks were gathered together on the
Isthmus. Thereupon he marched back again
through Decelea; for the rulers of Boeotia sent
for those of the Asopus country that dwelt near,
and these guided him to Sphendalae and thence to
Tanagra, where he camped for the night; and on
the next day he turned thence to Scolus, where he
was in Theban territory. There he laid waste the
lands of the Thebans, though they took the Persian
part; not for any ill-will that he bore them, but
because sheer necessity drove him to make a strong
place for his army, and to have this for a refuge if
the fortune of battle were other than he desired.
His army covered the ground from Erythrae past

---

[1] He would have to retreat into Boeotia by way of the
pass over Cithaeron.

παρὰ Ὑσιάς, κατέτεινε δὲ ἐς τὴν Πλαταιίδα γῆν,
παρὰ τὸν Ἀσωπὸν ποταμὸν τεταγμένον. οὐ
μέντοι τό γε τεῖχος τοσοῦτο ἐποιέετο, ἀλλ᾽ ὡς
ἐπὶ δέκα σταδίους μάλιστά κῃ μέτωπον ἕκαστον.

16. Ἐχόντων δὲ τὸν πόνον τοῦτον τῶν βαρβάρων, Ἀτταγῖνος ὁ Φρύνωνος ἀνὴρ Θηβαῖος
παρασκευασάμενος μεγάλως ἐκάλεε ἐπὶ ξείνια
αὐτόν τε Μαρδόνιον καὶ πεντήκοντα Περσέων
τοὺς λογιμωτάτους, κληθέντες δὲ οὗτοι εἵποντο·
ἦν δὲ τὸ δεῖπνον ποιεύμενον ἐν Θήβῃσι. τάδε
δὲ ἤδη τὰ ἐπίλοιπα ἤκουον Θερσάνδρου ἀνδρὸς
μὲν Ὀρχομενίου, λογίμου δὲ ἐς τὰ πρῶτα ἐν
Ὀρχομενῷ. ἔφη δὲ ὁ Θέρσανδρος κληθῆναι καὶ
αὐτὸς ὑπὸ Ἀτταγίνου ἐπὶ τὸ δεῖπνον τοῦτο, κληθῆναι δὲ καὶ Θηβαίων ἄνδρας πεντήκοντα, καί
σφεων οὐ χωρὶς ἑκατέρους κλῖναι, ἀλλὰ Πέρσην
τε καὶ Θηβαῖον ἐν κλίνῃ ἑκάστῃ. ὡς δὲ ἀπὸ
δείπνου ἦσαν, διαπινόντων τὸν Πέρσην τὸν ὁμό-
κλινον Ἑλλάδα γλῶσσαν ἱέντα εἰρέσθαι αὐτὸν
ὁποδαπός ἐστι, αὐτὸς δὲ ὑποκρίνασθαι ὡς εἴη
Ὀρχομένιος. τὸν δὲ εἰπεῖν "Ἐπεὶ νῦν ὁμοτρά-
πεζός τέ μοι καὶ ὁμόσπονδος ἐγένεο, μνημόσυνά
τοι γνώμης τῆς ἐμῆς καταλιπέσθαι θέλω, ἵνα καὶ
προειδὼς αὐτὸς περὶ σεωυτοῦ βουλεύεσθαι ἔχῃς
τὰ συμφέροντα. ὁρᾷς τούτους τοὺς δαινυμένους
Πέρσας καὶ τὸν στρατὸν τὸν ἐλίπομεν ἐπὶ τῷ
ποταμῷ στρατοπεδευόμενον· τούτων πάντων
ὄψεαι ὀλίγου τινὸς χρόνου διελθόντος ὀλίγους
τινὰς τοὺς περιγενομένους." ταῦτα ἅμα τε τὸν
Πέρσην λέγειν καὶ μετιέναι πολλὰ τῶν δακρύων.
αὐτὸς δὲ θωμάσας τὸν λόγον εἰπεῖν πρὸς αὐτὸν
"Οὐκῶν Μαρδονίῳ τε ταῦτα χρεόν ἐστι λέγειν

Hysiae and reached unto the lands of Plataeae, where it lay ranked by the Asopus river. I say not that the walled camp which he made was so great; each side of it was of a length of about ten furlongs.

16. While the foreigners were employed about this work, Attaginus son of Phrynon, a Theban, made great preparation and invited Mardonius with fifty who were the most notable of the Persians to be his guests at a banquet. They came as they were bidden; the dinner was given at Thebes. Now here follows the end of that matter, which was told me by Thersandrus of Orchomenus, one of the most notable men of that place. Thersandrus too (he said) was bidden to this dinner, and fifty Thebans besides; and Attaginus made them sit, not each man by himself, but on each couch a Persian and a Theban together. Now after dinner while they drank one with another, the Persian that sat with him asked Thersandrus in the Greek tongue of what country he was; and Thersandrus answered that he was of Orchomenus. Then said the Persian: "Since now you have eaten at the board with me and drunk with me thereafter, I would fain leave some record of my thought, that you yourself may have such knowledge as to take fitting counsel for your safety. See you these Persians at the banquet, and that host which we left encamped by the river side? of all these in a little while you shall see but a little remnant left alive"; and as he said this, the Persian wept bitterly. Marvelling at this saying, Thersandrus answered: "Must you not then tell this to Mardonius

καὶ τοῖσι μετ' ἐκεῖνον ἐν αἴνῃ ἐοῦσι Περσέων;"
τὸν δὲ μετὰ ταῦτα εἰπεῖν "Ξεῖνε, ὅ τι δεῖ γενέσθαι
ἐκ τοῦ θεοῦ ἀμήχανον ἀποτρέψαι ἀνθρώπῳ· οὐδὲ
γὰρ πιστὰ λέγουσι ἐθέλει πείθεσθαι οὐδείς.
ταῦτα δὲ Περσέων συχνοὶ ἐπιστάμενοι ἑπόμεθα
ἀναγκαίῃ ἐνδεδεμένοι, ἐχθίστη δὲ ὀδύνη ἐστὶ τῶν
ἐν ἀνθρώποισι αὕτη, πολλὰ φρονέοντα μηδενὸς
κρατέειν." ταῦτα μὲν Ὀρχομενίου Θερσάνδρου
ἤκουον, καὶ τάδε πρὸς τούτοισι, ὡς αὐτὸς αὐτίκα
λέγοι ταῦτα πρὸς ἀνθρώπους πρότερον ἢ γενέσθαι
ἐν Πλαταιῆσι τὴν μάχην.

17. Μαρδονίου δὲ ἐν τῇ Βοιωτίῃ στρατοπεδευο-
μένου οἱ μὲν ἄλλοι παρείχοντο ἅπαντες στρατιὴν
καὶ συνεσέβαλον ἐς Ἀθήνας, ὅσοι περ ἐμήδιζον
Ἑλλήνων τῶν ταύτῃ οἰκημένων, μοῦνοι δὲ Φωκέες
οὐ συνεσέβαλον (ἐμήδιζον γὰρ δὴ σφόδρα καὶ
οὗτοι) οὐκ ἑκόντες ἀλλ' ὑπ' ἀναγκαίης. ἡμέρῃσι
δὲ οὐ πολλῇσι μετὰ τὴν ἄπιξιν τὴν ἐς Θήβας
ὕστερον ἦλθον αὐτῶν ὁπλῖται χίλιοι, ἦγε δὲ
αὐτοὺς Ἁρμοκύδης ἀνὴρ τῶν ἀστῶν δοκιμώτατος.
ἐπεὶ δὲ ἀπίκατο καὶ οὗτοι ἐς Θήβας, πέμψας ὁ
Μαρδόνιος ἱππέας ἐκέλευσε σφέας ἐπ' ἑωυτῶν ἐν
τῷ πεδίῳ ἵζεσθαι. ἐπεὶ δὲ ἐποίησαν ταῦτα,
αὐτίκα παρῆν ἵππος ἡ ἅπασα. μετὰ δὲ ταῦτα
διεξῆλθε μὲν διὰ τοῦ στρατοπέδου τοῦ Ἑλληνικοῦ
τοῦ μετὰ Μήδων ἐόντος φήμη ὡς κατακοντιεῖ
σφεας, διεξῆλθε δὲ δι' αὐτῶν Φωκέων τὠυτὸ
τοῦτο. ἔνθα δή σφι ὁ στρατηγὸς Ἁρμοκύδης
παραίνεε λέγων τοιάδε. "Ὦ Φωκέες, πρόδηλα
γὰρ ὅτι ἡμέας οὗτοι οἱ ἄνθρωποι μέλλουσι προ-
όπτῳ θανάτῳ δώσειν, διαβεβλημένους ὑπὸ Θεσσαλῶν, ὡς ἐγὼ εἰκάζω· νῦν ἄνδρα πάντα τινὰ

and those honourable Persians that are with him?"
"Sir," said the Persian, "that which heaven wills
to send no man can turn aside; for even truth finds
none to believe it. What I have said is known to
many of us Persians; but we follow, in the bonds
of necessity. And it is the hatefulest of all human
sorrows to have much knowledge and no power."
This tale I heard from Thersandrus of Orchomenus;
who said to me, moreover, that he had straightway
told it to others before the fight of Plataeae.

17. So Mardonius was making his encampment in
Boeotia; all the Greeks of that region who took the
Persian part furnished fighting men, and they joined
with him in his attack upon Athens, except only
the Phocians: as to taking the Persian part, that
they did in good sooth, albeit not willingly but of
necessity. But when a few days were past after the
Persians' coming to Thebes, there came a thousand
Phocian men-at-arms, led by Harmocydes, the most
notable of their countrymen. These also being
arrived at Thebes, Mardonius sent horsemen and
bade the Phocians take their station on the plain
by themselves. When they had so done, straightway appeared the whole of the Persian cavalry;
and presently it was bruited about through all the
Greek army that was with Mardonius, and likewise
among the Phocians themselves, that Mardonius
would shoot them to death. Then their general
Harmocydes exhorted them: "Men of Phocis," he
said, "seeing it is plain that death at these fellows'
hands stares us in the face (we being, as I surmise,
maligned by the Thessalians); now it is meet for

ὑμέων χρεόν ἐστι γενέσθαι ἀγαθόν· κρέσσον γὰρ
ποιεῦντάς τι καὶ ἀμυνομένους τελευτῆσαι τὸν
αἰῶνα ἤ περ παρέχοντας διαφθαρῆναι αἰσχίστῳ
μόρῳ. ἀλλὰ μαθέτω τις αὐτῶν ὅτι ἐόντες βάρβαροι ἐπ᾽ Ἕλλησι ἀνδράσι φόνον ἔρραψαν."

18. Ὁ μὲν ταῦτα παραίνεε· οἱ δὲ ἱππέες
ἐπεί σφεας ἐκυκλώσαντο, ἐπήλαυνον ὡς ἀπο-
λέοντες, καὶ δὴ διετείνοντο τὰ βέλεα ὡς ἀπή-
σοντες, καί κού τις καὶ ἀπῆκε. καὶ οἳ
ἀντίοι ἔστησαν πάντη συστρέψαντες ἑωυτοὺς
καὶ πυκνώσαντες ὡς μάλιστα. ἐνθαῦτα οἱ ἱππόται ὑπέστρεφον καὶ ἀπήλαυνον ὀπίσω. οὐκ
ἔχω δ᾽ ἀτρεκέως εἰπεῖν οὔτε εἰ ἦλθον μὲν ἀπο-
λέοντες τοὺς Φωκέας δεηθέντων Θεσσαλῶν, ἐπεὶ
δὲ ὥρων πρὸς ἀλέξησιν τραπομένους, δείσαντες
μὴ καὶ σφίσι γένηται τρώματα, οὕτω δὴ ἀπήλαυνον ὀπίσω· ὡς γάρ σφι ἐνετείλατο Μαρδόνιος·
οὔτ᾽ εἰ αὐτῶν πειρηθῆναι ἠθέλησε εἴ τι ἀλκῆς
μετέχουσι. ὡς δὲ ὀπίσω ἀπήλασαν οἱ ἱππόται,
πέμψας Μαρδόνιος κήρυκα ἔλεγε τάδε. "Θαρ-
σέετε ὦ Φωκέες· ἄνδρες γὰρ ἐφάνητε ἐόντες ἀγα-
θοί, οὐκ ὡς ἐγὼ ἐπυνθανόμην. καὶ νῦν προθύμως
φέρετε τὸν πόλεμον τοῦτον· εὐεργεσίῃσι γὰρ οὐ
νικήσετε οὔτ᾽ ὦν ἐμὲ οὔτε βασιλέα." τὰ περὶ
Φωκέων μὲν ἐς τοσοῦτο ἐγένετο.

19. Λακεδαιμόνιοι δὲ ὡς ἐς τὸν Ἰσθμὸν ἦλθον,
ἐν τούτῳ ἐστρατοπεδεύοντο. πυνθανόμενοι δὲ
ταῦτα οἱ λοιποὶ Πελοποννήσιοι τοῖσι τὰ ἀμείνω
ἑάνδανε, οἱ δὲ καὶ ὁρῶντες ἐξιόντας Σπαρτιήτας,
οὐκ ἐδικαίευν λείπεσθαι τῆς ἐξόδου Λακεδαιμονίων. ἐκ δὴ ὦν τοῦ Ἰσθμοῦ καλλιερησάντων

every one of you to play the man; for it is better to
end our lives in action and fighting than tamely to
suffer a shameful death. Nay, but we will teach
them that they whose slaying they have devised are
men of Hellas." Thus he exhorted them.

18. But when the horsemen had encircled the
Phocians they rode at them as it were to slay
them, and drew their bows to shoot, and 'tis
like that some did even shoot. The Phocians
fronted them every way, drawing in together and
closing their ranks to the best of their power;
whereat the horsemen wheeled about and rode back
and away. Now I cannot with exactness say if they
came at the Thessalians' desire to slay the Phocians,
but, when they saw the men preparing to defend
themselves, feared lest they themselves should suffer
some hurt, and so rode away back (for such was
Mardonius' command),—or if Mardonius desired to
test the Phocians' mettle. But when the horsemen
had ridden away, Mardonius sent a herald, with this
message: " Men of Phocis, be of good courage; for
you have shown yourselves to be valiant men, and
not as it was reported to me. And now push this
war zealously forward; for you will outdo neither
myself nor the king in the rendering of service." [1]
Thus far went the Phocian business.

19. As for the Lacedaemonians, when they were
come to the Isthmus, they encamped there. When
the rest of the Peloponnesians who chose the better
cause heard that, seeing the Spartans setting forth
to war, they deemed it was not for them to be
behind the Lacedaemonians in so doing. Wherefore
they all marched from the Isthmus (the omens of

---

[1] That is, serve us and we will serve you.

τῶν ἱρῶν ἐπορεύοντο πάντες καὶ ἀπικνέονται ἐς
Ἐλευσῖνα· ποιήσαντες δὲ καὶ ἐνθαῦτα ἱρά, ὥς
σφι ἐκαλλιέρεε, τὸ πρόσω ἐπορεύοντο, Ἀθηναῖοι
δὲ ἅμα αὐτοῖσι, διαβάντες μὲν ἐκ Σαλαμῖνος,
συμμιγέντες δὲ ἐν Ἐλευσῖνι. ὡς δὲ ἄρα ἀπίκοντο
τῆς Βοιωτίης ἐς Ἐρυθράς, ἔμαθόν τε δὴ τοὺς
βαρβάρους ἐπὶ τῷ Ἀσωπῷ στρατοπεδευομένους,
φρασθέντες δὲ τοῦτο ἀντετάσσοντο ἐπὶ τῆς
ὑπωρέης τοῦ Κιθαιρῶνος.

20. Μαρδόνιος δέ, ὡς οὐ κατέβαινον οἱ Ἕλληνες
ἐς τὸ πεδίον, πέμπει ἐς αὐτοὺς πᾶσαν τὴν ἵππον,
τῆς ἱππάρχεε Μασίστιος εὐδοκιμέων παρὰ Πέρσῃσι, τὸν Ἕλληνες Μακίστιον καλέουσι, ἵππον
ἔχων Νησαῖον χρυσοχάλινον καὶ ἄλλως κεκο-
σμημένον καλῶς. ἐνθαῦτα ὡς προσήλασαν οἱ
ἱππόται πρὸς τοὺς Ἕλληνας, προσέβαλλον κατὰ
τέλεα, προσβάλλοντες δὲ κακὰ μεγάλα ἐργάζοντο
καὶ γυναῖκας σφέας ἀπεκάλεον.

21. Κατὰ συντυχίην δὲ Μεγαρέες ἔτυχον ταχθέντες τῇ τε ἐπιμαχώτατον ἦν τοῦ χωρίου
παντός, καὶ πρόσοδος μάλιστα ταύτῃ ἐγίνετο τῇ
ἵππῳ. προσβαλλούσης ὦν τῆς ἵππου οἱ Μεγαρέες πιεζόμενοι ἔπεμπον ἐπὶ τοὺς στρατηγοὺς τῶν
Ἑλλήνων κήρυκα, ἀπικόμενος δὲ ὁ κῆρυξ πρὸς
αὐτοὺς ἔλεγε τάδε. "Μεγαρέες λέγουσι· ἡμεῖς,
ἄνδρες σύμμαχοι, οὐ δυνατοί εἰμεν τὴν Περσέων
ἵππον δέκεσθαι μοῦνοι, ἔχοντες στάσιν ταύτην
ἐς τὴν ἔστημεν ἀρχήν· ἀλλὰ καὶ ἐς τόδε λιπαρίῃ
τε καὶ ἀρετῇ ἀντέχομεν καίπερ πιεζόμενοι. νῦν
τε εἰ μή τινας ἄλλους πέμψετε διαδόχους τῆς
τάξιος, ἴστε ἡμέας ἐκλείψοντας τὴν τάξιν." ὁ
μὲν δή σφι ταῦτα ἀπήγγελλε, Παυσανίης δὲ ἀπε-

sacrifice being favourable) and came to Eleusis ; and when they had offered sacrifice there also and the omens were favourable, they held on their march further, having now the Athenians with them, who had crossed over from Salamis and joined with them at Eleusis. When they came (as it is said) to Erythrae in Boeotia, they learnt that the foreigners were encamped by the Asopus, and taking note of that they arrayed themselves over against the enemy on the lower hills of Cithaeron.

20. The Greeks not coming down into the plain, Mardonius sent against them all his horse, whose commander was Masistius (whom the Greeks call Macistius), a man much honoured among the Persians ; he rode a Nesaean horse that had a golden bit and was at all points gaily adorned. Thereupon the horsemen rode up to the Greeks and charged them by squadrons, doing them much hurt thereby and calling them women.

21. Now it chanced that the Megarians were posted in that part of the field which was openest to attack, and here the horsemen found the readiest approach. Wherefore, being hard pressed by the charges, the Megarians sent a herald to the generals of the Greeks, who came to them and thus spoke : " From the men of Megara to their allies : We cannot alone withstand the Persian horse (albeit we have till now held our ground with patience and valour, though hard pressed) in this post whereunto we were first appointed ; and now be well assured that we will leave our post, except you send others to take our place therein." Thus the herald reported, and

πειρᾶτο τῶν Ἑλλήνων εἴ τινες ἐθέλοιεν ἄλλοι
ἐθελονταὶ ἰέναι τε ἐς τὸν χῶρον τοῦτον καὶ τάσ-
σεσθαι διάδοχοι Μεγαρεῦσι. οὐ βουλομένων δὲ
τῶν ἄλλων Ἀθηναῖοι ὑπεδέξαντο καὶ Ἀθηναίων
οἱ τριηκόσιοι λογάδες, τῶν ἐλοχήγεε Ὀλυμπιόδωρος
ὁ Λάμπωνος.

22. Οὗτοι ἦσαν οἵ τε ὑποδεξάμενοι καὶ οἱ πρὸ
τῶν ἄλλων τῶν παρεόντων Ἑλλήνων ἐς Ἐρυθρὰς
ταχθέντες, τοὺς τοξότας προσελόμενοι. μαχομένων
δὲ σφέων ἐπὶ χρόνον τέλος τοιόνδε ἐγένετο τῆς
μάχης. προσβαλλούσης τῆς ἵππου κατὰ τέλεα,
ὁ Μασιστίου προέχων τῶν ἄλλων ἵππος βάλλεται
τοξεύματι τὰ πλευρά, ἀλγήσας δὲ ἵσταταί τε
ὀρθὸς καὶ ἀποσείεται τὸν Μασίστιον· πεσόντι
δὲ αὐτῷ οἱ Ἀθηναῖοι αὐτίκα ἐπεκέατο. τόν τε
δὴ ἵππον αὐτοῦ λαμβάνουσι καὶ αὐτὸν ἀμυνόμενον
κτείνουσι, κατ' ἀρχὰς οὐ δυνάμενοι. ἐνεσκεύαστο
γὰρ οὕτω· ἐντὸς θώρηκα εἶχε χρύσεον λεπιδωτόν,
κατύπερθε δὲ τοῦ θώρηκος κιθῶνα φοινίκεον
ἐνεδεδύκεε. τύπτοντες δὲ ἐς τὸν θώρηκα ἐποίευν
οὐδέν, πρίν γε δὴ μαθών τις τὸ ποιεύμενον παίει
μιν ἐς τὸν ὀφθαλμόν. οὕτω δὴ ἔπεσέ τε καὶ ἀπέθανε. ταῦτα δέ κως γινόμενα ἐλελήθεε τοὺς
ἄλλους ἱππέας· οὔτε γὰρ πεσόντα μιν εἶδον ἀπὸ
τοῦ ἵππου οὔτε ἀποθνήσκοντα, ἀναχωρήσιός τε
γινομένης καὶ ὑποστροφῆς οὐκ ἔμαθον τὸ γινόμενον. ἐπείτε δὲ ἔστησαν, αὐτίκα ἐπόθεσαν, ὡς
σφεας οὐδεὶς ἦν ὁ τάσσων   μαθόντες δὲ τὸ γεγονός,
διακελευσάμενοι ἤλαυνον τοὺς ἵππους πάντας, ὡς
ἂν τὸν νεκρὸν ἀνελοίατο.

23. Ἰδόντες δὲ οἱ Ἀθηναῖοι οὐκέτι κατὰ τέλεα
προσελαύνοντας τοὺς ἱππέας ἀλλὰ πάντας, τὴν

Pausanias inquired among the Greeks if any would offer themselves to go to that place and relieve the Megarians by holding the post. None other would go; but the Athenians took it upon themselves, even three hundred picked men of Athens, whose captain was Olympiodorus son of Lampon.

22. These were they who took it upon themselves, and were posted at Erythrae in advance of the whole Greek army; and they took with them the archers also. For a long time they fought; and the end of the battle was as I shall show. The horsemen charged by squadrons; and Masistius' horse, being at the head of the rest, was smitten in the side by an arrow, and rearing up in its pain it threw Masistius; who when he fell was straightway set upon by the Athenians. His horse they took then and there, and he himself was slain fighting, though at first they could not kill him; for the fashion of his armour was such, that he wore a purple tunic over a cuirass of golden scales that was within it; and it was all in vain that they smote at the cuirass, till someone saw what they did and stabbed him in the eye, so that he fell dead. But as chance would have it the rest of the horsemen knew nought of this; for they had not seen him fall from his horse, or die; and they wheeled about and rode back without perceiving what was done. But as soon as they halted they saw what they lacked, since there was none to order them; and when they perceived what had chanced, they gave each other the word, and all rode together to recover the dead body.

23. When the Athenians saw the horsemen riding at them, not by squadrons as before, but all together,

ἄλλην στρατιὴν ἐπεβώσαντο. ἐν ᾧ δὲ ὁ πεζὸς
ἅπας ἐβοήθεε, ἐν τούτῳ μάχη ὀξέα περὶ τοῦ
νεκροῦ γίνεται. ἕως μέν νυν μοῦνοι ἦσαν οἱ τριηκόσιοι, ἐσσοῦντό τε πολλὸν καὶ τὸν νεκρὸν ἀπέ-
λειπον· ὡς δέ σφι τὸ πλῆθος ἐπεβοήθησε, οὕτω
δὴ οὐκέτι οἱ ἱππόται ὑπέμενον οὐδέ σφι ἐξεγένετο
τὸν νεκρὸν ἀνελέσθαι, ἀλλὰ πρὸς ἐκείνῳ ἄλλους
προσαπώλεσαν τῶν ἱππέων. ἀποστήσαντες ὦν
ὅσον τε δύο στάδια ἐβουλεύοντο ὅ τι χρεὸν εἴη
ποιέειν· ἐδόκεε δέ σφι ἀναρχίης ἐούσης ἀπελαύνειν
παρὰ Μαρδόνιον.

24. Ἀπικομένης δὲ τῆς ἵππου ἐς τὸ στρατόπεδον
πένθος ἐποιήσαντο Μασιστίου πᾶσά τε ἡ στρατιὴ
καὶ Μαρδόνιος μέγιστον, σφέας τε αὐτοὺς κείροντες
καὶ τοὺς ἵππους καὶ τὰ ὑποζύγια οἰμωγῇ τε χρεώμενοι ἀπλέτῳ· ἅπασαν γὰρ τὴν Βοιωτίην κατεῖχε
ἠχὼ ὡς ἀνδρὸς ἀπολομένου μετά γε Μαρδόνιον
λογιμωτάτου παρά τε Πέρσῃσι καὶ βασιλέι.

25. Οἱ μέν νυν βάρβαροι τρόπῳ τῷ σφετέρῳ
ἀποθανόντα ἐτίμων Μασίστιον· οἱ δὲ Ἕλληνες
ὡς τὴν ἵππον ἐδέξαντο προσβάλλουσαν καὶ δεξάμενοι ὤσαντο, ἐθάρσησάν τε πολλῷ μᾶλλον καὶ
πρῶτα μὲν ἐς ἄμαξαν ἐσθέντες τὸν νεκρὸν παρὰ
τὰς τάξις ἐκόμιζον· ὁ δὲ νεκρὸς ἦν θέης ἄξιος
μεγάθεος εἵνεκα καὶ κάλλεος, τῶν δὴ εἵνεκα καὶ
ταῦτα ἐποίευν· ἐκλείποντες τὰς τάξις ἐφοίτων
θεησόμενοι Μασίστιον. μετὰ δὲ ἔδοξέ σφι ἐπι-
καταβῆναι ἐς Πλαταιάς· ὁ γὰρ χῶρος ἐφαίνετο
πολλῷ ἐὼν ἐπιτηδεότερός σφι ἐνστρατοπεδεύεσθαι
ὁ Πλαταιικὸς τοῦ Ἐρυθραίου τά τε ἄλλα καὶ
εὐυδρότερος. ἐς τοῦτον δὴ τὸν χῶρον καὶ ἐπὶ
τὴν κρήνην τὴν Γαργαφίην τὴν ἐν τῷ χώρῳ τούτῳ
184

they cried to the rest of the army for help. While all their foot was rallying to aid, there waxed a sharp fight over the dead body. As long as the three hundred stood alone, they had the worst of the battle by far, and were nigh leaving the dead man; but when the main body came to their aid, then it was the horsemen that could no longer hold their ground, nor avail to recover the dead man, but they lost others of their comrades too besides Masistius. They drew off therefore and halted about two furlongs off, where they consulted what they should do; and resolved, as there was none to lead them, to ride away to Mardonius.

24. When the cavalry returned to the camp, Mardonius and all the army made very great mourning for Masistius, cutting their own hair and the hair of their horses and beasts of burden, and lamenting loud and long; for the sound of it was heard over all Boeotia, inasmuch as a man was dead who was next to Mardonius most esteemed by all Persia and the king.

25. So the foreigners honoured Masistius' death after their manner; but the Greeks were much heartened by their withstanding and repelling of the horsemen. And first they laid the dead man on a cart and carried him about their ranks; and the body was worth the viewing, for stature and goodliness; wherefore they would even leave their ranks and come to view Masistius. Presently they resolved that they would march down to Plataeae; for they saw that the ground there was in all ways fitter by much for encampment than at Erythrae, and chiefly because it was better watered. To this place, and to the Gargaphian spring that was there,

ἐοῦσαν ἔδοξέ σφι χρεὸν εἶναι ἀπικέσθαι καὶ
διαταχθέντας στρατοπεδεύεσθαι. ἀναλαβόντες
δὲ τὰ ὅπλα ἤισαν διὰ τῆς ὑπωρέης τοῦ Κιθαιρῶνος
παρὰ Ὑσιὰς ἐς τὴν Πλαταιίδα γῆν, ἀπικόμενοι
δὲ ἐτάσσοντο κατὰ ἔθνεα πλησίον τῆς τε κρήνης
τῆς Γαργαφίης καὶ τοῦ τεμένεος τοῦ Ἀνδρο-
κράτεος τοῦ ἥρωος, διὰ ὄχθων τε οὐκ ὑψηλῶν
καὶ ἀπέδου χώρου.

26. Ἐνθαῦτα ἐν τῇ διατάξι ἐγένετο λόγων
πολλῶν ὠθισμὸς Τεγεητέων τε καὶ Ἀθηναίων·
ἐδικαίευν γὰρ αὐτοὶ ἑκάτεροι ἔχειν τὸ ἕτερον
κέρας, καὶ καινὰ καὶ παλαιὰ παραφέροντες ἔργα.
τοῦτο μὲν οἱ Τεγεῆται ἔλεγον τάδε. "Ἡμεῖς αἰεί
κοτε ἀξιεύμεθα ταύτης τῆς τάξιος ἐκ τῶν συμμάχων ἀπάντων, ὅσαι ἤδη ἔξοδοι κοιναὶ ἐγένοντο
Πελοποννησίοισι καὶ τὸ παλαιὸν καὶ τὸ νέον, ἐξ
ἐκείνου τοῦ χρόνου ἐπείτε Ἡρακλεῖδαι ἐπειρῶντο
μετὰ τὸν Εὐρυσθέος θάνατον κατιόντες ἐς Πελο-
πόννησον· τότε εὑρόμεθα τοῦτο διὰ πρῆγμα
τοιόνδε. ἐπεὶ μετὰ Ἀχαιῶν καὶ Ἰώνων τῶν
τότε ἐόντων ἐν Πελοποννήσῳ ἐκβοηθήσαντες ἐς
τὸν Ἰσθμὸν ἱζόμεθα ἀντίοι τοῖσι κατιοῦσι, τότε
ὦν λόγος Ὕλλον ἀγορεύσασθαι ὡς χρεὸν εἴη τὸν
μὲν στρατὸν τῷ στρατῷ μὴ ἀνακινδυνεύειν συμ-
βάλλοντα, ἐκ δὲ τοῦ Πελοποννησίου στρατοπέδου
τὸν ἂν σφέων αὐτῶν κρίνωσι εἶναι ἄριστον, τοῦτόν
οἱ μουνομαχῆσαι ἐπὶ διακειμένοισι. ἔδοξέ τε
τοῖσι Πελοποννησίοισι ταῦτα εἶναι ποιητέα καὶ
ἔταμον ὅρκιον ἐπὶ λόγῳ τοιῷδε, ἢν μὲν Ὕλλος
νικήσῃ τὸν Πελοποννησίων ἡγεμόνα, κατιέναι
Ἡρακλείδας ἐπὶ τὰ πατρώια, ἢν δὲ νικηθῇ, τὰ

they resolved that they must betake themselves and
encamp in their several battalions; and they took
up their arms and marched along the lower slopes
of Cithaeron past Hysiae to the lands of Plataeae,
and when they were there they arrayed themselves
nation by nation near the Gargaphian spring and
the precinct of the hero Androcrates, among low
hills and in a level country.

26. There, in the ordering of their battle, arose
much dispute between the Tegeans and the Athenians; for each of them claimed that they should
hold the second [1] wing of the army, justifying themselves by tales of deeds new and old. First said the
Tegeans: "Of all the allies we have ever had the
right to hold this post, in all campaigns ancient and
late of the united Peloponnesian armies, ever since
that time when the Heraclidae after Eurystheus'
death essayed to return into the Peloponnese; that
right we then gained, for the achievement which we
will relate. When we mustered at the Isthmus for
war, along with the Achaeans and Ionians who then
dwelt in the Peloponnese, and encamped over against
the returning exiles, then (it is said) Hyllus [2] proclaimed his counsel that army should not be risked
against army in battle, but that that champion in
the host of the Peloponnesians whom they chose for
their best should fight with him in single combat on
agreed conditions. The Peloponnesians resolving
that this should be so, they swore a compact that if
Hyllus should vanquish the Peloponnesian champion,
the Heraclidae should return to the land of their
fathers, but if he were himself vanquished, then

---

[1] That is, the wing which was not held by the Lacedaemonians themselves.   [2] Son of Heracles.

ἔμπαλιν Ἡρακλείδας ἀπαλλάσσεσθαι καὶ ἀπάγειν
τὴν στρατιὴν ἑκατόν τε ἐτέων μὴ ζητῆσαι κάτοδον
ἐς Πελοπόννησον. προεκρίθη τε δὴ ἐκ πάντων
τῶν συμμάχων ἐθελοντὴς Ἔχεμος ὁ Ἠερόπου
τοῦ Φηγέος στρατηγός τε ἐὼν καὶ βασιλεὺς
ἡμέτερος, καὶ ἐμουνομάχησέ τε καὶ ἀπέκτεινε
Ὕλλον. ἐκ τούτου τοῦ ἔργου εὑρόμεθα ἐν Πελο-
ποννησίοισί γε τοῖσι τότε καὶ ἄλλα γέρεα μεγάλα,
τὰ διατελέομεν ἔχοντες, καὶ τοῦ κέρεος τοῦ ἑτέρου
αἰεὶ ἡγεμονεύειν κοινῆς ἐξόδου γινομένης. ὑμῖν
μέν νυν ὦ Λακεδαιμόνιοι οὐκ ἀντιεύμεθα, ἀλλὰ
διδόντες αἵρεσιν ὁκοτέρου βούλεσθε κέρεος ἄρχειν
παρίεμεν· τοῦ δὲ ἑτέρου φαμὲν ἡμέας ἱκνέεσθαι
ἡγεμονεύειν κατά περ ἐν τῷ πρόσθε χρόνῳ. χωρίς
τε τούτου τοῦ ἀπηγημένου ἔργου ἀξιονικότερα
εἰμὲν Ἀθηναίων ταύτην τὴν τάξιν ἔχειν. πολλοὶ
μὲν γὰρ καὶ εὖ ἔχοντες πρὸς ὑμέας ἡμῖν, ἄνδρες
Σπαρτιῆται, ἀγῶνες ἀγωνίδαται, πολλοὶ δὲ καὶ
πρὸς ἄλλους. οὕτω ὦν δίκαιον ἡμέας ἔχειν τὸ
ἕτερον κέρας ἤ περ Ἀθηναίους· οὐ γάρ σφι ἐστὶ
ἔργα οἷά περ ἡμῖν κατεργασμένα, οὔτ᾽ ὦν καινὰ
οὔτε παλαιά."

27. Οἱ μὲν ταῦτα ἔλεγον, Ἀθηναῖοι δὲ πρὸς
ταῦτα ὑπεκρίναντο τάδε. "Ἐπιστάμεθα μὲν σύνοδον τήνδε μάχης εἵνεκα συλλεγῆναι πρὸς τὸν
βάρβαρον, ἀλλ᾽ οὐ λόγων· ἐπεὶ δὲ ὁ Τεγεήτης
προέθηκε παλαιά καὶ καινὰ λέγειν τὰ ἑκατέροισι
ἐν τῷ παντὶ χρόνῳ κατέργασται χρηστά, ἀναγκαίως ἡμῖν ἔχει δηλῶσαι πρὸς ὑμέας ὅθεν ἡμῖν
πατρώιον ἐστὶ ἐοῦσι χρηστοῖσι αἰεὶ πρώτοισι
εἶναι μᾶλλον ἢ Ἀρκάσι. Ἡρακλείδας, τῶν οὗτοι
φασὶ ἀποκτεῖναι τὸν ἡγεμόνα ἐν Ἰσθμῷ, τοῦτο

contrariwise the Heraclidae should depart and lead
their army away, and not seek to return to the
Peloponnese till a hundred years were past. Then
our general and king Echemus, son of Phegeus' son
Eëropus, offered himself and was chosen out of all
the allied host; and he fought that duel and slew
Hyllus. For that feat of arms the Peloponnesians
of that day granted us this also among other great
privileges which we have never ceased to possess,
that in all united campaigns we should ever lead
the army's second wing. Now with you, men of
Lacedaemon, we have no rivalry, but forbear and bid
you choose the command of whichever wing you will ;
but this we say, that our place is at the head of the
other, as ever aforetime. And setting aside that feat
which we have related, we are worthier than the
Athenians to hold that post; for many are the fields
on which we have fought with happy event in regard
to you, men of Lacedaemon, and others besides. It
is just, therefore, that we and not the Athenians
should hold the second wing ; for never early or late
have they achieved such feats of arms as we."

27. Thus they spoke; and thus the Athenians
replied : " It is our belief that we are here gathered
in concourse for battle with the foreigner, and not
for discourses ; but since the man of Tegea has made
it his business to speak of all the valorous deeds, old
and new, which either of our nations has at any time
achieved, needs must that we prove to you how we,
rather than Arcadians, have in virtue of our valour
an hereditary right to the place of honour. These
Tegeans say that they slew the leader of the Heraclidae at the Isthmus ; now when those same Hera-

μὲν τούτους, πρότερον ἐξελαυνομένους ὑπὸ πάντων
Ἑλλήνων ἐς τοὺς ἀπικοίατο φεύγοντες δουλοσύνην
πρὸς Μυκηναίων, μοῦνοι ὑποδεξάμενοι τὴν Εὐρυσθέος ὕβριν κατείλομεν, σὺν ἐκείνοισι μάχῃ
νικήσαντες τοὺς τότε ἔχοντας Πελοπόννησον.
τοῦτο δὲ Ἀργείους τοὺς μετὰ Πολυνείκεος ἐπὶ
Θήβας ἐλάσαντας, τελευτήσαντας τὸν αἰῶνα καὶ
ἀτάφους κειμένους, στρατευσάμενοι ἐπὶ τοὺς
Καδμείους ἀνελέσθαι τε τοὺς νεκροὺς φαμὲν καὶ
θάψαι τῆς ἡμετέρης ἐν Ἐλευσῖνι. ἔστι δὲ ἡμῖν
ἔργον εὖ ἔχον καὶ ἐς Ἀμαζονίδας τὰς ἀπὸ Θερ-
μώδοντος ποταμοῦ ἐσβαλούσας κοτὲ ἐς γῆν τὴν
Ἀττικήν, καὶ ἐν τοῖσι Τρωικοῖσι πόνοισι οὐδαμῶν
ἐλειπόμεθα. ἀλλ' οὐ γάρ τι προέχει τούτων
ἐπιμεμνῆσθαι· καὶ γὰρ ἂν χρηστοὶ τότε ἐόντες
ὡυτοὶ νῦν ἂν εἶεν φλαυρότεροι, καὶ τότε ἐόντες
φλαῦροι νῦν ἂν εἶεν ἀμείνονες. παλαιῶν μέν νυν
ἔργων ἅλις ἔστω· ἡμῖν δὲ εἰ μηδὲν ἄλλο ἐστὶ
ἀποδεδεγμένον, ὥσπερ ἐστὶ πολλά τε καὶ εὖ
ἔχοντα εἰ τεοῖσι καὶ ἄλλοισι Ἑλλήνων, ἀλλὰ καὶ
ἀπὸ τοῦ ἐν Μαραθῶνι ἔργου ἄξιοι εἰμὲν τοῦτο τὸ
γέρας ἔχειν καὶ ἄλλα πρὸς τούτῳ, οἵτινες μοῦνοι
Ἑλλήνων δὴ μουνομαχήσαντες τῷ Πέρσῃ καὶ
ἔργῳ τοσούτῳ ἐπιχειρήσαντες περιεγενόμεθα καὶ
ἐνικήσαμεν ἔθνεα ἕξ τε καὶ τεσσεράκοντα. ἆρ'
οὐ δίκαιοι εἰμὲν ἔχειν ταύτην τὴν τάξιν ἀπὸ
τούτου μούνου τοῦ ἔργου; ἀλλ' οὐ γὰρ ἐν τῷ
τοιῷδε τάξιος εἵνεκα στασιάζειν πρέπει, ἄρτιοι
εἰμὲν πείθεσθαι ὑμῖν ὦ Λακεδαιμόνιοι, ἵνα δοκέει
ἐπιτηδεότατον ἡμέας εἶναι ἑστάναι καὶ κατ'
οὕστινας· πάντῃ γὰρ τεταγμένοι πειρησόμεθα

clidae had till then been rejected by every Greek
people to whom they resorted to escape the tyranny
of the Mycenaeans, we and none other received
them[1]; and with them we vanquished those that then
dwelt in the Peloponnese, and we broke the pride
of Eurystheus. Furthermore, when the Argives who
had marched with Polynices[2] against Thebes had
there made an end of their lives and lay unburied,
know that we sent our army against the Cadmeans
and recovered the dead and buried them in Eleusis;
and we have on record our great victory against the
Amazons who once came from the river Thermodon
and broke into Attica; and in the hard days of Troy
we were second to none. But since it is idle to
recall these matters—for they that were erstwhile
valiant may now be of lesser mettle, and they that
lacked mettle then may be better men now—enough
of these doings of old time; and we, if we are known
for no achievement (as we are, for more and greater
than are any men in Hellas), yet from our feat of
arms at Marathon we deserve to have this honour,
yea, and more beside; seeing that alone of all Greeks
we met the Persian single-handed, nor failed in that
high enterprise, but overcame six and forty nations.
Is it not our right to hold this post, for nought but
that one feat? Yet seeing that this is no time for
wrangling about our place in the battle, we are ready
to obey you, men of Lacedaemon! and take whatso
place and face whatso enemy you deem most fitting;
wheresoever you set us, we will strive to be valiant

[1] Hyllus, pursued by his enemy Eurystheus, took refuge
with the Athenians, and with their aid defeated and killed
Eurystheus and his sons.
[2] When Polynices tried to recover Thebes from his brother
Eteocles; see Aeschylus' "Seven against Thebes."

εἶναι χρηστοί. ἐξηγέεσθε δὲ ὡς πεισομένων."
οἱ μὲν ταῦτα ἀμείβοντο, Λακεδαιμονίων δὲ ἀνέ-
βωσε ἅπαν τὸ στρατόπεδον Ἀθηναίους ἀξιονι-
κοτέρους εἶναι ἔχειν τὸ κέρας ἤ περ Ἀρκάδας.
οὕτω δὴ ἔσχον οἱ Ἀθηναῖοι καὶ ὑπερεβάλοντο
τοὺς Τεγεήτας.

28. Μετὰ δὲ ταῦτα ἐτάσσοντο ὧδε οἱ ἐπι-
φοιτῶντές τε καὶ οἱ ἀρχὴν ἐλθόντες Ἑλλήνων.
τὸ μὲν δεξιὸν κέρας εἶχον Λακεδαιμονίων μύριοι·
τούτων δὲ τοὺς πεντακισχιλίους ἐόντας Σπαρτιήτας ἐφύλασσον ψιλοὶ τῶν εἱλώτων πεντακισχίλιοι καὶ τρισμύριοι, περὶ ἄνδρα ἕκαστον
ἑπτὰ τεταγμένοι. προσεχέας δὲ σφίσι εἵλοντο
ἑστάναι οἱ Σπαρτιῆται τοὺς Τεγεήτας καὶ τιμῆς
εἵνεκα καὶ ἀρετῆς· τούτων δ᾿ ἦσαν ὁπλῖται χίλιοι
καὶ πεντακόσιοι. μετὰ δὲ τούτους ἵσταντο Κορινθίων πεντακισχίλιοι, παρὰ δὲ σφίσι εὕροντο παρὰ
Παυσανίεω ἑστάναι Ποτιδαιητέων τῶν ἐκ Παλ-
λήνης τοὺς παρεόντας τριηκοσίους. τούτων δὲ
ἐχόμενοι ἵσταντο Ἀρκάδες Ὀρχομένιοι ἑξακόσιοι,
τούτων δὲ Σικυώνιοι τρισχίλιοι. τούτων δὲ
εἵχοντο Ἐπιδαυρίων ὀκτακόσιοι. παρὰ δὲ τούτους Τροιζηνίων ἐτάσσοντο χίλιοι, Τροιζηνίων δὲ
ἐχόμενοι Λεπρεητέων διηκόσιοι, τούτων δὲ Μυκηναίων καὶ Τιρυνθίων τετρακόσιοι, τούτων δὲ
ἐχόμενοι Φλειάσιοι χίλιοι. παρὰ δὲ τούτους
ἔστησαν Ἑρμιονέες τριηκόσιοι. Ἑρμιονέων δὲ
ἐχόμενοι ἵσταντο Ἐρετριέων τε καὶ Στυρέων
ἑξακόσιοι, τούτων δὲ Χαλκιδέες τετρακόσιοι, τούτων δὲ Ἀμπρακιητέων πεντακόσιοι. μετὰ δὲ
τούτους Λευκαδίων καὶ Ἀνακτορίων ὀκτακόσιοι
ἔστησαν, τούτων δὲ ἐχόμενοι Παλέες οἱ ἐκ Κεφαλ-

men. Command us then, as knowing that we will obey." Thus the Athenians answered; and the whole army shouted aloud that the Athenians were worthier to hold the wing than the Arcadians. Thus the Athenians were preferred to the men of Tegea, and gained that place.

28. Presently the whole Greek army was arrayed as I shall show, both the later and the earliest comers. On the right wing were ten thousand Lacedaemonians; five thousand of these, who were Spartans, had a guard of thirty-five thousand light-armed helots, seven appointed for each man. The Spartans chose the Tegeans for their neighbours in the battle, both to do them honour, and for their valour; there were of these fifteen hundred men-at-arms. Next to these in the line were five thousand Corinthians, at whose desire Pausanias suffered the three hundred Potidaeans from Pallene then present to stand by them. Next to these were six hundred Arcadians from Orchomenus, and after them three thousand men of Sicyon. By these a thousand Troezenians were posted, and after them two hundred men of Lepreum, then four hundred from Mycenae and Tiryns, and next to them a thousand from Phlius. By these stood three hundred men of Hermione. Next to the men of Hermione were six hundred Eretrians and Styreans; next to them, four hundred Chalcidians; next again, five hundred Ampraciots. After these stood eight hundred Leucadians and Anactorians, and next to them two hundred from

ληνίης διηκόσιοι. μετὰ δὲ τούτους Αἰγινητέων
πεντακόσιοι ἐτάχθησαν. παρὰ δὲ τούτους ἐτάσσοντο Μεγαρέων τρισχίλιοι. εἴχοντο δὲ τούτων
Πλαταιέες ἑξακόσιοι. τελευταῖοι δὲ καὶ πρῶτοι
Ἀθηναῖοι ἐτάσσοντο, κέρας ἔχοντες τὸ εὐώνυμον,
ὀκτακισχίλιοι· ἐστρατήγεε δ᾽ αὐτῶν Ἀριστείδης
ὁ Λυσιμάχου.

29. Οὗτοι, πλὴν τῶν ἑπτὰ περὶ ἕκαστον τεταγμένων Σπαρτιήτῃσι, ἦσαν ὁπλῖται, σύμπαντες
ἐόντες ἀριθμὸν τρεῖς τε μυριάδες καὶ ὀκτὼ χιλιάδες
καὶ ἑκατοντάδες ἑπτά. ὁπλῖται μὲν οἱ πάντες
συλλεγέντες ἐπὶ τὸν βάρβαρον ἦσαν τοσοῦτοι,
ψιλῶν δὲ πλῆθος ἦν τόδε, τῆς μὲν Σπαρτιητικῆς
τάξιος πεντακισχίλιοι καὶ τρισμύριοι ἄνδρες, ὡς
ἐόντων ἑπτὰ περὶ ἕκαστον ἄνδρα, καὶ τούτων πᾶς
τις παρήρτητο ὡς ἐς πόλεμον· οἱ δὲ τῶν λοιπῶν
Λακεδαιμονίων καὶ Ἑλλήνων ψιλοί, ὡς εἷς περὶ
ἕκαστον ἐὼν ἄνδρα, πεντακόσιοι καὶ τετρακισχίλιοι
καὶ τρισμύριοι ἦσαν.

30. Ψιλῶν μὲν δὴ τῶν ἁπάντων τῶν μαχίμων
ἦν τὸ πλῆθος ἕξ τε μυριάδες καὶ ἐννέα χιλιάδες
καὶ ἑκατοντάδες πέντε, τοῦ δὲ σύμπαντος τοῦ
Ἑλληνικοῦ τοῦ συνελθόντος ἐς Πλαταιὰς σύν τε
ὁπλίτῃσι καὶ ψιλοῖσι τοῖσι μαχίμοισι ἔνδεκα
μυριάδες ἦσαν, μιῆς χιλιάδος, πρὸς δὲ ὀκτακοσίων
ἀνδρῶν καταδέουσαι. σὺν δὲ Θεσπιέων τοῖσι
παρεοῦσι ἐξεπληροῦντο αἱ ἔνδεκα μυριάδες· παρῆσαν γὰρ καὶ Θεσπιέων ἐν τῷ στρατοπέδῳ οἱ
περιεόντες, ἀριθμὸν ἐς ὀκτακοσίους καὶ χιλίους·
ὅπλα δὲ οὐδ᾽ οὗτοι εἶχον. οὗτοι μέν νυν ταχθέντες
ἐπὶ τῷ Ἀσωπῷ ἐστρατοπεδεύοντο.

31. Οἱ δὲ ἀμφὶ Μαρδόνιον βάρβαροι ὡς ἀπε-

Pale in Cephallenia; after them in the array, five
hundred Aeginetans; by them stood three thousand
men of Megara, and next to these six hundred
Plataeans. At the end, and first in the line, were
the Athenians, on the left wing, eight thousand
men; their general was Aristides son of Lysimachus.

29. All these, save the seven appointed to attend
each Spartan, were men-at-arms, and the whole sum
of them was thirty-eight thousand and seven hundred.
This was the number of men-at-arms that mustered
for war against the foreigner; as regarding the
number of the light-armed men, there were in the
Spartan array seven for each man-at-arms, that is,
thirty-five thousand, and every one of these was
equipped for war; the light-armed from the rest of
Lacedaemon and Hellas were as one to every man-
at-arms, and their number was thirty-four thousand
and five hundred.

30. So the sum of all the light-armed men that were
fighters was sixty-nine thousand and five hundred, and
of the whole Greek army mustered at Plataeae, men-
at-arms and light-armed fighting men together, eleven
times ten thousand, lacking eighteen hundred. But
the Thespians who were there present made up the
full tale of an hundred and ten thousand; for the
survivors [1] of the Thespians were also present with
the army, eighteen hundred in number. These then
were arrayed, and encamped by the Asopus.

31. When Mardonius' foreigners had finished their

---

[1] That is, who had not fallen at Thermopylae.

κήδευσαν Μασίστιον, παρῆσαν, πυθόμενοι τοὺς
Ἕλληνας εἶναι ἐν Πλαταιῆσι, καὶ αὐτοὶ ἐπὶ τὸν
Ἀσωπὸν τὸν ταύτῃ ῥέοντα. ἀπικόμενοι δὲ
ἀντετάσσοντο ὧδε ὑπὸ Μαρδονίου. κατὰ μὲν
Λακεδαιμονίους ἔστησε Πέρσας. καὶ δὴ πολλὸν
γὰρ περιῆσαν πλήθεϊ οἱ Πέρσαι, ἐπί τε τάξις
πλεῦνας ἐκεκοσμέατο καὶ ἐπεῖχον τοὺς Τεγεήτας.
ἔταξε δὲ οὕτω· ὅ τι μὲν ἦν αὐτῶν δυνατώτατον
πᾶν ἀπολέξας ἔστησε ἀντίον Λακεδαιμονίων, τὸ
δὲ ἀσθενέστερον παρέταξε κατὰ τοὺς Τεγεήτας.
ταῦτα δ᾽ ἐποίεε φραζόντων τε καὶ διδασκόντων
Θηβαίων. Περσέων δὲ ἐχομένους ἔταξε Μήδους·
οὗτοι δὲ ἐπέσχον Κορινθίους τε καὶ Ποτιδαιήτας
καὶ Ὀρχομενίους τε καὶ Σικυωνίους. Μήδων δὲ
ἐχομένους ἔταξε Βακτρίους· οὗτοι δὲ ἐπέσχον
Ἐπιδαυρίους τε καὶ Τροιζηνίους καὶ Λεπρεήτας
τε καὶ Τιρυνθίους καὶ Μυκηναίους τε καὶ Φλειασίους. μετὰ δὲ Βακτρίους ἔστησε Ἰνδούς· οὗτοι
δὲ ἐπέσχον Ἑρμιονέας τε καὶ Ἐρετριέας καὶ
Στυρέας τε καὶ Χαλκιδέας. Ἰνδῶν δὲ ἐχομένους
Σάκας ἔταξε, οἳ ἐπέσχον Ἀμπρακιήτας τε καὶ
Ἀνακτορίους καὶ Λευκαδίους καὶ Παλέας καὶ
Αἰγινήτας. Σακέων δὲ ἐχομένους ἔταξε ἀντία
Ἀθηναίων τε καὶ Πλαταιέων καὶ Μεγαρέων
Βοιωτούς τε καὶ Λοκροὺς καὶ Μηλιέας τε καὶ
Θεσσαλοὺς καὶ Φωκέων τοὺς χιλίους· οὐ γὰρ ὧν
ἅπαντες οἱ Φωκέες ἐμήδισαν, ἀλλὰ τινὲς αὐτῶν
καὶ τὰ Ἑλλήνων ηὖξον περὶ τὸν Παρνησσὸν
κατειλημμένοι, καὶ ἐνθεῦτεν ὁρμώμενοι ἔφερόν τε
καὶ ἦγον τήν τε Μαρδονίου στρατιὴν καὶ τοὺς
μετ᾽ αὐτοῦ ἐόντας Ἑλλήνων. ἔταξε δὲ καὶ Μακε-

mourning for Masistius, and heard that the Greeks were at Plataeae, they also came to the part of the Asopus river nearest to them. When they were there they were arrayed for battle by Mardonius as I shall show. He posted the Persians facing the Lacedaemonians; and seeing that the Persians by far outnumbered the Lacedaemonians, they were arrayed in deeper ranks and their line ran fronting the Tegeans also. In his arraying of them he chose out the strongest part of the Persians to set it over against the Lacedaemonians, and posted the weaker by them facing the Tegeans; this he did being so informed and taught by the Thebans. Next to the Persians he posted the Medes, fronting the men of Corinth and Potidaea and Orchomenus and Sicyon; next to the Medes, the Bactrians, fronting the men of Epidaurus, Troezen, Lepreum, Tiryns, Mycenae, and Phlius. After the Bactrians he set the Indians, fronting the men of Hermione and Eretria and Styra and Chalcis. Next to the Indians he posted the Sacae, fronting the Ampraciots, Anactorians, Leucadians, Paleans, and Aeginetans; next to the Sacae, and over against the Athenians and Plataeans and Megarians, the Boeotians and Locrians and Malians and Thessalians and the thousand that came from Phocis; for not all the Phocians took the Persian part, but some of them gave their aid to the Greek cause; these had been beleaguered on Parnassus, and issued out from thence to harry Mardonius' army and the Greeks that were with him. Besides these,

δόνας τε καὶ τοὺς περὶ Θεσσαλίην οἰκημένους
κατὰ τοὺς Ἀθηναίους.

32. Ταῦτα μὲν τῶν ἐθνέων τὰ μέγιστα ὠνό-
μασται τῶν ὑπὸ Μαρδονίου ταχθέντων, τά περ
ἐπιφανέστατά τε ἦν καὶ λόγου πλείστου· ἐνῆσαν
δὲ καὶ ἄλλων ἐθνέων ἄνδρες ἀναμεμιγμένοι, Φρυγῶν
τε καὶ Θρηίκων καὶ Μυσῶν τε καὶ Παιόνων καὶ
τῶν ἄλλων, ἐν δὲ καὶ Αἰθιόπων τε καὶ Αἰγυπτίων
οἵ τε Ἑρμοτύβιες καὶ οἱ Καλασίριες καλεόμενοι
μαχαιροφόροι, οἵ περ εἰσὶ Αἰγυπτίων μοῦνοι
μάχιμοι. τούτους δὲ ἔτι ἐν Φαλήρῳ ἐὼν ἀπὸ
τῶν νεῶν ἀπεβιβάσατο ἐόντας ἐπιβάτας· οὐ γὰρ
ἐτάχθησαν ἐς τὸν πεζὸν τὸν ἅμα Ξέρξῃ ἀπικόμενον ἐς Ἀθήνας Αἰγύπτιοι. τῶν μὲν δὴ
βαρβάρων ἦσαν τριήκοντα μυριάδες, ὡς καὶ πρότερον δεδήλωται· τῶν δὲ Ἑλλήνων τῶν Μαρδονίου
συμμάχων οἶδε μὲν οὐδεὶς ἀριθμόν· οὐ γὰρ ὦν
ἠριθμήθησαν· ὡς δὲ ἐπεικάσαι, ἐς πέντε μυριάδας
συλλεγῆναι εἰκάζω. οὗτοι οἱ παραταχθέντες
πεζοὶ ἦσαν, ἡ δὲ ἵππος χωρὶς ἐτέτακτο.

33. Ὡς δὲ ἄρα πάντες οἱ ἐτετάχατο κατὰ ἔθνεα
καὶ κατὰ τέλεα, ἐνθαῦτα τῇ δευτέρῃ ἡμέρῃ ἐθύοντο
καὶ ἀμφότεροι. Ἕλλησι μὲν Τισαμενὸς Ἀντιόχου
ἦν ὁ θυόμενος· οὗτος γὰρ δὴ εἵπετο τῷ στρατεύ-
ματι τούτῳ μάντις· τὸν ἐόντα Ἠλεῖον καὶ γένεος
τοῦ Ἰαμιδέων [Κλυτιάδην] Λακεδαιμόνιοι ἐποιήσαντο λεωσφέτερον. Τισαμενῷ γὰρ μαντευομένῳ
ἐν Δελφοῖσι περὶ γόνου ἀνεῖλε ἡ Πυθίη ἀγῶνας
τοὺς μεγίστους ἀναιρήσεσθαι πέντε. ὁ μὲν δὴ

---

[1] The Egyptian military classes mentioned in Bk. II. 164.
[2] The Iamidae were a priestly family, the members of

198

he arrayed against the Athenians Macedonians also and the dwellers about Thessaly.

32. These that I have named were the greatest of the nations set in array by Mardonius that were of most note and account; but there was also in the army a mixed multitude of Phrygians, Thracians, Mysians, Paeonians, and the rest, besides Ethiopians and the Egyptian swordsmen called Hermotybies and Calasiries,[1] who are the only fighting men in Egypt. These had been fighters on shipboard, till Mardonius while yet at Phalerum disembarked them from their ships; for the Egyptians were not appointed to serve in the land army which Xerxes led to Athens. Of the foreigners, then, there were three hundred thousand, as I have already shown; as for the Greek allies of Mardonius, none knows the number of them, for they were not counted; but as far as guessing may serve, I suppose them to have been mustered to the number of fifty thousand. These were the footmen that were set in array; the cavalry were separately ordered.

33. When they had all been arrayed in their nations and their battalions, on the second day thereafter both armies offered sacrifice. For the Greeks, Tisamenus it was that sacrificed; for he was with their army as a diviner; he was an Elean by birth, a Clytiad of the Iamid clan,[2] and the Lacedaemonians gave him the freedom of their city. For when Tisamenus was inquiring of the oracle at Delphi concerning issue, the priestess prophesied to him that he should win five great victories. Not under-

which were found in all parts of Hellas. The Clytiadae were also Elean priests, but quite separate from the Iamidae; so Stein is probably right in bracketing Κλυτιάδην.

ἁμαρτὼν τοῦ χρηστηρίου προσεῖχε γυμνασίοισι
ὡς ἀναιρησόμενος γυμνικοὺς ἀγῶνας, ἀσκέων δὲ
πεντάεθλον παρὰ ἓν πάλαισμα ἔδραμε νικᾶν
Ὀλυμπιάδα, Ἱερωνύμῳ τῷ Ἀνδρίῳ ἐλθὼν ἐς ἔριν.
Λακεδαιμόνιοι δὲ μαθόντες οὐκ ἐς γυμνικοὺς ἀλλ᾽
ἐς ἀρηίους ἀγῶνας φέρον τὸ Τισαμενοῦ μαντήιον,
μισθῷ ἐπειρῶντο πείσαντες Τισαμενὸν ποιέεσθαι
ἅμα Ἡρακλειδέων τοῖσι βασιλεῦσι ἡγεμόνα τῶν
πολέμων. ὁ δὲ ὀρέων περὶ πολλοῦ ποιευμένους
Σπαρτιήτας φίλον αὐτὸν προσθέσθαι, μαθὼν
τοῦτο ἀνετίμα, σημαίνων σφι ὡς ἤν μιν πολιήτην
σφέτερον ποιήσωνται τῶν πάντων μεταδιδόντες,
ποιήσει ταῦτα, ἐπ᾽ ἄλλῳ μισθῷ δ᾽ οὔ. Σπαρτιῆται
δὲ πρῶτα μὲν ἀκούσαντες δεινὰ ἐποιεῦντο καὶ
μετίεσαν τῆς χρησμοσύνης τὸ παράπαν, τέλος δὲ
δείματος μεγάλου ἐπικρεμαμένου τοῦ Περσικοῦ
τούτου στρατεύματος καταίνεον μετιόντες. ὁ δὲ
γνοὺς τετραμμένους σφέας οὐδ᾽ οὕτω ἔτι ἔφη
ἀρκέεσθαι τούτοισι μούνοισι, ἀλλὰ δεῖν ἔτι τὸν
ἀδελφεὸν ἑωυτοῦ Ἡγίην γίνεσθαι Σπαρτιήτην
ἐπὶ τοῖσι αὐτοῖσι λόγοισι τοῖσι καὶ αὐτὸς γίνεται.

34. Ταῦτα δὲ λέγων οὗτος ἐμιμέετο Μελάμποδα,
ὡς εἰκάσαι βασιληίην τε καὶ πολιτηίην αἰτεομέ-
νους. καὶ γὰρ δὴ καὶ Μελάμπους τῶν ἐν Ἄργεϊ
γυναικῶν μανεισέων, ὥς μιν οἱ Ἀργεῖοι ἐμισθοῦντο
ἐκ Πύλου παῦσαι τὰς σφετέρας γυναῖκας τῆς
νούσου, μισθὸν προετείνατο τῆς βασιληίης τὸ
ἥμισυ. οὐκ ἀνασχομένων δὲ τῶν Ἀργείων ἀλλ᾽
ἀπιόντων, ὡς ἐμαίνοντο πλεῦνες τῶν γυναικῶν,

---

[1] The five events of the Pentathlum were running, jumping,
wrestling, and throwing of the spear and the discus.

standing that oracle, he betook himself to bodily
exercises, thinking so to win in such-like sports;
and having trained himself for the Five Contests,[1] he
came within one wrestling bout of winning the
Olympic prize, in a match with Hieronymus of
Andros. But the Lacedaemonians perceived that
the oracle given to Tisamenus spake of the lists not
of sport but of war; and they essayed to bribe Tisamenus to be a leader in their wars, jointly with
their kings of Heracles' line. But when he saw
that the Spartans set great store by his friendship,
with this knowledge he set his price higher, and
made it known to them that for no reward would he
do their will save for the gift of full citizenship and
all a citizen's rights. Hearing that, the Spartans
at first were angry and ceased wholly from their
request; but when the dreadful menace of this
Persian host overhung them they consented and
granted his demand. But when he saw their purpose changed, he said that not even so and with that
only would he be content; his brother Hegias too
must be made a Spartan on the same terms as
himself.

34. By so saying he imitated Melampus, in so far
as one may compare demands for kingship and for
citizenship. For when the women of Argos had gone
mad, and the Argives would fain hire him to come
from Pylos and heal them of that madness,[2] Melampus
demanded half of their kingship for his wages;
which the Argives could not suffer, and so departed;
but when the madness spread among their women,

---

[2] According to the legend, the Argive women were driven
mad by Dionysus for refusing to take part in his orgies, and
cured by Melampus. Many Greek authors refer to it, with
varying details.

οὕτω δὴ ὑποστάντες τὰ ὁ Μελάμπους προετείνατο
ἤισαν δώσοντές οἱ ταῦτα. ὁ δὲ ἐνθαῦτα δὴ ἐπο-
ρέγεται ὀρέων αὐτοὺς τετραμμένους, φάς, ἢν μὴ
καὶ τῷ ἀδελφεῷ Βίαντι μεταδῶσι τὸ τριτημόριον
τῆς βασιληίης, οὐ ποιήσειν τὰ βούλονται. οἱ δὲ
Ἀργεῖοι ἀπειληθέντες ἐς στεινὸν καταινέουσι καὶ
ταῦτα.

35. Ὡς δὲ καὶ Σπαρτιῆται, ἐδέοντο γὰρ δεινῶς
τοῦ Τισαμενοῦ, πάντως συνεχώρεόν οἱ. συγχωρη-
σάντων δὲ καὶ ταῦτα τῶν Σπαρτιητέων, οὕτω δὴ
πέντε σφι μαντευόμενος ἀγῶνας τοὺς μεγίστους
Τισαμενὸς ὁ Ἠλεῖος, γενόμενος Σπαρτιήτης,
συγκαταιρέει. μοῦνοι δὲ δὴ πάντων ἀνθρώπων
ἐγένοντο οὗτοι Σπαρτιήτῃσι πολιῆται. οἱ δὲ
πέντε ἀγῶνες οἵδε ἐγένοντο, εἷς μὲν καὶ πρῶτος
οὗτος ὁ ἐν Πλαταιῇσι, ἐπὶ δὲ ὁ ἐν Τεγέῃ πρὸς
Τεγεήτας τε καὶ Ἀργείους γενόμενος, μετὰ δὲ
ὁ ἐν Διπαιεῦσι πρὸς Ἀρκάδας πάντας πλὴν
Μαντινέων, ἐπὶ δὲ ὁ Μεσσηνίων ὁ πρὸς Ἰθώμῃ,
ὕστατος δὲ ὁ ἐν Τανάγρῃ πρὸς Ἀθηναίους τε
καὶ Ἀργείους γενόμενος· οὗτος δὲ ὕστατος
κατεργάσθη τῶν πέντε ἀγῶνων.

36. Οὗτος δὴ τότε τοῖσι Ἕλλησι ὁ Τισαμενός,
ἀγόντων τῶν Σπαρτιητέων, ἐμαντεύετο ἐν τῇ
Πλαταιίδι. τοῖσι μέν νυν Ἕλλησι καλὰ ἐγίνετο
τὰ ἱρὰ ἀμυνομένοισι, διαβᾶσι δὲ τὸν Ἀσωπὸν
καὶ μάχης ἄρχουσι οὔ.

37. Μαρδονίῳ δὲ προθυμεομένῳ μάχης ἄρχειν
οὐκ ἐπιτήδεα ἐγίνετο τὰ ἱρά, ἀμυνομένῳ δὲ καὶ
τούτῳ καλά. καὶ γὰρ οὗτος Ἑλληνικοῖσι ἱροῖσι
ἐχρᾶτο, μάντιν ἔχων Ἡγησίστρατον ἄνδρα Ἠλεῖον

thereat they promised what Melampus demanded and were ready to give it to him. Thereupon, seeing their purpose changed, he asked yet more, and said that he would not do their will except they gave a third of their kingship to his brother Bias; and the Argives, driven thus into a strait, consented to that also.

35. Thus the Spartans too were so eagerly desirous of winning Tisamenus that they granted all his demand. When they had granted him this also, then did Tisamenus of Elis, now become a Spartan, ply his divination for them and aid them to win five very great victories. None on earth save Tisamenus and his brother ever became citizens of Sparta. Now the five victories were these: one, the first, this victory at Plataeae; next that which was won at Tegea over the Tegeans and Argives; after that, over all the Arcadians save the Mantineans at Dipaea; next, over the Messenians at Ithome; lastly, the victory at Tanagra over the Athenians and Argives, which was the last won of the five victories.[1]

36. This Tisamenus had now been brought by the Spartans and was the diviner of the Greeks in the lands of Plataeae. Now the sacrifices boded good to the Greeks if they should but defend themselves, but evil if they should cross the Asopus and be the first to attack.

37. But Mardonius' sacrifices also boded nought to his liking if he should be zealous to attack first, and good if he should but defend himself; for he too used the Greek manner of sacrifice; Hegesistratus

---

[1] The battle at Ithome was apparently in the third Messenian war; that at Tanagra, in 457 B.C. (Thucyd. i. 107). Nothing is known of the battles at Tegea and Dipaea.

τε καὶ τῶν Τελλιαδέων ἐόντα λογιμώτατον, τὸν
δὴ πρότερον τούτων Σπαρτιῆται λαβόντες ἔδησαν
ἐπὶ θανάτῳ ὡς πεπονθότες πολλά τε καὶ ἀνάρσια
ὑπ' αὐτοῦ. ὁ δὲ ἐν τούτῳ τῷ κακῷ ἐχόμενος,
ὥστε τρέχων περὶ τῆς ψυχῆς πρό τε τοῦ θανάτου
πεισόμενος πολλά τε καὶ λυγρά, ἔργον ἐργάσατο
μέζον λόγου. ὡς γὰρ δὴ ἐδέδετο ἐν ξύλῳ σιδηρο-
δέτῳ, ἐσενειχθέντος κως σιδηρίου ἐκράτησε, αὐτίκα
δὲ ἐμηχανᾶτο ἀνδρηιότατον ἔργον πάντων τῶν
ἡμεῖς ἴδμεν· σταθμησάμενος γὰρ ὅκως ἐξελεύσεταί
οἱ τὸ λοιπὸν τοῦ ποδός, ἀπέταμε τὸν ταρσὸν
ἑωυτοῦ. ταῦτα δὲ ποιήσας, ὡς φυλασσόμενος
ὑπὸ φυλάκων, διορύξας τὸν τοῖχον ἀπέδρη ἐς
Τεγέην, τὰς μὲν νύκτας πορευόμενος, τὰς δὲ
ἡμέρας καταδύνων ἐς ὕλην καὶ αὐλιζόμενος, οὕτω
ὡς Λακεδαιμονίων πανδημεὶ διζημένων τρίτῃ εὐ-
φρόνῃ γενέσθαι ἐν Τεγέῃ, τοὺς δὲ ἐν θώματι
μεγάλῳ ἐνέχεσθαι τῆς τε τόλμης, ὁρῶντας τὸ
ἡμίτομον τοῦ ποδὸς κείμενον, κἀκεῖνον οὐ δυ-
ναμένους εὑρεῖν. τότε μὲν οὕτω διαφυγὼν Λακεδαιμονίους καταφεύγει ἐς Τεγέην ἐοῦσαν οὐκ
ἀρθμίην Λακεδαιμονίοισι τοῦτον τὸν χρόνον·
ὑγιὴς δὲ γενόμενος καὶ προσποιησάμενος ξύλινον
πόδα κατεστήκεε ἐκ τῆς ἰθέης Λακεδαιμονίοισι
πολέμιος. οὐ μέντοι ἔς γε τέλος οἱ συνήνεικε τὸ
ἔχθος τὸ ἐς Λακεδαιμονίους συγκεκυρημένον· ἥλω
γὰρ μαντευόμενος ἐν Ζακύνθῳ ὑπ' αὐτῶν καὶ
ἀπέθανε.

38. Ὁ μέντοι θάνατος ὁ Ἡγησιστράτου ὕστερον
ἐγένετο τῶν Πλαταιικῶν, τότε δὲ ἐπὶ τῷ Ἀσωπῷ
Μαρδονίῳ μεμισθωμένος οὐκ ὀλίγου ἐθύετό τε καὶ
προεθυμέετο κατά τε τὸ ἔχθος τὸ Λακεδαιμονίων καὶ

of Elis was his diviner, the most notable of the sons of Tellias. This man had been put in prison and doomed to die by the Spartans for the much harm that he had done them. Being in this evil case, inasmuch as he was in peril of his life and like to be very grievously maltreated ere his death, he did a deed well nigh past believing: being made fast in iron-bound stocks, he got an iron weapon that was brought in some wise into his prison, and straight-way conceived a plan of such hardihood as we have never known; reckoning how best the rest of it might get free, he cut off his own foot at the instep. This done, he burrowed through the wall out of the way of the guards that kept ward over him, and so escaped to Tegea; all night he journeyed and all day he hid and lay close in the woods, till on the third night he came to Tegea, while all the people of Lacedae-mon sought him; and they were greatly amazed, seeing the half of his foot cut off and lying there, but not being able to find the man himself. Thus did he then escape from the Lacedaemonians and take refuge in Tegea, which at that time was un-friendly to Lacedaemon; and after he was healed and had made himself a foot of wood, he declared himself an open enemy of the Lacedaemonians. Yet the enmity that he bore them brought him no good at the last; for they caught him at his divinations in Zacynthus, and slew him.

38. Howbeit, the death of Hegesistratus happened after the Plataean business; at the present he was by the Asopus, hired by Mardonius for no small wage, where he sacrificed and wrought zealously, both for the hatred he bore the Lacedaemonians,

κατὰ τὸ κέρδος. ὡς δὲ οὐκ ἐκαλλιέρεε ὥστε μάχεσθαι
οὔτε αὐτοῖσι Πέρσῃσι οὔτε τοῖσι μετ' ἐκείνων ἐοῦσι
Ἑλλήνων (εἶχον γὰρ καὶ οὗτοι ἐπ' ἑωυτῶν μάντιν
Ἱππόμαχον Λευκάδιον ἄνδρα), ἐπιρρεόντων δὲ τῶν
Ἑλλήνων καὶ γινομένων πλεύνων, Τιμηγενίδης ὁ
Ἕρπυος ἀνὴρ Θηβαῖος συνεβούλευσε Μαρδονίῳ
τὰς ἐκβολὰς τοῦ Κιθαιρῶνος φυλάξαι, λέγων ὡς
ἐπιρρέουσι οἱ Ἕλληνες αἰεὶ ἀνὰ πᾶσαν ἡμέρην
καὶ ὡς ἀπολάμψοιτο συχνούς.

39. Ἡμέραι δέ σφι ἀντικατημένοισι ἤδη ἐγεγόνεσαν ὀκτώ, ὅτε ταῦτα ἐκεῖνος συνεβούλευε
Μαρδονίῳ. ὁ δὲ μαθὼν τὴν παραίνεσιν εὖ ἔχουσαν,
ὡς εὐφρόνη ἐγένετο, πέμπει τὴν ἵππον ἐς τὰς
ἐκβολὰς τὰς Κιθαιρωνίδας αἳ ἐπὶ Πλαταιέων
φέρουσι, τὰς Βοιωτοὶ μὲν Τρεῖς κεφαλὰς καλέουσι,
Ἀθηναῖοι δὲ Δρυὸς κεφαλάς. πεμφθέντες δὲ οἱ
ἱππόται οὐ μάτην ἀπίκοντο· ἐσβάλλοντα γὰρ ἐς
τὸ πεδίον λαμβάνουσι ὑποζύγιά τε πεντακόσια,
σιτία ἄγοντα ἀπὸ Πελοποννήσου ἐς τὸ στρατόπεδον, καὶ ἀνθρώπους οἳ εἵποντο τοῖσι ζεύγεσι.
ἑλόντες δὲ ταύτην τὴν ἄγρην οἱ Πέρσαι ἀφειδέως
ἐφόνευον, οὐ φειδόμενοι οὔτε ὑποζυγίου οὐδενὸς
οὔτε ἀνθρώπου. ὡς δὲ ἄδην εἶχον κτείνοντες, τὰ
λοιπὰ αὐτῶν ἤλαυνον περιβαλόμενοι παρά τε
Μαρδόνιον καὶ ἐς τὸ στρατόπεδον.

40. Μετὰ δὲ τοῦτο τὸ ἔργον ἑτέρας δύο ἡμέρας
διέτριψαν, οὐδέτεροι βουλόμενοι μάχης ἄρξαι·
μέχρι μὲν γὰρ τοῦ Ἀσωποῦ ἐπήισαν οἱ βάρβαροι
πειρώμενοι τῶν Ἑλλήνων, διέβαινον δὲ οὐδέτεροι.
ἡ μέντοι ἵππος ἡ Μαρδονίου αἰεὶ προσέκειτο τε
καὶ ἐλύπεε τοὺς Ἕλληνας· οἱ γὰρ Θηβαῖοι, ἅτε
μηδίζοντες μεγάλως, προθύμως ἔφερον τὸν πόλε-

and for gain. But when no favourable omens for battle could be won either by the Persians themselves or by the Greeks that were with them (for they too had a diviner of their own, Hippomachus of Leucas), and the Greeks the while were ever flocking in and their army grew, Timagenides son of Herpys, a Theban, counselled Mardonius to guard the outlet of the pass over Cithaeron, telling him that the Greeks were ever flocking in daily and that he would thereby cut off many of them.

39. The armies had now lain over against each other for eight days when he gave this counsel. Mardonius perceived that the advice was good; and when night had fallen he sent his horsemen to the outlet of the pass over Cithaeron that leads towards Plataeae, which pass the Boeotians call the Three Heads, and the Athenians the Oaks' Heads. This despatch of the horsemen was no fruitless one; for they caught five hundred beasts of burden issuing into the low country, bringing provision from the Peloponnese for the army, and men that came with the waggons; having taken which quarry the Persians slew without mercy, sparing neither man nor beast. When they had their fill of slaughter, they set what remained in their midst and drove them to Mardonius and his camp.

40. After this deed they waited two days more, neither side desiring to begin the battle; for though the foreigners came to the Asopus to make trial of the Greeks' purpose, neither army crossed it. Howbeit Mardonius' horse was ever besetting and troubling the Greeks; for the Thebans, in their zeal for the Persian part, waged war heartily, and

μον καὶ αἰεὶ κατηγέοντο μέχρι μάχης, τὸ δὲ ἀπὸ
τούτου παραδεκόμενοι Πέρσαι τε καὶ Μῆδοι μάλα
ἔσκον οἱ ἀπεδείκνυντο ἀρετάς.

41. Μέχρι μέν νυν τῶν δέκα ἡμερέων οὐδὲν ἐπὶ
πλεῦν ἐγίνετο τούτων· ὡς δὲ ἑνδεκάτη ἐγεγόνεε
ἡμέρη ἀντικατημένοισι ἐν Πλαταιῇσι, οἵ τε δὴ
Ἕλληνες πολλῷ πλεῦνες ἐγεγόνεσαν καὶ Μαρδόνιος περιημέκτεε τῇ ἕδρῃ, ἐνθαῦτα ἐς λόγους
ἦλθον Μαρδόνιός τε ὁ Γοβρύεω καὶ Ἀρτάβαζος
ὁ Φαρνάκεος, ὃς ἐν ὀλίγοισι Περσέων ἦν ἀνὴρ
δόκιμος παρὰ Ξέρξῃ. βουλευομένων δὲ αἵδε ἦσαν
αἱ γνῶμαι, ἣ μὲν Ἀρταβάζου ὡς χρεὸν εἴη ἀναζεύξαντας τὴν ταχίστην πάντα τὸν στρατὸν ἰέναι
ἐς τὸ τεῖχος τὸ Θηβαίων, ἔνθα σῖτόν τέ σφι
ἐσενηνεῖχθαι πολλὸν καὶ χόρτον τοῖσι ὑποζυγίοισι,
κατ' ἡσυχίην τε ἱζομένους διαπρήσσεσθαι ποι-
εῦντας τάδε· ἔχειν γὰρ χρυσὸν πολλὸν μὲν ἐπίσημον πολλὸν δὲ καὶ ἄσημον, πολλὸν δὲ ἄργυρόν
τε καὶ ἐκπώματα· τούτων φειδομένους μηδενὸς
διαπέμπειν ἐς τοὺς Ἕλληνας, Ἑλλήνων δὲ μάλιστα ἐς τοὺς προεστεῶτας ἐν τῇσι πόλισι, καὶ
ταχέως σφέας παραδώσειν τὴν ἐλευθερίην· μηδὲ
ἀνακινδυνεύειν συμβάλλοντας. τούτου μὲν ἡ αὐτὴ
ἐγίνετο καὶ Θηβαίων γνώμη, ὡς προειδότος πλεῦν
τι καὶ τούτου, Μαρδονίου δὲ ἰσχυροτέρη τε καὶ
ἀγνωμονεστέρη καὶ οὐδαμῶς συγγινωσκομένη·
δοκέειν τε γὰρ πολλῷ κρέσσονα εἶναι τὴν σφετέρην
στρατιὴν τῆς Ἑλληνικῆς, συμβάλλειν τε τὴν ταχίστην μηδὲ περιορᾶν συλλεγομένους ἔτι πλεῦνας
τῶν συλλελεγμένων, τά τε σφάγια τὰ Ἡγησισ-

were ever guiding the horsemen to the encounter;
thereafter it was the turn of the Persians and
Medes, and they and none other would do deeds of
valour.

41. Until the ten days were past no more was
done than this; but on the eleventh day from their
first encampment over against each other, the
Greeks growing greatly in number and Mardonius
being sore vexed by the delay, there was a debate
held between Mardonius son of Gobryas and Artabazus son of Pharnaces, who stood as high as but
few others in Xerxes' esteem; and their opinions
in council were as I will show. Artabazus held it
best that they should strike their camp with all
speed and lead the whole army within the walls of
Thebes, where they had much provision stored and
fodder for their beasts of burden, and where they
could sit at their ease and despatch the business
by taking the great store they had of gold, minted
and other, and silver and drinking-cups, and sending
all this without stint to all places in Hellas, but
especially to the chief men in the cities of Hellas;
let them do this (said he) and the Greeks would
quickly surrender their liberty; but let not the
Persians risk the event of a battle. This opinion
of his was the same as the Thebans', inasmuch as he
too had especial foreknowledge; but Mardonius'
counsel was more vehement and intemperate and
nowise leaning to moderation; for (said he) he
deemed that their army was by much stronger than
the Greeks', and that they should give battle with
all speed, and not suffer yet more Greeks to muster
than were mustered already; as for the sacrifices of
Hegesistratus, let them pay no heed to these, nor

τράτου ἐᾶν χαίρειν μηδὲ βιάζεσθαι, ἀλλὰ νόμῳ
τῷ Περσέων χρεωμένους συμβάλλειν.

42. Τούτου δὲ οὕτω δικαιεῦντος ἀντέλεγε οὐδείς,
ὥστε ἐκράτεε τῇ γνώμῃ· τὸ γὰρ κράτος εἶχε τῆς
στρατιῆς οὗτος ἐκ βασιλέος, ἀλλ᾽ οὐκ Ἀρτάβαζος.
μεταπεμψάμενος ὦν τοὺς ταξιάρχους τῶν τελέων
καὶ τῶν μετ᾽ ἑωυτοῦ ἐόντων Ἑλλήνων τοὺς στρατηγοὺς εἰρώτα εἴ τι εἰδεῖεν λόγιον περὶ Περσέων
ὡς διαφθερέονται ἐν τῇ Ἑλλάδι. σιγώντων δὲ τῶν
ἐπικλήτων, τῶν μὲν οὐκ εἰδότων τοὺς χρησμούς,
τῶν δὲ εἰδότων μὲν ἐν ἀδείῃ δὲ οὐ ποιευμένων τὸ
λέγειν, αὐτὸς Μαρδόνιος ἔλεγε " ἐπεὶ τοίνυν ὑμεῖς
ἢ ἴστε οὐδὲν ἢ οὐ τολμᾶτε λέγειν, ἀλλ᾽ ἐγὼ ἐρέω
ὡς εὖ ἐπιστάμενος· ἔστι λόγιον ὡς χρεόν ἐστι
Πέρσας ἀπικομένους ἐς τὴν Ἑλλάδα διαρπάσαι τὸ
ἱρὸν τὸ ἐν Δελφοῖσι, μετὰ δὲ τὴν διαρπαγὴν ἀπολέσθαι πάντας. ἡμεῖς τοίνυν αὐτὸ τοῦτο ἐπιστάμενοι οὔτε ἴμεν ἐπὶ τὸ ἱρὸν τοῦτο οὔτε ἐπιχειρή-
σομεν διαρπάζειν, ταύτης τε εἵνεκα τῆς αἰτίης οὐκ
ἀπολεόμεθα. ὥστε ὑμέων ὅσοι τυγχάνουσι εὔνοοι
ἐόντες Πέρσῃσι, ἥδεσθε τοῦδε εἵνεκα ὡς περιεσομέ-
νους ἡμέας Ἑλλήνων." ταῦτά σφι εἴπας δεύτερα
ἐσήμαινε παραρτέεσθαί τε πάντα καὶ εὐκρινέα
ποιέεσθαι ὡς ἅμα ἡμέρῃ τῇ ἐπιούσῃ συμβολῆς
ἐσομένης.

43. Τοῦτον δ᾽ ἔγωγε τὸν χρησμόν, τὸν Μαρδόνιος εἶπε ἐς Πέρσας ἔχειν, ἐς Ἰλλυριούς τε καὶ
τὸν Ἐγχελέων στρατὸν οἶδα πεποιημένον, ἀλλ᾽

---

[1] Lit. to do violence, compel the gods, like " superos votis
fatigare " in Latin.

seek to wring good from them,[1] but rather give battle after Persian custom.

42. None withstood this argument, so that his opinion prevailed ; for it was he and not Artabazus who was generalissimo of the army by the king's commission. He sent therefore for the leaders of the battalions and the generals of those Greeks that were with him, and asked them if they knew any oracle which prophesied that the Persians should perish in Hellas. They that were summoned said nought, some not knowing the prophecies, and some knowing them but deeming it perilous to speak ; then said Mardonius himself: "Since, therefore, you either have no knowledge or are afraid to declare it, hear what I tell you out of the full knowledge that I have. There is an oracle that Persians are fated to come to Hellas and there all perish after they have plundered the temple at Delphi. We, therefore, knowing this same oracle, will neither approach that temple nor essay to plunder it ; and in so far as destruction hangs on that, none awaits us. Wherefore as many of you as wish the Persians well may rejoice for that, as knowing that we shall overcome the Greeks." Having thus spoken he gave command to have all prepared and set in fair order for the battle that should be joined at the next day's dawn.

43. Now for this prophecy, which Mardonius said was spoken of the Persians, I know it to have been made concerning not them but the Illyrians and the

οὐκ ἐς Πέρσας. ἀλλὰ τὰ μὲν Βάκιδι ἐς ταύτην
τὴν μάχην ἐστὶ πεποιημένα,

τὴν δ' ἐπὶ Θερμώδοντι καὶ Ἀσωπῷ λεχεποίη
Ἑλλήνων σύνοδον καὶ βαρβαρόφωνον ἰυγήν,
τῇ πολλοὶ πεσέονται ὑπὲρ λάχεσίν τε μόρον τε
τοξοφόρων Μήδων, ὅταν αἴσιμον ἦμαρ ἐπέλθῃ,

ταῦτα μὲν καὶ παραπλήσια τούτοισι ἄλλα Μουσαίῳ ἔχοντα οἶδα ἐς Πέρσας. ὁ δὲ Θερμώδων
ποταμὸς ῥέει μεταξὺ Τανάγρης τε καὶ Γλίσαντος.
44. Μετὰ δὲ τὴν ἐπειρώτησιν τῶν χρησμῶν καὶ
παραίνεσιν τὴν ἐκ Μαρδονίου νύξ τε ἐγίνετο καὶ
ἐς φυλακὰς ἐτάσσοντο. ὡς δὲ πρόσω τῆς νυκτὸς
προελήλατο καὶ ἡσυχίη ἐδόκεε εἶναι ἀνὰ τὰ στρατόπεδα καὶ μάλιστα οἱ ἄνθρωποι εἶναι ἐν ὕπνῳ,
τηνικαῦτα προσελάσας ἵππῳ πρὸς τὰς φυλακὰς
τὰς Ἀθηναίων Ἀλέξανδρος ὁ Ἀμύντεω, στρατηγός
τε ἐὼν καὶ βασιλεὺς Μακεδόνων, ἐδίζητο τοῖσι
στρατηγοῖσι ἐς λόγους ἐλθεῖν. τῶν δὲ φυλάκων
οἱ μὲν πλεῦνες παρέμενον, οἳ δ' ἔθεον ἐπὶ τοὺς
στρατηγούς, ἐλθόντες δὲ ἔλεγον ὡς ἄνθρωπος
ἥκοι ἐπ' ἵππου ἐκ τοῦ στρατοπέδου τοῦ Μήδων,
ὃς ἄλλο μὲν οὐδὲν παραγυμνοῖ ἔπος, στρατηγοὺς
δὲ ὀνομάζων ἐθέλειν φησὶ ἐς λόγους ἐλθεῖν.
45. Οἳ δὲ ἐπεὶ ταῦτα ἤκουσαν, αὐτίκα εἵποντο
ἐς τὰς φυλακάς· ἀπικομένοισι δὲ ἔλεγε Ἀλέξανδρος τάδε· "Ἄνδρες Ἀθηναῖοι, παραθήκην
ὑμῖν τὰ ἔπεα τάδε τίθεμαι, ἀπόρρητα ποιεύ-

---

[1] Referring to a legendary expedition of these north-
western tribes, directed against Hellas and Delphi in
particular.
[2] A little to the N.W. of Thebes.

army of the Encheleës.[1] But there is a prophecy
made by Bacis concerning this battle:

> By Thermodon's stream and the grassgrown banks
>   of Asopus
> Muster of Greeks for fight, and the ring of a
>   foreigner's war-cry,
> Many a Median archer by death untimely o'er-
>   taken
> There in the battle shall fall when the day of his
>   doom is upon him;

this prophecy, and others like to it that were
made by Musaeus, I know to have been spoken of
the Persians. As for the river Thermodon, it flows
between Tanagra and Glisas.[2]

44. After this questioning concerning oracles, and
Mardonius' exhortation, night came on and the
armies posted their sentries. Now when the night
was far spent and it seemed that all was still in the
camps and the men wrapt in deepest slumber, at
that hour Alexander son of Amyntas, the general
and king of the Macedonians, rode up to the
Athenian outposts and sought to have speech of
their generals. The greater part of the sentries
abiding where they were, the rest ran to their
generals, and told them that a horseman had ridden
in from the Persian camp, imparting no other word
save that he would have speech of the generals and
called them by their names.

45. Hearing that, the generals straightway went
with the men to the outposts; and when they were
come Alexander said to them: "Men of Athens, I
give you this my message in trust as a secret that

μενος πρὸς μηδένα λέγειν ὑμέας ἄλλον ἢ
Παυσανίην, μή με καὶ διαφθείρητε· οὐ γὰρ ἂν
ἔλεγον, εἰ μὴ μεγάλως ἐκηδόμην συναπάσης τῆς
Ἑλλάδος. αὐτός τε γὰρ Ἕλλην γένος εἰμὶ
τώρχαῖον καὶ ἀντ' ἐλευθέρης δεδουλωμένην οὐκ
ἂν ἐθέλοιμι ὁρᾶν τὴν Ἑλλάδα. λέγω δὲ ὦν ὅτι
Μαρδονίῳ τε καὶ τῇ στρατιῇ τὰ σφάγια οὐ
δύναται καταθύμια γενέσθαι· πάλαι γὰρ ἂν
ἐμάχεσθε. νῦν δέ οἱ δέδοκται τὰ μὲν σφάγια
ἐᾶν χαίρειν, ἅμ' ἡμέρῃ δὲ διαφωσκούσῃ συμβολὴν
ποιέεσθαι· καταρρώδηκε γὰρ μὴ πλεῦνες συλ-
λεχθῆτε, ὡς ἐγὼ εἰκάζω. πρὸς ταῦτα ἑτοιμά-
ζεσθε. ἢν δὲ ἄρα ὑπερβάληται τὴν συμβολὴν
Μαρδόνιος καὶ μὴ ποιέηται, λιπαρέετε μένοντες·
ὀλιγέων γάρ σφι ἡμερέων λείπεται σιτία. ἢν δὲ
ὑμῖν ὁ πόλεμος ὅδε κατὰ νόον τελευτήσῃ, μνη-
σθῆναί τινα χρὴ καὶ ἐμεῦ ἐλευθερώσιος πέρι, ὃς
Ἑλλήνων εἵνεκα οὕτω ἔργον παράβολον ἔργασμαι
ὑπὸ προθυμίης, ἐθέλων ὑμῖν δηλῶσαι τὴν διά-
νοιαν τὴν Μαρδονίου, ἵνα μὴ ἐπιπέσωσι ὑμῖν
ἐξαίφνης οἱ βάρβαροι μὴ προσδεκομένοισί κω.
εἰμὶ δὲ Ἀλέξανδρος ὁ Μακεδών." ὁ μὲν ταῦτα
εἴπας ἀπήλαυνε ὀπίσω ἐς τὸ στρατόπεδον καὶ
τὴν ἑωυτοῦ τάξιν.

46. Οἱ δὲ στρατηγοὶ τῶν Ἀθηναίων ἐλθόντες
ἐπὶ τὸ δεξιὸν κέρας ἔλεγον Παυσανίῃ τά περ
ἤκουσαν Ἀλεξάνδρου. ὁ δὲ τούτῳ τῷ λόγῳ
καταρρωδήσας τοὺς Πέρσας ἔλεγε τάδε. "Ἐπεὶ
τοίνυν ἐς ἠῶ ἡ συμβολὴ γίνεται, ὑμέας μὲν χρεόν
ἐστι τοὺς Ἀθηναίους στῆναι κατὰ τοὺς Πέρσας,
ἡμέας δὲ κατὰ τοὺς Βοιωτούς τε καὶ τοὺς κατ'
ὑμέας τεταγμένους Ἑλλήνων, τῶνδε εἵνεκα· ὑμεῖς

you must reveal to none but Pausanias, lest you even be my undoing; in truth I would not tell it to you were it not by reason of my great care for all Hellas; for I myself am by ancient descent a Greek, and I would not willingly see Hellas change her freedom for slavery. I tell you, then, that Mardonius and his army cannot get from the sacrifices omens to his liking; else had you fought long ere this. But now it is his purpose to pay no heed to the sacrifices, and join battle at the first glimmer of dawn; for he is in dread, as I surmise, lest you should muster to a greater host. Therefore I bid you make ready; and if (as may be) Mardonius should delay and not join battle, wait patiently where you are; for he has but a few days' provision left. But if this war end as you would wish, then must you take thought how to save me too from slavery, who of my zeal have done so desperate a deed as this for the cause of Hellas, in my desire to declare to you Mardonius' intent, that so the foreigners may not fall upon you suddenly ere you yet expect them. I that speak am Alexander the Macedonian." With that he rode away back to the camp and his own place therein.

46. The Athenian generals went to the right wing and told Pausanias what they had heard from Alexander. At the message Pausanias was struck with fear of the Persians, and said: "Since, therefore, the battle is to begin at dawn, it is best that you Athenians should take your stand fronting the Persians, and we fronting the Boeotians and the Greeks that are posted over against you, by reason that you

ἐπίστασθε τοὺς Μήδους καὶ τὴν μάχην αὐτῶν ἐν
Μαραθῶνι μαχεσάμενοι, ἡμεῖς δὲ ἄπειροί τε εἰμὲν
καὶ ἀδαέες τούτων τῶν ἀνδρῶν· Σπαρτιητέων γὰρ
οὐδεὶς πεπείρηται Μήδων· ἡμεῖς δὲ Βοιωτῶν καὶ
Θεσσαλῶν ἔμπειροι εἰμέν. ἀλλ᾽ ἀναλαβόντας τὰ
ὅπλα χρεόν ἐστι ἰέναι ὑμέας μὲν ἐς τόδε τὸ κέρας,
ἡμέας δὲ ἐς τὸ εὐώνυμον." πρὸς δὲ ταῦτα εἶπαν
οἱ Ἀθηναῖοι τάδε. "Καὶ αὐτοῖσι ἡμῖν πάλαι ἀπ᾽
ἀρχῆς, ἐπείτε εἴδομεν κατ᾽ ὑμέας τασσομένους
τοὺς Πέρσας, ἐν νόῳ ἐγένετο εἰπεῖν ταῦτα τά περ
ὑμεῖς φθάντες προφέρετε· ἀλλὰ ἀρρωδέομεν μὴ
ὑμῖν οὐκ ἡδέες γένωνται οἱ λόγοι. ἐπεὶ δ᾽ ὦν
αὐτοὶ ἐμνήσθητε, καὶ ἡδομένοισι ἡμῖν οἱ λόγοι
γεγόνασι καὶ ἕτοιμοι εἰμὲν ποιέειν ταῦτα."

47. Ὡς δ᾽ ἤρεσκε ἀμφοτέροισι ταῦτα, ἠώς τε
διέφαινε καὶ διαλλάσσοντο τὰς τάξις. γνόντες
δὲ οἱ Βοιωτοὶ τὸ ποιεύμενον ἐξαγορεύουσι Μαρδονίῳ. ὁ δ᾽ ἐπείτε ἤκουσε, αὐτίκα μετιστάναι καὶ
αὐτὸς ἐπειρᾶτο, παράγων τοὺς Πέρσας κατὰ
τοὺς Λακεδαιμονίους. ὡς δὲ ἔμαθε τοῦτο τοιοῦτο
γινόμενον ὁ Παυσανίης, γνοὺς ὅτι οὐ λανθάνει,
ὀπίσω ἦγε τοὺς Σπαρτιήτας ἐπὶ τὸ δεξιὸν κέρας·
ὡς δὲ οὕτως καὶ ὁ Μαρδόνιος ἐπὶ τοῦ εὐωνύμου.

48. Ἐπεὶ δὲ κατέστησαν ἐς τὰς ἀρχαίας τάξις,
πέμψας ὁ Μαρδόνιος κήρυκα ἐς τοὺς Σπαρτιήτας
ἔλεγε τάδε. "Ὦ Λακεδαιμόνιοι, ὑμεῖς δὴ λέγεσθε
εἶναι ἄνδρες ἄριστοι ὑπὸ τῶν τῇδε ἀνθρώπων,
ἐκπαγλεομένων ὡς οὔτε φεύγετε ἐκ πολέμου οὔτε
τάξιν ἐκλείπετε, μένοντές τε ἢ ἀπόλλυτε τοὺς
ἐναντίους ἢ αὐτοὶ ἀπόλλυσθε. τῶν δ᾽ ἄρ᾽ ἦν οὐδὲν
ἀληθές· πρὶν γὰρ ἢ συμμῖξαι ἡμέας ἐς χειρῶν τε
νόμον ἀπικέσθαι, καὶ δὴ φεύγοντας καὶ στάσιν

have fought with the Medes at Marathon and know them and their manner of fighting, but we have no experience or knowledge of those men; we Spartans have experience of the Boeotians and Thessalians, but not one of us has put the Medes to the test. Nay, let us take up our equipment and remove, you to this wing and we to the left." "We, too," the Athenians answered, "even from the moment when we saw the Persians posted over against you, had it in mind to make that proffer that now has first come from you; but we feared lest we should displease you by making it. But since you have spoken the wish yourselves, we too hear your words very gladly and are ready to do as you say."

47. Both being satisfied with this, they exchanged their places in the ranks at the first light of dawn. The Boeotians marked that and made it known to Mardonius; who, when he heard, forthwith essayed to make a change for himself also, by moving the Persians along to front the Lacedaemonians. But when Pausanias perceived what was this that was being done, he saw that his act was known, and led the Spartans back to the right wing; and Mardonius did in like manner on the left of his army.

48. When all were at their former posts again, Mardonius sent a herald to the Lacedaemonians with this message: "Men of Lacedaemon, you are said by the people of these parts to be very brave men; it is their boast of you that you neither flee from the field nor leave your post, but abide there and either slay your enemies or are yourselves slain. But it would seem that in all this there is no truth; for ere we can join battle and fight hand to hand, we have seen you even now fleeing and leaving your

ἐκλείποντας ὑμέας εἴδομεν, ἐν Ἀθηναίοισί τε τὴν
πρόπειραν ποιευμένους αὐτούς τε ἀντία δούλων
τῶν ἡμετέρων τασσομένους. ταῦτα οὐδαμῶς
ἀνδρῶν ἀγαθῶν ἔργα, ἀλλὰ πλεῖστον δὴ ἐν ὑμῖν
ἐψεύσθημεν. προσδεκόμενοι γὰρ κατὰ κλέος ὡς
δὴ πέμψετε ἐς ἡμέας κήρυκα προκαλεύμενοι καὶ
βουλόμενοι μούνοισι Πέρσῃσι μάχεσθαι, ἄρτιοι
ἐόντες ποιέειν ταῦτα οὐδὲν τοιοῦτο λέγοντας ὑμέας
εὕρομεν ἀλλὰ πτώσσοντας μᾶλλον. νῦν ὦν ἐπειδὴ
οὐκ ὑμεῖς ἤρξατε τούτου τοῦ λόγου, ἀλλ᾽ ἡμεῖς
ἄρχομεν. τί δὴ οὐ πρὸ μὲν τῶν Ἑλλήνων ὑμεῖς,
ἐπείτε δεδόξωσθε εἶναι ἄριστοι, πρὸ δὲ τῶν βαρβάρων ἡμεῖς ἴσοι πρὸς ἴσους ἀριθμὸν ἐμαχεσάμεθα;
καὶ ἢν μὲν δοκέῃ καὶ τοὺς ἄλλους μάχεσθαι, οἱ δ᾽
ὦν μετέπειτα μαχέσθων ὕστεροι· εἰ δὲ καὶ μὴ δοκέοι
ἀλλ᾽ ἡμέας μούνους ἀποχρᾶν, ἡμεῖς δὲ διαμαχε-
σώμεθα· ὁκότεροι δ᾽ ἂν ἡμέων νικήσωσι, τούτους
τῷ ἅπαντι στρατοπέδῳ νικᾶν."

49. Ὁ μὲν ταῦτα εἴπας τε καὶ ἐπισχὼν χρόνον,
ὥς οἱ οὐδεὶς οὐδὲν ὑπεκρίνατο, ἀπαλλάσσετο
ὀπίσω, ἀπελθὼν δὲ ἐσήμαινε Μαρδονίῳ τὰ κατα-
λαβόντα. ὁ δὲ περιχαρὴς γενόμενος καὶ ἐπαερ-
θεὶς ψυχρῇ νίκῃ ἐπῆκε τὴν ἵππον ἐπὶ τοὺς
Ἕλληνας. ὡς δὲ ἐπήλασαν οἱ ἱππόται, ἐσίνοντο
πᾶσαν τὴν στρατιὴν τὴν Ἑλληνικὴν ἐσακοντί-
ζοντές τε καὶ τοξεύοντες ὥστε ἱπποτοξόται τε
ἐόντες καὶ προσφέρεσθαι ἄποροι· τήν τε κρήνην
τὴν Γαργαφίην, ἀπ᾽ ἧς ὑδρεύετο πᾶν τὸ στράτευμα
τὸ Ἑλληνικόν, συνετάραξαν καὶ συνέχωσαν. ἦσαν
μὲν ὦν κατὰ τὴν κρήνην Λακεδαιμόνιοι τεταγμένοι
μοῦνοι, τοῖσι δὲ ἄλλοισι Ἕλλησι ἡ μὲν κρήνη
πρόσω ἐγίνετο, ὡς ἕκαστοι ἔτυχον τεταγμένοι, ὁ

station, using Athenians for the first assay of your
enemy, and arraying yourselves over against those
that are but our slaves. This is no brave men's
work; nay, we have been grievously mistaken in
you; for by what we heard of you, we looked that
you should send us a herald challenging the Persians
and none other to fight with you; and that we were
ready to do; but we find you making no such proffer,
but rather quailing before us. Now, therefore, since
the challenge comes not from you, take it from us
instead. What hinders that we should fight with
equal numbers on both sides, you for the Greeks
(since you have the name of being their best), and
we for the foreigners? and if it be willed that
the others fight also, let them fight later after us;
but if contrariwise it be willed that we alone suffice,
then let us fight it out, and which side soever
wins, let that serve as a victory for the whole
army."

49. Thus proclaimed the herald; and when he had
waited awhile and none made him any answer, he
departed back again, and at his return told Mardonius
what had befallen him. Mardonius was overjoyed
thereat and proud of this semblance of victory, and
sent his cavalry to attack the Greeks. The horsemen rode at them and shot arrows and javelins
among the whole Greek army to its great hurt,
inasmuch as they were mounted archers and ill to
close with; and they troubled and choked the
Gargaphian spring, whence all the army of the
Greeks drew its water. None indeed but the Lacedaemonians were posted near the spring, and it was
far from the several stations of the other Greeks,

δὲ Ἀσωπὸς ἀγχοῦ· ἐρυκόμενοι δὲ τοῦ Ἀσωποῦ
οὕτω δὴ ἐπὶ τὴν κρήνην ἐφοίτων· ἀπὸ τοῦ ποταμοῦ γάρ σφι οὐκ ἐξῆν ὕδωρ φορέεσθαι ὑπό τε
τῶν ἱππέων καὶ τοξευμάτων.

50. Τούτου δὲ τοιούτου γινομένου οἱ τῶν Ἑλλήνων στρατηγοί, ἅτε τοῦ τε ὕδατος στερηθείσης
τῆς στρατιῆς καὶ ὑπὸ τῆς ἵππου ταρασσομένης,
συνελέχθησαν περὶ αὐτῶν τε τούτων καὶ ἄλλων,
ἐλθόντες παρὰ Παυσανίην ἐπὶ τὸ δεξιὸν κέρας.
ἄλλα γὰρ τούτων τοιούτων ἐόντων μᾶλλον σφέας
ἐλύπεε· οὔτε γὰρ σιτία εἶχον ἔτι, οἵ τε σφέων
ὀπέωνες ἀποπεμφθέντες ἐς Πελοπόννησον ὡς
ἐπισιτιεύμενοι ἀπεκεκλήιατο ὑπὸ τῆς ἵππου, οὐ
δυνάμενοι ἀπικέσθαι ἐς τὸ στρατόπεδον.

51. Βουλευομένοισι δὲ τοῖσι στρατηγοῖσι ἔδοξε,
ἢν ὑπερβάλωνται ἐκείνην τὴν ἡμέρην οἱ Πέρσαι
συμβολὴν ποιεύμενοι, ἐς τὴν νῆσον ἰέναι. ἡ δὲ
ἐστὶ ἀπὸ τοῦ Ἀσωποῦ καὶ τῆς κρήνης τῆς Γαργαφίης, ἐπ' ᾗ ἐστρατοπεδεύοντο τότε, δέκα σταδίους ἀπέχουσα, πρὸ τῆς Πλαταιέων πόλιος.
νῆσος δὲ οὕτω ἂν εἴη ἐν ἠπείρῳ· σχιζόμενος ὁ
ποταμὸς ἄνωθεν ἐκ τοῦ Κιθαιρῶνος ῥέει κάτω ἐς
τὸ πεδίον, διέχων ἀπ' ἀλλήλων τὰ ῥέεθρα ὅσον
περ τρία στάδια, καὶ ἔπειτα συμμίσγει ἐς τώυτό.
οὔνομα δέ οἱ Ὠερόη· θυγατέρα δὲ ταύτην λέγουσι
εἶναι Ἀσωποῦ οἱ ἐπιχώριοι. ἐς τοῦτον δὴ τὸν
χῶρον ἐβουλεύσαντο μεταναστῆναι, ἵνα καὶ ὕδατι
ἔχωσι χρᾶσθαι ἀφθόνῳ καὶ οἱ ἱππέες σφέας μὴ

---

[1] Several streams flow N. or N.W. from Cithaeron, and
unite eventually to form the small river Oëroë. Between
two of these there is a long strip of land, which is perhaps

whereas the Asopus was near; but they would ever
go to the spring, because they were barred from the
Asopus, not being able to draw water from that
river by reason of the horsemen and the arrows.

50. In this turn of affairs, seeing that their army
was cut off from water and disordered by the horsemen, the generals of the Greeks betook themselves
to Pausanias on the right wing, and debated concerning this and other matters; for there were other
causes that troubled them more than what I have
told; they had no food left, and their followers
whom they had sent into the Peloponnese to bring
provision thence had been cut off by the horsemen,
and could not make their way to the army.

51. So they resolved in their council that if the
Persians delayed through that day to give battle,
they would go to the Island.[1] This is ten furlongs
distant from the Asopus and the Gargaphian spring,
whereby their army then lay, and in front of the town
of Plataeae. It is like to an island on dry land, by
reason that the river in its course down from Cithaeron
into the plain is parted into two channels, and there
is about three furlongs' space between till presently
the two channels unite again; and the name of that
river is Oëroë, who (say the people of the country)
was the daughter of Asopus. To that place then
they planned to remove, that they might have water
in plenty for their use, and not be harmed by the

the νῆσος; but it is not now actually surrounded by water,
as Herodotus describes it.

For some notice of controversy about the battlefield of
Plataeae, see the Introduction to this volume.

σινοίατο ὥσπερ κατιθὺ ἐόντων· μετακινέεσθαί τε
ἐδόκεε τότε ἐπεὰν τῆς νυκτὸς ᾖ δευτέρη φυλακή,
ὡς ἂν μὴ ἰδοίατο οἱ Πέρσαι ἐξορμωμένους καί
σφεας ἑπόμενοι ταράσσοιεν οἱ ἱππόται. ἀπικομένων δὲ ἐς τὸν χῶρον τοῦτον, τὸν δὴ ἡ Ἀσωπὶς
Ὠερόη περισχίζεται ῥέουσα ἐκ τοῦ Κιθαιρῶνος,
ὑπὸ τὴν νύκτα ταύτην ἐδόκεε τοὺς ἡμίσεας ἀπο-
στέλλειν τοῦ στρατοπέδου πρὸς τὸν Κιθαιρῶνα,
ὡς ἀναλάβοιεν τοὺς ὀπέωνας τοὺς ἐπὶ τὰ σιτία
οἰχομένους· ἦσαν γὰρ ἐν τῷ Κιθαιρῶνι ἀπολε-
λαμμένοι.

52. Ταῦτα βουλευσάμενοι κείνην μὲν τὴν
ἡμέρην πᾶσαν προσκειμένης τῆς ἵππου εἶχον
πόνον ἄτρυτον· ὡς δὲ ἥ τε ἡμέρη ἔληγε καὶ οἱ
ἱππέες ἐπέπαυντο, νυκτὸς δὴ γινομένης καὶ ἐούσης
τῆς ὥρης ἐς τὴν συνέκειτό σφι ἀπαλλάσσεσθαι,
ἐνθαῦτα ἀερθέντες οἱ πολλοὶ ἀπαλλάσσοντο, ἐς
μὲν τὸν χῶρον ἐς τὸν συνέκειτο οὐκ ἐν νόῳ ἔχοντες,
οἳ δὲ ὡς ἐκινήθησαν ἔφευγον ἄσμενοι τὴν ἵππον
πρὸς τὴν Πλαταιέων πόλιν, φεύγοντες δὲ ἀπικνέονται ἐπὶ τὸ Ἥραιον· τὸ δὲ πρὸ τῆς πόλιος ἐστὶ τῆς
Πλαταιέων, εἴκοσι σταδίους ἀπὸ τῆς κρήνης τῆς
Γαργαφίης ἀπέχον· ἀπικόμενοι δὲ ἔθεντο πρὸ τοῦ
ἱροῦ τὰ ὅπλα.

53. Καὶ οἱ μὲν περὶ τὸ Ἥραιον ἐστρατοπεδεύοντο, Παυσανίης δὲ ὁρῶν σφεας ἀπαλλασσο-
μένους ἐκ τοῦ στρατοπέδου παρήγγελλε καὶ τοῖσι
Λακεδαιμονίοισι ἀναλαβόντας τὰ ὅπλα ἰέναι κατὰ
τοὺς ἄλλους τοὺς προϊόντας, νομίσας αὐτοὺς ἐς
τὸν χῶρον ἰέναι ἐς τὸν συνεθήκαντο. ἐνθαῦτα οἱ
μὲν ἄλλοι ἄρτιοι ἦσαν τῶν ταξιάρχων πείθεσθαι
Παυσανίῃ, Ἀμομφάρετος δὲ ὁ Πολιάδεω λοχη-

horsemen, as now when they were face to face; and
they resolved to make their removal in the second
watch of the night, lest the Persians should see
them setting forth and the horsemen press after them
and disorder their array. Further, they resolved
that when they were come to that place, which is
encircled by the divided channels of Asopus' daughter
Oëroë as she flows from Cithaeron, they would in
that night send half of their army to Cithaeron, to
fetch away their followers who were gone to get the
provision; for these were cut off from them on
Cithaeron.

52. Having formed this design, all that day they
suffered unending hardship from the cavalry that
continually beset them; but when the day ended
and the horsemen ceased from troubling, then at
that hour of the night whereat it was agreed that
they should depart the most of them arose and took
their departure, not with intent to go to the place
whereon they had agreed; instead of that, once they
were afoot they got quit to their great content of the
horsemen, and escaped to the town of Plataeae, and
came in their flight to the temple of Here which is
without that town, twenty furlongs distant from
the Gargaphian spring; thither they came, and piled
their arms before the temple.

53. So they encamped about the temple of Here.
But Pausanias, seeing their departure from the camp,
gave orders to the Lacedaemonians to take up their
arms likewise and follow after the others that went
before, supposing that these were making for the
place whither they had agreed to go. Thereupon,
all the rest of the captains being ready to obey
Pausanias, Amompharetus son of Poliades, the leader

γέων τοῦ Πιτανητέων λόχου οὐκ ἔφη τοὺς ξείνους
φεύξεσθαι οὐδὲ ἑκὼν εἶναι αἰσχυνέειν τὴν Σπάρτην, ἐθώμαζέ τε ὁρέων τὸ ποιεύμενον ἅτε οὐ παρα-
γενόμενος τῷ προτέρῳ λόγῳ. ὁ δὲ Παυσανίης τε
καὶ ὁ Εὐρυάναξ δεινὸν μὲν ἐποιεῦντο τὸ μὴ πείθεσθαι ἐκεῖνον σφίσι, δεινότερον δὲ ἔτι, κείνου
ταῦτ' ἀναινομένου, ἀπολιπεῖν τὸν λόχον τὸν Πι-
τανήτην, μὴ ἢν ἀπολίπωσι ποιεῦντες τὰ συνεθήκαντο τοῖσι ἄλλοισι Ἕλλησι, ἀπόληται ὑπολει-
φθεὶς αὐτός τε Ἀμομφάρετος καὶ οἱ μετ' αὐτοῦ.
ταῦτα λογιζόμενοι ἀτρέμας εἶχον τὸ στρατόπεδον
τὸ Λακωνικόν, καὶ ἐπειρῶντο πείθοντές μιν ὡς οὐ
χρεὸν εἴη ταῦτα ποιέειν.

54. Καὶ οἱ μὲν παρηγόρεον Ἀμομφάρετον μοῦνον Λακεδαιμονίων τε καὶ Τεγεητέων λελειμμένον,
Ἀθηναῖοι δὲ ἐποίευν τοιάδε· εἶχον ἀτρέμας σφέας
αὐτοὺς ἵνα ἐτάχθησαν, ἐπιστάμενοι τὰ Λακεδαιμονίων φρονήματα ὡς ἄλλα φρονεόντων καὶ ἄλλα
λεγόντων· ὡς δὲ ἐκινήθη τὸ στρατόπεδον, ἔπεμπον σφέων ἱππέα ὀψόμενόν τε εἰ πορεύεσθαι ἐπι-
χειρέοιεν οἱ Σπαρτιῆται, εἴτε καὶ τὸ παράπαν μὴ
διανοεῦνται ἀπαλλάσσεσθαι, ἐπειρέσθαι τε Παυσανίην τὸ χρεὸν εἴη ποιέειν.

55. Ὡς δὲ ἀπίκετο ὁ κῆρυξ ἐς τοὺς Λακεδαιμονίους, ὥρα τε σφέας κατὰ χώρην τεταγμένους καὶ
ἐς νείκεα ἀπιγμένους αὐτῶν τοὺς πρώτους. ὡς
γὰρ δὴ παρηγορέοντο τὸν Ἀμομφάρετον ὅ τε
Εὐρυάναξ καὶ ὁ Παυσανίης μὴ κινδυνεύειν μένοντας μούνους Λακεδαιμονίων, οὔ κως ἔπειθον, ἐς ὃ

of the Pitanate [1] battalion, refused to flee from the
strangers or (save by compulsion) bring shame on
Sparta; the whole business seemed strange to him,
for he had not been present in the council lately
held. Pausanias and Euryanax liked little enough
that Amompharetus should disobey them; but they
misliked yet more that his refusing should compel
them to abandon the Pitanate battalion; for they
feared that if they fulfilled their agreement with the
rest of the Greeks and abandoned him, Amompharetus
and his men would be left behind to perish. Thus
considering, they held the Laconian army unmoved,
and strove to persuade Amompharetus that he did
not aright.

54. So they reasoned with Amompharetus, he
being the only man left behind of all the Lacedaemonians and Tegeans. As for the Athenians, they
stood unmoved at their post, well knowing that the
purposes and the promises of Lacedaemonians were
not alike. But when the army removed from its
place, they sent a horseman of their own who should
see if the Spartans were essaying to march or if
they were wholly without any purpose of departure,
and should ask Pausanias withal what the Athenians
must do.

55. When the messenger was come to the Lacedaemonians, he saw them arrayed where they had been,
and their chief men by now in hot dispute. For
though Euryanax and Pausanias reasoned with Amompharetus, that the Lacedaemonians should not be
imperilled by abiding there alone, they could in no

---

[1] Thucydides (1. 20) denies the existence of a Πιτανάτης
λόχος as a formal part of the Spartan army; it is not clear
what Herodotus means. For Pitana v. iii. 55.

ἐς νείκεά τε συμπεσόντες ἀπίκατο καὶ ὁ κῆρυξ τῶν
Ἀθηναίων παρίστατό σφι ἀπιγμένος. νεικέων δὲ
ὁ Ἀμομφάρετος λαμβάνει πέτρον ἀμφοτέρῃσι τῇσι
χερσὶ καὶ τιθεὶς πρὸ ποδῶν τῶν Παυσανίεω ταύτῃ
τῇ ψήφῳ ψηφίζεσθαι ἔφη μὴ φεύγειν τοὺς ξείνους,
λέγων τοὺς βαρβάρους. ὁ δὲ μαινόμενον καὶ οὐ
φρενήρεα καλέων ἐκεῖνον, πρός τε τὸν Ἀθηναῖον
κήρυκα ἐπειρωτῶντα τὰ ἐντεταλμένα λέγειν ὁ
Παυσανίης ἐκέλευε τὰ παρεόντα σφι πρήγματα,
ἐχρήιζέ τε τῶν Ἀθηναίων προσχωρῆσαί τε πρὸς
ἑωυτοὺς καὶ ποιέειν περὶ τῆς ἀπόδου τά περ ἂν
καὶ σφεῖς.

56. Καὶ ὁ μὲν ἀπαλλάσσετο ἐς τοὺς Ἀθηναίους·
τοὺς δὲ ἐπεὶ ἀνακρινομένους πρὸς ἑωυτοὺς ἠὼς
κατελάμβανε, ἐν τούτῳ τῷ χρόνῳ κατήμενος ὁ
Παυσανίης, οὐ δοκέων τὸν Ἀμομφάρετον λείψεσθαι τῶν ἄλλων Λακεδαιμονίων ἀποστειχόντων, τὰ
δὴ καὶ ἐγένετο, σημήνας ἀπῆγε διὰ τῶν κολωνῶν
τοὺς λοιποὺς πάντας· εἵποντο δὲ καὶ Τεγεῆται.
Ἀθηναῖοι δὲ ταχθέντες ἤισαν τὰ ἔμπαλιν ἢ Λακε-
δαιμόνιοι· οἱ μὲν γὰρ τῶν τε ὄχθων ἀντείχοντο
καὶ τῆς ὑπωρέης τοῦ Κιθαιρῶνος φοβεόμενοι τὴν
ἵππον, Ἀθηναῖοι δὲ κάτω τραφθέντες ἐς τὸ
πεδίον.

57. Ἀμομφάρετος δὲ ἀρχήν γε οὐδαμὰ δοκέων
Παυσανίην τολμήσειν σφέας ἀπολιπεῖν, περιεί-
χετο αὐτοῦ μένοντας μὴ ἐκλιπεῖν τὴν τάξιν· προ-
τερεόντων δὲ τῶν σὺν Παυσανίῃ, καταδόξας αὐτοὺς
ἰθέῃ τέχνῃ ἀπολείπειν αὐτόν, ἀναλαβόντα τὸν

wise prevail with him; and at the last, when the
Athenian messenger came among them, hot words
began to pass; and in this wrangling Amompharetus
took up a stone with both hands and cast it down
before Pausanias' feet, crying that it was his pebble
wherewith he voted against fleeing from the strangers
(meaning thereby the foreigners).   Pausanias called
him a madman and distraught; then the Athenian
messenger putting the question wherewith he was
charged, he bade the man tell the Athenians of his
present condition, and prayed them to join themselves
to the Lacedaemonians and do as they did in respect
of departure.

56. So the messenger went back to the Athenians.
But when dawn found the dispute still continuing,
Pausanias having all this time held his army halted,
now gave the word and led all the rest away
between the hillocks, the Tegeans following; for
he supposed that Amompharetus would not stay
behind when the rest of the Lacedaemonians left
him; and indeed such was the event.   The
Athenians set themselves in array and marched,
but not by the same way as the Lacedaemonians,
who clung close to the broken ground and the
lower slopes of Cithaeron, to escape from the Persian
horse, but the Athenians marched down into the
plain instead.

57. Now Amompharetus at first supposed that
Pausanias would never have the heart to leave him
and his men, and he was instant that they should
remain where they were and not quit their post;
but when Pausanias' men went forward on their
way, he deemed that they had left him in good
earnest, and so bidding his battalion take up its

λόχον τὰ ὅπλα ἦγε βάδην πρὸς τὸ ἄλλο στῖφος·
τὸ δὲ ἀπελθὸν ὅσον τε δέκα στάδια ἀνέμενε τὸν
Ἀμομφαρέτου λόχον, περὶ ποταμὸν Μολόεντα
ἱδρυμένον Ἀργιόπιόν τε χῶρον καλεόμενον, τῇ
καὶ Δήμητρος Ἐλευσινίης ἱρὸν ἧσται. ἀνέμενε
δὲ τοῦδε εἵνεκα, ἵνα ἢν μὴ ἀπολείπῃ τὸν χῶρον
ἐν τῷ ἐτετάχατο ὁ Ἀμομφάρετός τε καὶ ὁ λόχος,
ἀλλ᾽ αὐτοῦ μένωσι, βοηθέοι ὀπίσω παρ᾽ ἐκείνους.
καὶ οἵ τε ἀμφὶ τὸν Ἀμομφάρετον παρεγίνοντό σφι
καὶ ἡ ἵππος ἡ τῶν βαρβάρων προσέκειτο πᾶσα.
οἱ γὰρ ἱππόται ἐποίευν οἷον καὶ ἐώθεσαν ποιέειν
αἰεί, ἰδόντες δὲ τὸν χῶρον κεινὸν ἐν τῷ ἐτετάχατο
οἱ Ἕλληνες τῇσι προτέρῃσι ἡμέρῃσι, ἤλαυνον τοὺς
ἵππους αἰεὶ τὸ πρόσω καὶ ἅμα καταλαβόντες
προσεκέατό σφι.

58. Μαρδόνιος δὲ ὡς ἐπύθετο τοὺς Ἕλληνας
ἀποιχομένους ὑπὸ νύκτα εἶδέ τε τὸν χῶρον ἔρημον,
καλέσας τὸν Ληρισαῖον Θώρηκα καὶ τοὺς ἀδελ-
φεοὺς αὐτοῦ Εὐρύπυλον καὶ Θρασυδήιον ἔλεγε
"Ὦ παῖδες Ἀλεύεω, ἔτι τί λέξετε τάδε ὁρῶντες
ἔρημα; ὑμεῖς γὰρ οἱ πλησιόχωροι ἐλέγετε Λακεδαιμονίους οὐ φεύγειν ἐκ μάχης, ἀλλὰ ἄνδρας εἶναι
τὰ πολέμια πρώτους· τοὺς πρότερόν τε μετιστα-
μένους ἐκ τῆς τάξιος εἴδετε, νῦν τε ὑπὸ τὴν παροιχομένην νύκτα καὶ οἱ πάντες ὁρῶμεν διαδράντας·
διέδεξάν τε, ἐπεί σφεας ἔδεε πρὸς τοὺς ἀψευδέως
ἀρίστους ἀνθρώπων μάχῃ διακριθῆναι, ὅτι οὐδένες
ἄρα ἐόντες ἐν οὐδαμοῖσι ἐοῦσι Ἕλλησι ἐναπεδεί-
κνύατο. καὶ ὑμῖν μὲν ἐοῦσι Περσέων ἀπείροισι
πολλὴ ἔκ γε ἐμεῦ ἐγίνετο συγγνώμη, ἐπαινεόντων
τούτους τοῖσί τι καὶ συνῃδέατε· Ἀρταβάζου δὲ
θῶμα καὶ μᾶλλον ἐποιεύμην τὸ καὶ καταρρωδῆσαι

arms he led it at a foot's pace after the rest of the
column; which having gone as far as ten furlongs
away was waiting for Amompharetus, halting by
the stream Moloïs and the place called Argiopium,
where is set a shrine of Eleusinian Demeter. The
reason of their waiting was that, if Amompharetus
and his battalion should not leave the place where
it was posted but abide there still, they might return
and succour him. No sooner had Amompharetus'
men come up than the foreigners' cavalry attacked
the army; for the horsemen did according as they
had ever been wont, and when they saw no enemy
on the ground where the Greek array had been on
the days before this, they rode ever forward and
attacked the Greeks as soon as they overtook them.

58. When Mardonius learnt that the Greeks had
departed under cover of night, and saw the ground
deserted, he called to him Thorax of Larissa and
his brothers Eurypylus and Thrasydeïus, and said:
"What will you now say, sons of Aleuas! when you
see this place deserted? for you, who are their
neighbours, ever told me that Lacedaemonians fled
from no battlefield and were surpassing masters of
war; yet these same men you lately saw changing
from their post, and now you and all of us see that
they have fled away in the night that is past; no
sooner must they measure themselves in battle with
those that are in very truth the bravest on earth,
than they plainly showed that they are men of no
account, and all other Greeks likewise. Now you
for your part were strangers to the Persians, and I
could readily pardon you for praising these fellows,
who were in some sort known to you; but I marvelled much more at Artabazus, that he should be

Λακεδαιμονίους καταρρωδήσαντά τε ἀποδέξασθαι
γνώμην δειλοτάτην, ὡς χρεὸν εἴη ἀναζεύξαντας τὸ
στρατόπεδον ἰέναι ἐς τὸ Θηβαίων ἄστυ πολιορκη-
σομένους· τὴν ἔτι πρὸς ἐμεῦ βασιλεὺς πεύσεται.
καὶ τούτων μὲν ἑτέρωθι ἔσται λόγος. νῦν δὲ ἐκείνοισι ταῦτα ποιεῦσι οὐκ ἐπιτρεπτέα ἐστί, ἀλλὰ
διωκτέοι εἰσὶ ἐς ὃ καταλαμφθέντες δώσουσι ἡμῖν
τῶν δὴ ἐποίησαν Πέρσας πάντων δίκας."

59. Ταῦτα εἴπας ἦγε τοὺς Πέρσας δρόμῳ δια-
βάντας τὸν Ἀσωπὸν κατὰ στίβον τῶν Ἑλλήνων
ὡς δὴ ἀποδιδρησκόντων, ἐπεῖχέ τε ἐπὶ Λακεδαιμονίους τε καὶ Τεγεήτας μούνους· Ἀθηναίους γὰρ
τραπομένους ἐς τὸ πεδίον ὑπὸ τῶν ὄχθων οὐ
κατώρα. Πέρσας δὲ ὁρῶντες ὁρμημένους διώκειν
τοὺς Ἕλληνας οἱ λοιποὶ τῶν βαρβαρικῶν τελέων
ἄρχοντες αὐτίκα πάντες ἤειραν τὰ σημήια, καὶ
ἐδίωκον ὡς ποδῶν ἕκαστοι εἶχον, οὔτε κόσμῳ
οὐδενὶ κοσμηθέντες οὔτε τάξι.

60. Καὶ οὗτοι μὲν βοῇ τε καὶ ὁμίλῳ ἐπήισαν
ὡς ἀναρπασόμενοι τοὺς Ἕλληνας· Παυσανίης δέ,
ὡς προσέκειτο ἡ ἵππος, πέμψας πρὸς τοὺς Ἀθηναίους ἱππέα λέγει τάδε. "Ἄνδρες Ἀθηναῖοι,
ἀγῶνος μεγίστου προκειμένου ἐλευθέρην εἶναι ἢ
δεδουλωμένην τὴν Ἑλλάδα, προδεδόμεθα ὑπὸ τῶν
συμμάχων ἡμεῖς τε οἱ Λακεδαιμόνιοι καὶ ὑμεῖς οἱ
Ἀθηναῖοι ὑπὸ τὴν παροιχομένην νύκτα διαδράν-
των. νῦν ὦν δέδοκται τὸ ἐνθεῦτεν τὸ ποιητέον
ἡμῖν· ἀμυνομένους γὰρ τῇ δυνάμεθα ἄριστα περι-
στέλλειν ἀλλήλους. εἰ μέν νυν ἐς ὑμέας ὅρμησε
ἀρχὴν ἡ ἵππος, χρῆν δὴ ἡμέας τε καὶ τοὺς μετ'
ἡμέων τὴν Ἑλλάδα οὐ προδιδόντας Τεγεήτας
βοηθέειν ὑμῖν· νῦν δέ, ἐς ἡμέας γὰρ ἅπασα κεχώ-

so sore affrighted by the Lacedaemonians as to give us a craven's advice to strike our camp, and march away to be beleaguered in Thebes; of which advice the king shall yet learn from me. This shall be matter for speech elsewhere; but now, we must not suffer our enemies to do as they desire; they must be pursued till they be overtaken and pay the penalty for all the harm they have wrought the Persians."

59. With that, he led the Persians at speed across the Asopus in pursuit of the Greeks, supposing that they were in flight; it was the army of Lacedaemon and Tegea alone that was his goal; for the Athenians marched another way over the broken ground, and were out of his sight. Seeing the Persians setting forth in pursuit of the Greeks, the rest of the foreign battalions straightway raised their standards and pursued likewise, each at the top of his speed, no battalion having order in its ranks nor place assigned in the line.

60. So they ran pell-mell and shouting, as though they would utterly make an end of the Greeks; but Pausanias, when the cavalry attacked him, sent a horseman to the Athenians, with this message: "Men of Athens, in this great issue which must give freedom or slavery to Hellas, we Lacedaemonians and you Athenians have been betrayed by the flight of our allies in the night that is past. Now therefore I am resolved what we must forthwith do; we must protect each other by fighting as best we can. If the cavalry had attacked you first, it had been for us and the Tegeans with us, who are faithful to Hellas, to succour you; but now, seeing that the whole

ρηκε, δίκαιοί έστε ύμείς πρὸς τὴν πιεζομένην
μάλιστα τῶν μοιρέων ἀμυνέοντες ἰέναι. εἰ δ᾽ ἄρα
αὐτοὺς ὑμέας καταλελάβηκε ἀδύνατόν τι βοηθέειν,
ὑμεῖς δ᾽ ἡμῖν τοὺς τοξότας ἀποπέμψαντες χάριν
θέσθε. συνοίδαμεν δὲ ὑμῖν ὑπὸ τὸν παρεόντα
τόνδε πόλεμον ἐοῦσι πολλὸν προθυμοτάτοισι,
ὥστε καὶ ταῦτα ἐσακούειν."

61. Ταῦτα οἱ Ἀθηναῖοι ὡς ἐπύθοντο, ὁρμέατο
βοηθέειν καὶ τὰ μάλιστα ἐπαμύνειν· καί σφι ἤδη
στείχουσι ἐπιτίθενται οἱ ἀντιταχθέντες Ἑλλήνων τῶν μετὰ βασιλέος γενομένων, ὥστε μηκέτι
δύνασθαι βοηθῆσαι· τὸ γὰρ προσκείμενον σφέας
ἐλύπεε. οὕτω δὴ μουνωθέντες Λακεδαιμόνιοι καὶ
Τεγεῆται, ἐόντες σὺν ψιλοῖσι ἀριθμὸν οἱ μὲν
πεντακισμύριοι Τεγεῆται δὲ τρισχίλιοι (οὗτοι γὰρ
οὐδαμὰ ἀπεσχίζοντο ἀπὸ Λακεδαιμονίων), ἐσφα-
γιάζοντο ὡς συμβαλέοντες Μαρδονίῳ καὶ τῇ
στρατιῇ τῇ παρεούσῃ. καὶ οὐ γάρ σφι ἐγίνετο τὰ
σφάγια χρηστά, ἔπιπτον δὲ αὐτῶν ἐν τούτῳ τῷ
χρόνῳ πολλοὶ καὶ πολλῷ πλεῦνες ἐτρωματίζοντο·
φράξαντες γὰρ τὰ γέρρα οἱ Πέρσαι ἀπίεσαν τῶν
τοξευμάτων πολλὰ ἀφειδέως, οὕτω ὥστε πιεζο-
μένων τῶν Σπαρτιητέων καὶ τῶν σφαγίων οὐ γινομένων ἀποβλέψαντα τὸν Παυσανίην πρὸς τὸ
Ἥραιον τὸ Πλαταιέων ἐπικαλέσασθαι τὴν θεόν,
χρηίζοντα μηδαμῶς σφέας ψευσθῆναι τῆς
ἐλπίδος.

62. Ταῦτα δ᾽ ἔτι τούτου ἐπικαλεομένου προεξ-
αναστάντες πρότεροι οἱ Τεγεῆται ἐχώρεον ἐς τοὺς
βαρβάρους, καὶ τοῖσι Λακεδαιμονίοισι αὐτίκα

brunt of their assault falls on us, it is right that you
should come to the aid of that division which is
hardest pressed. But if, as may be, aught has
befallen you whereby it is impossible that you should
aid us, yet do us the service of sending us your
archers. We are assured that you will hearken to us,
as knowing that you have been by far more zealous
than all others in this present war."

61. When the Athenians heard that, they essayed
to succour the Lacedaemonians and defend them
with all their might; but when their march was
already begun they were set upon by the Greeks
posted over against them, who had joined themselves to the king; wherefore they could now send
no aid, being troubled by the foe that was closest.
Thus it was that the Lacedaemonians and Tegeans
stood alone; men-at-arms and light-armed together,
there were of the Lacedaemonians fifty thousand
and of the Tegeans, who had never been parted
from the Lacedaemonians, three thousand; and
they offered sacrifice, the better to join battle with
Mardonius and the army that was with him. But
as they could get no favourable omen from their
sacrifices, and in the meanwhile many of them were
slain and by far more wounded (for the Persians set
up their shields for a fence, and shot showers of
arrows innumerable), it was so, that, the Spartans
being hard pressed and their sacrifices of no avail,
Pausanias lifted up his eyes to the temple of Here
at Plataeae and called on the goddess, praying that
they might nowise be disappointed of their hope.

62. While he yet prayed, the men of Tegea leapt
out before the rest and charged the foreigners; and
immediately after Pausanias' prayer the sacrifices of

233

μετὰ τὴν εὐχὴν τὴν Παυσανίεω ἐγίνετο θυομένοισι
τὰ σφάγια χρηστά· ὡς δὲ χρόνῳ κοτὲ ἐγένετο,
ἐχώρεον καὶ οὗτοι ἐπὶ τοὺς Πέρσας, καὶ οἱ Πέρσαι
ἀντίοι τὰ τόξα μετέντες. ἐγίνετο δὲ πρῶτον περὶ
τὰ γέρρα μάχη. ὡς δὲ ταῦτα ἐπεπτώκεε, ἤδη
ἐγίνετο ἡ μάχη ἰσχυρὴ παρ' αὐτὸ τὸ Δημήτριον
καὶ χρόνον ἐπὶ πολλόν, ἐς ὃ ἀπίκοντο ἐς ὠθισμόν·
τὰ γὰρ δόρατα ἐπιλαμβανόμενοι κατέκλων οἱ
βάρβαροι. λήματι μέν νυν καὶ ῥώμῃ οὐκ ἥσσονες
ἦσαν οἱ Πέρσαι, ἄνοπλοι δὲ ἐόντες καὶ πρὸς
ἀνεπιστήμονες ἦσαν καὶ οὐκ ὅμοιοι τοῖσι ἐναν-
τίοισι σοφίην, προεξαΐσσοντες δὲ κατ' ἕνα καὶ
δέκα, καὶ πλεῦνές τε καὶ ἐλάσσονες συστρεφό-
μενοι, ἐσέπιπτον ἐς τοὺς Σπαρτιήτας καὶ διεφθείροντο.

63. Τῇ δὲ ἐτύγχανε αὐτὸς ἐὼν Μαρδόνιος, ἀπ'
ἵππου τε μαχόμενος λευκοῦ ἔχων τε περὶ ἑωυτὸν
λογάδας Περσέων τοὺς ἀρίστους χιλίους, ταύτῃ
δὲ καὶ μάλιστα τοὺς ἐναντίους ἐπίεσαν. ὅσον μέν
νυν χρόνον Μαρδόνιος περιῆν, οἱ δὲ ἀντεῖχον καὶ
ἀμυνόμενοι κατέβαλλον πολλοὺς τῶν Λακεδαιμο-
νίων· ὡς δὲ Μαρδόνιος ἀπέθανε καὶ τὸ περὶ ἐκεῖνον
τεταγμένον ἐὸν ἰσχυρότατον ἔπεσε, οὕτω δὴ καὶ
οἱ ἄλλοι ἐτράποντο καὶ εἶξαν τοῖσι Λακεδαιμονίοισι. πλεῖστον γὰρ σφέας ἐδηλέετο ἡ ἐσθὴς
ἔρημος ἐοῦσα ὅπλων· πρὸς γὰρ ὁπλίτας ἐόντες
γυμνῆτες ἀγῶνα ἐποιεῦντο.

64. Ἐνθαῦτα ἥ τε δίκη τοῦ Λεωνίδεω κατὰ τὸ
χρηστήριον τοῖσι Σπαρτιήτῃσι ἐκ Μαρδονίου
ἐπετελέετο, καὶ νίκην ἀναιρέεται καλλίστην ἁπασέων τῶν ἡμεῖς ἴδμεν Παυσανίης ὁ Κλεομβρότου
τοῦ Ἀναξανδρίδεω· τῶν δὲ κατύπερθέ οἱ προγό-

the Lacedaemonians grew to be favourable; which being at last vouchsafed to them, they too charged the Persians, and the Persians met them, throwing away their bows. And first they fought for the fence of shields; and when that was down, thereafter the battle waxed fierce and long about the temple of Demeter itself, till they grappled and thrust; for the foreigners laid hold of the spears and broke them short. Now the Persians were neither the less valorous nor the weaker; but they had no armour, and moreover they were unskilled and no match for their adversaries in craft; they would rush out singly and in tens or in groups great or small, hurling themselves on the Spartans and so perishing.

63. Where Mardonius was himself, riding a white horse in the battle and surrounded by a thousand picked men who were the flower of the Persians, there they pressed their adversaries hardest. So long as Mardonius was alive the Persians stood their ground and defended themselves, overthrowing many Lacedaemonians; but when Mardonius was slain and his guards, who were the strongest part of the army, fallen likewise, then the rest too yielded and gave ground before the men of Lacedaemon. For what chiefly wrought them harm was that they wore no armour over their raiment, and fought as it were naked against men fully armed.

64. On that day the Spartans gained from Mardonius their full measure of vengeance for the slaying of Leonidas, according to the oracle, and the most glorious of victories ever known to men was won by Pausanias, the son of Cleombrotus, who was the son of Anaxandrides. (I have named the

νων τὰ οὐνόματα εἴρηται ἐς Λεωνίδην· ὡυτοὶ γάρ
σφι τυγχάνουσι ἐόντες. ἀποθνῄσκει δὲ Μαρδόνιος ὑπὸ Ἀειμνήστου ἀνδρὸς ἐν Σπάρτῃ λογίμου,
ὃς χρόνῳ ὕστερον μετὰ τὰ Μηδικὰ ἔχων ἄνδρας
τριηκοσίους συνέβαλε ἐν Στενυκλήρῳ πολέμου
ἐόντος Μεσσηνίοισι πᾶσι, καὶ αὐτός τε ἀπέθανε
καὶ οἱ τριηκόσιοι.

65. Ἐν δὲ Πλαταιῆσι οἱ Πέρσαι ὡς ἐτράποντο
ὑπὸ τῶν Λακεδαιμονίων, ἔφευγον οὐδένα κόσμον
ἐς τὸ στρατόπεδον τὸ ἑωυτῶν καὶ ἐς τὸ τεῖχος τὸ
ξύλινον τὸ ἐποιήσαντο ἐν μοίρῃ τῇ Θηβαΐδι.
θῶμα δέ μοι ὅκως παρὰ τῆς Δήμητρος τὸ ἄλσος
μαχομένων οὐδὲ εἷς ἐφάνη τῶν Περσέων οὔτε
ἐσελθὼν ἐς τὸ τέμενος οὔτε ἐναποθανών, περί τε
τὸ ἱρὸν οἱ πλεῖστοι ἐν τῷ βεβήλῳ ἔπεσον. δοκέω
δέ, εἴ τι περὶ τῶν θείων πρηγμάτων δοκέειν δεῖ, ἡ
θεὸς αὐτή σφεας οὐκ ἐδέκετο ἐμπρήσαντας τὸ ἱρὸν
τὸ ἐν Ἐλευσῖνι ἀνάκτορον.

66. Αὕτη μέν νυν ἡ μάχη ἐπὶ τοσοῦτο ἐγένετο.
Ἀρτάβαζος δὲ ὁ Φαρνάκεος αὐτίκα τε οὐκ
ἠρέσκετο κατ' ἀρχὰς λειπομένου Μαρδονίου ἀπὸ
βασιλέος, καὶ τότε πολλὰ ἀπαγορεύων οὐδὲν ἤνυε,
συμβάλλειν οὐκ ἐῶν· ἐποίησέ τε αὐτὸς τοιάδε ὡς
οὐκ ἀρεσκόμενος τοῖσι πρήγμασι τοῖσι ἐκ Μαρδονίου ποιευμένοισι. τῶν ἐστρατήγεε ὁ Ἀρτάβαζος (εἶχε δὲ δύναμιν οὐκ ὀλίγην ἀλλὰ καὶ ἐς
τέσσερας μυριάδας ἀνθρώπων περὶ ἑωυτόν), τούτους, ὅκως ἡ συμβολὴ ἐγίνετο, εὖ ἐξεπιστάμενος
τὰ ἔμελλε ἀποβήσεσθαι ἀπὸ τῆς μάχης, ἦγε
κατηρτημένως, παραγγείλας κατὰ τὠυτὸ ἰέναι
πάντας τῇ ἂν αὐτὸς ἐξηγῆται, ὅκως ἂν αὐτὸν
ὁρῶσι σπουδῆς ἔχοντα. ταῦτα παραγγείλας ὡς

rest of Pausanias' ancestors in the lineage of Leonidas; for they are the same for both.) As for Mardonius, he was slain by Aeimnestus, a Spartan of note; who long after the Persian business did in time of war lead three hundred men to battle at Stenyclerus against the whole army of Messenia, and was there slain, he and his three hundred.

65. But at Plataeae, the Persians being routed by the Lacedaemonians fled in disorder to their own camp and within the wooden walls that they had made in the lands of Thebes. And herein is a marvellous thing, that though the battle was hard by the grove of Demeter there was no sign that any Persian had been slain in the precinct, or entered into it; most of them fell near the temple in unconsecrated ground; and I judge—if it be not a sin to judge of the ways of heaven—that the goddess herself denied them entry, for that they had burnt her temple, the shrine at Eleusis.

66. Thus far then went this battle. But Artabazus son of Pharnaces had from the very first misliked the king's leaving Mardonius, and now all his counselling not to join battle had been of no avail; and in his displeasure at what Mardonius was doing he himself did as I will show. He had with him a great army, even as many as forty thousand men; knowing well what would be the event of the battle, no sooner had the Greeks and Persians met than he led these with purpose fixed, bidding them follow him all together whither he should lead them, according to whatsoever they should see to be his intent; and with that command he made pretence

ἐς μάχην ἦγε δῆθεν τὸν στρατόν. προτερέων δὲ
τῆς ὁδοῦ ὥρα καὶ δὴ φεύγοντας τοὺς Πέρσας·
οὕτω δὴ οὐκέτι τὸν αὐτὸν κόσμον κατηγέετο, ἀλλὰ
τὴν ταχίστην ἐτρόχαζε φεύγων οὔτε ἐς τὸ ξύλινον
οὔτε ἐς τὸ Θηβαίων τεῖχος ἀλλ' ἐς Φωκέας,
ἐθέλων ὡς τάχιστα ἐπὶ τὸν Ἑλλήσποντον
ἀπικέσθαι.

67. Καὶ δὴ οὗτοι μὲν ταύτῃ ἐτράποντο· τῶν
δὲ ἄλλων Ἑλλήνων τῶν μετὰ βασιλέος ἐθελοκα-
κεόντων Βοιωτοὶ Ἀθηναίοισι ἐμαχέσαντο χρόνον
ἐπὶ συχνόν. οἱ γὰρ μηδίζοντες τῶν Θηβαίων,
οὗτοι εἶχον προθυμίην οὐκ ὀλίγην μαχόμενοί τε
καὶ οὐκ ἐθελοκακέοντες, οὕτω ὥστε τριηκόσιοι
αὐτῶν οἱ πρῶτοι καὶ ἄριστοι ἐνθαῦτα ἔπεσον ὑπὸ
Ἀθηναίων. ὡς δὲ ἐτράποντο καὶ οὗτοι, ἔφευγον
ἐς τὰς Θήβας, οὐ τῇ περ οἱ Πέρσαι καὶ τῶν
ἄλλων συμμάχων ὁ πᾶς ὅμιλος, οὔτε διαμαχεσά-
μενος οὐδενὶ οὔτε τι ἀποδεξάμενος, ἔφευγον.

68. Δηλοῖ τέ μοι ὅτι πάντα τὰ πρήγματα τῶν
βαρβάρων ἤρτητο ἐκ Περσέων, εἰ καὶ τότε οὗτοι
πρὶν ἢ καὶ συμμῖξαι τοῖσι πολεμίοισι ἔφευγον, ὅτι
καὶ τοὺς Πέρσας ὥρων. οὕτω τε πάντες ἔφευγον
πλὴν τῆς ἵππου τῆς τε ἄλλης καὶ τῆς Βοιωτίης·
αὕτη δὲ τοσαῦτα προσωφέλεε τοὺς φεύγοντας,
αἰεί τε πρὸς τῶν πολεμίων ἄγχιστα ἐοῦσα
ἀπέργουσά τε τοὺς φιλίους φεύγοντας ἀπὸ τῶν
Ἑλλήνων.

69. Οἱ μὲν δὴ νικῶντες εἵποντο τοὺς Ξέρξεω
διώκοντές τε καὶ φονεύοντες. ἐν δὲ τούτῳ τῷ
γινομένῳ φόβῳ ἀγγέλλεται τοῖσι ἄλλοισι Ἕλλησι
τοῖσι τεταγμένοισι περὶ τὸ Ἥραιον καὶ ἀπο-
γενομένοισι τῆς μάχης, ὅτι μάχη τε γέγονε καὶ

of leading them to battle. But as he came farther on his way he saw the Persians already fleeing; whereat he led his men no longer in the same array, but took to his heels and fled with all speed not to the wooden fort nor to the walled city of Thebes, but to Phocis, that so he might make his way with all despatch to the Hellespont.

67. So Artabazus and his army turned that way. All the rest of the Greeks that were on the king's side fought of set purpose ill; but not so the Boeotians; they fought for a long time against the Athenians. For those Thebans that took the Persian part showed no small zeal in the battle, and had no will to fight slackly, insomuch that three hundred of their first and best were there slain by the Athenians. But at last the Boeotians too yielded; and they fled to Thebes, not by the way that the Persians had fled and all the multitude of the allies, a multitude that had fought no fight to the end nor achieved any feat of arms.

68. This flight of theirs ere they had even closed, because they saw the Persians flee, proves to me that it was on the Persians that all the fortune of the foreigners hung. Thus they all fled, save only the cavalry, Boeotian and other; which did in so far advantage the fleeing men as it kept ever between them and their enemies, and shielded its friends from the Greeks in their flight.

69. So the Greeks followed in victory after Xerxes' men, pursuing and slaying. In this rout that grew apace there came a message to the rest of the Greeks, who lay at the temple of Here and had kept away from the fight, that there had been a

νικῷεν οἱ μετὰ Παυσανίεω· οἳ δὲ ἀκούσαντες
ταῦτα, οὐδένα κόσμον ταχθέντες, οἱ μὲν ἀμφὶ
Κορινθίους ἐτράποντο διὰ τῆς ὑπωρέης καὶ τῶν
κολωνῶν τὴν φέρουσαν ἄνω ἰθὺ τοῦ ἱροῦ τῆς
Δήμητρος, οἱ δὲ ἀμφὶ Μεγαρέας τε καὶ Φλειασίους
διὰ τοῦ πεδίου τὴν λειοτάτην τῶν ὁδῶν. ἐπείτε
δὲ ἀγχοῦ τῶν πολεμίων ἐγίνοντο οἱ Μεγαρέες καὶ
Φλειάσιοι, ἀπιδόντες σφέας οἱ τῶν Θηβαίων
ἱππόται ἐπειγομένους οὐδένα κόσμον ἤλαυνον ἐπ'
αὐτοὺς τοὺς ἵππους, τῶν ἱππάρχεε Ἀσωπόδωρος
ὁ Τιμάνδρου, ἐσπεσόντες δὲ κατεστόρεσαν αὐτῶν
ἑξακοσίους, τοὺς δὲ λοιποὺς κατήραξαν διώκοντες
ἐς τὸν Κιθαιρῶνα.

70. Οὗτοι μὲν δὴ ἐν οὐδενὶ λόγῳ ἀπώλοντο· οἱ
δὲ Πέρσαι καὶ ὁ ἄλλος ὅμιλος, ὡς κατέφυγον ἐς
τὸ ξύλινον τεῖχος, ἔφθησαν ἐπὶ τοὺς πύργους
ἀναβάντες πρὶν ἢ τοὺς Λακεδαιμονίους ἀπικέσθαι,
ἀναβάντες δὲ ἐφράξαντο ὡς ἠδυνέατο ἄριστα τὸ
τεῖχος· προσελθόντων δὲ τῶν Λακεδαιμονίων
κατεστήκεέ σφι τειχομαχίη ἐρρωμενεστέρη. ἕως
μὲν γὰρ ἀπῆσαν οἱ Ἀθηναῖοι, οἳ δ' ἠμύνοντο καὶ
πολλῷ πλέον εἶχον τῶν Λακεδαιμονίων ὥστε οὐκ
ἐπισταμένων τειχομαχέειν· ὡς δέ σφι Ἀθηναῖοι
προσῆλθον, οὕτω δὴ ἰσχυρὴ ἐγίνετο τειχομαχίη
καὶ χρόνον ἐπὶ πολλόν. τέλος δὲ ἀρετῇ τε καὶ
λιπαρίῃ ἐπέβησαν Ἀθηναῖοι τοῦ τείχεος καὶ
ἤριπον· τῇ δὴ ἐσεχέοντο οἱ Ἕλληνες. πρῶτοι δὲ
ἐσῆλθον Τεγεῆται ἐς τὸ τεῖχος, καὶ τὴν σκηνὴν
τὴν Μαρδονίου οὗτοι ἦσαν οἱ διαρπάσαντες, τά τε
ἄλλα ἐξ αὐτῆς καὶ τὴν φάτνην τῶν ἵππων ἐοῦσαν
χαλκέην πᾶσαν καὶ θέης ἀξίην. τὴν μέν νυν

battle and that Pausanias' men were victorious;
which when they heard, they set forth in no ordered
array, they that were with the Corinthians keeping
to the spurs of the mountain and the hill country,
by the road that led upward straight to the temple
of Demeter, and they that were with the Megarians
and Phliasians following the levelest way over the
plain. But when the Megarians and Phliasians
were come near to the enemy, the Theban horsemen
(whose captain was Asopodorus son of Timander)
espied them approaching in haste and disorder, and
rode at them; by which onfall they laid six hundred
of them low, and pursued and swept the rest to
Cithaeron.

70. So these perished, none regarding them. But
when the Persians and the rest of the multitude had
fled within the wooden wall, they made a shift to
get them up on the towers before the coming of the
Lacedaemonians, which done they strengthened the
wall as best they could; and when the Athenians
were now arrived there began a stiff battle for the
wall. For as long as the Athenians were not there,
the foreigners defended themselves, and had greatly
the advantage of the Lacedaemonians, they having
no skill in the assault of walls; but when the
Athenians came up, the fight for the wall waxed
hot and continued long. But at the last the
Athenians did by valour and steadfast endeavour
scale the wall and breach it, by which breach the
Greeks poured in; the first to enter were the
Tegeans, and it was they who plundered the tent
of Mardonius, taking from it beside all else the
manger of his horses, that was all of bronze and a
thing worth the beholding. The Tegeans dedicated

φάτνην ταύτην τὴν Μαρδονίου ἀνέθεσαν ἐς τὸν
νηὸν τῆς Ἀλέης Ἀθηναίης Τεγεῆται, τὰ δὲ ἄλλα
ἐς τὠυτό, ὅσα περ ἔλαβον, ἐσήνεικαν τοῖσι
Ἕλλησι. οἱ δὲ βάρβαροι οὐδὲν ἔτι στῖφος
ἐποιήσαντο πεσόντος τοῦ τείχεος, οὐδέ τις αὐτῶν
ἀλκῆς ἐμέμνητο, ἀλύκταζόν τε οἷα ἐν ὀλίγῳ χώρῳ
πεφοβημένοι τε καὶ πολλαὶ μυριάδες κατειλη-
μέναι ἀνθρώπων· παρῆν τε τοῖσι Ἕλλησι
φονεύειν οὕτω ὥστε τριήκοντα μυριάδων στρατοῦ,
καταδεουσέων τεσσέρων τὰς ἔχων Ἀρτάβαζος
ἔφευγε, τῶν λοιπέων μηδὲ τρεῖς χιλιάδας περι-
γενέσθαι. Λακεδαιμονίων δὲ τῶν ἐκ Σπάρτης
ἀπέθανον οἱ πάντες ἐν τῇ συμβολῇ εἷς καὶ
ἐνενήκοντα, Τεγεητέων δὲ ἑκκαίδεκα, Ἀθηναίων
δὲ δύο καὶ πεντήκοντα.

71. Ἠρίστευσε δὲ τῶν βαρβάρων πεζὸς μὲν ὁ
Περσέων, ἵππος δὲ ἡ Σακέων, ἀνὴρ δὲ λέγεται
Μαρδόνιος· Ἑλλήνων δέ, ἀγαθῶν γενομένων καὶ
Τεγεητέων καὶ Ἀθηναίων, ὑπερεβάλοντο ἀρετῇ
Λακεδαιμόνιοι. ἄλλῳ μὲν οὐδενὶ ἔχω ἀποση-
μήνασθαι (ἅπαντες γὰρ οὗτοι τοὺς κατ᾽ ἑωυτοὺς
ἐνίκων), ὅτι δὲ κατὰ τὸ ἰσχυρότερον προσ-
ηνείχθησαν καὶ τούτων ἐκράτησαν. καὶ ἄριστος
ἐγένετο μακρῷ Ἀριστόδημος κατὰ γνώμας τὰς
ἡμετέρας, ὃς ἐκ Θερμοπυλέων μοῦνος τῶν τριη-
κοσίων σωθεὶς εἶχε ὄνειδος καὶ ἀτιμίην. μετὰ δὲ
τοῦτον ἠρίστευσαν Ποσειδώνιός τε καὶ Φιλοκύων
καὶ Ἀμομφάρετος ὁ Σπαρτιήτης. καίτοι γενομένης λέσχης ὃς γένοιτο αὐτῶν ἄριστος, ἔγνωσαν

---

¹ These figures must refer to the ὁπλῖται alone, leaving out
of account the Laconian περίοικοι and the rest of the light-

this manger of Mardonius in the temple of Athene
Alea ; all else that they took they brought into the
common stock, as did the rest of the Greeks.   As
for the foreigners, they drew no more to a head
once the wall was down, but they were crazed with
panic fear, as men hunted down in a narrow space
where many myriads were herded together ; and
such a slaughter were the Greeks able to make, that
of two hundred and sixty thousand, that remained
after Artabazus had fled with his forty thousand,
scarce three thousand were left alive.   Of the
Lacedaemonians from Sparta there were slain in
the battle ninety-one in all ; of the Tegeans,
seventeen ; and of the Athenians, fifty-two.[1]

71. Among the foreigners they that fought best
were the Persian foot and the horse of the Sacae,
and of men, it is said, the bravest was Mardonius ;
among the Greeks, the Tegeans and Athenians bore
themselves gallantly, but the Lacedaemonians excelled all in valour.   Of this my only clear proof
is (for all these vanquished the foes opposed to
them) that the Lacedaemonians met the strongest
part of the army, and overcame it.   According to
my judgment, he that bore himself by far the best
was Aristodemus, who had been reviled and dis-
honoured for being the only man of the three
hundred that came alive from Thermopylae ;[2] and
the next after him in valour were Posidonius and
Philocyon and Amompharetus.   Nevertheless when
there was talk, and question who had borne himself

armed troops.   Plutarch says that 60,300 Greeks fell at
Plataea.
   [2] Cp. vii. 231.

οἱ παραγενόμενοι Σπαρτιητέων Ἀριστόδημον μὲν
βουλόμενον φανερῶς ἀποθανεῖν ἐκ τῆς παρεούσης
οἱ αἰτίης, λυσσῶντά τε καὶ ἐκλείποντα τὴν τάξιν
ἔργα ἀποδέξασθαι μεγάλα, Ποσειδώνιον δὲ οὐ
βουλόμενον ἀποθνήσκειν ἄνδρα γενέσθαι ἀγαθόν·
τοσούτῳ τοῦτον εἶναι ἀμείνω. ἀλλὰ ταῦτα μὲν
καὶ φθόνῳ ἂν εἴποιεν· οὗτοι δὲ τοὺς κατέλεξα
πάντες, πλὴν Ἀριστοδήμου, τῶν ἀποθανόντων ἐν
ταύτῃ τῇ μάχῃ τίμιοι ἐγένοντο· Ἀριστόδημος δὲ
βουλόμενος ἀποθανεῖν διὰ τὴν προειρημένην αἰτίην
οὐκ ἐτιμήθη.

72. Οὗτοι μὲν τῶν ἐν Πλαταιῆσι ὀνομαστότατοι
ἐγένοντο. Καλλικράτης γὰρ ἔξω τῆς μάχης
ἀπέθανε, ἐλθὼν ἀνὴρ κάλλιστος ἐς τὸ στρατόπεδον
τῶν τότε Ἑλλήνων, οὐ μοῦνον αὐτῶν Λακεδαιμονίων ἀλλὰ καὶ τῶν ἄλλων Ἑλλήνων· ὅς,
ἐπειδὴ ἐσφαγιάζετο Παυσανίης, κατήμενος ἐν τῇ
τάξι ἐτρωματίσθη τοξεύματι τὰ πλευρά. καὶ δὴ
οἳ μὲν ἐμάχοντο, ὃ δ᾽ ἐξενηνειγμένος ἐδυσθανάτεέ
τε καὶ ἔλεγε πρὸς Ἀρίμνηστον ἄνδρα Πλαταιέα
οὔ μέλειν οἳ ὅτι πρὸ τῆς Ἑλλάδος ἀποθνήσκει,
ἀλλ᾽ ὅτι οὐκ ἐχρήσατο τῇ χειρὶ καὶ ὅτι οὐδέν ἐστί
οἱ ἀποδεδεγμένον ἔργον ἑωυτοῦ ἄξιον προθυμευ-
μένου ἀποδέξασθαι.

73. Ἀθηναίων δὲ λέγεται εὐδοκιμῆσαι Σώφανης
ὁ Εὐτυχίδεω, ἐκ δήμου Δεκελεῆθεν, Δεκελέων δὲ
τῶν κοτὲ ἐργασαμένων ἔργον χρήσιμον ἐς τὸν
πάντα χρόνον, ὡς αὐτοὶ Ἀθηναῖοι λέγουσι. ὡς
γὰρ δὴ τὸ πάλαι κατὰ Ἑλένης κομιδὴν Τυνδαρίδαι

244

most bravely, those Spartans that were there judged that Aristodemus had achieved great feats because by reason of the reproach under which he lay he plainly wished to die, and so pressed forward in frenzy from his post, whereas Posidonius had borne himself well with no desire to die, and must in so far be held the better man. This they may have said of mere jealousy; but all the aforesaid who were slain in that fight received honour, save only Aristodemus; he, because he desired death by reason of the reproach afore-mentioned, received none.

72. These won the most renown of all that fought at Plataeae. Callicrates is not among them; for he died away from the battle, he that, when he came to the army, was the goodliest Lacedaemonian, aye, or Greek, in the Hellas of that day. He, when Pausanias was offering sacrifice, was wounded in the side by an arrow where he sat in his place; and while his comrades were fighting, he was carried out of the battle and died a lingering death, saying to Arimnestus, a Plataean, that it was no grief to him to die for Hellas' sake; his sorrow was rather that he had struck no blow and achieved no deed worthy of his merit, for all his eager desire so to do.

73. Of the Athenians, Sophanes son of Euty-chides is said to have won renown, a man of the township of Decelea; that Decelea whose people once did a deed that was for all time serviceable, as the Athenians themselves say. For of old when the sons of Tyndarus strove to win Helen [1] back and

---

[1] According to legend, the Dioscuri came to recover their sister Helen, who had been carried off to Aphidnae in Attica by Theseus and Pirithous.

ἐσέβαλον ἐς γῆν τὴν ᾿Αττικὴν σὺν στρατοῦ
πλήθεϊ καὶ ἀνίστασαν τοὺς δήμους, οὐκ εἰδότες
ἵνα ὑπεξέκειτο ἡ ῾Ελένη, τότε λέγουσι τοὺς
Δεκελέας, οἱ δὲ αὐτὸν Δέκελον ἀχθόμενόν τε τῇ
Θησέος ὕβρι καὶ δειμαίνοντα περὶ πάσῃ τῇ
᾿Αθηναίων χώρῃ, ἐξηγησάμενόν σφι τὸ πᾶν
πρῆγμα κατηγήσασθαι ἐπὶ τὰς ᾿Αφίδνας, ὰς δὴ
Τιτακὸς ἐὼν αὐτόχθων καταπροδιδοῖ Τυνδαρίδῃσι.
τοῖσι δὲ Δεκελεῦσι ἐν Σπάρτῃ ἀπὸ τούτου τοῦ
ἔργου ἀτελείη τε καὶ προεδρίη διατελέει ἐς τόδε
αἰεὶ ἔτι ἐοῦσα, οὕτω ὥστε καὶ ἐς τὸν πόλεμον
τὸν ὕστερον πολλοῖσι ἔτεσι τούτων γενόμενον
᾿Αθηναίοισί τε καὶ Πελοποννησίοισι, σινομένων
τὴν ἄλλην ᾿Αττικὴν Λακεδαιμονίων, Δεκελέης
ἀπέχεσθαι.

74. Τούτου τοῦ δήμου ἐὼν ὁ Σωφάνης καὶ
ἀριστεύσας τότε ᾿Αθηναίων διξοὺς λόγους λεγο-
μένους ἔχει, τὸν μὲν ὡς ἐκ τοῦ ζωστῆρος τοῦ
θώρηκος ἐφόρεε χαλκέῃ ἀλύσι δεδεμένην ἄγκυραν
σιδηρέην, τὴν ὅκως πελάσειε ἀπικνεόμενος τοῖσι
πολεμίοισι βαλλέσκετο, ἵνα δή μιν οἱ πολέμιοι
ἐκπίπτοντες ἐκ τῆς τάξιος μετακινῆσαι μὴ δυ-
ναίατο· γινομένης δὲ φυγῆς τῶν ἐναντίων δέδοκτο
τὴν ἄγκυραν ἀναλαβόντα οὕτω διώκειν. οὗτος
μὲν οὕτω λέγεται, ὁ δ᾿ ἕτερος τῶν λόγων τῷ
πρότερον λεχθέντι ἀμφισβατέων λέγεται, ὡς ἐπ᾿
ἀσπίδος αἰεὶ περιθεούσης καὶ οὐδαμὰ ἀτρεμιζούσης
ἐφόρεε ἄγκυραν, καὶ οὐκ ἐκ τοῦ θώρηκος δεδεμένην
σιδηρέην.

broke with a great host into Attica, and were turning the townships upside down because they knew not where Helen had been hidden, then (it is said) the Deceleans (and, as some say, Decelus himself, because he was angered by the pride of Theseus and feared for the whole land of Attica) revealed the whole matter to the sons of Tyndarus, and guided them to Aphidnae, which Titacus, one of the country's oldest stock, betrayed to the Tyndaridae. For that deed the Deceleans have ever had and still have at Sparta freedom from all dues and chief places at feasts, insomuch that even as late as in the war that was waged many years after this time between the Athenians and Peloponnesians, the Lacedaemonians laid no hand on Decelea when they harried the rest of Attica.[1]

74. Of that township was Sophanes, who now was the best Athenian fighter in the battle; concerning which, two tales are told. By the first, he bore an anchor of iron made fast to the girdle of his cuirass with a chain of bronze; which anchor he would ever cast whenever he drew nigh to his enemies in onset, that so the enemies as they left their ranks might not avail to move him from his place; and when they were put to flight, it was his plan that he would weigh his anchor and so pursue them. So runs this tale; but the second that is told is at variance with the first, and relates that he bore no anchor of iron made fast to his cuirass, but that his shield, which he ever whirled round and never kept still, had on it an anchor for device.

[1] But in the later part of the Peloponnesian war the Lacedaemonians established themselves at Decelea and held it as a menace to Athens (413 B.C.).

75. Ἔστι δὲ καὶ ἕτερον Σωφάνεϊ λαμπρὸν ἔργον ἐξεργασμένον, ὅτι περικατημένων Ἀθηναίων Αἴγιναν Εὐρυβάτην τὸν Ἀργεῖον ἄνδρα πεντάεθλον ἐκ προκλήσιος ἐφόνευσε. αὐτὸν δὲ Σωφάνεα χρόνῳ ὕστερον τούτων κατέλαβε ἄνδρα γενόμενον ἀγαθόν, Ἀθηναίων στρατηγέοντα ἅμα Λεάγρῳ τῷ Γλαύκωνος, ἀποθανεῖν ὑπὸ Ἠδωνῶν ἐν Δάτῳ περὶ τῶν μετάλλων τῶν χρυσέων μαχόμενον.

76. Ὡς δὲ τοῖσι Ἕλλησι ἐν Πλαταιῇσι κατέστρωντο οἱ βάρβαροι, ἐνθαῦτά σφι ἐπῆλθε γυνὴ αὐτόμολος· ἣ ἐπειδὴ ἔμαθε ἀπολωλότας τοὺς Πέρσας καὶ νικῶντας τοὺς Ἕλληνας, ἐοῦσα παλλακὴ Φαρανδάτεος τοῦ Τεάσπιος ἀνδρὸς Πέρσεω, κοσμησαμένη χρυσῷ πολλῷ καὶ αὐτὴ καὶ ἀμφίπολοι καὶ ἐσθῆτι τῇ καλλίστῃ τῶν παρεουσέων, καταβᾶσα ἐκ τῆς ἁρμαμάξης ἐχώρεε ἐς τοὺς Λακεδαιμονίους ἔτι ἐν τῇσι φονῇσι ἐόντας, ὁρῶσα δὲ πάντα ἐκεῖνα διέποντα Παυσανίην, πρότερόν τε τὸ οὔνομα ἐξεπισταμένη καὶ τὴν πάτρην ὥστε πολλάκις ἀκούσασα, ἔγνω τε τὸν Παυσανίην καὶ λαβομένη τῶν γουνάτων ἔλεγε τάδε. "Ὦ βασιλεῦ Σπάρτης, ῥῦσαί με τὴν ἱκέτιν αἰχμαλώτου δουλοσύνης. σὺ γὰρ καὶ ἐς τόδε ὤνησας, τούσδε ἀπολέσας τοὺς οὔτε δαιμόνων οὔτε θεῶν ὄπιν ἔχοντας. εἰμὶ δὲ γένος μὲν Κώη, θυγάτηρ δὲ Ἡγητορίδεω τοῦ Ἀνταγόρεω· βίῃ δέ με λαβὼν ἐν Κῷ εἶχε ὁ Πέρσης." ὁ δὲ ἀμείβεται τοῖσιδε. "Γύναι, θάρσεε καὶ ὡς ἱκέτις καὶ εἰ δὴ πρὸς τούτῳ τυγχάνεις ἀληθέα λέγουσα καὶ εἶς

248

75. Another famous feat of arms Sophanes achieved: when the Athenians were beleaguering Aegina, he challenged and slew Eurybates the Argive, a victor in the Five Contests. But long after this Sophanes, who had borne himself thus gallantly, came by his death; being general of the Athenians with Leagrus, son of Glaucon, he was slain at Datus [1] by the Edonians in a battle for the gold-mines.

76. Immediately after the Greeks had laid low the foreigners at Plataeae, there came to them a woman, deserting from the enemy, who was the concubine of Pharandates, a Persian, son of Teaspis. She, learning that the Persians were destroyed and the Greeks victorious, decked herself (as did also her attendants) with many gold ornaments and the fairest raiment that she had, and so lighting from her carriage came to the Lacedaemonians while they were yet at the slaughtering; and seeing Pausanias ordering all that business, whose name and country she knew from her often hearing of it, she knew that it was he, and thus besought him, clasping his knees: "Save me, your suppliant, O king of Sparta! from captive slavery; for you have done me good service till this hour, by making an end of yonder men, that regard not aught that is divine in heaven or earth. Coan am I by birth, daughter to Hegetorides, son of Antagoras; in Cos the Persian laid violent hands on me and held me prisoner." "Be of good cheer, lady," Pausanias answered, "for that you are my suppliant, and for your tale withal, if

---

[1] In the attempt to establish an Athenian settlement at Amphipolis in 465 (Thucyd. i. 100, v. 102). Datus was on the Thracian seaboard opposite Thasos.

θυγάτηρ Ἡγητορίδεω τοῦ Κῴου, ὃς ἐμοὶ ξεῖνος
μάλιστα τυγχάνει ἐὼν τῶν περὶ ἐκείνους τοὺς
χώρους οἰκημένων." ταῦτα δὲ εἴπας τότε μὲν
ἐπέτρεψε τῶν ἐφόρων τοῖσι παρεοῦσι, ὕστερον
δὲ ἀπέπεμψε ἐς Αἴγιναν, ἐς τὴν αὐτὴ ἤθελε
ἀπικέσθαι.

77. Μετὰ δὲ τὴν ἄπιξιν τῆς γυναικός, αὐτίκα
μετὰ ταῦτα ἀπίκοντο Μαντινέες ἐπ᾽ ἐξεργα-
σμένοισι· μαθόντες δὲ ὅτι ὕστεροι ἥκουσι τῆς
συμβολῆς, συμφορὴν ἐποιεῦντο μεγάλην, ἄξιοί τε
ἔφασαν εἶναι σφέας ζημιῶσαι. πυνθανόμενοι δὲ
τοὺς Μήδους τοὺς μετὰ Ἀρταβάζου φεύγοντας,
τούτους ἐδίωκον μέχρι Θεσσαλίης· Λακεδαιμόνιοι
δὲ οὐκ ἔων φεύγοντας διώκειν. οἳ δὲ ἀναχωρή-
σαντες ἐς τὴν ἑωυτῶν τοὺς ἡγεμόνας τῆς στρατιῆς
ἐδίωξαν ἐκ τῆς γῆς. μετὰ δὲ Μαντινέας ἧκον
Ἠλεῖοι, καὶ ὡσαύτως οἱ Ἠλεῖοι τοῖσι Μαντινεῦσι
συμφορὴν ποιησάμενοι ἀπαλλάσσοντο· ἀπελ-
θόντες δὲ καὶ οὗτοι τοὺς ἡγεμόνας ἐδίωξαν. τὰ
κατὰ Μαντινέας μὲν καὶ Ἠλείους τοσαῦτα.

78. Ἐν δὲ Πλαταιῆσι ἐν τῷ στρατοπέδῳ τῶν
Αἰγινητέων ἦν Λάμπων Πυθέω, Αἰγινητέων ἐὼν
τὰ πρῶτα· ὃς ἀνοσιώτατον ἔχων λόγον ἵετο πρὸς
Παυσανίην, ἀπικόμενος δὲ σπουδῇ ἔλεγε τάδε.
"Ὦ παῖ Κλεομβρότου, ἔργον ἔργασταί τοι
ὑπερφυὲς μέγαθός τε καὶ κάλλος, καί τοι θεὸς
παρέδωκε ῥυσάμενον τὴν Ἑλλάδα κλέος κατα-
θέσθαι μέγιστον Ἑλλήνων τῶν ἡμεῖς ἴδμεν. σὺ
δὲ καὶ τὰ λοιπὰ τὰ ἐπὶ τούτοισι ποίησον, ὅκως
λόγος τε σὲ ἔχῃ ἔτι μέζων καί τις ὕστερον
φυλάσσηται τῶν βαρβάρων μὴ ὑπάρχειν ἔργα
ἀτάσθαλα ποιέων ἐς τοὺς Ἕλληνας. Λεωνίδεω

you be verily daughter to Hegetorides of Cos, for he is my closest friend, of all that dwell in those lands." Thus saying, he gave her for the nonce in charge to those of the ephors who were present, and thereafter sent her to Aegina, whither she herself desired to go.

77. Immediately after the coming of this woman, came the men of Mantinea, when all was over; who, learning that they were come too late for the battle, were greatly distressed, and said that they deserved to punish themselves therefor. Hearing that the Medes with Artabazus were fleeing, they would have pursued after them as far as Thessaly; but the Lacedaemonians would not suffer them to pursue fleeing men; and returning to their own land the Mantineans banished the leaders of their army from the country. After the Mantineans came the men of Elis, who also went away sorrowful in like manner as the Mantineans, and after their departure banished their leaders likewise. Such were the doings of the Mantineans and Eleans.

78. Now there was at Plataeae in the army of the Aeginetans one Lampon, son of Pytheas, a leading man of Aegina; he sought Pausanias with most unrighteous counsel, and having made haste to come said to him: "Son of Cleombrotus, you have done a deed of surpassing greatness and glory; by heaven's favour you have saved Hellas, and thereby won greater renown than any Greek known to men. But now you must finish what remains to do, that your fame may be yet the greater, and that no foreigner may hereafter make bold unprovoked to wreak his mad and wicked will on the Greeks. When Leonidas

γὰρ ἀποθανόντος ἐν Θερμοπύλῃσι Μαρδόνιός τε
καὶ Ξέρξης ἀποταμόντες τὴν κεφαλὴν ἀνεσταύ-
ρωσαν· τῷ σὺ τὴν ὁμοίην ἀποδιδοὺς ἔπαινον ἕξεις
πρῶτα μὲν ὑπὸ πάντων Σπαρτιητέων, αὖτις δὲ
καὶ πρὸς τῶν ἄλλων Ἑλλήνων· Μαρδόνιον γὰρ
ἀνασκολοπίσας τετιμωρήσεαι ἐς πάτρων τὸν σὸν
Λεωνίδην."

79. Ὁ μὲν δοκέων χαρίζεσθαι ἔλεγε τάδε, ὁ δ'
ἀνταμείβετο τοῖσιδε. "Ὦ ξεῖνε Αἰγινῆτα, τὸ μὲν
εὐνοέειν τε καὶ προορᾶν ἄγαμαί σευ, γνώμης
μέντοι ἡμάρτηκας χρηστῆς· ἐξαείρας γάρ με ὑψοῦ
καὶ τὴν πάτρην καὶ τὸ ἔργον, ἐς τὸ μηδὲν κατέ-
βαλες παραινέων νεκρῷ λυμαίνεσθαι, καὶ ἢν
ταῦτα ποιέω, φὰς ἄμεινόν με ἀκούσεσθαι· τὰ
πρέπει μᾶλλον βαρβάροισι ποιέειν ἤ περ
Ἕλλησι· καὶ ἐκείνοισι δὲ ἐπιφθονέομεν. ἐγὼ
δ' ὦν τούτου εἵνεκα μήτε Αἰγινήτῃσι ἅδοιμι μήτε
τοῖσι ταῦτα ἀρέσκεται, ἀποχρᾷ δέ μοι Σπαρτιήτῃσι ἀρεσκόμενον ὅσια μὲν ποιέειν, ὅσια δὲ καὶ
λέγειν. Λεωνίδῃ δέ, τῷ με κελεύεις τιμωρῆσαι,
φημὶ μεγάλως τετιμωρῆσθαι, ψυχῇσί τε τῇσι
τῶνδε ἀναριθμήτοισι τετίμηται αὐτός τε καὶ οἱ
ἄλλοι οἱ ἐν Θερμοπύλῃσι τελευτήσαντες. σὺ
μέντοι ἔτι ἔχων λόγον τοιόνδε μήτε προσέλθῃς
ἔμοιγε μήτε συμβουλεύσῃς, χάριν τε ἴσθι ἐὼν
ἀπαθής."

80. Ὁ μὲν ταῦτα ἀκούσας ἀπαλλάσσετο.
Παυσανίης δὲ κήρυγμα ποιησάμενος μηδένα
ἅπτεσθαι τῆς ληίης, συγκομίζειν ἐκέλευε τοὺς
εἵλωτας τὰ χρήματα. οἱ δὲ ἀνὰ τὸ στρατόπεδον
σκιδνάμενοι εὕρισκον σκηνὰς κατεσκευασμένας
χρυσῷ καὶ ἀργύρῳ, κλίνας τε ἐπιχρύσους καὶ

was slain at Thermopylae, Mardonius and Xerxes
cut off his head and set it on a pole; make them a
like return, and you will win praise from all Spartans,
and the rest of Hellas besides; for if you impale
Mardonius you will be avenged for your father's
brother Leonidas."

79. So said Lampon, thinking to please. But
Pausanias answered him thus: "Sir Aeginetan, I
thank you for your goodwill and forethought; but
you have missed the mark of right judgment; for
first you exalt me on high and my fatherland and
my deeds withal, yet next you cast me down to
mere nothingness when you counsel me to insult the
dead, and say that I shall win more praise if I so do;
but that were an act more proper for foreigners than
for Greeks, and one that we deem matter of blame
even in foreigners. Nay, for myself, I would fain in
this business find no favour either with the people of
Aegina or whoso else is pleased by such acts; it is
enough for me if I please the Spartans by righteous
deed and righteous speech. As for Leonidas, whom
you would have me avenge, I hold that he has had
full measure of vengeance; the uncounted souls of
these that you see have done honour to him and the
rest of those who died at Thermopylae. But to you
this is my warning, that you come not again to me
with words like these nor give me such counsel;
and be thankful now that you go unpunished."

80. With that answer Lampon departed. Then
Pausanias made a proclamation, that no man should
touch the spoil, and bade the helots gather all the
stuff together. They, scattering all about the camp,
found there tents adorned with gold and silver, and
couches gilded and silver-plated, and golden bowls

ἐπαργύρους, κρητῆράς τε χρυσέους καὶ φιάλας τε
καὶ ἄλλα ἐκπώματα· σάκκους τε ἐπ' ἀμαξέων
εὕρισκον, ἐν τοῖσι λέβητες ἐφαίνοντο ἐνεόντες
χρύσεοί τε καὶ ἀργύρεοι· ἀπό τε τῶν κειμένων
νεκρῶν ἐσκύλευον ψέλιά τε καὶ στρεπτοὺς καὶ
τοὺς ἀκινάκας ἐόντας χρυσέους, ἐπεὶ ἐσθῆτός γε
ποικίλης λόγος ἐγίνετο οὐδείς. ἐνθαῦτα πολλὰ
μὲν κλέπτοντες ἐπώλεον πρὸς τοὺς Αἰγινήτας οἱ
εἵλωτες, πολλὰ δὲ καὶ ἀπεδείκνυσαν, ὅσα αὐτῶν
οὐκ οἷά τε ἦν κρύψαι· ὥστε Αἰγινήτῃσι οἱ
μεγάλοι πλοῦτοι ἀρχὴν ἐνθεῦτεν ἐγένοντο, οἳ τὸν
χρυσὸν ἅτε ἐόντα χαλκὸν δῆθεν παρὰ τῶν εἰλώτων
ὠνέοντο.

81. Συμφορήσαντες δὲ τὰ χρήματα καὶ δεκάτην
ἐξελόντες τῷ ἐν Δελφοῖσι θεῷ, ἀπ' ἧς ὁ τρίπους ὁ
χρύσεος ἀνετέθη ὁ ἐπὶ τοῦ τρικαρήνου ὄφιος τοῦ
χαλκέου ἐπεστεὼς ἄγχιστα τοῦ βωμοῦ, καὶ τῷ
ἐν Ὀλυμπίῃ θεῷ ἐξελόντες, ἀπ' ἧς δεκάπηχυν
χάλκεον Δία ἀνέθηκαν, καὶ τῷ ἐν Ἰσθμῷ θεῷ,
ἀπ' ἧς ἑπτάπηχυς χάλκεος Ποσειδέων ἐξεγένετο,
ταῦτα ἐξελόντες τὰ λοιπὰ διαιρέοντο, καὶ ἔλαβον
ἕκαστοι τῶν ἄξιοι ἦσαν, καὶ τὰς παλλακὰς τῶν
Περσέων καὶ τὸν χρυσὸν καὶ ἄργυρον καὶ ἄλλα
χρήματά τε καὶ ὑποζύγια. ὅσα μέν νυν ἐξαίρετα
τοῖσι ἀριστεύσασι αὐτῶν ἐν Πλαταιῆσι ἐδόθη, οὐ
λέγεται πρὸς οὐδαμῶν, δοκέω δ' ἔγωγε καὶ τούτοισι δοθῆναι· Παυσανίῃ δὲ πάντα δέκα ἐξαιρέθη
τε καὶ ἐδόθη, γυναῖκες ἵπποι τάλαντα κάμηλοι,
ὡς δὲ αὕτως καὶ τἆλλα χρήματα.

[1] The bronze three-headed serpent supporting the cauldron
was intended apparently to commemorate the whole Greek
alliance against Persia. The serpent pedestal still exists,

and cups and other drinking-vessels; and sacks they found on wains, wherein were seen cauldrons of gold and silver; and they stripped from the dead that lay there their armlets and torques, and daggers of gold; as for many-coloured raiment, it was nothing regarded. Much of all this the helots showed, as much as they could not conceal; but much they stole and sold to the Aeginetans; insomuch that the Aeginetans thereby laid the foundation of their great fortunes, by buying gold from the helots as though it were bronze.

81. Having brought all the stuff together they set apart a tithe for the god of Delphi, whereof was made and dedicated that tripod that rests upon the bronze three-headed serpent,[1] nearest to the altar; another they set apart for the god of Olympia, whereof was made and dedicated a bronze figure of Zeus, ten cubits high; and another for the god of the Isthmus, whereof came a bronze Poseidon seven cubits high; all which having set apart they divided the remnant, and each received according to his desert of the concubines of the Persians, and the gold and silver, and all the rest of the stuff, and the beasts of burden. How much was set apart and given to those who had fought best at Plataeae, no man says; but I think that they also received gifts; but tenfold of every kind, women, horses, talents, camels, and all other things likewise, was set apart and given to Pausanias.

in the Atmeidan (formerly Hippodrome) at Constantinople, whither it was transported by Constantine; it has been fully exposed and its inscription deciphered since 1856. The names of thirty-one Greek states are incised on eleven spirals, from the third to the thirteenth. For a fuller account see How and Wells' note *ad loc.*

HERODOTUS

82. Λέγεται δὲ καὶ τάδε γενέσθαι, ὡς Ξέρξης
φεύγων ἐκ τῆς Ἑλλάδος Μαρδονίῳ τὴν κατασκευὴν καταλίποι τὴν ἑωυτοῦ· Παυσανίην ὦν
ὁρῶντα τὴν Μαρδονίου κατασκευὴν χρυσῷ τε καὶ
ἀργύρῳ καὶ παραπετάσμασι ποικίλοισι κατε-
σκευασμένην, κελεῦσαι τούς τε ἀρτοκόπους καὶ
τοὺς ὀψοποιοὺς κατὰ ταὐτὰ καθὼς Μαρδονίῳ
δεῖπνον παρασκευάζειν. ὡς δὲ κελευόμενοι οὗτοι
ἐποίευν ταῦτα, ἐνθαῦτα τὸν Παυσανίην ἰδόντα
κλίνας τε χρυσέας καὶ ἀργυρέας εὖ ἐστρωμένας
καὶ τραπέζας τε χρυσέας καὶ ἀργυρέας καὶ παρα-
σκευὴν μεγαλοπρεπέα τοῦ δείπνου, ἐκπλαγέντα τὰ
προκείμενα ἀγαθὰ κελεῦσαι ἐπὶ γέλωτι τοὺς ἑωυτοῦ
διηκόνους παρασκευάσαι Λακωνικὸν δεῖπνον. ὡς
δὲ τῆς θοίνης ποιηθείσης ἦν πολλὸν τὸ μέσον,
τὸν Παυσανίην γελάσαντα μεταπέμψασθαι τῶν
Ἑλλήνων τοὺς στρατηγούς, συνελθόντων δὲ τούτων εἰπεῖν τὸν Παυσανίην, δεικνύντα ἐς ἑκατέρην
τοῦ δείπνου παρασκευήν, "Ἄνδρες Ἕλληνες,
τῶνδε εἵνεκα ἐγὼ ὑμέας συνήγαγον, βουλόμενος
ὑμῖν τοῦδε τοῦ Μήδων ἡγεμόνος τὴν ἀφροσύνην
δέξαι, ὃς τοιήνδε δίαιταν ἔχων ἦλθε ἐς ἡμέας
οὕτω οἰζυρὴν ἔχοντας ἀπαιρησόμενος." ταῦτα
μὲν Παυσανίην λέγεται εἰπεῖν πρὸς τοὺς στρατηγοὺς τῶν Ἑλλήνων.

83. Ὑστέρῳ μέντοι χρόνῳ μετὰ ταῦτα καὶ τῶν
Πλαταιέων εὗρον συχνοὶ θήκας χρυσοῦ καὶ
ἀργύρου καὶ τῶν ἄλλων χρημάτων. ἐφάνη δὲ
καὶ τόδε ὕστερον τούτων ἐπὶ τῶν νεκρῶν περι-
ψιλωθέντων τὰς σάρκας· συνεφόρεον γὰρ τὰ
ὀστέα οἱ Πλαταιέες ἐς ἕνα χῶρον· εὑρέθη κεφαλὴ
οὐκ ἔχουσα ῥαφὴν οὐδεμίαν ἀλλ' ἐξ ἑνὸς ἐοῦσα
256

82. This other story is also told. Xerxes in his flight from Hellas, having left to Mardonius his own establishment, Pausanias, seeing Mardonius' establishment with its display of gold and silver and gaily-coloured tapestry, bade the bakers and the cooks to prepare a dinner in such wise as they were wont to do for Mardonius. They did his bidding; whereat Pausanias, when he saw golden and silvern couches richly covered, and tables of gold and silver, and all the magnificent service of the banquet, was amazed at the splendour before him, and for a jest bade his own servants prepare a dinner after Laconian fashion. When that meal was ready and was far different from the other, Pausanias fell a-laughing, and sent for the generals of the Greeks. They being assembled, Pausanias pointed to the fashion after which either dinner was served, and said : " Men of Hellas, I have brought you hither because I desired to show you the foolishness of the leader of the Medes ; who, with such provision for life as you see, came hither to take away from us ours, that is so pitiful." Thus, it is said, Pausanias spoke to the generals of the Greeks.

83. But in later days many of the Plataeans also found chests full of gold and silver and all else. Moreover there were sights to see among these dead, when their bones (which the Plataeans gathered into one place) were laid bare of flesh : there was found a skull whereof the bone was all

ὀστέου, ἐφάνη δὲ καὶ γνάθος κατὰ τὸ ἄνω¹ τῆς
γνάθου ἔχουσα ὀδόντας μουνοφυέας ἐξ ἑνὸς
ὀστέου πάντας τούς τε προσθίους καὶ γομφίους,
καὶ πενταπήχεος ἀνδρὸς ὀστέα ἐφάνη.

84. Ἐπείτε δὲ² Μαρδονίου δευτέρῃ ἡμέρῃ ὁ
νεκρὸς ἠφάνιστο, ὑπὸ ὅτευ μὲν ἀνθρώπων τὸ
ἀτρεκὲς οὐκ ἔχω εἰπεῖν, πολλοὺς δὲ τινὰς ἤδη
καὶ παντοδαποὺς ἤκουσα θάψαι Μαρδόνιον, καὶ
δῶρα μεγάλα οἶδα λαβόντας πολλοὺς παρὰ
Ἀρτόντεω τοῦ Μαρδονίου παιδὸς διὰ τοῦτο τὸ
ἔργον· ὅστις μέντοι ἦν αὐτῶν ὁ ὑπελόμενός τε καὶ
θάψας τὸν νεκρὸν τὸν Μαρδονίου, οὐ δύναμαι
ἀτρεκέως πυθέσθαι, ἔχει δὲ τινὰ φάτιν καὶ
Διονυσοφάνης ἀνὴρ Ἐφέσιος θάψαι Μαρδόνιον.
ἀλλ' ὁ μὲν τρόπῳ τοιούτῳ ἐτάφη.

85. Οἱ δὲ Ἕλληνες ὡς ἐν Πλαταιῇσι τὴν ληίην
διείλοντο, ἔθαπτον τοὺς ἑωυτῶν χωρὶς ἕκαστοι.
Λακεδαιμόνιοι μὲν τριξὰς ἐποιήσαντο θήκας· ἔνθα
μὲν τοὺς ἰρένας ἔθαψαν, τῶν καὶ Ποσειδώνιος καὶ
Ἀμομφάρετος ἦσαν καὶ Φιλοκύων τε καὶ Καλλικράτης. ἐν μὲν δὴ ἑνὶ τῶν τάφων ἦσαν οἱ
ἰρένες, ἐν δὲ τῷ ἑτέρῳ οἱ ἄλλοι Σπαρτιῆται, ἐν
δὲ τῷ τρίτῳ οἱ εἵλωτες. οὗτοι μὲν οὕτω ἔθαπτον,
Τεγεῆται δὲ χωρὶς πάντας ἁλέας, καὶ Ἀθηναῖοι
τοὺς ἑωυτῶν ὁμοῦ, καὶ Μεγαρέες τε καὶ Φλειάσιοι
τοὺς ὑπὸ τῆς ἵππου διαφθαρέντας. τούτων μὲν
δὴ πάντων πλήρεες ἐγένοντο οἱ τάφοι· τῶν δὲ
ἄλλων ὅσοι καὶ φαίνονται ἐν Πλαταιῇσι ἐόντες

¹ MS. καὶ τὸ ἄνω; Stein suggests κατά, which is here
adopted.
² MS. ἔπειτε δέ, introducing a protasis which has no
apodosis; Stein's suggested ἐπεί γε δή (= for as to Mardonius,
etc.) seems preferable.

one without suture, and a jawbone wherein the
teeth of the upper jaw were one whole, a single
bone, front teeth and grinders; and there were
to be seen the bones of a man of five cubits'
stature.

84. As for the body of Mardonius, it was made
away with on the day after the battle; by whom, I
cannot with exactness say; but I have heard of very
many of all countries that buried Mardonius, and I
know of many that were richly rewarded for that
act by Mardonius' son Artontes; but which of them
it was that stole away and buried the body of
Mardonius I cannot learn for a certainty, albeit
some report that it was buried by Dionysophanes,
an Ephesian. Such was the manner of Mardonius'
burial.

85. But the Greeks, when they had divided the
spoil at Plataeae, buried their dead each severally in
their place. The Lacedaemonians made three vaults;
there they buried their "irens," [1] among whom were
Posidonius and Amompharetus and Philocyon and
Callicrates. In one of the tombs, then, were the
"irens," in the second the rest of the Spartans,
and in the third the helots. Thus the Lacedaemonians buried their dead; the Tegeans buried all
theirs together in a place apart, and the Athenians
did likewise with their own dead; and so did the
Megarians and Phliasians with those who had been
slain by the horsemen. All the tombs of these
peoples were filled with dead; but as for the rest of
the states whose tombs are to be seen at Plataeae,

---

[1] Spartan young men between the ages of twenty and
thirty.

HERODOTUS

τάφοι, τούτους δέ, ὡς ἐγὼ πυνθάνομαι, ἐπαισχυνο-
μένους τῇ ἀπεστοῖ τῆς μάχης ἑκάστους χώματα
χῶσαι κεινὰ τῶν ἐπιγινομένων εἵνεκεν ἀνθρώπων,
ἐπεὶ καὶ Αἰγινητέων ἐστὶ αὐτόθι καλεόμενος τάφος,
τὸν ἐγὼ ἀκούω καὶ δέκα ἔτεσι ὕστερον μετὰ ταῦτα
δεηθέντων τῶν Αἰγινητέων χῶσαι Κλεάδην τὸν
Αὐτοδίκου ἄνδρα Πλαταιέα, πρόξεινον ἐόντα
αὐτῶν.

86. Ὡς δ᾽ ἄρα ἔθαψαν τοὺς νεκροὺς ἐν Πλαταιῇσι οἱ Ἕλληνες, αὐτίκα βουλευομένοισί σφι
ἐδόκεε στρατεύειν ἐπὶ τὰς Θήβας καὶ ἐξαιτέειν
αὐτῶν τοὺς μηδίσαντας, ἐν πρώτοισι δὲ αὐτῶν
Τιμηγενίδην καὶ Ἀτταγῖνον, οἳ ἀρχηγέται ἀνὰ
πρώτους ἦσαν· ἢν δὲ μὴ ἐκδιδῶσι, μὴ ἀπανί-
στασθαι ἀπὸ τῆς πόλιος πρότερον ἢ ἐξέλωσι.
ὡς δέ σφι ταῦτα ἔδοξε, οὕτω δὴ ἑνδεκάτῃ ἡμέρῃ
ἀπὸ τῆς συμβολῆς ἀπικόμενοι ἐπολιόρκεον Θη-
βαίους, κελεύοντες ἐκδιδόναι τοὺς ἄνδρας· οὐ
βουλομένων δὲ τῶν Θηβαίων ἐκδιδόναι, τήν τε
γῆν αὐτῶν ἔταμνον καὶ προσέβαλλον πρὸς τὸ
τεῖχος.

87. Καὶ οὐ γὰρ ἐπαύοντο σινόμενοι, εἰκοστῇ
ἡμέρῃ ἔλεξε τοῖσι Θηβαίοισι Τιμηγενίδης τάδε.
"Ἄνδρες Θηβαῖοι, ἐπειδὴ οὕτω δέδοκται τοῖσι
Ἕλλησι, μὴ πρότερον ἀπαναστῆναι πολιορκέοντας
ἢ ἐξέλωσι Θήβας ἢ ἡμέας αὐτοῖσι παραδῶτε, νῦν
ὦν ἡμέων εἵνεκα γῆ ἡ Βοιωτίη πλέω μὴ ἀναπλήσῃ,
ἀλλ᾽ εἰ μὲν χρημάτων χρηίζοντες πρόσχημα
ἡμέας ἐξαιτέονται, χρήματά σφι δῶμεν ἐκ τοῦ
κοινοῦ (σὺν γὰρ τῷ κοινῷ καὶ ἐμηδίσαμεν οὐδὲ
μοῦνοι ἡμεῖς), εἰ δὲ ἡμέων ἀληθέως δεόμενοι
πολιορκέουσι, ἡμεῖς ἡμέας αὐτοὺς ἐς ἀντιλογίην
260

their tombs are but empty barrows that they built for the sake of men that should come after, because they were ashamed to have been absent from the battle. In truth there is one there that is called the tomb of the Aeginetans, which, as I have been told, was built as late as ten years after, at the Aeginetans' desire, by their patron and protector Cleades son of Autodicus, a Plataean.

86. As soon as the Greeks had buried their dead at Plataeae, they resolved in council that they would march against Thebes and demand surrender of those who had taken the Persian part, but specially of Timagenidas and Attaginus, who were chief among their foremost men; and that, if these men were not delivered to them, they would not withdraw from before the city till they should have taken it. Being thus resolved, they came with this intent on the eleventh day after the battle and laid siege to the Thebans, demanding the surrender of the men; and the Thebans refusing this surrender, they laid their lands waste and assaulted the walls.

87. Seeing that the Greeks would not cease from their harrying, when nineteen days were past, Timagenidas thus spoke to the Thebans: "Men of Thebes, since the Greeks have so resolved that they will not raise the siege till Thebes be taken or we be delivered to them, now let not the land of Boeotia increase the measure of its ills for our sake; nay, if it is money they desire and their demand for our surrender is but a pretext, let us give them money out of our common treasury (for it was by the common will and not ours alone that we took the Persian part); but if they be besieging the town for no other cause save to have us, then we will give

παρέξομεν." κάρτα τε ἔδοξε εὖ λέγειν καὶ ἐς
καιρόν, αὐτίκα τε ἐπεκηρυκεύοντο πρὸς Παυσανίην
οἱ Θηβαῖοι θέλοντες ἐκδιδόναι τοὺς ἄνδρας.

88. Ὡς δὲ ὡμολόγησαν ἐπὶ τούτοισι, Ἀτταγῖνος μὲν ἐκδιδρήσκει ἐκ τοῦ ἄστεος, παῖδας δὲ
αὐτοῦ ἀπαχθέντας Παυσανίης ἀπέλυσε τῆς αἰτίης,
φὰς τοῦ μηδισμοῦ παῖδας οὐδὲν εἶναι μεταιτίους.
τοὺς δὲ ἄλλους ἄνδρας τοὺς ἐξέδοσαν οἱ Θηβαῖοι,
οἳ μὲν ἐδόκεον ἀντιλογίης τε κυρήσειν καὶ δὴ
χρήμασι ἐπεποίθεσαν διωθέεσθαι· ὁ δὲ ὡς παρέ-
λαβε, αὐτὰ ταῦτα ὑπονοέων τὴν στρατιὴν τὴν
τῶν συμμάχων ἅπασαν ἀπῆκε καὶ ἐκείνους ἀγα-
γὼν ἐς Κόρινθον διέφθειρε. ταῦτα μὲν τὰ ἐν
Πλαταιῇσι καὶ Θήβῃσι γενόμενα.

89. Ἀρτάβαζος δὲ ὁ Φαρνάκεος φεύγων ἐκ
Πλαταιέων καὶ δὴ πρόσω ἐγίνετο. ἀπικόμενον
δέ μιν οἱ Θεσσαλοὶ παρὰ σφέας ἐπί τε ξείνια
ἐκάλεον καὶ ἀνειρώτων περὶ τῆς στρατιῆς τῆς
ἄλλης, οὐδὲν ἐπιστάμενοι τῶν ἐν Πλαταιῇσι γενομένων. ὁ δὲ Ἀρτάβαζος γνοὺς ὅτι εἰ ἐθέλει σφι
πᾶσαν τὴν ἀληθείην τῶν ἀγώνων εἰπεῖν, αὐτός
τε κινδυνεύσει ἀπολέσθαι καὶ ὁ μετ' αὐτοῦ στρα-
τός· ἐπιθήσεσθαι γάρ οἱ πάντα τινὰ ᾤετο πυν-
θανόμενον τὰ γεγονότα. ταῦτα ἐκλογιζόμενος οὔτε
πρὸς τοὺς Φωκέας ἐξηγόρευε οὐδὲν πρός τε τοὺς
Θεσσαλοὺς ἔλεγε τάδε. "Ἐγὼ μὲν ὦ ἄνδρες
Θεσσαλοί, ὡς ὁρᾶτε, ἐπείγομαί τε κατὰ τάχος
ἐλῶν ἐς Θρηίκην καὶ σπουδὴν ἔχω, πεμφθεὶς
κατά τι πρῆγμα ἐκ τοῦ στρατοπέδου μετὰ τῶνδε·
αὐτὸς δὲ ὑμῖν Μαρδόνιος καὶ ὁ στρατὸς αὐτοῦ,
οὗτος κατὰ πόδας ἐμεῦ ἐλαύνων προσδόκιμός ἐστι.

ourselves up to be tried by them." This seeming to be very well and seasonably said, the Thebans immediately sent a herald to Pausanias, offering to surrender the men.

88. On these terms they made an agreement; but Attaginus escaped out of the town; his sons were seized, but Pausanias held them free of guilt, saying that the sons were nowise accessory to the treason. As for the rest of the men whom the Thebans surrendered, they supposed that they would be put on their trial, and were confident that they would defeat the impeachment by bribery; but Pausanias had that very suspicion of them, and when they were put into his hands he sent away the whole allied army, and carried the men to Corinth, where he put them to death. Such were the doings at Plataeae and Thebes.

89. Artabazus the son of Pharnaces was by now far on his way in his flight from Plataeae. The Thessalians, when he came among them, entertained him hospitably and inquired of him concerning the rest of the army, knowing nothing of what had been done at Plataeae. Artabazus understood that if he told them the whole truth about the fighting, he would imperil his own life and the lives of all that were with him; for he thought that every man would set upon him if they heard the story; wherefore, thus reasoning, even as he had revealed nothing to the Phocians so he spoke thus to the Thessalians: "I myself, men of Thessaly, am pressing on with all speed and diligence to march into Thrace, being despatched from the army for a certain purpose with these whom you see; and you may look to see Mardonius and that host of his yonder, marching

HERODOTUS

τοῦτον καὶ ξεινίζετε καὶ εὖ ποιεῦντες φαίνεσθε·
οὐ γὰρ ὑμῖν ἐς χρόνον ταῦτα ποιεῦσι μεταμε-
λήσει." ταῦτα δὲ εἴπας ἀπήλαυνε σπουδῇ τὴν
στρατιὴν διὰ Θεσσαλίης τε καὶ Μακεδονίης ἰθὺ
τῆς Θρηίκης, ὡς ἀληθέως ἐπειγόμενος, καὶ τὴν
μεσόγαιαν τάμνων τῆς ὁδοῦ. καὶ ἀπικνέεται ἐς
Βυζάντιον, καταλιπὼν τοῦ στρατοῦ τοῦ ἑωυτοῦ
συχνοὺς ὑπὸ Θρηίκων κατακοπέντας κατ' ὁδὸν
καὶ λιμῷ συστάντας καὶ καμάτῳ· ἐκ Βυζαντίου
δὲ διέβη πλοίοισι. οὗτος μὲν οὕτω ἀπενόστησε
ἐς τὴν Ἀσίην.

90. Τῆς δὲ αὐτῆς ἡμέρης τῆς περ ἐν Πλαταιῇσι
τὸ τρῶμα ἐγένετο, συνεκύρησε γενέσθαι καὶ ἐν
Μυκάλῃ τῆς Ἰωνίης. ἐπεὶ γὰρ δὴ ἐν τῇ Δήλῳ
κατέατο οἱ Ἕλληνες οἱ ἐν τῇσι νηυσὶ ἅμα Λευτυ-
χίδῃ τῷ Λακεδαιμονίῳ ἀπικόμενοι, ἦλθόν σφι
ἄγγελοι ἀπὸ Σάμου Λάμπων τε Θρασυκλέος καὶ
Ἀθηναγόρης Ἀρχεστρατίδεω καὶ Ἡγησίστρατος
Ἀρισταγόρεω, πεμφθέντες ὑπὸ Σαμίων λάθρῃ
τῶν τε Περσέων καὶ τοῦ τυράννου Θεομήστορος
τοῦ Ἀνδροδάμαντος, τὸν κατέστησαν Σάμου
τύραννον οἱ Πέρσαι. ἐπελθόντων δὲ σφέων ἐπὶ
τοὺς στρατηγοὺς ἔλεγε Ἡγησίστρατος πολλὰ καὶ
παντοῖα, ὡς ἢν μοῦνον ἴδωνται αὐτοὺς οἱ Ἴωνες
ἀποστήσονται ἀπὸ Περσέων, καὶ ὡς οἱ βάρβαροι
οὐκ ὑπομενέουσι· ἢν δὲ καὶ ἄρα ὑπομείνωσι, οὐκ
ἑτέρην ἄγρην τοιαύτην εὑρεῖν ἂν αὐτούς· θεούς τε
κοινοὺς ἀνακαλέων προέτραπε αὐτοὺς ῥύσασθαι
ἄνδρας Ἕλληνας ἐκ δουλοσύνης καὶ ἀπαμῦναι τὸν
βάρβαρον· εὐπετές τε αὐτοῖσι ἔφη ταῦτα γίνεσθαι·
τάς τε γὰρ νέας αὐτῶν κακῶς πλέειν καὶ οὐκ ἀξι-
ομάχους κείνοισι εἶναι. αὐτοί τε, εἴ τι ὑποπτεύουσι

264

close after me. It is for you to entertain him, and
show that you do him good service; for if you so do,
you will not afterwards repent of it." So saying, he
used all diligence to lead his army away straight
towards Thrace through Thessaly and Macedonia,
brooking in good sooth no delay and following the
shortest inland road. So he came to Byzantium, but
he left behind many of his army, cut down by the
Thracians or overcome by hunger and weariness;
and from Byzantium he crossed over in boats. In
such case Artabazus returned into Asia.

90. Now on the selfsame day when the Persians
were so stricken at Plataeae, it so fell out that they
suffered a like fate at Mycale in Ionia. For the
Greeks who had come in their ships with Leutychides
the Lacedaemonian being then in quarters at Delos,
there came to them certain messengers from Samos,
to wit, Lampon son of Thrasycles, Athenagoras son of
Archestratides, and Hegesistratus son of Aristagoras;
these the Samians had sent, keeping their despatch
secret from the Persians and the despot Theomestor
son of Androdamas, whom the Persians had made
despot of Samos. When they came before the
generals, Hegesistratus spoke long and vehemently:
"If the Ionians but see you," said he, "they will
revolt from the Persians; and the foreigners will
not stand; but if perchance they do stand, you
will have such a prey as never again"; and he
prayed them in the name of the gods of their
common worship to deliver Greeks from slavery and
drive the foreigner away. That, said he, would be
an easy matter for them; "for the Persian ships are
unseaworthy and no match for yours; and if you

μὴ δόλῳ αὐτοὺς προάγοιεν, ἕτοιμοι εἶναι ἐν τῇσι
νηυσὶ τῇσι ἐκείνων ἀγόμενοι ὅμηροι εἶναι.

91. Ὡς δὲ πολλὸς ἦν λισσόμενος ὁ ξεῖνος ὁ
Σάμιος, εἴρετο Λευτυχίδης, εἴτε κληδόνος εἵνεκεν
θέλων πυθέσθαι εἴτε καὶ κατὰ συντυχίην θεοῦ
ποιεῦντος, "Ὦ ξεῖνε Σάμιε, τί τοι τὸ οὔνομα;"
ὁ δὲ εἶπε "Ἡγησίστρατος." ὁ δὲ ὑπαρπάσας τὸν
ἐπίλοιπον λόγον, εἴ τινα ὅρμητο λέγειν ὁ Ἡγησίστρατος, εἶπε "Δέκομαι τὸν οἰωνὸν τὸν Ἡγησιστράτου, ὦ ξεῖνε Σάμιε. σὺ δὲ ἡμῖν ποίεε ὅκως
αὐτός τε δοὺς πίστιν ἀποπλεύσεαι καὶ οἱ σὺν σοὶ
ἐόντες οἵδε, ἦ μὲν Σαμίους ἡμῖν προθύμους ἔσεσθαι
συμμάχους."

92. Ταῦτά τε ἅμα ἠγόρευε καὶ τὸ ἔργον
προσῆγε· αὐτίκα γὰρ οἱ Σάμιοι πίστιν τε καὶ
ὅρκια ἐποιεῦντο συμμαχίης πέρι πρὸς τοὺς Ἕλληνας. ταῦτα δὲ ποιήσαντες οἱ μὲν ἀπέπλεον·
μετὰ σφέων γὰρ ἐκέλευε πλέειν τὸν Ἡγησίστρατον, οἰωνὸν τὸ οὔνομα ποιεύμενος.

93. Οἱ δὲ Ἕλληνες ἐπισχόντες ταύτην τὴν
ἡμέρην τῇ ὑστεραίῃ ἐκαλλιερέοντο, μαντευομένου
σφι Δηιφόνου τοῦ Εὐηνίου ἀνδρὸς Ἀπολλωνιήτεω,
Ἀπολλωνίης δὲ τῆς ἐν τῷ Ἰονίῳ κόλπῳ. τούτου
τὸν πατέρα Εὐήνιον κατέλαβε πρῆγμα τοιόνδε.
ἔστι ἐν τῇ Ἀπολλωνίῃ ταύτῃ ἱρὰ ἡλίου πρόβατα,
τὰ τὰς μὲν ἡμέρας βόσκεται παρὰ Χῶνα ποταμόν,
ὃς ἐκ Λάκμονος ὄρεος ῥέει διὰ τῆς Ἀπολλωνίης
χώρης ἐς θάλασσαν παρ' Ὤρικον λιμένα, τὰς
δὲ νύκτας ἀραιρημένοι ἄνδρες οἱ πλούτῳ τε καὶ
γένεϊ δοκιμώτατοι τῶν ἀστῶν, οὗτοι φυλάσσουσι
ἐνιαυτὸν ἕκαστος· περὶ πολλοῦ γὰρ δὴ ποιεῦνται

have any suspicion that we may be tempting you guilefully, we are ready to be carried in your ships as hostages."

91. This Samian stranger being so earnest in entreaty, Leutychides asked him (whether it was that he desired to know for the sake of a presage, or that heaven happily prompted him thereto), "Sir Samian, what is your name?" "Hegesistratus,"[1] said he. Then Leutychides cut short whatever else Hegesistratus had begun to say, and cried: "I accept the omen of your name, Sir Samian; now do you see to it that ere you sail hence you and these that are with you pledge yourselves that the Samians will be our zealous allies."

92. Thus he spoke, and then and there added the deed thereto; for straightway the Samians bound themselves by pledge and oath to alliance with the Greeks. This done, the rest sailed away, but Leutychides bade Hegesistratus take ship with the Greeks, for the good omen of his name.

93. The Greeks waited through that day, and on the next they sought and won favourable augury; their diviner was Deïphonus son of Evenius, a man of that Apollonia which is in the Ionian gulf. This man's father Evenius had once fared as I will now relate. There is at the aforesaid Apollonia a certain flock sacred to the Sun, which in the daytime is pastured beside the river Chon, which flows from the mountain called Lacmon through the lands of Apollonia and issues into the sea by the haven of Oricum; by night, those townsmen who are most notable for wealth or lineage are chosen to watch it, each man serving for a year; for the people of

[1] Hegesistratus = Army-leader.

'Απολλωνιῆται τὰ πρόβατα ταῦτα ἐκ θεοπροπίου
τινός· ἐν δὲ ἄντρῳ αὐλίζονται ἀπὸ τῆς πόλιος ἑκάς.
ἔνθα δὴ τότε ὁ Εὐήνιος οὗτος ἀραιρημένος ἐφύλασσε. καὶ κοτὲ αὐτοῦ κατακοιμήσαντος φυλακὴν
παρελθόντες λύκοι ἐς τὸ ἄντρον διέφθειραν τῶν
προβάτων ὡς ἑξήκοντα. ὁ δὲ ὡς ἐπήισε, εἶχε
σιγῇ καὶ ἔφραζε οὐδενί, ἐν νόῳ ἔχων ἀντικατα-
στήσειν ἄλλα πριάμενος. καὶ οὐ γὰρ ἔλαθε τοὺς
'Απολλωνιήτας ταῦτα γενόμενα, ἀλλ᾽ ὡς ἐπύθοντο, ὑπαγαγόντες μιν ὑπὸ δικαστήριον κατέ-
κριναν, ὡς τὴν φυλακὴν κατακοιμήσαντα, τῆς
ὄψιος στερηθῆναι. ἐπείτε δὲ τὸν Εὐήνιον ἐξετύ-
φλωσαν, αὐτίκα μετὰ ταῦτα οὔτε πρόβατά σφι
ἔτικτε οὔτε γῆ ἔφερε ὁμοίως καρπόν. πρόφαντα
δέ σφι ἔν τε Δωδώνῃ καὶ ἐν Δελφοῖσι ἐγίνετο,
ἐπείτε ἐπειρώτων τοὺς προφήτας τὸ αἴτιον τοῦ
παρεόντος κακοῦ, οἱ δὲ αὐτοῖσι ἔφραζον ὅτι
ἀδίκως τὸν φύλακον τῶν ἱρῶν προβάτων Εὐήνιον
τῆς ὄψιος ἐστέρησαν· αὐτοὶ γὰρ ἐπορμῆσαι τοὺς
λύκους, οὐ πρότερόν τε παύσεσθαι τιμωρέοντες
ἐκείνῳ πρὶν ἢ δίκας δῶσι τῶν ἐποίησαν ταύτας
τὰς ἂν αὐτὸς ἕληται καὶ δικαιοῖ· τούτων δὲ
τελεομένων αὐτοὶ δώσειν Εὐηνίῳ δόσιν τοιαύτην
τὴν πολλούς μιν μακαριεῖν ἀνθρώπων ἔχοντα.

94. Τὰ μὲν χρηστήρια ταῦτά σφι ἐχρήσθη, οἱ
δὲ 'Απολλωνιῆται ἀπόρρητα ποιησάμενοι προ-
έθεσαν τῶν ἀστῶν ἀνδράσι διαπρῆξαι. οἱ δέ
σφι διέπρηξαν ὧδε· κατημένου Εὐηνίου ἐν θώκῳ
ἐλθόντες οἱ παρίζοντο καὶ λόγους ἄλλους ἐποιεῦντο, ἐς ὃ κατέβαινον συλλυπεύμενοι τῷ πάθεϊ·
ταύτῃ δὲ ὑπάγοντες εἰρώτων τίνα δίκην ἂν ἕλοιτο,

Apollonia set great store by this flock, being so taught by a certain oracle. It is folded in a cave far distant from the town. Now at the time whereof I speak, Evenius was the chosen watchman. But one night he fell asleep, and wolves came past his guard into the cave, killing about sixty of the flock. When Evenius was aware of it, he held his peace and told no man, being minded to restore what was lost by buying others. But this matter was not hid from the people of Apollonia; and when it came to their knowledge they haled him to judgment and condemned him to lose his eyesight for sleeping at his watch. So they blinded Evenius; but from the day of their so doing their flocks bore no offspring, nor did their land yield her fruits as aforetime; and a declaration was given to them at Dodona and Delphi, when they inquired of the prophets what might be the cause of their present ill: the gods told them by their prophets that they had done unjustly in blinding Evenius, the guardian of the sacred flock, "for we ourselves" (said they) "sent those wolves, and we will not cease from avenging him ere you make him such restitution for what you did as he himself chooses and approves; when that is fully done, we will ourselves give Evenius such a gift as will make many men to deem him happy."

94. This was the oracle given to the people of Apollonia. They kept it secret, and charged certain of their townsmen to carry the business through; who did so as I will now show. Coming and sitting down by Evenius at the place where he sat, they spoke of other matters, till at last they fell to commiserating his misfortune; and thus guiding the discourse they asked him what requital he would

εἰ ἐθέλοιεν Ἀπολλωνιῆται δίκας ὑποστῆναι
δώσειν τῶν ἐποίησαν. ὁ δὲ οὐκ ἀκηκοὼς τὸ
θεοπρόπιον εἵλετο εἴπας εἴ τις οἱ δοίη ἀγρούς,
τῶν ἀστῶν ὀνομάσας τοῖσι ἠπίστατο εἶναι καλ-
λίστους δύο κλήρους τῶν ἐν τῇ Ἀπολλωνίῃ, καὶ
οἴκησιν πρὸς τούτοισι τὴν ᾔδεε καλλίστην ἐοῦσαν
τῶν ἐν πόλι· τούτων δὲ ἔφη ἐπήβολος γενόμενος
τοῦ λοιποῦ ἀμήνιτος εἶναι, καὶ δίκην οἱ ταύτην
ἀποχρᾶν γενομένην. καὶ ὁ μὲν ταῦτα ἔλεγε, οἱ
δὲ πάρεδροι εἶπαν ὑπολαβόντες "Εὐήνιε, ταύτην
δίκην Ἀπολλωνιῆται τῆς ἐκτυφλώσιος ἐκτίνουσί
τοι κατὰ θεοπρόπια τὰ γενόμενα." ὁ μὲν δὴ
πρὸς ταῦτα δεινὰ ἐποίεε, τὸ ἐνθεῦτεν πυθόμενος
τὸν πάντα λόγον, ὡς ἐξαπατηθείς· οἱ δὲ πριάμενοι
παρὰ τῶν ἐκτημένων διδοῦσί οἱ τὰ εἵλετο. καὶ
μετὰ ταῦτα αὐτίκα ἔμφυτον μαντικὴν εἶχε, ὥστε
καὶ ὀνομαστὸς γενέσθαι.

95. Τούτου δὴ ὁ Δηίφονος ἐὼν παῖς τοῦ Εὐηνίου
ἀγόντων Κορινθίων ἐμαντεύετο τῇ στρατιῇ. ἤδη
δὲ καὶ τόδε ἤκουσα, ὡς ὁ Δηίφονος ἐπιβατεύων
τοῦ Εὐηνίου οὐνόματος ἐξελάμβανε ἐπὶ τὴν Ἑλλάδα ἔργα, οὐκ ἐὼν Εὐηνίου παῖς.

96. Τοῖσι δὲ Ἕλλησι ὡς ἐκαλλιέρησε, ἀνῆγον
τὰς νέας ἐκ τῆς Δήλου πρὸς τὴν Σάμον. ἐπεὶ
δὲ ἐγένοντο τῆς Σαμίης πρὸς Καλαμίσοισι, οἱ
μὲν αὐτοῦ ὁρμισάμενοι κατὰ τὸ Ἥραιον τὸ ταύτῃ
παρεσκευάζοντο ἐς ναυμαχίην, οἱ δὲ Πέρσαι
πυθόμενοι σφέας προσπλέειν ἀνῆγον καὶ αὐτοὶ
πρὸς τὴν ἤπειρον τὰς νέας τὰς ἄλλας, τὰς δὲ
Φοινίκων ἀπῆκαν ἀποπλέειν. βουλευομένοισι γάρ
σφι ἐδόκεε ναυμαχίην μὴ ποιέεσθαι· οὐ γὰρ ὦν

choose, if the people of Apollonia should promise to requite him for what they had done. He, knowing nought of the oracle, said he would choose for a gift the lands of certain named townsmen whom he deemed to have the two fairest estates in Apollonia, and a house besides which he knew to be the fairest in the town; let him (he said) have possession of these, and he would forgo his wrath, and be satisfied with that by way of restitution. They that sat by him waited for no further word than that, and said: "Evenius, the people of Apollonia hereby make you that restitution for the loss of your sight, obeying the oracle given to them." At that he was very angry, for he learnt thereby the whole story and saw that they had cheated him; but they bought from the possessors and gave him what he had chosen; and from that day he had a natural gift of divination, so that he won fame thereby.

95. Deïphonus, the son of this Evenius, had been brought by the Corinthians, and practised divination for the army. But I have heard it said ere now, that Deïphonus was no son of Evenius, but made a wrongful use of that name, and wrought for wages up and down Hellas.

96. Having won favourable omens, the Greeks stood out to sea from Delos for Samos. When they were now near Calamisa in the Samian territory, they anchored there hard by the temple of Here that is in those parts, and prepared for a sea-fight; the Persians, learning of their approach, stood likewise out to sea and made for the mainland, with all their ships save the Phoenicians, whom they sent sailing away. It was determined by them in council that they would not do battle by sea; for they

ἐδόκεον ὅμοιοι εἶναι. ἐς δὲ τὴν ἤπειρον ἀπέπλεον,
ὅκως ἔωσι ὑπὸ τὸν πεζὸν στρατὸν τὸν σφέτερον
ἐόντα ἐν τῇ Μυκάλῃ, ὃς κελεύσαντος Ξέρξεω
καταλελειμμένος τοῦ ἄλλου στρατοῦ Ἰωνίην ἐφύ-
λασσε· τοῦ πλῆθος μὲν ἦν ἓξ μυριάδες, ἐστρατήγεε
δὲ αὐτοῦ Τιγράνης κάλλεϊ καὶ μεγάθεϊ ὑπερ-
φέρων Περσέων. ὑπὸ τοῦτον μὲν δὴ τὸν στρατὸν
ἐβουλεύσαντο καταφυγόντες οἱ τοῦ ναυτικοῦ
στρατηγοὶ ἀνειρύσαι τὰς νέας καὶ περιβαλέσθαι
ἕρκος ἔρυμά τε τῶν νεῶν καὶ σφέων αὐτῶν
κρησφύγετον.

97. Ταῦτα βουλευσάμενοι ἀνήγοντο. ἀπικόμενοι δὲ παρὰ τὸ τῶν Ποτνιέων ἱρὸν τῆς Μυκάλης
ἐς Γαίσωνά τε καὶ Σκολοπόεντα, τῇ Δήμητρος
Ἐλευσινίης ἱρόν, τὸ Φίλιστος ὁ Πασικλέος ἱδρύ-
σατο Νείλεῳ τῷ Κόδρου ἐπισπόμενος ἐπὶ Μιλήτου
κτιστύν, ἐνθαῦτα τάς τε νέας ἀνείρυσαν καὶ περι-
εβάλοντο ἕρκος καὶ λίθων καὶ ξύλων, δένδρεα
ἐκκόψαντες ἥμερα, καὶ σκόλοπας περὶ τὸ ἕρκος
κατέπηξαν, καὶ παρεσκευάδατο ὡς πολιορκη-
σόμενοι καὶ ὡς νικήσοντες, ἐπ᾿ ἀμφότερα ἐπιλε-
γόμενοι γὰρ παρεσκευάζοντο.

98. Οἱ δὲ Ἕλληνες ὡς ἐπύθοντο οἰχωκότας
τοὺς βαρβάρους ἐς τὴν ἤπειρον, ἤχθοντο ὡς
ἐκπεφευγότων ἀπορίῃ τε εἴχοντο ὅ τι ποιέωσι,
εἴτε ἀπαλλάσσωνται ὀπίσω εἴτε καταπλέωσι
ἐπ᾿ Ἑλλησπόντου. τέλος δὲ ἔδοξε τούτων μὲν
μηδέτερα ποιέειν, ἐπιπλέειν δὲ ἐπὶ τὴν ἤπειρον.
παρασκευασάμενοι ὦν ἐς ναυμαχίην καὶ ἀπο-
βάθρας καὶ ἄλλα ὅσων ἔδεε, ἔπλεον ἐπὶ τῆς

deemed themselves overmatched; and the reason of their making for the mainland was, that they might lie under the shelter of their army at Mycale, which had been left by Xerxes' command behind the rest of his host to hold Ionia; there were sixty thousand men in it, and Tigranes, the goodliest and tallest man in Persia, was their general. It was the design of the Persian admirals to flee to the shelter of that army, and there to beach their ships and build a fence round them which should be a protection for the ships and a refuge for themselves.

97. With this design they put to sea. So when they came past the temple of the Goddesses [1] at Mycale to the Gaeson and Scolopoïs, [2] where is a temple of Eleusinian Demeter (which was built by Philistus son of Pasicles, when he went with Nileus son of Codrus to the founding of Miletus), there they beached their ships and fenced them round with stones and trunks of orchard trees that they cut down; and they drove in stakes round the fence, and prepared for siege or victory, making ready of deliberate purpose for either event.

98. When the Greeks learnt that the foreigners were off and away to the mainland, they were ill-pleased to think that their enemy had escaped them, and doubted whether to return back or make sail for the Hellespont. At the last they resolved that they would do neither, but sail to the mainland; and equipping themselves therefore with gangways and all else needful for a sea-fight, they

---

[1] Demeter and Persephone.

[2] The Gaeson was probably a stream running south of the hill called Mycale; Scolopoïs, a place on its east bank (How and Wells).

HERODOTUS

Μυκάλης. ἐπεὶ δὲ ἀγχοῦ τε ἐγίνοντο τοῦ στρατοπέδου καὶ οὐδεὶς ἐφαίνετό σφι ἐπαναγόμενος,
ἀλλ' ὥρων νέας ἀνελκυσμένας ἔσω τοῦ τείχεος,
πολλὸν δὲ πεζὸν παρακεκριμένον παρὰ τὸν αἰγιαλόν, ἐνθαῦτα πρῶτον μὲν ἐν τῇ νηὶ παραπλέων,
ἐγχρίμψας τῷ αἰγιαλῷ τὰ μάλιστα, Λευτυχίδης
ὑπὸ κήρυκος προηγόρευε τοῖσι Ἴωσι λέγων
'"Ἄνδρες Ἴωνες, οἳ ὑμέων τυγχάνουσι ἐπακούοντες,
μάθετε τὰ λέγω· πάντως γὰρ οὐδὲν συνήσουσι
Πέρσαι τῶν ἐγὼ ὑμῖν ἐντέλλομαι. ἐπεὰν συμμίσγωμεν, μεμνῆσθαι τινὰ χρὴ ἐλευθερίης μὲν
πάντων πρῶτον, μετὰ δὲ τοῦ συνθήματος Ἥβης.
καὶ τάδε ἴστω καὶ ὁ μὴ ἀκούσας ὑμέων πρὸς τοῦ
ἀκούσαντος." ὡυτὸς δὲ οὗτος ἐὼν τυγχάνει
νόος τοῦ πρήγματος καὶ ὁ Θεμιστοκλέος ὁ ἐπ'
Ἀρτεμισίῳ· ἢ γὰρ δὴ λαθόντα τὰ ῥήματα τοὺς
βαρβάρους ἔμελλε τοὺς Ἴωνας πείσειν, ἢ ἔπειτα
ἀνενειχθέντα ἐς τοὺς βαρβάρους ποιήσειν ἀπίστους τοῖσι Ἕλλησι.

99. Λευτυχίδεω δὲ ταῦτα ὑποθεμένου δεύτερα
δὴ τάδε ἐποίευν οἱ Ἕλληνες· προσσχόντες τὰς
νέας ἀπέβησαν ἐς τὸν αἰγιαλόν. καὶ οὗτοι μὲν
ἐτάσσοντο, οἱ δὲ Πέρσαι ὡς εἶδον τοὺς Ἕλληνας
παρασκευαζομένους ἐς μάχην καὶ τοῖσι Ἴωσι πα-
ραινέσαντας, τοῦτο μὲν ὑπονοήσαντες τοὺς Σαμίους
τὰ Ἑλλήνων φρονέειν ἀπαιρέονται τὰ ὅπλα. οἱ
γὰρ ὦν Σάμιοι ἀπικομένων Ἀθηναίων αἰχμαλώ-
των ἐν τῇσι νηυσὶ τῶν βαρβάρων, τοὺς ἔλαβον
ἀνὰ τὴν Ἀττικὴν λελειμμένους οἱ Ξέρξεω, τούτους λυσάμενοι πάντας ἀποπέμπουσι ἐποδιά-
σαντες ἐς Ἀθήνας· τῶν εἵνεκεν οὐκ ἥκιστα ὑπο-
ψίην εἶχον, πεντακοσίας κεφαλὰς τῶν Ξέρξεω

held their course for Mycale. When they came
near to the camp and found none putting out to
meet them, and saw the ships beached within the
wall and a great host of men drawn up in array
along the strand, Leutychides thereupon first coasted
along in his ship, keeping as near to the shore as he
could, and made this proclamation to the Ionians by
the voice of a herald : " Men of Ionia, you that hear
us, take heed of what I say ! for in no case will the
Persians understand aught of my charge to you :
when we join battle, let a man remember first his
freedom, and next the battle-cry ' Hebe ' : and let him
that hears me not be told of this by him that hears."
The purpose of this act was the same as Themistocles' purpose at Artemisium[1]; either the message
would be unknown to the foreigners and would
prevail with the Ionians, or if it were thereafter
reported to the foreigners it would make them to
mistrust their Greek allies.

99. After this counsel of Leutychides', the Greeks
next brought their ships to land and disembarked
on the beach, where they put themselves in array.
But the Persians, seeing the Greeks prepare for
battle and exhort the Ionians, first of all took away
the Samians' armour, suspecting that they favoured
the Greeks; for indeed when the foreigners' ships
brought certain Athenian captives, who had been
left in Attica and taken by Xerxes' army, the
Samians had set them all free and sent them away
to Athens with provision for the way; for which
cause in especial they were held suspect, as having
set free five hundred souls of Xerxes' enemies.

[1] Cp. viii. 22.

πολεμίων λυσάμενοι. τοῦτο δὲ τὰς διόδους τὰς ἐς
τὰς κορυφὰς τῆς Μυκάλης φερούσας προστάσσουσι
τοῖσι Μιλησίοισι φυλάσσειν ὡς ἐπισταμένοισι
δῆθεν μάλιστα τὴν χώρην. ἐποίευν δὲ τοῦτο
τοῦδε εἵνεκεν, ἵνα ἐκτὸς τοῦ στρατοπέδου ἔωσι.
τούτους μὲν Ἰώνων, τοῖσι καὶ κατεδόκεον νεοχμὸν
ἄν τι ποιέειν δυνάμιος ἐπιλαβομένοισι, τρόποισι
τοιούτοισι προεφυλάσσοντο οἱ Πέρσαι, αὐτοὶ δὲ
συνεφόρησαν τὰ γέρρα ἔρκος εἶναι σφίσι.

100. Ὡς δὲ ἄρα παρεσκευάδατο τοῖσι Ἕλλησι,
προσήισαν πρὸς τοὺς βαρβάρους· ἰοῦσι δέ σφι
φήμη τε ἐσέπτατο ἐς τὸ στρατόπεδον πᾶν καὶ
κηρυκήιον ἐφάνη ἐπὶ τῆς κυματώγης κείμενον· ἡ
δὲ φήμη διῆλθέ σφι ὧδε, ὡς οἱ Ἕλληνες τὴν
Μαρδονίου στρατιὴν νικῷεν ἐν Βοιωτοῖσι μαχόμενοι. δῆλα δὴ πολλοῖσι τεκμηρίοισι ἐστὶ τὰ
θεῖα τῶν πρηγμάτων, εἰ καὶ τότε, τῆς αὐτῆς
ἡμέρης συμπιπτούσης τοῦ τε ἐν Πλαταιῆσι καὶ
τοῦ ἐν Μυκάλῃ μέλλοντος ἔσεσθαι τρώματος,
φήμη τοῖσι Ἕλλησι τοῖσι ταύτῃ ἐσαπίκετο, ὥστε
θαρσῆσαί τε τὴν στρατιὴν πολλῷ μᾶλλον καὶ
ἐθέλειν προθυμότερον κινδυνεύειν.

101. Καὶ τόδε ἕτερον συνέπεσε γενόμενον,
Δήμητρος τεμένεα Ἐλευσινίης παρὰ ἀμφοτέρας
τὰς συμβολὰς εἶναι· καὶ γὰρ δὴ ἐν τῇ Πλαταιίδι
παρ' αὐτὸ τὸ Δημήτριον ἐγίνετο, ὡς καὶ πρότερόν
μοι εἴρηται, ἡ μάχη, καὶ ἐν Μυκάλῃ ἔμελλε
ὡσαύτως ἔσεσθαι. γεγονέναι δὲ νίκην τῶν μετὰ
Παυσανίεω Ἑλλήνων ὀρθῶς σφι ἡ φήμη συνέβαινε ἐλθοῦσα· τὸ μὲν γὰρ ἐν Πλαταιῆσι πρωὶ
ἔτι τῆς ἡμέρης ἐγίνετο, τὸ δὲ ἐν Μυκάλῃ περὶ
δείλην· ὅτι δὲ τῆς αὐτῆς ἡμέρης συνέβαινε

Furthermore, they appointed the Milesians to guard the passes leading to the heights of Mycale, alleging that they were best acquainted with the country; but their true reason for so doing was, that the Milesians should be away from the rest of their army. In such manner did the Persians safeguard themselves from those Ionians who (they supposed) might turn against them if opportunity were given; for themselves, they set their shields close to make a barricade.

100. The Greeks, having made all preparation, advanced their line against the foreigners. As they went, a rumour sped all about the army, and a herald's wand was seen lying by the water-line; and the rumour that ran was to the effect that the Greeks were victors over Mardonius' army at a battle in Boeotia. Now there are many clear proofs of the divine ordering of things; seeing that at this time, the Persians' disaster at Plataeae falling on the same day as that other which was to befall them at Mycale, the rumour came to the Greeks at that place, whereby their army was greatly heartened and the readier to face danger.

101. Moreover there was this other coincidence, that there were precincts of Eleusinian Demeter on both battlefields; for at Plataeae the fight was hard by the temple of Demeter, as I have already said, and so it was to be at Mycale likewise. It so fell out that the rumour of victory won by the Greeks with Pausanias spoke truth; for the defeat oi Plataeae happened while it was yet early in the day, and the defeat of Mycale in the afternoon. That the two fell on the same day of the same

γίνεσθαι μηνός τε τοῦ αὐτοῦ, χρόνῳ οὐ πολλῷ
σφι ὕστερον δῆλα ἀναμανθάνουσι ἐγίνετο. ἦν δὲ
ἀρρωδίη σφι, πρὶν τὴν φήμην ἐσαπικέσθαι, οὔτι
περὶ σφέων αὐτῶν οὕτω ὡς τῶν Ἑλλήνων, μὴ
περὶ Μαρδονίῳ πταίσῃ ἡ Ἑλλάς. ὡς μέντοι ἡ
κληδὼν αὕτη σφι ἐσέπτατο, μᾶλλόν τι καὶ ταχύ-
τερον τὴν πρόσοδον ἐποιεῦντο. οἱ μὲν δὴ Ἕλληνες
καὶ οἱ βάρβαροι ἔσπευδον ἐς τὴν μάχην, ὡς σφι
καί αἱ νῆσοι καὶ ὁ Ἑλλήσποντος ἄεθλα προέκειτο.

102. Τοῖσι μέν νυν Ἀθηναίοισι καὶ τοῖσι προσ-
εχέσι τούτοισι τεταγμένοισι, μέχρι κου τῶν
ἡμισέων, ἡ ὁδὸς ἐγίνετο κατ' αἰγιαλόν τε καὶ
ἄπεδον χῶρον, τοῖσι δὲ Λακεδαιμονίοισι καὶ τοῖσι
ἐπεξῆς τούτοισι τεταγμένοισι κατά τε χαράδραν
καὶ ὄρεα. ἐν ᾧ δὲ οἱ Λακεδαιμόνιοι περιήισαν,
οὗτοι οἱ ἐπὶ τῷ ἑτέρῳ κέρεϊ ἔτι καὶ δὴ ἐμάχοντο.
ἕως μέν νυν τοῖσι Πέρσῃσι ὀρθὰ ἦν τὰ γέρρα, ἠμύ-
νοντό τε καὶ οὐδὲν ἔλασσον εἶχον τῇ μάχῃ· ἐπεὶ δὲ
τῶν Ἀθηναίων καὶ τῶν προσεχέων ὁ στρατός, ὅκως
ἑωυτῶν γένηται τὸ ἔργον καὶ μὴ Λακεδαιμονίων,
παρακελευσάμενοι ἔργου εἴχοντο προθυμότεροι,
ἐνθεῦτεν ἤδη ἑτεροιοῦτο τὸ πρῆγμα. διωσάμενοι
γὰρ τὰ γέρρα οὗτοι φερόμενοι ἐσέπεσον ἁλέες ἐς
τοὺς Πέρσας, οἳ δὲ δεξάμενοι καὶ χρόνον συχνὸν
ἀμυνόμενοι τέλος ἔφευγον ἐς τὸ τεῖχος. Ἀθηναῖοι
δὲ καὶ Κορίνθιοι καὶ Σικυώνιοι καὶ Τροιζήνιοι
(οὕτω γὰρ ἦσαν ἐπεξῆς τεταγμένοι) συνεπισπό-
μενοι συνέσπιπτον ἐς τὸ τεῖχος. ὡς δὲ καὶ τὸ
τεῖχος ἀραίρητο, οὔτ' ἔτι πρὸς ἀλκὴν ἐτράποντο
οἱ βάρβαροι πρὸς φυγήν τε ὁρμέατο οἱ ἄλλοι πλὴν
Περσέων· οὗτοι δὲ κατ' ὀλίγους γινόμενοι ἐμά-

month was proved to the Greeks when they examined the matter not long afterwards. Now before this rumour came they had been faint-hearted, fearing less for themselves than for the Greeks with Pausanias, lest Mardonius should be the stumbling-block of Hellas; but when the report sped among them they grew stronger and swifter in their onset. So Greeks and foreigners alike were eager for battle, seeing that the islands and the Hellespont were the prizes of victory.

102. As for the Athenians and those whose place was nearest them, that is, for about half of the line, their way lay over the beach and level ground; for the Lacedaemonians and those that were next to them, through a ravine and among hills; and while the Lacedaemonians were making a circuit, those others on the other wing were already fighting. While the Persians' shields stood upright, they defended themselves and held their own in the battle; but when the Athenians and their neighbours in the line passed the word and went more zealously to work, that they and not the Lacedaemonians might win the victory, immediately the face of the fight was changed. Breaking down the shields they charged all together into the midst of the Persians, who received the onset and stood their ground for a long time, but at the last fled within their wall; and the Athenians and Corinthians and Sicyonians and Troezenians, who were next to each other in the line, followed hard after and rushed in together likewise. But when the walled place was won, the foreigners made no further defence, but took to flight, all save the Persians, who gathered themselves into bands of a few men and fought

χοντο τοῖσι αἰεὶ ἐς τὸ τεῖχος ἐσπίπτουσι Ἑλλήνων.
καὶ τῶν στρατηγῶν τῶν Περσικῶν δύο μὲν ἀπο-
φεύγουσι, δύο δὲ τελευτῶσι· Ἀρταΰντης μὲν καὶ
Ἰθαμίτρης τοῦ ναυτικοῦ στρατηγέοντες ἀπο-
φεύγουσι, Μαρδόντης δὲ καὶ ὁ τοῦ πεζοῦ στρατηγὸς Τιγράνης μαχόμενοι τελευτῶσι.

103. Ἔτι δὲ μαχομένων τῶν Περσέων ἀπίκοντο
Λακεδαιμόνιοι καὶ οἱ μετ᾽ αὐτῶν, καὶ τὰ λοιπὰ
συνδιεχείριζον. ἔπεσον δὲ καὶ αὐτῶν τῶν Ἑλλήνων συχνοὶ ἐνθαῦτα ἄλλοι τε καὶ Σικυώνιοι
καὶ στρατηγὸς Περίλεως· τῶν τε Σαμίων οἱ
στρατευόμενοι ἐόντες τε ἐν τῷ στρατοπέδῳ τῷ
Μηδικῷ καὶ ἀπαραιρημένοι τὰ ὅπλα, ὡς εἶδον
αὐτίκα κατ᾽ ἀρχὰς γινομένην ἑτεραλκέα τὴν μάχην, ἔρδον ὅσον ἐδυνέατο προσωφελέειν ἐθέλοντες
τοῖσι Ἕλλησι. Σαμίους δὲ ἰδόντες οἱ ἄλλοι
Ἴωνες ἄρξαντας οὕτω δὴ καὶ αὐτοὶ ἀποστάντες
ἀπὸ Περσέων ἐπέθεντο τοῖσι βαρβάροισι.

104. Μιλησίοισι δὲ προσετέτακτο μὲν ἐκ τῶν
Περσέων τὰς διόδους τηρέειν σωτηρίης εἵνεκά σφι,
ὡς ἢν ἄρα σφέας καταλαμβάνῃ οἷά περ κατέλαβε,
ἔχοντες ἡγεμόνας σώζωνται ἐς τὰς κορυφὰς τῆς
Μυκάλης. ἐτάχθησαν μέν νυν ἐπὶ τοῦτο τὸ
πρῆγμα οἱ Μιλήσιοι τούτου τε εἵνεκεν καὶ ἵνα μὴ
παρεόντες ἐν τῷ στρατοπέδῳ τι νεοχμὸν ποιέοιεν·
οἱ δὲ πᾶν τοὐναντίον τοῦ προστεταγμένου ἐποίεον,
ἄλλας τε κατηγεόμενοί σφι ὁδοὺς φεύγουσι, αἳ
δὴ ἔφερον ἐς τοὺς πολεμίους, καὶ τέλος αὐτοί σφι
ἐγίνοντο κτείνοντες πολεμιώτατοι. οὕτω δὴ τὸ
δεύτερον Ἰωνίη ἀπὸ Περσέων ἀπέστη.

with whatever Greeks came rushing within the walls. Of the Persian leaders two escaped by flight and two were slain; Artaÿntes and Ithamitres, who were admirals of the fleet, escaped; Mardontes and Tigranes, the general of the land army, were slain fighting.

103. While the Persians still fought, the Lacedaemonians and their comrades came up, and finished what was left of the business. The Greeks too lost many men there, notably the men of Sicyon and their general Perilaus. As for the Samians who served in the Median army, and had been disarmed, they, seeing from the first that victory hung in the balance,[1] did what they could in their desire to aid the Greeks; and when the other Ionians saw the Samians set the example, they also thereupon deserted the Persians and attacked the foreigners.

104. The Persians had for their own safety appointed the Milesians to watch the passes, so that if haply aught should befall the Persian army such as did befall it, they might have guides to bring them safe to the heights of Mycale. This was the task to which the Milesians were appointed, for the aforesaid reason, and that they might not be present with the army and so turn against it. But they did wholly contrariwise to the charge laid upon them; they misguided the fleeing Persians by ways that led them among their enemies, and at last themselves became their worst enemies and slew them. Thus did Ionia for the second time revolt from the Persians.

[1] ἑτεραλκής here probably means "doubtful," giving victory to one side or other; cp. vii. 11; in Homer it means "decisive," giving victory to one as opposed to the other.

105. Ἐν δὲ ταύτῃ τῇ μάχῃ Ἑλλήνων ἠρίστευσαν Ἀθηναῖοι καὶ Ἀθηναίων Ἑρμόλυκος ὁ Εὐθοίνου, ἀνὴρ παγκράτιον ἐπασκήσας. τοῦτον δὲ τὸν Ἑρμόλυκον κατέλαβε ὕστερον τούτων, πολέμου ἐόντος Ἀθηναίοισί τε καὶ Καρυστίοισι, ἐν Κύρνῳ τῆς Καρυστίης χώρης ἀποθανόντα ἐν μάχῃ κεῖσθαι ἐπὶ Γεραιστῷ. μετὰ δὲ Ἀθηναίους Κορίνθιοι καὶ Τροιζήνιοι καὶ Σικυώνιοι ἠρίστευσαν.

106. Ἐπείτε δὲ κατεργάσαντο οἱ Ἕλληνες τοὺς πολλοὺς τοὺς μὲν μαχομένους τοὺς δὲ καὶ φεύγοντας τῶν βαρβάρων, τὰς νέας ἐνέπρησαν καὶ τὸ τεῖχος ἅπαν, τὴν ληίην προεξαγαγόντες ἐς τὸν αἰγιαλόν, καὶ θησαυρούς τινας χρημάτων εὗρον· ἐμπρήσαντες δὲ τὸ τεῖχος καὶ τὰς νέας ἀπέπλεον. ἀπικόμενοι δὲ ἐς Σάμον οἱ Ἕλληνες ἐβουλεύοντο περὶ ἀναστάσιος τῆς Ἰωνίης, καὶ ὅκῃ χρεὸν εἴη τῆς Ἑλλάδος κατοικίσαι τῆς αὐτοὶ ἐγκρατέες ἦσαν, τὴν δὲ Ἰωνίην ἀπεῖναι τοῖσι βαρβάροισι· ἀδύνατον γὰρ ἐφαίνετό σφι εἶναι ἑωυτούς τε Ἰώνων προκατῆσθαι φρουρέοντας τὸν πάντα χρόνον, καὶ ἑωυτῶν μὴ προκατημένων Ἴωνας οὐδεμίαν ἐλπίδα εἶχον χαίροντας πρὸς τῶν Περσέων ἀπαλλάξειν. πρὸς ταῦτα Πελοποννησίων μὲν τοῖσι ἐν τέλεϊ ἐοῦσι ἐδόκεε τῶν μηδισάντων ἐθνέων τῶν Ἑλληνικῶν τὰ ἐμπολαῖα ἐξαναστήσαντας δοῦναι τὴν χώρην Ἴωσι ἐνοικῆσαι, Ἀθηναίοισι δὲ οὐκ ἐδόκεε ἀρχὴν Ἰωνίην γενέσθαι ἀνάστατον οὐδὲ Πελοποννησίοισι περὶ τῶν σφετερέων ἀποικιέων βουλεύειν· ἀντιτεινόντων δὲ τούτων προθύμως, εἶξαν οἱ Πελοποννήσιοι.

105. In that battle those of the Greeks that fought best were the Athenians, and the Athenian that fought best was one who practised the pancratium,[1] Hermolycus son of Euthoenus. This Hermolycus on a later day met his death in battle at Cyrnus in Carystus during a war between the Athenians and Carystians, and lay dead on Geraestus. Those that fought best next after the Athenians were the men of Corinth and Troezen and Sicyon.

106. When the Greeks had made an end of most of the foreigners, either in battle or in flight, they brought out their booty on to the beach, and found certain stores of wealth; then they burnt the ships and the whole of the wall, which having burnt they sailed away. When they were arrived at Samos, they debated in council whether they should dispeople Ionia, and in what Greek lands under their dominion it were best to plant the Ionians, leaving the country itself to the foreigners; for it seemed to them impossible to stand on guard between the Ionians and their enemies for ever; yet if they should not so stand, they had no hope that the Persians would suffer the Ionians to go unpunished. In this matter the Peloponnesians that were in authority were for removing the people from the marts of those Greek nations that had sided with the Persians, and giving their land to the Ionians to dwell in; but the Athenians misliked the whole design of dispeopling Ionia, or suffering the Peloponnesians to determine the lot of Athenian colonies; and as they resisted hotly, the Peloponnesians

[1] The "pancratium" was a mixture of boxing and wrestling.

καὶ οὕτω δὴ Σαμίους τε καὶ Χίους καὶ Λεσβίους
καὶ τοὺς ἄλλους νησιώτας, οἳ ἔτυχον συστρα-
τευόμενοι τοῖσι Ἕλλησι, ἐς τὸ συμμαχικὸν ἐποιήσαντο, πίστι τε καταλαβόντες καὶ ὁρκίοισι ἐμ-
μενέειν τε καὶ μὴ ἀποστήσεσθαι. τούτους δὲ
καταλαβόντες ὁρκίοισι ἔπλεον τὰς γεφύρας λύ-
σοντες· ἔτι γὰρ ἐδόκεον ἐντεταμένας εὑρήσειν.
οὗτοι μὲν δὴ ἐπ᾽ Ἑλλησπόντου ἔπλεον.

107. Τῶν δὲ ἀποφυγόντων βαρβάρων ἐς τὰ
ἄκρα τῆς Μυκάλης κατειληθέντων, ἐόντων οὐ
πολλῶν, ἐγίνετο κομιδὴ ἐς Σάρδις. πορευομένων
δὲ κατ᾽ ὁδόν Μασίστης ὁ Δαρείου παρατυχὼν τῷ
πάθεϊ τῷ γεγονότι τὸν στρατηγὸν Ἀρταΰντην
ἔλεγε πολλά τε καὶ κακά, ἄλλα τε καὶ γυναικὸς
κακίω φὰς αὐτὸν εἶναι τοιαῦτα στρατηγήσαντα,
καὶ ἄξιον εἶναι παντὸς κακοῦ τὸν βασιλέος οἶκον
κακώσαντα. παρὰ δὲ τοῖσι Πέρσῃσι γυναικὸς
κακίω ἀκοῦσαι δέννος μέγιστός ἐστι. ὁ δὲ ἐπεὶ
πολλὰ ἤκουσε, δεινὰ ποιεύμενος σπᾶται ἐπὶ τὸν
Μασίστην τὸν ἀκινάκην, ἀποκτεῖναι θέλων. καί
μιν ἐπιθέοντα φρασθεὶς Ξειναγόρης ὁ Πρηξίλεω
ἀνὴρ Ἁλικαρνησσεὺς ὄπισθε ἑστεὼς αὐτοῦ Ἀρταΰντεω ἁρπάζει μέσον καὶ ἐξαείρας παίει ἐς
τὴν γῆν· καὶ ἐν τούτῳ οἱ δορυφόροι οἱ Μασίστεω
προέστησαν. ὁ δὲ Ξειναγόρης ταῦτα ἐργάσατο
χάριτα αὐτῷ τε Μασίστῃ τιθέμενος καὶ Ξέρξῃ,
ἐκσώζων τὸν ἀδελφεὸν τὸν ἐκείνου· καὶ διὰ τοῦτο
τὸ ἔργον Ξειναγόρης Κιλικίης πάσης ἦρξε δόντος
βασιλέος. τῶν δὲ κατ᾽ ὁδὸν πορευομένων οὐδὲν
ἐπὶ πλέον τούτων ἐγένετο, ἀλλ᾽ ἀπικνέονται ἐς
Σάρδις.

108. Ἐν δὲ τῇσι Σάρδισι ἐτύγχανε ἐὼν βασι-

yielded. Thus it came about that they admitted
to their alliance the Samians, Chians, Lesbians, and
all other islanders who had served with their armaments, and bound them by pledge and oaths to
remain faithful and not desert their allies; who
being thus sworn, the Greeks set sail to break the
bridges, supposing that these still held fast. So
they laid their course for the Hellespont.

107. The few foreigners who escaped were driven
to the heights of Mycale, and made their way thence
to Sardis. While they were journeying on the road,
Masistes son of Darius, who had chanced to be
present at the Persian disaster, reviled the admiral
Artaÿntes very bitterly, telling him (with much
beside) that such generalship as his proved him
worse than a woman, and that no punishment was
too bad for the hurt he had wrought to the king's
house. Now it is the greatest of all taunts in Persia
to be called worse than a woman. These many
insults so angered Artaÿntes, that he drew his sword
upon Masistes to kill him; but Xenagoras son of
Praxilaus of Halicarnassus, who stood behind
Artaÿntes himself, saw him run at Masistes, and
caught him round the middle and lifted and hurled
him to the ground; meanwhile Masistes' guards
came between them. By so doing Xenagoras won
the gratitude of Masistes himself and Xerxes, for
saving the king's brother; for which deed he was
made ruler of all Cilicia by the king's gift. They
went then on their way without any outcome of the
matter, and came to Sardis.

108. Now it chanced that the king had been at

λεὺς ἐξ ἐκείνου τοῦ χρόνου, ἐπείτε ἐξ Ἀθηνέων
προσπταίσας τῇ ναυμαχίῃ φυγὼν ἀπίκετο. τότε
δὴ ἐν τῇσι Σάρδισι ἐὼν ἄρα ἤρα τῆς Μασίστεω
γυναικός, ἐούσης καὶ ταύτης ἐνθαῦτα. ὡς δέ οἱ
προσπέμποντι οὐκ ἐδύνατο κατεργασθῆναι, οὐδὲ
βίην προσεφέρετο προμηθεόμενος τὸν ἀδελφεὸν
Μασίστην· τὠυτὸ δὲ τοῦτο εἶχε καὶ τὴν γυναῖκα·
εὖ γὰρ ἐπίστατο βίης οὐ τευξομένη· ἐνθαῦτα δὴ
Ξέρξης ἐργόμενος τῶν ἄλλων πρήσσει τὸν γάμον
τοῦτον τῷ παιδὶ τῷ ἑωυτοῦ Δαρείῳ, θυγατέρα τῆς
γυναικὸς ταύτης καὶ Μασίστεω, δοκέων αὐτὴν
μᾶλλον λάμψεσθαι ἢν ταῦτα ποιήσῃ. ἁρμόσας
δὲ καὶ τὰ νομιζόμενα ποιήσας ἀπήλαυνε ἐς Σοῦσα·
ἐπεὶ δὲ ἐκεῖ τε ἀπίκετο καὶ ἠγάγετο ἐς ἑωυτοῦ
Δαρείῳ τὴν γυναῖκα, οὕτω δὴ τῆς Μασίστεω μὲν
γυναικὸς ἐπέπαυτο, ὁ δὲ διαμειψάμενος ἤρα τε
καὶ ἐτύγχανε τῆς Δαρείου μὲν γυναικὸς Μασίστεω
δὲ θυγατρός· οὔνομα δὲ τῇ γυναικὶ ταύτῃ ἦν
Ἀρταΰντη.

109. Χρόνου δὲ προϊόντος ἀνάπυστα γίνεται
τρόπῳ τοιῷδε. ἐξυφήνασα Ἄμηστρις ἡ Ξέρξεω
γυνὴ φᾶρος μέγα τε καὶ ποικίλον καὶ θέης ἄξιον
διδοῖ Ξέρξῃ. ὁ δὲ ἡσθεὶς περιβάλλεταί τε καὶ
ἔρχεται παρὰ τὴν Ἀρταΰντην· ἡσθεὶς δὲ καὶ
ταύτῃ ἐκέλευσε αὐτὴν αἰτῆσαι ὅ τι βούλεταί οἱ
γενέσθαι ἀντὶ τῶν αὐτῷ ὑπουργημένων· πάντα
γὰρ τεύξεσθαι αἰτήσασαν. τῇ δὲ κακῶς γὰρ ἔδεε
πανοικίῃ γενέσθαι, πρὸς ταῦτα εἶπε Ξέρξῃ "Δώ-
σεις μοι τὸ ἄν σε αἰτήσω;" ὁ δὲ πᾶν μᾶλλον
δοκέων κείνην αἰτῆσαι ὑπισχνέετο καὶ ὤμοσε. ἡ
δὲ ὡς ὤμοσε ἀδεῶς αἰτέει τὸ φᾶρος. Ξέρξης δὲ
παντοῖος ἐγίνετο οὐ βουλόμενος δοῦναι, κατ᾽ ἄλλο

Sardis ever since he came thither in flight from
Athens after his overthrow in the sea-fight. Being
then at Sardis he became enamoured of Masistes'
wife, who was also at that place. But as all his
messages could not bring her to yield to him, and
he would not force her to his will, out of regard for
his brother Masistes (which indeed wrought with
the woman also, for she knew well that no force
would be used with her), Xerxes found no other
way to his purpose than that he should make a
marriage between his own son Darius and the
daughter of this woman and Masistes; for he
thought that by so doing he would be likeliest
to get her. So he betrothed them with all due
ceremony, and rode away to Susa. But when he
was come thither and had taken Darius' bride into
his house, he thought no more of Masistes' wife,
but changed about, and wooed and won this girl
Artaÿnte, Darius' wife and Masistes' daughter.

109. But as time went on the truth came to light,
and in such manner as I will show. Xerxes' wife,
Amestris, wove and gave to him a great gaily-
coloured mantle, wondrous to behold. Xerxes was
pleased with it, and went wearing it to Artaÿnte;
and being pleased with her too, he bade her ask for
what she would have in return for her favours, for
he would deny nothing at her asking. Thereat—
for she and all her house were doomed to evil—she
said to Xerxes, "Will you give me whatever I ask
of you?" and he promised and swore it, supposing
that she would ask anything but that; but when
he had sworn, she asked boldly for his mantle.
Xerxes strove hard to refuse her, for no cause save

HERODOTUS

μὲν οὐδέν, φοβεόμενος δὲ Ἄμηστριν, μὴ καὶ πρὶν
κατεικαζούσῃ τὰ γινόμενα οὕτω ἐπευρεθῇ πρήσ-
σων· ἀλλὰ πόλις τε ἐδίδου καὶ χρυσὸν ἄπλετον
καὶ στρατόν, τοῦ ἔμελλε οὐδεὶς ἄρξειν ἀλλ' ἢ
ἐκείνη. Περσικὸν δὲ κάρτα ὁ στρατὸς δῶρον.
ἀλλ' οὐ γὰρ ἔπειθε, διδοῖ τὸ φᾶρος. ἡ δὲ περιχαρὴς
ἐοῦσα τῷ δώρῳ ἐφόρεέ τε καὶ ἀγάλλετο.

110. Καὶ ἡ Ἄμηστρις πυνθάνεταί μιν ἔχουσαν·
μαθοῦσα δὲ τὸ ποιεύμενον τῇ μὲν γυναικὶ ταύτῃ
οὐκ εἶχε ἔγκοτον, ἡ δὲ ἐλπίζουσα τὴν μητέρα
αὐτῆς εἶναι αἰτίην καὶ ταῦτα ἐκείνην πρήσσειν,
τῇ Μασίστεω γυναικὶ ἐβούλευε ὄλεθρον. φυλάξασα δὲ τὸν ἄνδρα τὸν ἑωυτῆς Ξέρξην βασιλήιον
δεῖπνον προτιθέμενον· τοῦτο δὲ τὸ δεῖπνον παρα-
σκευάζεται ἅπαξ τοῦ ἐνιαυτοῦ ἡμέρῃ τῇ ἐγένετο
βασιλεύς. οὔνομα δὲ τῷ δείπνῳ τούτῳ περσιστὶ
μὲν τυκτά, κατὰ δὲ τὴν Ἑλλήνων γλῶσσαν τέλει-
ον· τότε καὶ τὴν κεφαλὴν σμᾶται μοῦνον βασιλεὺς καὶ Πέρσας δωρέεται· ταύτην δὴ τὴν ἡμέρην
φυλάξασα ἡ Ἄμηστρις χρηίζει τοῦ Ξέρξεω δο-
θῆναί οἱ τὴν Μασίστεω γυναῖκα. ὃ δὲ δεινόν τε
καὶ ἀνάρσιον ἐποιέετο τοῦτο μὲν ἀδελφεοῦ γυναῖκα
παραδοῦναι, τοῦτο δὲ ἀναιτίην ἐοῦσαν τοῦ πρήγματος τούτου· συνῆκε γὰρ τοῦ εἵνεκεν ἐδέετο.

111. Τέλος μέντοι ἐκείνης τε λιπαρεούσης καὶ
ὑπὸ τοῦ νόμου ἐξεργόμενος, ὅτι ἀτυχῆσαι τὸν
χρηίζοντα οὔ σφι δυνατόν ἐστι βασιλήιου δείπνου
προκειμένου, κάρτα δὴ ἀέκων κατανεύει, καὶ
παραδοὺς ποιέει ὧδε· τὴν μὲν κελεύει ποιέειν τὰ
βούλεται, ὁ δὲ μεταπεμψάμενος τὸν ἀδελφεὸν
λέγει τάδε. "Μασίστα, σὺ εἶς Δαρείου τε παῖς
καὶ ἐμὸς ἀδελφεός, πρὸς δ' ἔτι τούτοισι καὶ εἶς
288

that he feared lest Amestris might have plain proof of his doing what she already guessed; and he offered her cities instead, and gold in abundance, and an army for none but herself to command. Armies are the properest of gifts in Persia. But as he could not move her, he gave her the mantle; and she, rejoicing greatly in the gift, went flaunting her finery.

110. Amestris heard that she had the mantle; but when she learnt the truth her anger was not with the girl; she supposed rather that the girl's mother was guilty and that this was her doing, and so it was Masistes' wife that she plotted to destroy. She waited therefore till Xerxes her husband should be giving his royal feast. This banquet is served once a year, on the king's birthday; the Persian name for it is "tukta," which is in the Greek language "perfect"; on that day (and none other) the king anoints his head, and makes gifts to the Persians. Waiting for that day, Amestris then desired of Xerxes that Masistes' wife should be given to her. Xerxes held it a terrible and wicked act to give up his brother's wife, and that too when she was guiltless of the deed supposed; for he knew the purpose of the request.

111. Nevertheless, Amestris being instant, and the law constraining him (for at this royal banquet in Persia every boon asked must of necessity be granted), he did very unwillingly consent, and delivered the woman to Amestris; then, bidding her do what she would, he sent for his brother and thus spoke: "Masistes, you are Darius' son and my brother, yea, and a right good man; hear me then;

ἀνὴρ ἀγαθός· γυναικὶ δὴ ταύτῃ τῇ νῦν συνοικέεις
μὴ συνοίκεε, ἀλλά τοι ἀντ' αὐτῆς ἐγὼ δίδωμι θυγατέρα τὴν ἐμήν. ταύτῃ συνοίκεε· τὴν δὲ νῦν ἔχεις,
οὐ γὰρ δοκέει ἐμοί, μὴ ἔχε γυναῖκα." ὁ δὲ Μασίστης ἀποθωμάσας τὰ λεγόμενα λέγει τάδε. "Ὦ
δέσποτα, τίνα μοι λόγον λέγεις ἄχρηστον, κελεύων
με γυναῖκα, ἐκ τῆς μοι παῖδές τε νεηνίαι εἰσὶ καὶ
θυγατέρες, τῶν καὶ σὺ μίαν τῷ παιδὶ τῷ σεωυτοῦ
ἠγάγεο γυναῖκα, αὐτή τέ μοι κατὰ νόον τυγχάνει
κάρτα ἐοῦσα· ταύτην με κελεύεις μετέντα θυγατέρα τὴν σὴν γῆμαι; ἐγὼ δὲ βασιλεῦ μεγάλα μὲν
ποιεῦμαι ἀξιεύμενος θυγατρὸς τῆς σῆς, ποιήσω
μέντοι τούτων οὐδέτερα. σὺ δὲ μηδαμῶς βιῶ
πρήγματος τοιοῦδε δεόμενος· ἀλλὰ τῇ τε σῇ θυ-
γατρὶ ἀνὴρ ἄλλος φανήσεται ἐμεῦ οὐδὲν ἥσσων,
ἐμέ τε ἔα γυναικὶ τῇ ἐμῇ συνοικέειν." ὁ μὲν δὴ
τοιούτοισι ἀμείβεται, Ξέρξης δὲ θυμωθεὶς λέγει
τάδε. "Οὕτω τοι, Μασίστα, πέπρηκται· οὔτε
γὰρ ἄν τοι δοίην θυγατέρα τὴν ἐμὴν γῆμαι, οὔτε
ἐκείνη πλεῦνα χρόνον συνοικήσεις, ὡς μάθῃς τὰ
διδόμενα δέκεσθαι." ὁ δὲ ὡς ταῦτα ἤκουσε, εἴπας
τοσόνδε ἐχώρεε ἔξω "Δέσποτα, οὐ δή κώ με
ἀπώλεσας."

112. Ἐν δὲ τούτῳ τῷ διὰ μέσου χρόνῳ, ἐν τῷ
Ξέρξης τῷ ἀδελφεῷ διελέγετο, ἡ Ἄμηστρις μετα-
πεμψαμένη τοὺς δορυφόρους τοῦ Ξέρξεω διαλυ-
μαίνεται τὴν γυναῖκα τοῦ Μασίστεω· τούς τε
μαζοὺς ἀποταμοῦσα κυσὶ προέβαλε καὶ ῥῖνα καὶ
ὦτα καὶ χείλεα καὶ γλῶσσαν ἐκταμοῦσα ἐς οἶκόν
μιν ἀποπέμπει διαλελυμασμένην.

113. Ὁ δὲ Μασίστης οὐδέν κω ἀκηκοὼς τούτων,
ἐλπόμενος δέ τί οἱ κακὸν εἶναι, ἐσπίπτει δρόμῳ ἐς

you must live no longer with her who is now your wife. I give you my daughter in her place; take her for your own; but put away the wife that you have, for it is not my will that you should have her." At that Masistes was amazed; "Sire," he said, "what is this evil command that you lay upon me, bidding me deal thus with my wife? I have by her young sons and daughters, of whom you have taken a wife for your own son; and I am exceeding well content with herself; yet do you bid me put her away and wed your daughter? Truly, O king, I deem it a high honour to be accounted worthy of your daughter; but I will do neither the one nor the other. Nay, constrain me not to consent to such a desire; you will find another husband for your daughter as good as I; but suffer me to keep my own wife." Thus answered Masistes; but Xerxes was very angry, and said: "To this pass you are come, Masistes; I will give you no daughter of mine to wife, nor shall you longer live with her that you now have; thus shall you learn to accept that which is offered you." Hearing that, Masistes said nought but this: "Nay, sire, you have not destroyed me yet!" and so departed.

112. But in the meantime, while Xerxes talked with his brother, Amestris sent for Xerxes' guards and used Masistes' wife very cruelly; she cut off the woman's breasts and threw them to dogs, and her nose and ears and lips likewise, and cut out her tongue, and sent her home thus cruelly used.

113. Knowing nought as yet of this, but fearing evil, Masistes ran speedily to his house. Seeing the

τὰ οἰκία. ἰδὼν δὲ διεφθαρμένην τὴν γυναῖκα,
αὐτίκα μετὰ ταῦτα συμβουλευσάμενος τοῖσι παισὶ
ἐπορεύετο ἐς Βάκτρα σύν τε τοῖσι ἑωυτοῦ υἱοῖσι
καὶ δή κου τισὶ καὶ ἄλλοισι ὡς ἀποστήσων νομὸν
τὸν Βάκτριον καὶ ποιήσων τὰ μέγιστα κακῶν
βασιλέα· τά περ ἂν καὶ ἐγένετο, ὡς ἐμοὶ δοκέειν,
εἴ περ ἔφθη ἀναβὰς ἐς τοὺς Βακτρίους καὶ τοὺς
Σάκας· καὶ γὰρ ἔστεργόν μιν καὶ ἦν ὕπαρχος τῶν
Βακτρίων. ἀλλὰ γὰρ Ξέρξης πυθόμενος ταῦτα
ἐκεῖνον πρήσσοντα, πέμψας ἐπ' αὐτὸν στρατιὴν
ἐν τῇ ὁδῷ κατέκτεινε αὐτόν τε ἐκεῖνον καὶ τοὺς
παῖδας αὐτοῦ καὶ τὴν στρατιὴν τὴν ἐκείνου. κατὰ
μὲν τὸν ἔρωτα τὸν Ξέρξεω καὶ τὸν Μασίστεω
θάνατον τοσαῦτα ἐγένετο.

114. Οἱ δὲ ἐκ Μυκάλης ὁρμηθέντες Ἕλληνες
ἐπ' Ἑλλησπόντου πρῶτον μὲν περὶ Λεκτὸν
ὅρμεον, ὑπὸ ἀνέμων ἀπολαμφθέντες, ἐνθεῦτεν δὲ
ἀπίκοντο ἐς Ἄβυδον καὶ τὰς γεφύρας εὗρον διαλελυμένας, τὰς ἐδόκεον εὑρήσειν ἔτι ἐντεταμένας,
καὶ τούτων οὐκ ἥκιστα εἵνεκεν ἐς τὸν Ἑλλήσποντον ἀπίκοντο. τοῖσι μέν νυν ἀμφὶ Λευτυχίδην
Πελοποννησίοισι ἔδοξε ἀποπλέειν ἐς τὴν Ἑλλάδα,
Ἀθηναίοισι δὲ καὶ Ξανθίππῳ τῷ στρατηγῷ αὐτοῦ
ὑπομείναντας πειρᾶσθαι τῆς Χερσονήσου. οἱ
μὲν δὴ ἀπέπλεον, Ἀθηναῖοι δὲ ἐκ τῆς Ἀβύδου
διαβάντες ἐς τὴν Χερσόνησον Σηστὸν ἐπολιόρκεον.

115. Ἐς δὲ τὴν Σηστὸν ταύτην, ὡς ἐόντος ἰσχυ-
ροτάτου τείχεος τῶν ταύτῃ, συνῆλθον, ὡς ἤκουσαν
παρεῖναι τοὺς Ἕλληνας ἐς τὸν Ἑλλήσποντον, ἔκ
τε τῶν ἀλλέων τῶν περιοικίδων, καὶ δὴ καὶ ἐκ
Καρδίης πόλιος Οἰόβαζος ἀνὴρ Πέρσης, ὃς τὰ ἐκ
τῶν γεφυρέων ὅπλα ἐνθαῦτα ἦν κεκομικώς. εἶχον

havoc made of his wife, straightway he took counsel
with his children and set forth to journey to Bactra
with his own sons (and others too, belike), purposing
to raise the province of Bactra in revolt and work
the king the greatest of harm; which he would have
done, to my thinking, had he escaped up into the
country of the Bactrians and Sacae; for they loved
him well, and he was viceroy over the Bactrians.
But it was of no avail; for Xerxes learnt his intent,
and sent against him an army that slew him on his
way, and his sons and his army withal. Such is
the story of Xerxes' love and Masistes' death.

114. The Greeks that had set out from Mycale for
the Hellespont first lay to off Lectum [1] under stress
of weather, and thence came to Abydos, where they
found the bridges broken which they thought would
be still holding fast, and indeed these were the chief
cause of their coming to the Hellespont. The
Peloponnesians then who were with Leutychides
thus resolved that they would sail away to Hellas,
but the Athenians, with Xanthippus their general,
that they would remain there and attack the
Chersonesus. So the rest sailed away, but the
Athenians crossed over to the Chersonesus and laid
siege to Sestus.

115. Now when the Persians heard that the Greeks
were at the Hellespont, they had come in from the
neighbouring towns and assembled at this same
Sestus, seeing that it was the strongest walled place
in that region; among them there was come from
Cardia a Persian named Oeobazus, and he had carried
thither the tackle of the bridges. Sestus was held

---

[1] At the western end of the bay of Adramyttium.

δὲ ταύτην ἐπιχώριοι Αἰολέες, συνῆσαν δὲ Πέρσαι
τε καὶ τῶν ἄλλων συμμάχων συχνὸς ὅμιλος.

116. Ἐτυράννευε δὲ τούτου τοῦ νομοῦ Ξέρξεω
ὕπαρχος Ἀρταΰκτης, ἀνὴρ μὲν Πέρσης, δεινὸς δὲ
καὶ ἀτάσθαλος, ὃς καὶ βασιλέα ἐλαύνοντα ἐπ'
Ἀθήνας ἐξηπάτησε, τὰ Πρωτεσίλεω τοῦ Ἰφίκλου
χρήματα ἐξ Ἐλαιοῦντος ὑπελόμενος. ἐν γὰρ
Ἐλαιοῦντι τῆς Χερσονήσου ἐστὶ Πρωτεσίλεω
τάφος τε καὶ τέμενος περὶ αὐτόν, ἔνθα ἦν χρήματα
πολλὰ καὶ φιάλαι χρύσεαι καὶ ἀργύρεαι καὶ
χαλκὸς καὶ ἐσθὴς καὶ ἄλλα ἀναθήματα, τὰ
Ἀρταΰκτης ἐσύλησε βασιλέος δόντος. λέγων δὲ
τοιάδε Ξέρξην διεβάλετο. "Δέσποτα, ἔστι οἶκος
ἀνδρὸς Ἕλληνος ἐνθαῦτα, ὃς ἐπὶ γῆν σὴν στρατευ-
σάμενος δίκης κυρήσας ἀπέθανε· τούτου μοι δὸς
τὸν οἶκον, ἵνα καί τις μάθῃ ἐπὶ γῆν τὴν σὴν μὴ
στρατεύεσθαι." ταῦτα λέγων εὐπετέως ἔμελλε
ἀναπείσειν Ξέρξην δοῦναι ἀνδρὸς οἶκον, οὐδὲν
ὑποτοπηθέντα τῶν ἐκεῖνος ἐφρόνεε. ἐπὶ γῆν δὲ
τὴν βασιλέος στρατεύεσθαι Πρωτεσίλεων ἔλεγε
νοέων τοιάδε· τὴν Ἀσίην πᾶσαν νομίζουσι ἑωυτῶν
εἶναι Πέρσαι καὶ τοῦ αἰεὶ βασιλεύοντος. ἐπεὶ δὲ
ἐδόθη, τὰ χρήματα ἐξ Ἐλαιοῦντος ἐς Σηστὸν
ἐξεφόρησε, καὶ τὸ τέμενος ἔσπειρε καὶ ἐνέμετο,
αὐτός τε ὅκως ἀπίκοιτο ἐς Ἐλαιοῦντα ἐν τῷ
ἀδύτῳ γυναιξὶ ἐμίσγετο. τότε δὲ ἐπολιορκέετο
ὑπὸ Ἀθηναίων οὔτε παρεσκευασμένος ἐς πολιορ-
κίην οὔτε προσδεκόμενος τοὺς Ἕλληνας, ἀφύκτως
δέ κως αὐτῷ ἐπέπεσον.

117. Ἐπεὶ δὲ πολιορκεομένοισί σφι φθινόπωρον
ἐπεγίνετο, καὶ ἤσχαλλον οἱ Ἀθηναῖοι ἀπό τε τῆς

by the Aeolians of the country, but with him were
Persians and a great multitude of their allies withal.

116. This province was ruled by Xerxes' viceroy
Artaÿctes, a cunning man and a wicked ; witness the
deceit that he practised on the king in his march to
Athens, how he stole away from Elaeus the treasure
of Protesilaus [1] son of Iphiclus.   This was the way of
it : there is at Elaeus in the Chersonesus the tomb
of Protesilaus, and a precinct about it, where was
much treasure, with vessels of gold and silver,
bronze, raiment, and other dedicated offerings ; all
of which Artaÿctes carried off, by the king's gift.
"Sire," he said deceitfully to Xerxes, "there is here
the house of a certain Greek, who met a just death
for invading your territory with an army ; give me
this man's house, whereby all may be taught not to
invade your territory."   It was to be thought that
this plea would easily persuade Xerxes to give him
a man's house, having no suspicion of Artaÿctes'
meaning ; whose reason for saying that Protesilaus
had invaded the king's territory was, that the
Persians believe all Asia to belong to themselves and
whosoever is their king.   So when the treasure was
given him, he carried it away from Elaeus to Sestus,
and planted and farmed the precinct ; and he would
come from Elaeus and have intercourse with women
in the shrine.   Now, when the Athenians laid siege
to him, he had made no preparation for it, nor
thought that the Greeks would come, and he had no
way of escape from their attack.

117. But the siege continuing into the late
autumn, the Athenians grew weary of their absence

[1] The first Greek to fall in the Trojan war, νηὸς ἀποθρώσκων
(Hom. *Il.* ii. 701).

ἑωυτῶν ἀποδημέοντες καὶ οὐ δυνάμενοι ἐξελεῖν
τὸ τεῖχος, ἐδέοντό τε τῶν στρατηγῶν ὅκως ἀπά-
γοιεν σφέας ὀπίσω, οἱ δὲ οὐκ ἔφασαν πρὶν ἢ
ἐξέλωσι ἢ τὸ Ἀθηναίων κοινόν σφεας μεταπέμ-
ψηται· οὕτω δὴ ἔστεργον τὰ παρεόντα.
118. Οἱ δὲ ἐν τῷ τείχεϊ ἐς πᾶν ἤδη κακοῦ
ἀπιγμένοι ἦσαν, οὕτω ὥστε τοὺς τόνους ἕψοντες
τῶν κλινέων ἐσιτέοντο. ἐπείτε δὲ οὐδὲ ταῦτα ἔτι
εἶχον, οὕτω δὴ ὑπὸ νύκτα οἴχοντο ἀποδράντες οἵ
τε Πέρσαι καὶ ὁ Ἀρταΰκτης καὶ ὁ Οἰόβαζος,
ὄπισθε τοῦ τείχεος καταβάντες, τῇ ἦν ἐρημότατον
τῶν πολεμίων. ὡς δὲ ἡμέρη ἐγένετο, οἱ Χερσονη-
σῖται ἀπὸ τῶν πύργων ἐσήμηναν τοῖσι Ἀθηναίοισι
τὸ γεγονὸς καὶ τὰς πύλας ἄνοιξαν. τῶν δὲ οἱ μὲν
πλεῦνες ἐδίωκον, οἱ δὲ τὴν πόλιν εἶχον.
119. Οἰόβαζον μέν νυν ἐκφεύγοντα ἐς τὴν
Θρηίκην Θρήικες Ἀψίνθιοι λαβόντες ἔθυσαν
Πλειστώρῳ ἐπιχωρίῳ θεῷ τρόπῳ τῷ σφετέρῳ,
τοὺς δὲ μετ' ἐκείνου ἄλλῳ τρόπῳ ἐφόνευσαν. οἱ
δὲ ἀμφὶ τὸν Ἀρταΰκτην ὕστεροι ὁρμηθέντες φεύγειν, καὶ ὡς κατελαμβάνοντο ὀλίγον ἐόντες ὑπὲρ
Αἰγὸς ποταμῶν, ἀλεξόμενοι χρόνον ἐπὶ συχνὸν
οἱ μὲν ἀπέθανον οἱ δὲ ζῶντες ἐλάμφθησαν. καὶ
συνδήσαντες σφέας οἱ Ἕλληνες ἦγον ἐς Σηστόν,
μετ' αὐτῶν δὲ καὶ Ἀρταΰκτην δεδεμένον αὐτόν τε
καὶ τὸν παῖδα αὐτοῦ.
120. Καί τεῳ τῶν φυλασσόντων λέγεται ὑπὸ
Χερσονησιτέων ταρίχους ὀπτῶντι τέρας γενέσθαι

from home and their ill success at taking the
fortress, and entreated their generals to lead them
away again; but the generals refused to do that,
till they should take the place or be recalled by the
Athenian state. Thereat the men endured their
plight patiently.

118. But they that were within the walls were by
now brought to the last extremity, insomuch that
they boiled the thongs of their beds for food; but
at the last even these failed them, and Artaÿctes
and Oeobazus and all the Persians made their way
down from the back part of the fortress, where their
enemies were scarcest, and fled away at nightfall.
When morning came, the people of the Chersonesus
signified from their towers to the Athenians what
had happened, and opened their gates; and the
greater part of the Athenians going in pursuit, the
rest stayed to hold the town.

119. Oeobazus made to escape into Thrace; but
the Apsinthians of that country caught and sacrificed
him after their fashion to Plistorus the god of their
land; as for his companions, they slew them in
another manner. Artaÿctes and his company had
begun their flight later, and were overtaken a little
way beyond the Goat's Rivers,[1] where after they had
defended themselves a long time some of them were
slain and the rest taken alive. The Greeks bound
and carried them to Sestus, and Artaÿctes and his
son likewise with them in bonds.

120. It is told by the people of the Chersonesus
that a marvellous thing befell one of them that

[1] A roadstead opposite Lampsacus; the rivers were
probably two small streams that flow into the sea there (How
and Wells).

τοιόνδε· οἱ τάριχοι ἐπὶ τῷ πυρὶ κείμενοι ἐπάλ-
λοντό τε καὶ ἤσπαιρον ὅκως περ ἰχθύες νεοάλωτοι.
καὶ οἳ μὲν περιχυθέντες ἐθώμαζον, ὁ δὲ Ἀρταΰκτης ὡς εἶδε τὸ τέρας, καλέσας τὸν ὀπτῶντα τοὺς
ταρίχους ἔφη " Ξεῖνε Ἀθηναῖε, μηδὲν φοβέο τὸ
τέρας τοῦτο· οὐ γὰρ σοὶ πέφηνε, ἀλλ' ἐμοὶ σημαί-
νει ὁ ἐν Ἐλαιοῦντι Πρωτεσίλεως ὅτι καὶ τεθνεὼς
καὶ τάριχος ἐὼν δύναμιν πρὸς θεῶν ἔχει τὸν
ἀδικέοντα τίνεσθαι. νῦν ὦν ἄποινά μοι τάδε
ἐθέλω ἐπιθεῖναι, ἀντὶ μὲν χρημάτων τῶν ἔλαβον
ἐκ τοῦ ἱροῦ ἑκατὸν τάλαντα καταθεῖναι τῷ θεῷ,
ἀντὶ δ' ἐμεωυτοῦ καὶ τοῦ παιδὸς ἀποδώσω τάλαντα
διηκόσια Ἀθηναίοισι περιγενόμενος." ταῦτα
ὑπισχόμενος τὸν στρατηγὸν Ξάνθιππον οὐκ
ἔπειθε· οἱ γὰρ Ἐλαιούσιοι τῷ Πρωτεσίλεῳ τιμωρέοντες ἐδέοντό μιν καταχρησθῆναι, καὶ αὐτοῦ
τοῦ στρατηγοῦ ταύτῃ νόος ἔφερε. ἀπαγαγόντες
δὲ αὐτὸν ἐς τὴν ἀκτὴν ἐς τὴν Ξέρξης ἔζευξε τὸν
πόρον, οἳ δὲ λέγουσι ἐπὶ τὸν κολωνὸν τὸν ὑπὲρ
Μαδύτου πόλιος, πρὸς σανίδας προσπασσαλεύ-
σαντες ἀνεκρέμασαν· τὸν δὲ παῖδα ἐν ὀφθαλμοῖσι
τοῦ Ἀρταΰκτεω κατέλευσαν.

121. Ταῦτα δὲ ποιήσαντες ἀπέπλεον ἐς τὴν
Ἑλλάδα, τά τε ἄλλα χρήματα ἄγοντες καὶ δὴ
καὶ τὰ ὅπλα τῶν γεφυρέων ὡς ἀναθήσοντες ἐς τὰ
ἱρά. καὶ κατὰ τὸ ἔτος τοῦτο οὐδὲν ἐπὶ πλέον
τούτων ἐγένετο.

122. Τούτου δὲ τοῦ Ἀρταΰκτεω τοῦ ἀνακρεμα-
σθέντος προπάτωρ Ἀρτεμβάρης ἐστὶ ὁ Πέρσῃσι
ἐξηγησάμενος λόγον τὸν ἐκεῖνοι ὑπολαβόντες

guarded Artaÿctes: he was frying dried fishes, and
these as they lay over the fire began to leap and
writhe as though they were fishes newly caught.
The rest gathered round, amazed at the sight; but
when Artaÿctes saw the strange thing, he called
him that was frying the fishes and said to him: " Sir
Athenian, be not afraid of this portent; it is not to you
that it is sent; it is to me that Protesilaus of Elaeus
would signify that though he be dead and dry he has
power given him by heaven to take vengeance on me
that wronged him.   Now therefore I offer a ransom,
to wit, payment of a hundred talents to the god for
the treasure that I took from his temple; and I will
pay to the Athenians two hundred talents for myself
and my son, if they spare us."   But Xanthippus the
general was unmoved by this promise; for the
people of Elaeus entreated that Artaÿctes should
be put to death in justice to Protesilaus, and the
general himself likewise was so minded.   So they
carried Artaÿctes away to the headland where
Xerxes had bridged the strait (or, by another story,
to the hill above the town of Madytus), and there
nailed him to boards and hanged him aloft; and as
for his son, they stoned him to death before his
father's eyes.

121. This done, they sailed away to Hellas,
carrying with them the tackle of the bridges to be
dedicated in their temples, and the rest of the stuff
withal.   And in that year nothing further was done.

122. This Artaÿctes who was crucified was grandson to that Artembares [1] who instructed the Persians
in a design which they took from him and laid

---

[1] There is an Artembares in i. 114; but he is a Mede, and
so can hardly be meant here.

Κύρῳ προσήνεικαν λέγοντα τάδε. "'Επεὶ Ζεὺς Πέρσῃσι ἡγεμονίην διδοῖ, ἀνδρῶν δὲ σοὶ Κῦρε, κατελὼν 'Αστυάγην, φέρε, γῆν γὰρ ἐκτήμεθα ὀλίγην καὶ ταύτην τρηχέαν, μεταναστάντες ἐκ ταύτης ἄλλην σχῶμεν ἀμείνω. εἰσὶ δὲ πολλαὶ μὲν ἀστυγείτονες πολλαὶ δὲ καὶ ἑκαστέρω, τῶν μίαν σχόντες πλέοσι ἐσόμεθα θωμαστότεροι. οἰκὸς δὲ ἄνδρας ἄρχοντας τοιαῦτα ποιέειν· κότε γὰρ δὴ καὶ παρέξει κάλλιον ἢ ὅτε γε ἀνθρώπων τε πολλῶν ἄρχομεν πάσης τε τῆς 'Ασίης ;" Κῦρος δὲ ταῦτα ἀκούσας καὶ οὐ θωμάσας τὸν λόγον ἐκέλευε ποιέειν ταῦτα, οὕτω δὲ αὐτοῖσι παραίνεε κελεύων παρασκευάζεσθαι ὡς οὐκέτι ἄρξοντας ἀλλ' ἀρξομένους· φιλέειν γὰρ ἐκ τῶν μαλακῶν χώρων μαλακοὺς γίνεσθαι· οὐ γάρ τι τῆς αὐτῆς γῆς εἶναι καρπόν τε θωμαστὸν φύειν καὶ ἄνδρας ἀγαθοὺς τὰ πολέμια. ὥστε συγγνόντες Πέρσαι οἴχοντο ἀποστάντες, ἑσσωθέντες τῇ γνώμῃ πρὸς Κύρου, ἄρχειν τε εἵλοντο λυπρὴν οἰκέοντες μᾶλλον ἢ πεδιάδα σπείροντες ἄλλοισι δουλεύειν.

before Cyrus; this was its purport: "Seeing that Zeus grants lordship to the Persian people, and to you, Cyrus, among them, by bringing Astyages low, let us now remove out of the little and rugged land that we possess and take to ourselves one that is better. There be many such on our borders, and many further distant; if we take one of these we shall have more reasons for renown. It is but reasonable that a ruling people should act thus; for when shall we have a fairer occasion than now, when we are lords of so many men and of all Asia?" Cyrus heard them, and found nought to marvel at in their design; "Do so," said he; "but if you do, make ready to be no longer rulers, but subjects. Soft lands breed soft men; wondrous fruits of the earth and valiant warriors grow not from the same soil." Thereat the Persians saw that Cyrus reasoned better than they, and they departed from before him, choosing rather to be rulers on a barren mountain side than slaves dwelling in tilled valleys.

INDEX

INDEX

INDEX

INDEX

INDEX

INDEX

INDEX

Apaturia, an Athenian festival celebrated in the month Pyanepsion, I. 147

Aphetae, in Magnesia, on the Pagasaean gulf, station of Xerxes' fleet, VII. 193, 196; storm and shipwreck there, VIII. 12

Aphidnae, a deme of Attica, IX. 73

Aphrodisias, an island off the coast of Libya, IV. 169

Aphrodite, worshipped in Cyprus and Cythera, I. 105; in Cyrene, II. 181; in Egypt (Hathor), II. 41, 112; other local cults under various names, I. 105, 131, 199, III. 8, IV. 59, 67

Aphthite province of Egypt, inhabited by one of the warrior clans, II. 166

Apia, a Scythian goddess, IV. 59

Apidanus, a river of Thessaly, VII. 129, 196

Apis, (1) the sacred calf of Egypt, II. 38, 153; Cambyses' sacrilegious treatment of Apis, III. 27–29. (2) An Egyptian town, II. 18

Apollo, I. 87, VII. 26; cult at Delos and Delphi, I. 50, 91, IV. 163, 155, VI. 80, 118; other local cults, I. 52, 69, 92, 144, II. 83, 144, 155 (Horus), II. 159, 178, III. 52, IV. 59, 158, V. 59–61, VIII. 33, 134

Apollonia, (1) a town on the Euxine sea, IV. 90, 93. (2) A town on the Ionic gulf, IX. 90

Apollophanes, a man of Abydos, VI. 26

Apries, a king of Egypt, deposed by Amasis, II. 161–163; his death, II. 169; marriage of his daughter to Cambyses, III. 1; his expedition against Cyrene, IV. 159

Apsinthii, a tribe near the Chersonese (promontory of Gallipoli), VI. 34, 36, IX. 119

Arabia, its customs, I. 131, 198, III. 8; invasion of Egypt by Arabians and Assyrians, II. 141; geography, II. 8, 11, 15, 19, III. 7; home of the phoenix and flying serpents, II. 73, 75; natural history, III. 107–113; part of Persian empire, III. 91, 97

Arabian gulf (Red Sea), II. 11, 102, 158, IV. 39, 42. Arabians in Xerxes' forces, VII. 69, 86, 184

Aradians, of the island Aradus, off the Phoenician coast, VII. 98

Ararus, an alleged tributary of the Danube, IV. 48

Araxes, a river flowing from the west into the Caspian (but apparently confused by Herodotus with other rivers), I. 202, 205, II. 36, IV. 11, 40; crossed by Cyrus when invading the Massagetae, I. 209–211

Arcadia, its relations with Sparta, I. 66; a Pelasgian people, I.

310

INDEX

INDEX

Artoxerxes, king of Persia, son of Xerxes, VII. 106; his friendly relations with Argos, VII. 151

Artozostre, daughter of Darius and wife of Mardonius, VI. 43

Artybius, a Persian general in Cyprus, V. 108–112

Artyphius, a Persian officer in Xerxes' army, son of Artabanus, VII. 66

Artystone, Cyrus' daughter, wife of Darius, III. 88

Aryandes, Persian satrap of Egypt under Darius, his silver coinage, IV. 166; his forces sent to reinstate Pheretime in Barca, IV. 167, 200

Aryenis, daughter of Alyattes king of Lydia, married to Astyages the Mede, I. 74

Asbystae, a tribe of Libya, IV. 170

Ascalon, a town in Syria, I. 105

Asia : beginning of troubles between Asia and Greece, I. 4. Croesus' conquest of Asiatic Greeks, I. 6; division of Upper and Lower Asia by the Halys, I. 72; Assyrian rule of Upper Asia, I. 95; Asia ruled by Medes, I. 102; by Scythians, I. 103–106, IV. 4, VII. 20; by Persians, I. 130; Ionians of Asia, I. 142; Median conquest of Lower, Persian of Upper Asia, I. 177; wealth of Assyria a third of entire wealth of Asia, I. 192; division of Asia and Libya, II. 16, 17; Darius' Asiatic empire, III. 88–94; extremities of Asia (e.g. Arabia), III. 115; prosperity of Asia under Darius, IV. 1; mistake of those who think Europe no bigger than Asia, IV. 36; geography of the world, IV. 37–42; name of Asia, IV. 45; Asia and Libya compared, IV. 198; Aristagoras' map of Asia, V. 49; the "royal road" in Asia, V. 52; Asia "shaken for three years" by Darius' preparations against Greece, VII. 1; every nation of Asia in Xerxes' armament, VII. 21, 157; numbers of Asiatic contingents, VII. 184; Persian belief that all Asia is theirs, IX. 116 (many other unimportant reff.)

Asia, wife of Prometheus, IV. 45

Asias, (1) son of Cotys, a legendary Lydian, IV. 45. (2) A clan at Sardis, IV. 45

Asine, a town in Laconia, VIII. 73

Asmach, name of a people in Ethiopia, II. 30

Asonides, captain of an Aeginetan ship captured by Xerxes' fleet near Sciathus, VII. 181

Asopii, inhabitants of the Asopus valley, IX. 15

Asopodorus, a Theban cavalry leader under Mardonius at Plataea, IX. 69

INDEX

Asopus, (1) a river in Trachis near Thermopylae, VII. 199, 216, 217. (2) A river in Boeotia, made the boundary between Theban and Plataean territory, VI. 108; frequently referred to in connection with the Plataean campaign of Mardonius, who encamped on its bank, IX. 15–59

Aspathines, one of the seven conspirators against the Magians, III. 70, 78

Assa, a town in the Singitic gulf west of Athos, VII. 122

Assesus, a town with a local cult of Athene, in the lands of Miletus, I. 19, 22

Assyria: Assyrian rule of Upper Asia, I. 95; resistance to Medes, I. 102; Median conquest of all Assyria but Babylonia, I. 106; Cyrus' invasion, I. 178, 188; Herodotus' proposed Assyrian history, I. 183; some account of Assyria, I. 192–194; Sanacharibus' invasion of Egypt with Arabians and Assyrians, II. 141; Assyrian script, IV. 87; Perseus an Assyrian, VI. 54; Assyrians in Xerxes' army, VII. 63

Astacus, a legendary Theban, V. 67

Aster, a Spartan, V. 63

Astrabacus, a Spartan hero or demigod, VI. 69

Astyages, a Median king, son of Cyaxares and son-in-law of Croesus, I. 73–75; his treatment of Cyrus as a child and as a youth, and his dealings with Harpagus, I. 107–125; deposed by Cyrus, I. 127–130

Asychis, king of Egypt, builder of a brick pyramid, II. 136

Atarantes, a people in Libya, IV. 184

Atarbechis, a town in Egypt with a temple of "Aphrodite," II. 41

Atarneus, a district of Mysia, I. 160, VI. 28, 29, VIII. 106; on Xerxes' line of march, VII. 42

Athamas, a legendary Greek hero, VII. 58; ritual of human sacrifice connected with his family, VII. 197

Athenades, of Trachis, VII. 213

Athenagoras, of Samos, IX. 90

Athene (and Pallas), Libyan tradition of, IV. 180; cult at Athens, I. 60, V. 77, 82, VII. 141, VIII. 37, 39, 55; elsewhere, I. 19, 22, 62, 66, 92, 160, 175, II. 28, 59, 83, 169, 175, 182, III. 59, IV. 180, 188, V. 45, 95, VII. 43, VIII. 94, 104, IX. 70

Athens and Athenians, passim in Bks. V–IX; Solon's legislation at Athens, I. 29; Athenians the leading Ionian people, I. 56, 146; Pisistratus' usurpation of power, I. 59–64; Ionian appeal to Athens, V. 55, 97; murder of Hipparchus, V. 56; expulsion of Hippias with help from Sparta, V. 62 foll.; legis-

INDEX

INDEX

Magian, then of Darius, III. 68, 88; her desire that Darius should invade Greece, III. 133–134; her influence with Darius, VII. 2

Atramyttium, a town on Xerxes' route through W. Asia Minor, VII. 42

Atridae, Agamemnon and Menelaus, VII. 20

Attaginus, a leading Theban friendly to Mardonius, IX. 15; Greek demand for his surrender, IX. 86; his escape, IX. 88

Attica: Attic language, VI. 138; Attic weights and measures, I. 192; Attic dance movements, VI. 129. (See Athens.)

Atys, (1) son of Croesus, accidentally killed by Adrastus, I. 34–45; father of Pythius, VII. 27. (2) Earliest mentioned king of Lydia, son of Manes, I. 7, VII. 74; a dearth in his reign, I. 94

Auchatae, one of the earliest Scythian tribes, IV. 6

Augila, a date-growing place in Libya, on the caravan route from Egypt to the west, IV. 172, 182–184

Auras, a river flowing from the Balkan range into the Danube, IV. 49

Auschisae, a Libyan people on the sea coast, near Barca, IV. 171

Ausees, a Libyan people on the sea coast, IV. 180, 191

Autesion, a Theban, descended from Polynices, IV. 147, VI. 52

Autodicus, a Plataean, IX. 85

Autonous, a hero worshipped at Delphi, his alleged aid against the Persians, VIII. 39

Auxesia, a goddess of fertility worshipped in Aegina and Epidaurus, V. 82–83

Axius (Vardar), a river in Macedonia, VII. 123

Azanes, a Persian officer in Xerxes' army, VII. 66

Aziris, a place in Libya, a Greek settlement there, IV. 157, 169

Azotus, a town in Syria, II. 157

Babylon, the capital of Assyria; alliance with Croesus, I. 77; description of the city, I. 178–183; Nitocris and navigation of the Euphrates, I. 184–186; her tomb, I. 187; Cyrus' siege and capture of Babylon, I. 188–191; details of Babylonian life, I. 93, 192–200, II. 109, III. 89, 95, IV. 198; tribute paid to Persia, III. 92; siege and capture by Darius, III. 150–160

Bacchiadae, a powerful clan at Corinth, V. 92

Bacchic mysteries, II. 81

Bacis, reputed author or compiler of oracles, VIII. 20, 77, 96, IX. 43

INDEX

Bactra, in the eastern part of the Persian empire, still to be subdued by Cyrus, I. 153; tribute paid to Persia, III. 92; conquered peoples exiled thither, IV. 204, VI. 9; Bactrians in Xerxes' army, VII. 64, 66, 86; with Mardonius, VIII. 113; Masistes' plan for a Bactrian revolt, IX. 113

Badres, (1) a Persian commander in the expedition against Cyrene, IV. 167, 203. (2) A Persian officer in Xerxes' army, son of Hystanes, VII. 77

Bagaeus, a Persian, employed by Darius against Oroetes, III. 128; father of Mardontes, VII. 80, VIII. 130

Barca, a town of northern Libya, a colony from Cyrene, IV. 160; its tribute to Persia, III. 91; submission to Cambyses, III. 13; troubles with Cyrene, IV. 164, 167; captured and enslaved by Persians, 200–205

Basileïdes, an Ionian, father of Herodotus the historian's namesake, VIII. 132

Bassaces, a Persian officer in Xerxes' army, son of Artabanus, VII. 75

Battiadae, descendants of Battus, IV. 202

Battus; three of this name, all kings of Cyrene (see Arcesilaus). (1) A man of Thera, son of Polymnestus, and first colonist of Cyrene, IV. 150–159. (2) Grandson of the above, called " the fortunate "; his defeat of an Egyptian army, IV. 159. (3) Grandson of the last; curtailment of his royal power at Cyrene, IV. 161. (" Battus " said to be a Libyan word meaning " king," IV. 155.)

Belbinite, an inhabitant of the islet of Belbina off Attica, used by Themistocles as an instance of an insignificant place, VIII. 125

Belian gates of Babylon, opened to admit Darius' besieging army, III. 155, 158

Belus, a legendary descendant of Heracles, I. 7, and perhaps, VII. 61, apparently = the Asiatic god Bel, who has affinities with Heracles; the Babylonian form of " Bel " (Baal); identified with Zeus, I. 181 (the temple of Zeus Belus).

Bermius, a mountain range in Macedonia, VIII. 138

Bessi, a priestly clan among the Satrae of Thrace, VII. 111

Bias, (1) brother of the seer Melampus, IX. 34. (2) Bias of Priene, one of the " Seven Sages," his advice to Croesus, I. 27; to the Ionians, I. 170

Bisaltae, a Thracian tribe, VIII. 116; their country Bisaltia, VII. 115

INDEX

INDEX

Bubastis, (1) an Egyptian goddess identified with Artemis, II. 59, 83, 137, 156. (2) An Egyptian town, II. 59, 67, 137, 154, 158, 166. (Bubastite province, II. 166)

Bucolic mouth of the Nile artificial, II. 17

Budii, a Median tribe, I. 101

Budini, a people adjacent to Scythia, IV. 21, 102, 105, 119, 122, 136; their town of wood, and their Greek customs, IV. 108

Bulis, a Spartan, his offer to expiate the Spartan killing of Persian envoys by surrendering himself to Xerxes, VII. 134–137

Bura, a town in Argolis, I. 145

Busae, a Median tribe, I. 101

Busiris, a town in the Delta with a temple of Isis, II. 59, 61; Busirite province, II. 165

Butacides, a man of Croton, V. 47

Buto, a town in the Delta, with a cult of Apollo and Artemis, and an oracular shrine of Leto (Uat), II. 59, 63, 67, 75, 83, 111, 133, 152, III. 64; description of the temple, II. 155

Bybassia, a peninsula in Caria, I. 174

Byzantium, IV. 87, VI. 33; beauty of its site, IV. 144; taken by Otanes, V. 26; annexed by Ionian rebels, V. 103; occupied by Histiaeus, VI. 5, 26; Artabazus there in return to Asia, IX. 89

Cabales, a small tribe in northern Libya, near Barca, IV. 171

Cabalees, a people on the Lycian border, their tribute to Persia, III. 90; in Xerxes' army, VII. 77

Cabiri, minor deities worshipped in many places, in Samothrace and Memphis, II. 51, III. 37

Cadmeans, alleged Phoenician immigrants into Greece with Cadmus, I. 56, 146, V. 57; a Cadmean script, V. 59; once settled at Thebes, IX. 27; a " Cadmean victory " one where victors are no better off than vanquished, I. 166

Cadmus, (1) a Tyrian, son of Agenor, in Boeotia, II. 49; chronology, II. 145 (cp. Cadmeans). (2) A Coan, son of Scythes; an emissary from Gelon of Sicily, VII. 163

Cadytis, a town in Syria (Gaza), III. 5; taken by Necos, II. 159

Caïcus, a river between Lydia and Mysia, VI. 28, VII. 42

Caeneus, a Corinthian, father of Eëtion, V. 92

Calamisa (or Calama), in Samos, IX. 96

Calasiries, one of the Egyptian warrior tribes, II. 164; some account of them, II. 166, 168; in Mardonius' army at Plataea, IX. 32

INDEX

Callantiae, an Indian people, III. 97; perhaps the same as the Callatiae, *q.v.*

Callatebus, a town in Lydia on Xerxes' line of march, VII. 31

Callatiae, Indian cannibals, III. 38

Calchas, the legendary seer, VII. 51

Calchedon (or Chalcedon), on the Hellespont, IV. 85; its site compared with that of Byzantium, IV. 144; taken by Otanes, V. 26; burnt by Phoenicians, VI. 33

Calliades, archon at Athens in 480 B.C., VIII. 51

Callias, (1) an Elean seer, acting with Croton in its war with Sybaris, V. 44. (2) An Athenian, son of Hipponicus; an envoy to Xerxes' son Artoxerxes in 448 B.C., VII. 151. (3) Grandfather of the above, a noted Athenian champion of freedom and enemy of Pisistratus, VI. 121

Callicrates, a Spartan killed (but not in actual fighting) at Plataea, IX. 72

Callimachus of Aphidnae, the Athenian polemarch, with the army at Marathon, his vote for battle, VI. 109, 110; his death, VI. 114

Calliphon, a man of Croton, III. 125

Callipidae, "Greek Scythians" near the town of Borysthenes, IV. 17

Callipolitae, settlers in Sicily from the adjacent town of Naxos VII. 154

Calliste, old name of the island of Thera, IV. 147

Calydnians, islanders in Xerxes' fleet, VII. 99

Calynda, on the frontier of Lycia, I. 172; Calyndians in Xerxes' fleet, VIII. 87

Camarina, in Sicily, VII. 154; its citizens transferred to Syracuse by Gelon, VII. 156

Cambyses, (1) a Persian, son of Teïspes, son-in-law of Astyages and father of Cyrus, I. 107; elsewhere mostly a patronymic of Cyrus. (2) King of Persia, son of Cyrus, his accession, I. 208, II. 1; conquest of Egypt, I. 1–4, 9–16; expeditions to Ethiopia and Libya, 19–26; his sacrilegious and criminal acts while in Egypt, especially the murder of his brother, III. 27–38; Magian usurpation of the Persian throne, and Cambyses' death, III. 61–66; Greeks in Egypt during Cambyses' occupation, III. 139; Cambyses' punishment of an unjust judge, V. 25 (other unimportant reff.)

Camicus, a town in Sicily, scene of Minos' death, VII. 169

Camirus, a Dorian town in Rhodes, I. 144

INDEX

INDEX

Casian mountain, low sandhills on the eastern frontier of Egypt, II. 6, III. 5

Casmena, a town in Sicily, VII. 155

Caspatyrus, a town probably on the Indus, III. 102, IV. 44

Caspian Sea, its size, I. 203; northern boundary of the Persian empire, IV. 40; Caspian tribute paid to Persia, III. 92; Caspii in Xerxes' army, VII. 67, 86

Cassandane, mother of Cambyses, II. 1, III. 2

Cassiterides (tin-producing) islands, perhaps Britain, their existence questioned by Herodotus, III. 115

Castalian spring at Delphi, VIII. 39

Casthanaea, a town in Magnesia, VII. 183, 188

Catadupa, the first or Assuan cataract of the Nile, source of the river, according to Herodotus, II. 17

Catarrhactes, a tributary of the Maeander, rising at Celaenae, VII. 26

Catiari, one of the oldest Scythian tribes, IV. 6

Caucasa, on the S.E. coast of Chios, V. 33

Caucasus range, I. 104, 203, III. 97, IV. 12

Caucones, an Arcadian people, one of the most ancient of Greek races, I. 147, IV. 148

Caunus, near Caria and Lycia, origin of its people, I. 172; attacked and subdued by the Medes, I. 171, 176; participation in Ionian revolt against Darius, V. 103

Caystrius, a river near Sardis, V. 100

Caÿstrobius, a Proconnesian, father of Aristeas, IV. 13

Ceans, natives of Ceos in the Aegean, IV. 35; in the Greek fleet, VIII. 1, 46

Cecrops, king of Athens, VII. 141, VIII. 53; Athenians called Cecropidae, VIII. 44

Celaenae, a town in Phrygia at the junction of the Marsyas and Maeander, on Xerxes' route, VII. 26

Celeas, a Spartan companion of Dorieus' voyage to Italy, V. 46

Celti, the farthest west (but one) of all European nations, beyond the Pillars of Heracles, II. 33; source of the Danube in their country, IV. 49

Ceos, apparently a place in Salamis (but not identified), VIII. 76; clearly not the island in the Aegean.

Cephallenia, an island west of Greece, its contingent at Plataea, IX. 28

Cephenes, an old name for the Persians, VII. 61

INDEX

325

INDEX

INDEX

Cnidus, in Caria, on the Triopian promontory, I. 174; a Dorian town, I. 144, II. 178; attempted restoration by Cnidians of a Tarentine exile, III. 138

Cnoethus, an Aeginetan, VI. 88

Cnosus, in Crete, the capital city of Minos' empire, III. 122

Cobon, a Delphian, his corruption of the oracle in Cleomenes' interest, VI. 66

Codrus, an ancient king of Athens, ancestor of the Caucones (q.v.), I. 147; of Pisistratus, V. 65; Dorian invasion of Attica during his rule, V. 76; father of the founder of Miletus, IX. 97

Coenyra, a place in Thasos, VI. 47

Coes, of Mytilene, his advice to Darius to leave Ionians guarding the bridge of the Ister, IV. 97; made despot of Mytilene, V. 11; his death, V. 38

Colaeus, a Samian shipmaster, IV. 152

Colaxaïs, the youngest of the three brothers who founded the Scythian race, IV. 5, 7

Colchis, on the Euxine, its situation, I. 104, IV. 37, 40; Egyptian origin of Colchians, II. 104; tribute to Persia, III. 97; in Xerxes' army, VII. 79

Colias, adjective of an Attic promontory where wrecks were driven ashore after Salamis, VIII. 96

Colophon, an Ionian town in Lydia, I. 142; taken by Gyges, I. 14; Apaturia not celebrated at Colophon, I. 147; civil strife there, I. 150

Colossae, a town in Phrygia, on Xerxes' route, VII. 30

Combrea, a town in Chalcidice, VII. 123

Compsantus, a river in Thrace, VII. 109

Coniaean, of Conium in Phrygia, V. 63 (but " Gonnaean " should probably be read).

Contadesdus, a river in Thrace, IV. 90

Copaïs lake in Boeotia, VIII. 135

Coresus, near Ephesus, on the coast, V. 100

Corinth, its treasury at Delphi, I. 14, IV. 162; despotism of Periander and his cruelty, I. 23, V. 92; his troubles with his son, and with Corcyra, III. 48–54; Corinthian estimation of artificers, II. 167; story of Cypselus, V. 92; Corinthian reluctance to invade Attica, V. 75; friendship with Athens, VI. 89; adjustment by Corinth of a quarrel between Athens and Thebes, VI. 108; Corinthians at Thermopylae, VII. 202; in the Greek fleet, VIII. 1, 21, 43; in the army at the Isthmus, VIII. 72; dispute between Themistocles and Adeimantus,

INDEX

VIII. 61; Corinthians' alleged desertion of the Greeks at Salamis, VIII. 94; Corinthians at Plataea, IX. 28, 31, 69; at Mycale, IX. 102, 105

Corobius, a Cretan merchant, employed by Greeks to guide them to Libya, IV. 151–153

Coronea, a town in Boeotia, V. 79

Corycian cave on Parnassus, a refuge for the Delphians, VIII. 36

Corydallus, a man of Anticyra, VII. 214

Corys, a river in Arabia, III. 9

Cos, an island off Caria, colonized by Dorians, I. 144; abdication of its despot Cadmus, VII. 164; Coans in Xerxes' fleet, VII. 99

Cotys, a legendary Lydian, IV. 45

Cranai, old name for Athenians, VIII. 44

Cranaspes, a Persian, III. 126

Crannon, in Thessaly, VI. 128

Crathis, (1) a river in Achaea, I. 145. (2) A river by Sybaris, V. 45

Cremni (cliffs), name of a port in Scythia, on the "Maeetian lake," IV. 20, 110

Crestonian country, in Thrace, V. 3, 5, VII. 124, 127, VIII. 116. The reading *Creston* in I. 57 is doubtful; *Croton* is suggested (not the town in Magna Graecia, but Cortona in Umbria).

Crete, Cretan origin of Lycurgus' Spartan laws, I. 65; beginning of Minos' rule, I. 173; Samian settlers in Crete, III. 59; connexion of Crete with the settlement of Cyrene, IV. 151, 154, 161; Cretan reason for not joining the Greeks against Xerxes, VII. 169–171; Lycians originally Cretan, VII. 92

Cretines, (1) a man of Magnesia in Greece, VII. 190. (2) A man of Rhegium, VII. 165

Crinippus, a man of Himera, VII. 165

Crisaean plain, in Locris, VIII. 32

Critalla, a town on Xerxes' route in Cappadocia, VII. 26

Critobulus, (1) a man of Cyrene, II. 181. (2) A man of Torone, made governor of Olynthus by the Persians, VIII. 127

Crius, a leading Aeginetan, sent to Athens as hostage for Aeginetan good faith, VI. 50, 73; his meeting with Themistocles at Salamis, VIII. 92

Crobyzi, a Thracian tribe, IV. 49

"Crocodiles' town," near Lake Moeris in Egypt; labyrinth there, II. 148

Croesus, king of Lydia, son of Alyattes, extent of his rule, I. 6, 26–28; Solon's visit to him, I. 28–33; story of his son Atys,

INDEX

INDEX

331

INDEX

live in a fertile country, IX. 122 (many other reff., mostly where the name is used as a patronymic). (2) Paternal grandfather of the above, I. 111

Cytissorus, a Colchian, custom respecting his descendants at Alus in Achaea, VII. 197

Dadicae, a people in the N.E. of the Persian empire; their tribute, III. 91; in Xerxes' army, VII. 66

Daedalus, sought by Minos, VII. 170

Daï, a nomad Persian tribe, I. 125

Damasithymus, (1) king of the Calyndians, in Xerxes' fleet at Salamis, VIII. 87. (2) A Carian officer in Xerxes' fleet, son of Candaules, VII. 98

Damasus of Siris, a suitor for Cleisthenes' daughter, VI. 127

Damia, a deity worshipped in Aegina and Epidaurus, V. 82, 83

Danaë, mother of Perseus, daughter of Acrisius, II. 91, VI. 53, VII. 61, 150

Danaus, his legendary migration to Greece from Chemmis in Egypt, II. 91, VII. 94; his daughters, II. 171, 182

Daphnae, near Pelusium, on the Egyptian frontier, II. 30, 107

Daphnis, despot of Abydos, IV. 138

Dardaneans, an Assyrian people, apparently, I. 189

Dardanus, a town on the Hellespont, V. 117, VII. 43

Darius, (1) king of Persia, son of Hystaspes; suspected by Cyrus, I. 209; story of his part in the conspiracy against the Magians, and his accession to the throne, III. 73–87; canal made by him in Egypt, II. 158, IV. 39; inquiry into varieties of custom, III. 38; tribute paid by his empire, III. 89–97; called " the huxter," III. 89; severity of his rule, III. 118, 119; punishment of Oroetes, III. 127, 128; Democedes at Darius' court, III. 129–132; plans against Greece, III. 134, 135; conquest of Samos, III. 139–149; reduction of Babylon, III. 150–160; Scythian expedition planned, IV. 1; Darius' passage of the Bosporus, march to the Ister, and invasion of Scythia, IV. 83–98; Scythian campaign and return to Asia, IV. 118–143; Cyrenaean expedition, IV. 200–204; transportation of Paeonians to Asia, V. 12–15; Histiaeus summoned by Darius to Susa, V. 24; Darius' anger against Athens for the burning of Sardis, and his dispatch of Histiaeus to Ionia, V. 105–107; reception of Scythes, VI. 24; estimation of Histiaeus, VI. 30; demand of earth and water from Greek states, VI. 48, 49; Demaratus at Darius' court, VI. 70; reasons for

INDEX

INDEX

INDEX

Eëropus, a king of Tegea, IX. 26

Eëtion, a Corinthian, father of Cypselus, V. 92

Egesta, a town in Sicily, allied with Phoenicians against Greeks, V. 46, VII. 158

Egis, a Spartan king, VII. 204

Egypt, its extent, II. 5–19; course of the Nile, II. 19–34; Egyptian custom and religion, I. 140, 182, 193, 198, II. 4, 35–98, IV. 168, 180, 186; kings of Egypt, II. 99–182; eschatology, II. 123; chronology, II. 142–146; the pyramids, II. 124–128; Egyptian origin of Dorian heroes, VI. 53–55; Solon in Egypt, I. 30; Scythian invasion, I. 105; alliance with Croesus, I. 77; Cambyses' invasion, III. 1–16; his sacrilege, III. 27, 28; Egypt a Persian province, III. 91; Athenian campaign in Egypt, III. 160; Darius' canal from the Nile, IV. 39; circumnavigation of Africa from Egypt, IV. 42, 43; Egypt and Cyrene, IV. 159; revolt of Egypt against Persia, VII. 1, 7; Egyptian bridge over the Hellespont, VII. 34; Egyptian marines in Persian fleet, VII. 89, VIII. 68, 100, IX. 32; their exploits at Artemisium, VIII. 17

Eïon, a town on the Strymon, VII. 25; its defence, and capture by the Greeks, VII. 107, 113; Xerxes said to have embarked there for Asia, VIII. 118

Elaeus, a town in the Thracian Chersonese, VI. 140, VII. 22; profanation of its shrine of Protesilaus, VII. 33, IX. 116, 120

Elatea, a town in Phocis, VIII. 33

Elbo, an island in the Delta, the refuge of the deposed king Anysis, II. 140

Eleon, a town in Boeotia, V. 43

Elephantine, on the Nile opposite Assuan, II. 9; the southern limit of Egypt, II. 17; close to the source of the Nile, II. 28; a Persian frontier guard there, II. 30; stone-quarries of Elephantine, II. 175; tribe of "Fish-eaters" there, III. 19

Eleusis, in Attica, scene of a battle, I. 30; the first objective of Cleomenes' invasion, V. 74, VI. 75; mysteries of Demeter-worship there and the vision of Dicaeus, VIII. 65; Greek forces there before Plataea, IX. 19; burning of the temple of Demeter by Persians, IX. 65

Elis; Elean management of Olympic games, II. 160; no mules in Elis, IV. 30; destruction of neighbouring towns, IV. 148; Elis the only Aetolian part of Peloponnese, VIII. 73; Eleans in the Greek force on the Isthmus, VIII. 72; too late at Plataea, IX. 77

INDEX

INDEX

Erechtheus, a legendary Attic hero; sacrifice offered to him by Epidaurians in return for Attic olive trees, v. 82; father of Orithyia, VII. 189; name of Athenians first used in his time, VIII. 44; his shrine on the Acropolis, VIII. 55

Eretria, in Euboea, Pisistratus in exile there, I. 61; native place of Gephyraei, v. 57; objective of Mardonius' campaign under Darius, VI. 43; of Datis, VI. 94, 98; subdued by Persians, VI. 100–102; Eretrian captives in Persia, VI. 119; contingent in Greek fleet, VIII. 1, 46; at Plataea, IX. 28, 31

Eridanus, a river in Europe, its existence doubted by Herodotus, III. 115

Erineus, a place in Doris, VIII. 43

Erinyes, avenging deities (of Laius and Oedipus), IV. 149

Erochus, a town in Phocis, burnt by the Persians, VIII. 33

Erxandrus, a Mytilenaean, IV. 97, v. 37

Erythea, an island alleged to be outside the Pillars of Heracles, IV. 8

Erythrae, (1) a town in Boeotia, near Plataea, IX. 15, 19, 22. (2) An Ionian town in Asia Minor, I. 18, 142, VI. 8

Erythre bolos, "Red Earth," a town in Egypt, II. 111

Erythre thalassa, the Persian Gulf and the nearer part of the Indian Ocean; Phoenicians coming from it, I. 1, VII. 89; mouth of the Euphrates and the Tigris in the Red Sea, I. 180, 189; united with the Mediterranean, I. 203; Arabian mountains in the direction of the Red Sea, II. 8; our "Red Sea" ('Αράβιος κόλπος) an offshoot from it, II. 11; identical with the "Southern Sea," II. 158; captives settled by Persians in islands of the Red Sea, III. 93, VII. 80; Persia extends to its shores, IV. 37; Phoenician circumnavigation of Africa starting from the Red Sea, IV. 42; Ampe on the Red Sea, VI. 20

Eryx, in western Sicily, v. 43, 45

Eryxo, wife of the second Arcesilaus of Cyrene, IV. 160

Etearchus, (1) king of the Ammonians; visit of Cyrenaeans to him, II. 32. (2) King of Oaxus in Crete, IV. 154

Eteocles, son of Oedipus, v. 61

Ethiopians, of Meroë, II. 29; Ethiopian kings of Egypt, II. 100, 137–140; circumcision in Ethiopia, II. 104; Cambyses' mission to the "long-lived" Ethiopians, III. 17–26, 97; Ethiopia in relation to Egypt, II. 11, 28, 30, 110, 139, 146, 161; "Troglodyte" Ethiopians, IV. 183; "Ethiopians" of Asia, their tribute to Persia, III. 94; in Xerxes' army, VII. 70; Ethiopians in Cyprus, VII. 90

INDEX

INDEX

341

INDEX

Getae, a Thracian tribe said to believe in immortality, IV. 93, 118, V. 3

Gigonus, a town in Chalcidice, VII. 123

Giligamae, a Libyan tribe inland of Cyrene, IV. 169

Gillus, a Tarentine refugee in Persia, III. 138

Gindanes, a Libyan tribe, IV. 176

Glaucon, an Athenian, IX. 75

Glaucus, (1) son of Hippolochus, ancestor of a Lycian dynasty, I. 47. (2) Son of Epicydes, a Spartan; story of his attempted fraud told by Leutychides at Athens, VI. 86. (3) A Chian worker in metals, I. 25

Glisas, a town in Boeotia near Tanagra, IX. 43

Gnurus, a Scythian, father of Anacharsis, IV. 76

Gobryas, (1) son of Darius, an officer in Xerxes' army, VII. 72. (2) One of the seven conspirators against the Magians, III. 70–79; his advice to Darius in Scythia, IV. 132, 134; father of Mardonius, VI. 43; his daughter married to Darius, VII. 2 (elsewhere as a patronymic).

Goetosyrus, a Scythian deity identified with Apollo, IV. 59

Gonnus, a town in Thessaly, VII. 128, 173

Gordias, (1) father of Midas, VIII. 138. (2) King of Phrygia, son of Midas; father of Adrastus, I. 35, 45

Gorgo, daughter of Cleomenes, king of Sparta, V. 48; her advice to Cleomenes, V. 51; her interpretation of a message, VII. 239

Gorgon's head, brought from Libya by Perseus, II. 91

Gorgus, king of Salamis in Cyprus, V. 104, 115, VIII. 11; in Xerxes' fleet, VII. 98

Grinnus, king of Thera, his consultation of the Delphic oracle about a colony in Libya, IV. 150

Grynea, an Aeolian town in Asia Minor, I. 149

Gygaea, daughter of Amyntas of Macedonia, married to Bubares, a Persian, V. 21, VIII. 136

Gygaean lake, in Lydia, I. 93

Gyges, (1) king of Lydia; his accession after murdering Candaules, I. 8–13; his gifts to Delphi, I. 14. (2) A Lydian, III. 122, V. 121

Gyndes, a river in Assyria diverted by Cyrus from its course, I. 189, 202

Gyzantes, a tribe in the western part of Libya, IV. 194

Haemus, a mountain range in Thrace (the Balkans), rivers flowing from it into the Danube, IV. 49

INDEX

INDEX

344

INDEX

commander of Xerxes' "Ten Thousand," VII. 83; governor
of the seaboard of W. Asia Minor, VII. 135; his command at
Thermopylae, VII. 211, 215, 218; with Xerxes in his flight
after Salamis, VIII. 113, 118

Hydrea, an island S.E. of Argolis, III. 59

Hyela, an Italian town (Velia) colonised by Phocaeans, I. 167

Hylaea (Woodland), a district of Scythia, east of the Borysthenes,
IV. 9, 18, 54, 76

Hyllees, a Sicyonian tribe so named after Cleisthenes' death,
V. 68

Hyllus, (1) son of Heracles, ancestor of the Spartan royal families,
VI. 52, VII. 204, VIII. 131; his death, IX. 26. (2) A tributary
of the river Hermus in Lydia, I. 80

Hymaees, a Persian commander in the second Ionian revolt,
V. 116, 122

Hymessus (Hymettus), a hill outside Athens, VI. 137

Hypachaei, an old name for Cilicians, VII. 91

Hypacyris, a Scythian river, apparently east of the Borysthenes,
IV. 47, 55

Hypanis, a Scythian river (Boug), IV. 18, 47, 52, 81

Hyperanthes, a son of Darius, killed at Thermopylae, VII. 224

Hyperboreans, a people alleged to inhabit the farthest north of
Europe, IV. 13; story of their communication with Delos,
IV. 32–36

Hyperoche, one of two maidens alleged to have come to Delos
from the Hyperboreans, IV. 33

Hyrcanians, a people in the Persian empire, S. of the Caspian,
III. 117; in Xerxes' army, VII. 62

Hyrgis (or Syrgis), a Scythian river (probably the Donetz), IV. 57

Hyria, a town in S. Italy (Oria), alleged to be founded by Cretans,
VII. 170

Hyroeades, a Mardian, his discovery of a way into Sardis, I. 84

Hysiae, a village on the slopes of Cithaeron, in Attica; taken
by Boeotians, V. 74; VI. 108; part played by it on the battlefield of Plataea, IX. 15, 25

Hysseldomus, a Carian, VII. 98

Hystanes, a Persian, VII. 77

Hystaspes, (1) father of Darius; his pledge to Cyrus of Darius'
fidelity, I. 209, 210; governor of the province of Persia, III.
70. (Elsewhere a patronymic.) (2) A son of Darius, VII. 64

Hytennees, a Pisidian tribe; their tribute to the Persian empire,
III. 90

INDEX

Iadmon, a Samian, his slaves Rhodopis and Aesopus, II. 134
Iamidae, a family of diviners in Elis, V. 44, IX. 33
Iapygia, in the heel of Italy, III. 138, IV. 99, VII. 170
Iardanus, a Lydian, I. 7
Iason, his voyage in the Argo, IV. 179, VII. 193
Iatragoras, an agent of the Ionians in revolt against Darius, V. 37
Ibanollis, a man of Mylasa, V. 37, 121
Iberians, their traffic with Phocaea, I. 163; attack on Gelon of Sicily, VII. 165
Icarian sea, VI. 95
Ichnae, a town in Macedonia, near the coast, VII. 123
Ichthyophagi, a tribe inhabiting Elephantine, Cambyses' interpreters in his mission to the Ethiopians, III. 19–23
Ida, a mountain in the Troad, I. 151; Xerxes' route past it, VII. 42
Idanthyrsus, a Scythian king, IV. 76; in command of Scythians against Darius, IV. 120; his defiance of Darius, IV. 127
Idriad district in Caria, V. 118
Ielysus, a Dorian town in Rhodes, I. 144
Ienysus, a town in Syria, near the Egyptian frontier, III. 5.
Iliad, story of Paris and Helen in it, II. 116
Ilissus, a river in Attica; temple of Boreas built near it, VII. 189
Ilium, the Trojan war there, I. 5, II. 10, 117–120, VII. 20, 161; Troad subdued by Persians, V. 122; traversed by Xerxes, VII. 42
Illyria, customs of the Eneti there, I. 196; river Angrus there, IV. 49; flight to Illyria of the Temenid brothers, VIII. 137; Illyrian invasion of Greece, IX. 43
Imbros, in the N.E. Aegean, V. 26, VI. 41, 104
Inachus, father of Io, I. 1.
Inaros of Libya, his revolt against Persia in 460 B.C., III. 12, 15, VII. 7
Indians, their tribute to Persia, III. 94; their customs, III. 97–102, 104; conquest by Darius, IV. 44; most numerous people in the world, V. 3; in Xerxes' army, VII. 65, 86; with Mardonius, VIII. 113, IX. 31.   Indian dogs, I. 192, VII. 187
Indus, the river, Darius' exploration of it, IV. 44
Ino, wife of Athamas, VII. 197
Intaphrenes, one of the seven conspirators against the Magians III. 70, 78; his presumption and punishment, III. 118

INDEX

Inyx (or Inycus), a town in Sicily, probably near Acragas, VI. 123

Io, daughter of Inachus, her abduction, I. 1, 5; depicted in the form of a cow, II. 41

Iolcus, a town offered by the Thessalians to the exiled Hippias, V. 94

Ion, eponymous ancestral hero of the Ionians, V. 66, VII. 94, VIII. 44

Ionians, subdued by Croesus, I. 6; Dorian and Ionian races, I. 56; threatened by Cyrus, I. 141, 142; their settlements in Asia, I. 143–153, II. 178; conquest by Cyrus, I. 159–171; Ionian beliefs about Egypt refuted, II. 15, 16; Sesostris' inscriptions in Ionia, II. 106; Ionian pirates in Egypt, II. 152; Amasis' Ionian guards, II. 163; tribute paid by Ionians to Persia, III. 90; Ionians with Darius' Scythian expedition, IV. 89; left to guard the Ister bridge, IV. 97, 128, 133, 136–142; Ionian revolt against Darius, V. 28–38; Ionian and Phoenician writing, V. 58, 59; Ionian tribes in Attica, V. 69; Ionian dress, V. 87; course of Ionian revolt, and burning of Sardis, V. 97–103, 108–115; reduction of Ionian towns, V. 116–123; continuance of revolt and its final suppression, VI. 1–32 passim; Persian organisation of Ionia, VI. 42; Ionia "exposed to many risks" (in story of Glaucus), VI. 86; Ionians in Xerxes' fleet, VII. 94; Themistocles' appeal to them, VIII. 22; Athenians called Ionians, VIII. 44; Ionians in Peloponnese, VIII. 73; Ionian ships with Xerxes at Salamis, VIII. 85, 90; appeals from Ionia to the Greeks for help, VIII. 132, IX. 90; Ionian desertion of Persians at Mycale, IX. 98, 103; revolt against Persia, IX. 104, 106; (other unimportant reff.)

Ionian sea, VII. 20, IX. 92

Iphiclus, father of Protesilaus, IX. 116

Iphigenia, daughter of Agamemnon; human sacrifice offered to her in Scythia, IV. 103

Ipni (Ovens), name of rocks at the foot of Pelion, the scene of a Persian shipwreck, VII. 188

Irasa, in Libya, the site of the founding of Cyrene, IV. 158

Irens, Spartan young men between 20 and 30 years of age, IX. 85

Is (Hit), a place eight days distant from Babylon, on a river of the same name, producing bitumen, I. 179

Isagoras, an Athenian, rival of Cleisthenes the reformer, and supported by Sparta, V. 66, 70–74

INDEX

INDEX

INDEX

INDEX

INDEX

Lysimachus, an Athenian, father of Aristides, VIII. 79

Lysistratus, an Athenian oracle-monger, VIII. 96

Macae, a tribe on the Libyan coast, IV. 175, V. 42

Macedonians, a name for Dorians in their early settlements near Mt. Pindus, I. 56, VIII. 43

Macedonia, access to it from the east, V. 17; fate of Persian envoys there, V. 18–20; subdued by Mardonius, VI. 44; passes from Macedonia into Thessaly, VII. 128, 173; Macedonians in Xerxes' army, VII. 185, at Plataea, IX. 31; story of the beginnings of the Temenid dynasty, VIII. 137–139; Macedonians governing Boeotia for Persians, VIII. 34 (see also Alexander).

Machlyes, a tribe on the Libyan coast, IV. 178, 180

Macistius, see Masistius.

Macistus, a town in the west of the Peloponnese, founded by the Minyae, IV. 148

Macrones, a tribe S.E. of the Euxine, II. 104; their tribute to Persia, III. 94; in Xerxes' army, VII. 78

Mactorium, a town near Gela in Sicily, VII. 153

Madyes, a Scythian king; his invasion of Media and conquest of Asia, I. 104

Madytus, a town in the Thracian Chersonese, near Xerxes' bridge, VII. 33, IX. 120

Maeander, a river between Lydia and Caria; its windings, II. 29; source at Celaenae, VII. 26; crossed by Xerxes, VII. 30

Maeandrius, secretary to Polycrates of Samos, III. 124; Polycrates' deputy, III. 142; his death, III. 143

Maeëtae, a tribe north of the Maeëtian lake, IV. 123; the Tanaïs called Maeëtian, IV. 45

Maeëtian lake (Palus Maeotis, Sea of Azov), its distance from the Phasis, I. 104; mouth of the Tanaïs there, IV. 57, 100; nearly as large as the Euxine, IV. 86, 110, 116, 120, 123

Magdolus (Migdol of O.T.), on the Egyptian and Syrian frontier; alleged scene of a battle (really fought not here but at Megiddo) between Egyptians and Syrians, II. 159

Magi, a Median tribe of magicians and interpreters of dreams, I. 101; their services in this respect, I. 107, 120, 128, 132, 140, VII. 19, 37, 43, 113, 191; the Magian usurpation of royalty and its end, III. 61, 63–69, 71, 74–80

Magnesia, (1) a district in Thessaly, Xerxes' fleet there, VII. 183, 193; Magnesians in Xerxes' army, VII. 132, 185. (2) A

355

INDEX

Mardontes, a Persian, one of Xerxes' officers, VII. 80; in command of Persian fleet after Salamis, VIII. 130; his death at Mycale, IX. 102

Marea, a frontier post in western Egypt, II. 18, 30

Mares, a tribe apparently on the S.E. coast of the Euxine; tribute to Persia, III. 94; in Xerxes' army, VII. 79

Mariandyni, a tribe in Paphlagonia; tribute to Persia, III. 90; in Xerxes' army, VII. 72

Maris, a northern tributary of the Danube, according to Herodotus (but this is wrong, if Maris is modern Marosch), IV. 49

Maron, a Spartan distinguished at Thermopylae, VII. 227

Maronea, a Greek town in Thrace, on Xerxes' route, VII. 109

Marsyas, (1) the "Silenus" according to legend worsted in a musical competition and flayed by Apollo, VII. 26. (2) A river in Caria, V. 118. (The better known Marsyas in Phrygia is called Catarrhactes by Herodotus, VII. 26.)

Mascames, Persian governor of Doriscus in Thrace; his defence of the town, VII. 105

Masistes, son of Darius, one of the six generals of Xerxes' army, VII. 82, 121; his quarrel with Artaÿntes, IX. 107; victim of Xerxes' adultery and cruelty, IX. 110–113.

Masistius, a Persian officer in Xerxes' army, VII. 79; in command of cavalry at Plataea, IX. 20; his death, and mourning for him, IX. 22, 24

Maspii, a Persian tribe, I. 125

Massages, a Persian officer in Xerxes' army, VII. 71

Massagetae, a people apparently N. of the Caspian; Cyrus' campaign against them, I. 201, 204–208, 211–214; their customs, I. 215, 216; Scythians driven from their country by Massagetae, IV. 11

Massalia (Massilia, Marseilles), V. 9

Matieni, a people of doubtful locality; on the right of the Halys, I. 72; source of the Araxes, I. 202; of the Gyndes, I. 189; of the modern "Greater Zab," V. 52; west of Armenia, V. 49; tribute to Persia, III. 94; in Xerxes' army, VII. 72

Matten, a Tyrian officer in Xerxes' fleet, VII. 98

Mausolus, a man of Cindye in Caria, V. 118

Mecisteus, brother of Adrastus according to legend, and slain by Melanippus, V. 67

Mecyberna, a town on the Sithonian promontory of Chalcidice, VII. 122

Medea, her abduction by Iason, I. 2; Media called after her, VII. 62

357

INDEX

Medians (as distinct from Persians), their war with Lydia, I. 16; the Halys their frontier, I. 72; Cyaxares' feud with Scythians, I. 73; Medians' revolt from Assyria, and growth of their power, I. 95–102; conquered by Scythians, I. 104, IV. 1; their liberation, I. 106, IV. 4; subjection of Media to Persia by Cyrus, I. 123–130; Median system of government, I. 134; their dress, I. 135, III. 84, V. 9; Babylonians alarmed by Median power, I. 185; Median tribute to Persia, III. 92; horses, III. 106, VII. 40; Media on the northern frontier of Persia, IV. 37; Medians in Xerxes' army, VII. 62; at Thermopylae, VII. 210; in Mardonius' army, VIII. 113, IX. 31, 40

Megabates, a Persian general, Darius' cousin, V. 32, 35

Megabazus, (1) a Persian general, left by Darius in Thrace on his Scythian expedition, IV. 143; Darius' estimation of him, *ib.*; his operations in Thrace, V. 1, 10, 12, 14, 17, 23. (2) One of Xerxes' admirals, son of Megabates, VII. 97

Megabyzus, (1) a Persian, one of the seven conspirators against the Magians, III. 70; advocate of oligarchy for Persia, III. 81. (2) A Persian, father of Zopyrus, III. 153. (3) Son of Zopyrus; one of the generals of Xerxes' army, VII. 82, 121; in command subsequently in Egypt, III. 160

Megacles, (1) an Athenian, father of Alcmeon, VI. 125. (2) Son of Alcmeon; leader of the " Men of the Coast," I. 59; father-in-law of Pisistratus, I. 61; married to the daughter of Cleisthenes of Sicyon, VI. 127, 130. (3) Grandson of Megacles (2), and grandfather of Pericles, VI. 131

Megacreon, of Abdera, his saying about the feeding of Xerxes' army, VII. 120

Megadostes, a Persian, VII. 105

Megapanus, a Persian officer in Xerxes' army, afterwards governor of Babylon, VII. 62

Megara, a Dorian settlement, on the borders of Attica, V. 76; Megarians in the Greek fleet, VIII. 1, 45; in Pausanias' army, IX. 21, 28, 31; their disaster, IX. 69, 85. Megarians of Sicily, their treatment by Gelon, VII. 156

Megasidrus, a Persian, VII. 72

Megistias, an Acarnanian diviner, with Leonidas at Thermopylae, VII. 219, 221; his epitaph, VII. 228

Meïonians, old name of Lydians, I. 7; in Xerxes' army, VII. 74

Melampus, a legendary hero and teacher; his introduction of the cult of Dionysus into Greece, II. 49; ancestor of Megistias, VII. 221; his demand of privileges at Argos, IX. 34

INDEX

Melampygus, name of a rock on the mountain side above Thermopylae, VII. 216

Melanchlaeni (Black-Cloaks), a tribe N. of Scythia, IV. 20, 100; their customs, IV. 107; their part in the war with Darius, IV. 119, 125

Melanippus, (1) a legendary Theban hero; his cult introduced at Sicyon, V. 67. (2) A Mytilenaean, a friend of the poet Alcaeus, V. 95

Melanthius, an Athenian commander sent to assist the Ionian rebels against Darius, V. 97

Melanthus, father of Codrus, I. 147, V. 65

Melas (black), epithet of (1) a river in Thrace, crossed by Xerxes, VII. 58. (2) A bay into which the above flows, VI. 41, VII. 58. (3) A river in Malis near Thermopylae, VII. 198

Meles, king of Sardis, I. 84

Meliboea, near the coast of Magnesia; wreck of Xerxes' fleet near it, VII. 188

Melians (of Melis, or Malis), their submission to Xerxes, VII. 132; mountains of Melis, VII. 198; Thermopylae in Melis, VII. 201; discovery of the Anopaea path, VII. 215; Melians in Persian armies, VIII. 66, IX. 31; Melian gulf a stage on the way from the Hyperboreans to Delos, IV. 33

Melians of Melos, colonists from Lacedaemon, in the Greek fleet, VIII. 46, 48

Melissa, wife of Periander of Corinth, III. 50, V. 92

Membliarus, a Phoenician, founder of a settlement in the island of Calliste or Thera, IV. 147

Memnon, legendary king of Ethiopia; a rock figure in Ionia wrongly taken to represent him, II. 106; Susa called " Memnonian," V. 53, VII. 151

Memphis, in Egypt, its temple of " Hephaestus," II. 3, 112, 153; pyramids there, II. 8; hills above it, II. 12, 158; Nile flood below Memphis, II. 97, 99; works of Min there, II. 99; precinct of Proteus, II. 112; quarries of Memphis, II. 175; water supply from Memphis, III. 6; Memphis taken by Cambyses, III. 13; his return thither from Ethiopia, III. 25; his sacrilege there, III. 37; Persian garrison there, III. 91; Darius and Syloson at Memphis, III. 139

Menares, a Spartan, father of Leutychides, VI. 65, 71, VIII. 131

Mende, a town on the promontory of Pallene in Chalcidice, VII. 123

Mendes, an Egyptian deity; identified with Pan, II. 42, 46;

359

INDEX

Mendesian province, II. 42, 46; inhabited by one of the
Egyptian warrior tribes, II. 166; Mendesian mouth of the
Nile, II. 17

Menelaus, (1) brother of Agamemnon; his visit to Egypt, II.
118, 119; Cretans reminded of their assistance of Menelaus
before Troy, VII. 169, 171. (2) A harbour near Cyrene, IV.
169

Menius, a Spartan, brother-in-law of Leutychides, VI. 71

Merbalus, an officer in Xerxes' fleet, from the island of Aradus,
VII. 98

Mermnadae, the reigning dynasty in Lydia from Gyges to Croesus,
I. 7, 14

Meroë, on the Nile, the capital of Ethiopia, II. 29 (probably
Napata)

Mesambria, a town on the Thracian coast of the Aegean, IV. 93,
VI. 33, VII. 108

Messapii, a people near Tarentum, said to be of Cretan origin,
VII. 170

Messene, in Sicily (Messina), otherwise called Zancle; a Coän
settlement there, VII. 164

Messenia, its alliance with Samos, III. 47; wars with Sparta,
V. 49, IX. 35, 64

Metapontium, near Croton in Italy, its story of the reincarna-
tion of Aristeas, IV. 15

Metiochus, son of the younger Miltiades, his capture by Persians,
VI. 41

Metrodorus, one of the Hellespontian despots with Darius'
Scythian expedition, IV. 138

Micythus, governor of Rhegium, his defeat by Messapians and
his offerings at Olympia, VII. 170

Midas, king of Phrygia, son of Gordias, his offerings at Delphi,
I. 14; his gardens in Macedonia, VIII. 138

Miletus, in Caria, attacked by Gyges, I. 14; war with Alyattes,
I. 17–22; an Ionian town, I. 142; agreement with Cyrus,
I. 169; port of Borysthenes a Milesian settlement, IV. 78;
wealth and dissensions of Miletus, V. 28, 29; Aristagoras its
governor, V. 30; Milesians defeated by Persians in Ionic
revolt, V. 120; threatened attack of Miletus by Persians, VI.
5–7; siege, capture, and depopulation of the town, VI. 18–
22; Phrynichus' drama on the subject, VI. 22; Persian fleet
off Miletus, VI. 31; story of the Milesian and Glaucus, VI. 86;
Miletus' foundation by Neleus, IX. 97; Milesians' desertion

INDEX

Mophi, one of two hills alleged to be near the source of the Nile (see Crophi), II. 28

Moschi, a tribe at the E. end of the Euxine, their tribute to Persia, III. 94; in Xerxes' army, VII. 78

Mossynoeci, a tribe between Armenia and the Euxine, their tribute to Persia, III. 94; in Xerxes' army, VII. 78

Munychia, on the Attic coast E. of the Piraeus, the eastern extremity of Xerxes' line before Salamis, VIII. 76

Murychides, a Hellespontian envoy from Mardonius to the Athenians, IX. 4

Musaeus, his oracles, VII. 6, VIII. 96, IX. 43

Mycale, an Ionian promontory opposite Samos; Panionium there, I. 148; flight of Chians thither after Lade, VI. 16; defeat of Persians by Greeks at Mycale, IX. 90, 96–101

Mycenaeans, at Thermopylae, VII. 202; Heraclidae and Mycenaeans, IX. 27; Mycenaeans in Pausanias' army, IX. 31

Mycerinus, king of Egypt, son of Cheops, his virtues and misfortunes, and his way of prolonging his life, II. 129–133; his buildings, and economic state of Egypt in his time, II. 136

Myci, a tribe probably in the south of Persia, their tribute, III. 93; in Xerxes' army, VII. 98

Myconus, an island in the Aegean, near Delos, VI. 118

Myecphorite province of Egypt, inhabited by one of the warrior tribes, II. 166

Mygdonia, a district on the Thermaic gulf, VII. 123, 127

Mylasa, a town in Caria; temple of Zeus there, I. 171

Mylitta, an Assyrian deity identified with Aphrodite, I. 131, 199

Myrcinus, a town of the Edonians in Thrace, given to Histiaeus, V. 11, 23; Aristagoras' retreat thither, V. 126

Myriandric gulf, the bay of Issus in Asia Minor, IV. 38

Myrina, (1) an Aeolian town in Mysia, I. 149. (2) A town in Lemnos, taken by Miltiades, VI. 140

Myrmex (the Ant), name of a reef between Magnesia and Sciathus, VII. 183

Myron, grandfather of Cleisthenes of Sicyon, VI. 126

Myrsilus, Greek name for Candaules, despot of Sardis, I. 7

Myrsus, (1) father of Candaules, I. 7. (2) A Lydian emissary of Oroetes, III. 122; his death in battle in Caria, V. 121

Mys, a man of Europus sent by Mardonius to consult oracles, VIII. 133–135

Mysia, plagued by a wild boar, I. 36; Mysians " brothers " of the Carians, I. 171; their tribute to Persia, III. 90; legendary

362

INDEX

INDEX

Nothon, an Eretrian, vi. 100

Notium, an Aeolian town in Asia Minor, i. 149

Nudium, a town in the W. of the Peloponnese, founded by the Minyae, iv. 148

Nymphodorus, of Abdera, his betrayal of Spartan envoys to the Athenians, vii. 137

Nysa, in Ethiopia, called "the sacred," its cult of Dionysus, ii. 146, iii. 97

Oarizus, a Persian, vii. 71

Oarus, a river in Scythia running into the Palus Maeotis, iv. 123

Oasis, a town eight days west of the Egyptian Thebes (apparently the modern "Great oasis" of Khargeh), inhabited by Samians; reached by Cambyses' force sent against the Ammonians, iii. 26

Oaxus, a town in Crete, ruled by Etearchus, iv. 154

Oceanus, the circle of sea (or river) supposed to surround the whole world; this theory questioned by Herodotus, ii. 21, 23, iv. 8, 36

Octamasades, a king of Scythia; his murder of his brother Scyles, iv. 80

Ocytus, a Corinthian, father of Adimantus, viii. 5

Odomanti, a Thracian or Paeonian tribe inhabiting the range of Pangaeum, v. 16 (if the reading be right), vii. 112

Odrysae, a Thracian tribe on Darius' route to the Danube, iv. 92

Odyssey, quoted by Herodotus, ii. 116, iv. 29

Oea, a place in Aegina; figures of Damia and Auxesia carried thither, v. 83

Oebares, (1) Darius' groom; his trick to ensure Darius' election as king, iii. 85–88. (2) Persian governor at Dascyleum, son of Megabazus, vi. 33

Oedipus, son of Laïus of Thebes, his "avenging deities," iv. 149; v. 60

Oenoe, a northern division of Attica, taken by the Boeotians, v. 74

Oenone, ancient name of Aegina, viii. 46

Oenotria, the toe of Italy, i. 167

Oenussae, islands between Chios and Asia Minor; the Phocaeans' proposal to buy them from Chios, i. 165

Oeobazus, (1) a Persian, Darius' cruel treatment of him, iv. 84.

INDEX

(2) A Persian, father of Siromitres, VII. 68. (3) A Persian fugitive from the Greeks in Thrace, his death there, IX. 115, 119

Oeolycus, son of Theras of Sparta; origin of his name, IV. 149

Oëroë, a tributary of the Asopus, on or near the battlefield of Plataea, IX. 51

Oeta, the mountain range S. of Thermopylae, VII. 176, 217

Oetosyrus, a variant of Goetosyrus, q.v.

Olbiopolitae, Greek name for the people of the Borysthenite port (Olbia) on the Euxine, IV. 18

Olen, a Lycian hymn-writer, IV. 35

Olenus, a town on the seacoast of Achaea, I. 145

Oliatus of Mylasa, his seizure by the Ionians, V. 37

Olophyxus, a town on the promontory of Athos, VII. 22

Olorus, a Thracian king, father-in-law of the younger Miltiades, VI. 39

Olympia, offerings there, VII. 170, IX. 81; sacrifice to obtain oracles, VIII. 134

Olympic games, I. 59; before battle of Thermopylae, VII. 206; of Salamis, VIII. 72; victories won by Philippus, V. 47; Cylon, V. 71; Miltiades the elder, VI. 36; Demaratus, VI. 70; Cimon, VI. 103; Callias, VI. 122; Alcmeon, VI. 125; Cleisthenes, VI. 126; Hieronymus, IX. 33; crown of olive given as the prize, VIII. 26; management of games by Eleans, II. 160, VI. 127; competition limited to Greeks, V. 22

Olympiodorus, an Athenian leader at Plataea, IX. 21

Olympus, Mount, (1) in Thessaly, I. 56; northern boundary of Thessaly, VII. 129; pass between Olympus and Ossa, VII. 173. (2) In Mysia; haunted by a wild boar, I. 36, 43; Mysians called Olympians, VII. 74

Olynthus, in Chalcidice, VII. 122; besieged and taken by Artabazus, VIII. 127

Ombrici, the people of central and northern Italy; Lydian settlement there, I. 94; source of a river Alpis in the country above the Ombrici, IV. 49

Oneatae, name given to a Sicyonian tribe by Cleisthenes, V. 68

Onesilus, a leader in the Cyprian revolt against Darius, V. 104, 108; his duel, and death in battle, V. 110–115

Onetes of Carystus, Herodotus' denial that he was the Persians' guide over the Anopaea pass at Thermopylae, VII. 214

Onochonus, a river in Thessaly alleged to have been drunk dry by Xerxes' army, VII. 129, 196

INDEX

Onomacritus, an Athenian purveyor or forger of oracles, at Xerxes' court, VII. 7

Onomastus of Elis, a suitor for Cleisthenes' daughter, VI. 127

Onuphite province of Egypt, inhabited by one of the warrior tribes, II. 166

Ophryneum, a town in the Troad, VII. 43

Opis, (1) a town on the Tigris (at the highest point of navigation), I. 189. (2) One of the Hyperborean pilgrims to Delos, IV. 35

Opoea, wife of Ariapithes and afterwards Scyles of Scythia, IV. 78

Opuntians, see Locrians.

Orbelus, a mountain in Thrace, in the neighbourhood of the lake-dwellers, V. 16

Orchomenus, (1) in Arcadia; its contingent at Thermopylae, VII. 202; at Plataea, IX. 28. (2) In Boeotia; Minyans there, I. 146; territory overrun by Persians, VIII. 34

Ordessus, a Scythian tributary of the Danube, IV. 48

Orestes, son of Agamemnon, discovery of his tomb at Tegea, I. 67

Orestheum, apparently on the route from Sparta to Megalopolis, IX. 11

Orgeus, a Thasian, VII. 118

Oricus, son of Ariapithes, king of Scythia, IV. 78

Oricus, the port of Apollonia in N.W. Greece, IX. 93

Orithyia, legendary daughter of Erechtheus and wife of Boreas, VII. 189

Orneatae, inhabitants of Orneae in Argolis, of inferior status like the Spartan Perioeci, VIII. 73

Oroetes, Persian governor of Sardis, his treacherous murder of Polycrates, III. 120–125; his downfall and death, III. 126–129

Oromedon, a Cilician, VII. 98

Oropus, on the Attic coast opposite Euboea, VI. 101

Orotalt, an Arabian deity identified with Dionysus, III. 8

Orphic rites, their similarity to Egyptian, II. 81

Orsiphantus, a Spartan, VII. 227

Orus, an Egyptian deity, identified with Apollo, q.v.

Osiris, identified with Dionysus, q.v.

Ossa, a mountain in Thessaly, I. 56; separated from Olympus by the Peneus, VII. 128, 173

Otanes, (1) a Persian, father of Xerxes' wife Amestris, VII. 40, 61, 82. (2) A Persian, made a judge in place of his father Sisamnes by Cambyses, V. 25; his command against the

INDEX

INDEX

Pammon of Scyros, his guidance of the Persian fleet to Magnesia, VII. 183

Pamphyli, name assumed by a Dorian tribe at Sicyon, V. 68

Pamphylia, in Asia Minor, subdued by Croesus, I. 28; tribute to Persia, III. 90; contingent in Xerxes' army, VII. 91; disparaged by Artemisia, VIII. 68

Pan, one of the "youngest" Greek gods, II. 145; his cult at Athens, VI. 105; identified with the Egyptian Mendes, II. 42, 46, 145

Panaetius of Tenos, his news of the Persian encirclement of Salamis, VIII. 82

Panathenaea, a festival celebrated every fourth year at Athens; murder of Hipparchus at it, V. 56

Pandion, a legendary Athenian, father of Lycus the hero of the Lycians, I. 173

Pangaeum, a mountain range in Thrace, V. 16, VII. 112

Panionia, the festival of the Ionian stock, I. 148

Panionium, an Ionian place of meeting for council or ceremonial, near Mycale, I. 148, 170, VI. 7

Panionius of Chios, his crime and punishment, VIII. 105, 106

Panites, a Messenian, his advice to the Spartans about the royal succession, VI. 52

Panopeus, on the borders of Phocis and Boeotia, Xerxes' army there, VIII. 34

Panormus, a harbour near Miletus, I. 157

Pantagnotus, brother of, and put to death by Polycrates of Samos, III. 39

Pantaleon, half brother of Croesus, put to death by him for conspiracy, I. 92

Pantares, a man of Gela, VII. 154

Panthialaei, a Persian tribe, I. 125

Panticapes, a river in Scythia east of the Borysthenes, IV. 18, 47, 54

Pantimathi, a tribe in the Persian empire, S. of the Caspian, their tribute, III. 92

Pantites, said to have been sent as a messenger to Sparta from Thermopylae, VII. 232

Papaeus, a Scythian deity identified with Zeus, IV. 59

Paphlagonians, west of the Halys in N. Asia Minor, I. 6, 72; their tribute to Persia, III. 90; in Xerxes' army, VII. 72

Paphos, Paphian ships in Xerxes' fleet, VII. 195

Papremis, a town in Egypt, its cult of Ares, II. 59; ceremonial

INDEX

line, IX. 46; special appeal to Athenians, IX. 60; instance of his generosity and courtesy, IX. 76, 79; bronze caldron dedicated by him on the Bosporus, IV. 81; his pride and ambition after the Persian war, V. 32, VIII. 3

Pausicae, a tribe S. of the Caspian; their tribute to Persia, III. 92

Pausiris, an Egyptian, permitted by the Persians to succeed to the governorship of his rebel father Amyrtaeus, III. 15

Pedasus (or Pedasa), a place in Caria, V. 121, VI. 20; singular story of a priestess there, I. 175, VIII. 104

Pedieis, a Phocian town burnt by the Persians, VIII. 33

Pelasgian, a name applied by Herodotus to the oldest known inhabitants and remains in Greece, contrasted with " Hellenic," I. 56; Pelasgian language probably non-Greek, I. 57; Pelasgian forts, *ib.*; Arcadia Pelasgian, I. 146; deities, II. 50–52; Hellas formerly called Pelasgia, II. 56; expulsion of Minyae by Pelasgians, IV. 145; Lemnos and Imbros Pelasgian, V. 26; expulsion of Pelasgi from Attica, VI. 137–139; *cp.* V. 64 and VIII. 44

Peleus, Thetis carried off by him from Magnesia, VII. 191

Pelion, the Argo built there, IV. 179; Pelion and Ossa in the E. of Thessaly, VII. 129; wreck of Xerxes' fleet near Pelion, VIII. 8, 12

Pella, a town in Macedonia, VII. 123

Pellene, an Achaean town, near Sicyon, I. 145

Peloponnese, migration of Dorians thither, I. 56, II. 171; most of the Peloponnese subject to Sparta temp. Croesus, I. 68; Peloponnesian tale of Anacharsis, IV. 77; Peloponnesian invasion of Attica, V. 74; Peloponnesian scale of ransom, VI. 79; security of property there, VI. 86; contingents at Thermopylae, VII. 202; Peloponnesians anxious to guard the Isthmus, VIII. 40, 49, 71, IX. 8; contingents at Salamis, VIII. 43; Artemisia's advice to Xerxes about the Peloponnese, VIII. 68; various nations of Peloponnese, VIII. 73; prophecy of expulsion of Dorians, VIII. 141; Peloponnesian armies in antiquity, IX. 26; Athenian jealousy of Peloponnesians, IX. 106; Peloponnesian return from Mycale, IX. 114 (other reff. of less importance)

Pelops, called by Xerxes a Phrygian settler in Greece, VII. 8, 11; Pelopides a title of Agamemnon, VII. 159

Pelusium, at the E. mouth of the Nile, near the Arabian frontier of Egypt, II. 15, 141; Pelusian mouth, II. 17; Greek settle-

375

INDEX

Phronime, daughter of Etearchus of Crete, the plot against her life, and her escape, IV. 154, 155

Phrygia, antiquity of the Phrygians proved by Psammetichus, II. 2; their tribute to Persia, III. 90; "Royal road" through Phrygia, V. 52; exiled Paeonians settled there, V. 98; Xerxes' route through Phrygia, VII. 26, 30; Phrygians in Xerxes' army, VII. 73; their European origin, I. 6; in Mardonius' army, IX. 32

Phrynon, a Theban, IX. 16

Phrynichus, the Athenian tragedian, his play "Capture of Miletus" suppressed, VI. 21

Phthiotis, in northern Greece, earliest home of the Dorians, I. 56; its submission to Xerxes, VII. 132

Phthius, a legendary personage, son of Achaeus, II. 98

Phya, an Athenian woman caused by Pisistratus to impersonate Athene, I. 60

Phylacus, (1) a Delphian hero, his supposed aid against the Persians, VIII. 39. (2) A Samian trierarch on the Persian side at Salamis, VIII. 85

Phyllis, a district of Thrace, on the Strymon, VII. 113

Pieres, a Thracian tribe, mines in their country, VII. 112; in Xerxes' army, VII. 185

Pieria, a district of Macedonia, on Xerxes' route, VII. 131, 177; pitch from thence, IV. 195

Pigres, (1) brother of Mantyes, q.v., V. 12. (2) A Carian officer in Xerxes' fleet, VII. 98

Pilorus, a town on the Singitic gulf west of Athos, VII. 122

Pindar, the poet, quoted ("Custom is the lord of all"), III. 38

Pindus, (1) a Thessalian town, an early home of the Dorians, I. 56, VIII. 93. (2) A mountain range on the W. frontier of Thessaly, VII. 129

Piraeus, one of the ports of Athens, at the eastern end of Xerxes' line at the battle of Salamis, VIII. 85

Pirene, a spring at Corinth, V. 92

Pirus, a river in Achaea, I. 145

Pisa, a town in Elis, its distance from Athens, II. 7

Pisistratus, (1) the son of Nestor of Pylus, V. 65. (2) Despot of Athens; his seizure of power, I. 59; expulsion and return, I. 60; second retirement and return, and use of his power, I. 61–64, VI. 35. (Elsewhere as a patronymic.) For the Pisistratidae, see Hippias and Hipparchus, also V. 63–65;

376

INDEX

their expulsion from Athens, at Xerxes' court, VII. 6; their attempt to induce Athens to surrender, VIII. 52

Pistyrus, a town in Thrace, on Xerxes' route, VII. 109

Pitana, (1) an Aeolian town in Mysia, I. 149. (2) A Spartan township, III. 55; a " Pitanate battalion " in the Lacedaemonian army at Plataea, IX. 53 (see Amompharetus)

Pithagoras, despot of Selinus, deposed, V. 46

Pittacus of Mytilene, one of the Seven Sages, his advice to Croesus, I. 27

Pixodarus of Cindya, his advice to the Carians on choice of a battlefield, V. 118

Placia, a town of Pelasgian origin on the Hellespont, I. 57

Plataeae (or Plataea), burnt by the Persians, VIII. 50; *passim* in IX. in connection with military operations there (16–88). Plataeans, their first alliance with Athens, VI. 108; at Marathon, VI. 111, 113; refusal to "medize," VII. 132, VIII. 66; (later) Theban attack on their town, VII. 233; in the Greek fleet, VIII. 1; but not at Salamis, VIII. 44; their envoys to Sparta, IX. 7; in Pausanias' army, IX. 28, 31

Platea, an island (modern Bomba) off Libya, occupied by the earliest colonists of Cyrene, IV. 151–153, 156, 169

Pleistarchus, king of Sparta, Pausanias' ward and son of Leonidas, IX. 10

Pleistorus, a god of the Thracian Apsinthians, sacrifice of a Persian to him, IX. 119

Plinthinete bay, on the coast of Egypt, near (the later) Alexandria, II. 6

Plynus, a Libyan harbour (modern Gulf of Sollum), near the west of Egypt, IV. 168

Poeciles, a Phoenician, ancestor of the inhabitants of Thera, IV. 147

Pogon, the port of Troezen, rendezvous for Greek ships before Salamis, VIII. 42

Poliades, a Spartan, father of Amompharetus, IX. 53

Polichne, in Chios, a stronghold of Histiaeus, VI. 26

Polichnitae, a people of Crete, VII. 170

Polyas of Anticyra, a messenger between the Greeks at Artemisium and Leonidas, VIII. 21

Polybus, an ancient king of Sicyon, V. 67

Polycrates, despot of Samos, son of Aeaces, his friendship with Amasis, II. 182, III. 39, 40; his successes and alarming good luck, III. 39–43; his war with Lacedaemon, III. 44–46, 54–56;

INDEX

378

INDEX

INDEX

of twelve states in N.E. Greece; their action in regard to Epialtes, VII. 213

Pylus (1) in Messenia, VII. 168. (2) In Elis, IX. 34. Pylians, descendants of Nestor of Pylus, Pisistratus of that family, V. 65; Caucones called Pylians, I. 147

Pyrene, according to Herodotus a town of the Celts in western Europe, source of the Danube said to be there, II. 33

Pyretus, see Porata.

Pyrgus, a town in western Greece founded by the Minyae, IV. 148

Pythagoras, (1) the philosopher, son of Mnesarchus, Pythagorean and Orphic belief, II. 81; Zalmoxis his slave, IV. 95. (2) A Milesian, put in charge of Miletus by Aristagoras, V. 126

Pytheas, (1) an Aeginetan, son of Ischenoüs, his bravery, and attention paid him by the Persians, VII. 181; his return to Aegina, VIII. 92. (2) An Aeginetan (apparently not the same as 1), father of Lampon, IX. 78

Pythermus, a Phocaean, spokesman at Sparta for Ionian and Aeolian envoys, I. 152

Pythes, a man of Abdera, VII. 137

Pythian priestess, see Delphi.

Pythians, Spartan officials for communication with Delphi, their privileges, VI. 57

Pythius, a Lydian, his offer of his wealth to Xerxes, VII. 27–29; his request to Xerxes and its consequence, VII. 38, 39

Pytho, a synonym for Delphi, I. 54

Pythogenes, brother of the despot of Zancle, his imprisonment by Hippocrates, VI. 23

Rhampsinitus, king of Egypt, story of the theft of his treasure, II. 121

Rhegium, in southern Italy, I. 166, VI. 23; its disaster in battle, VII. 170

Rhenaea, an island near Delos, VI. 97

Rhodes, I. 174; its part in the Greek settlement at Naucratis, II. 178; Rhodian colonists in Sicily, VII. 153

Rhodope, a mountain range in Thrace, source of a tributary of the Danube, IV. 49; flight thither of a Bisaltian king, VIII. 116

Rhodopis, a Thracian courtesan in Egypt, her offerings at Delphi, II. 134, 135

Rhoecus, a Samian, builder of the Heraeum at Samos, III. 60

INDEX

INDEX

INDEX

INDEX

Scylax, (1) a man of Caryanda, his navigation of the Indus and the eastern seas, IV. 44. (2) A man of Myndus, his maltreatment by Megabates, V. 33

Scyles, a king of Scythia, his adoption of Greek customs and his consequent fate, IV. 78–80

Scyllias of Scione, his exploits as a diver, VIII. 8

Scyros, an island in the Aegean E. of Euboea, VII, 183

Scythes, (1) son of Heracles and reputed ancestor of all Scythian kings, IV. 10. (2) Despot of Zancle, his imprisonment by Hippocrates, VI. 23, 24, VII. 163

Scythians, their expulsion of Cimmerians, I. 15; quarrel with Cyaxares, I. 73; invasion of Media and conquest of "Asia," I. 103–106; Scythians subdued by Sesostris, II. 103, 110; contempt of peaceful occupations in Scythia, II. 167; alliance against Persia proposed to Sparta by Scythians, VI. 84; Scythians called Sacae by Persians, VII. 64. Book IV. 1–142 (relating almost wholly to Scythia and adjacent regions): IV. 1–4, Scythians' invasion of Media and troubles after their return; 5–10, early Scythian legends; 11–12, their expulsion of Cimmerians; 16–31, 46, 47, general description of Scythia and inhabitants (nomad, farming, and "royal" Scythian), and regions adjacent; 48–58, rivers of Scythia; 59–75, manners and customs; 76–80, Scythian dislike of foreign manners; 81, size of population; 99–109, geography of Scythia and description of adjacent tribes; 118–142, Scythian warfare against Darius.

Sebennyte province of Egypt, in the Delta, inhabited by one of the warrior tribes, II. 166; Sebennytic or central mouth of the Nile, II. 17, 155

Selinus, a town in Sicily, its occupation by one of Dorieus' followers, V. 46

Selymbria, a Greek town near the Hellespont, VI. 33

Semele, daughter of Cadmus and mother of Dionysus, II. 145

Semiramis, queen of Babylon, her embankment of the Euphrates, . I. 184; gate of Babylon called after her, III. 155

Sepea, near Tiryns in Argolis, scene of a battle between Lacedaemonians and Argives, VI. 77

Sepias promontory, in Magnesia, Xerxes' fleet there, VII. 183; wreck of many of his ships, VII. 188–190

Serbonian marsh, on the eastern frontier of Egypt, II. 6, III. 5

Seriphus, one of the Cyclades islands, Seriphians in the Greek fleet, VIII. 46, 48

INDEX

INDEX

INDEX

INDEX

VII. 24; Bithynians of Asia originally Strymonians, VII. 75; Persian defence of Eïon on the Strymon, VII. 107; sacrifice offered to the river by the Magi, VII. 113; Strymonian or north wind, Xerxes' danger from it, VIII. 118 (a few other unimportant reff.)

Stymphalian lake, alleged subterranean channel from it to Argos, VI. 76

Styreans, from Styra in S.W. Euboea, VI. 107; in the Greek fleet, VIII. 1, 46; in Pausanias' army, IX. 28, 31

Styx, the water of, a mountain stream in Arcadia, supposed to communicate with the world of the dead; oath there administered by Cleomenes, VI. 74

Sunium, the southern promontory of Attica, IV. 99; Athenian festival there, VI. 87; settlement of banished Aeginetans on Sunium, VI. 90; rounding of Sunium by Datis after Marathon, VI. 115; Greek trophy set up there, VIII. 121

Susa, the capital of the Persian kings, on the Choaspes, I. 188, V. 49; Smerdis murdered there, III. 30; revolt against the Magi there, III. 70 seqq.; Histiaeus at Susa, V. 30; end of the Royal road, V. 52; called the Memnonian, V. 54, VII. 151; Milesian captives brought thither, VI. 20; Demaratus and the Pisistratidae at Susa, VII. 3, 6; Spartans there, VII. 136; reception there of Xerxes' despatches from Greece, VIII. 99; Xerxes' amours at Susa, IX. 108 (other unimportant reff. to Susa as the royal residence)

Syagrus, Spartan envoy to Sicily, VII. 153; his reply to Gelon, VII. 159

Sybaris, in southern Italy, attacked by Dorieus, V. 44; its capture by the Crotoniats, VI. 21; its former prosperity, VI. 127

Syene (Assuan), alleged to be near the source of the Nile, opposite Elephantine, II. 28

Syennesis, (1) king of Cilicia, his reconciliation of Medians and Lydians, I. 74; his daughter, V. 118. (2) A Cilician officer in Xerxes' army, VII. 98

Sylean plain in Thrace, near Stagirus, on Xerxes' route, VII. 115

Syloson, banished by his brother Polycrates from Samos, III. 39; his gift to Darius and its reward, III. 139–141; his restoration to the government of Samos, III. 144–149. (Elsewhere a patronymic.)

Syme, an island near Rhodes, I. 174

INDEX

Syracuse, its despots comparable for splendour to Polycrates, III. 125; its seizure by Gelon, and growth under his rule, VII. 154–156; Greek envoys there, VII. 157; Amilcas of Carthage partly a Syracusan, VII. 166

Syrgis, see Hyrgis

Syria, its geography, II. 12, 116; many rivers there, II. 20; Syrian desert, III. 6; see also Palestine; Syrians' defeat by Egyptians, II. 159; their tribute to Persia, III. 91; Syrians of Cappadocia, I. 6; Cappadocians called Syrians by Greeks, I. 72, V. 49; invaded by Croesus, I. 76; their tribute to Persia, III. 90; in Xerxes' army, VII. 72

Syrtis, the bay of the Libyan coast W. of Cyrene, alleged canal between it and Lake of Moeris, II. 150; silphium produced near it, IV. 169; inhabitants of its coast, II. 32, IV. 173

Tabalus, made governor of Sardis by Cyrus, I. 153; rising of Lydians against him, I. 154

Tabiti, a Scythian deity identified with the Greek Hestia, IV. 59

Tachompso, an alleged island in the Nile between Elephantine and Meroë, II. 29

Taenarum, southern promontory of Laconia, Arion's arrival there on a dolphin, I. 24; Corcyraean ships' delay there, VII. 168

Talaüs, an Argive, father of Adrastus, V. 67

Talthybius, the Greek herald in the Iliad, his supposed vengeance of the death of heralds, VII. 134, 137

Tamynae, a town in Euboea, its occupation by Datis, VI. 101

Tanagra, a town in Boeotia, its lands occupied by Cadmus, followers, V. 57; Mardonius there, IX. 15; scene of a battle (later) between the Spartans and the Athenians and Argives, IX. 35; near the river Thermodon, IX. 43

Tanaïs, a Scythian river (the Don), between Scythians and Sauromatae, IV. 21; its source and mouth, IV. 57, 100; crossed by Amazons and Sauromatae, IV. 116

Tanite province of Egypt, inhabited by one of the warrior tribes, II. 166

Taras (Tarentum), Arion's departure thence, I. 24; Tarentines' services to Democedes, III. 136; their refusal to admit a banished man, III. 138, IV. 99; Tarentines' losses in a battle with their neighbours, VII. 170

Targitaus, by legend the earliest Scythian, son of Zeus and Borysthenes, IV. 5; a thousand years before Darius' invasion, IV. 7

389

INDEX

Taricheae (salting-places), near the Canopic mouth of the Nile, Paris' landing there, II. 113

Tartessus, at the mouth of the Baetis (Guadalquivir), friendship of Phocaeans with its king, I. 163; Samians' voyage thither, IV. 152; Tartessian weasels, IV. 192

Tauchira, a town in Libya near Barca, IV. 171

Tauri, a Scythian people, in the Tauric Chersonese W. of the Palus Maeotis, their country described, IV. 99–101; their part in the campaign against Darius, IV. 102–119

Taxacis, a leader in the Scythian armies against Darius, IV. 120

Taÿgetus, the mountain range E. of Laconia, its occupation by the Minyae, IV. 145, 146

Tearus, a Thracian river, its water praised by Darius, IV. 89–90

Teaspis, a Persian, IV. 43, VII. 79, IX. 76

Tegea, a town in Arcadia, varying event of its wars with Sparta, I. 66–68; Leutychides' death there, VI. 72; Phidippides' vision near Tegea, VI. 105; Tegeans at Thermopylae, VII. 202; Tegeans' claim to the post of honour in Pausanias' army, IX. 26–28; (later) victory of Spartans over Tegea and Argos, IX. 35; Tegean valour at Plataea, IX. 56, 60, 61, 62, 70

Teïspes, two of this name in the list of Xerxes' forefathers, VII. 11 (see How and Wells, Appendix IV. 3)

Telamon, one of the legendary heroes of Salamis, his aid invoked by the Greeks, VIII. 64

Teleboae, an Acarnanian people, Amphitryon's defeat of them, V. 59

Telecles, a Samian, III. 41

Teleclus, a Spartan king, VII. 204

Telemachus, son of Nestor, Menelaus' narrative to him, II. 116

Telesarchus of Samos, his opposition to Maeandrius, III. 143

Telines, his priesthood at Gela in Sicily, VII. 153

Telliadae, a family or clan of diviners in Elis, one of them with Mardonius, IX. 37

Tellias of Elis (perhaps of the above family), his device for a Phocian night attack on Thessalians, VIII. 27

Tellus, an Athenian, Solon's judgment of his happiness, I. 30

Telmessians, probably in Lycia, their prophetic answers, I. 78, 84

Telos, an island near Rhodes, home of Telines, VII. 153

Telys, despot of Sybaris, V. 44

Temenus, ancestor of the Temenid family of Macedonian kings, VIII. 137

INDEX

INDEX

Thebe, (1) legendary daughter of Asopus and sister of Aegina, v. 80. (2) A plain in Mysia, on Xerxes' route, VII. 42

Thebes, (1) in Upper Egypt (modern Luxor), a custom of the temple there, I. 182; Herodotus' inquiries at Thebes, II. 3; distance from Heliopolis, II. 9; Thebes once called Egypt, II. 15; rules of abstinence there, II. 42; alleged connection between the temple at Thebes and Dodona, II. 54–56; crocodiles held sacred there, II. 69; sacred snakes, II. 74; Hecataeus' investigations at Thebes, II. 143; single instance of rain at Thebes, III. 10; Cambyses there, III. 25; distance from Thebes of the temple of Ammon, IV. 143; Thebaïc province, Syene and Chemmis in it, II. 28, 91; inhabited by one of the warrior tribes, II. 166. (2) In Boeotia, temple of Apollo there, I. 52; Croesus' gifts there, I. 92; Theban assistance to Pisistratus, I. 61; Phoenician inscriptions at Thebes, V. 59; Theban feud with Athens, V. 79, 81–89, VI. 108; Theban recovery of an image of Apollo, VI. 118; submission to Xerxes, VII. 132; Thebans unwillingly at Thermopylae, VII. 205; Thebans and oracles of Amphiaraus, VIII. 134; Theban advice to Mardonius, IX. 2; Mardonius in Theban territory, IX. 15; story of Polynices' attack on Thebes, IX. 27; proposed retreat of Persians to Thebes, IX. 58; Theban valour on Persian side, IX. 67; surrender of Thebes to Greek army, IX. 86–88

Themis, a deity in Greece but not in Egypt, II. 50

Themiscyra, on the S. coast of the Euxine, breadth of the sea measured thence, IV. 86

Themison, a Theraean trader, his bargain with Etearchus of Crete, IV. 154

Themistocles, his interpretation of the Delphic oracle given to Athens, VII. 143; his creation of the Athenian navy, VII. 144; in command of a force in Thessaly, VII. 173; bribery of Greeks to stay at Artemisium, VIII. 4; his efforts to detach Ionians from Xerxes, VIII. 19, 22; advice to Greeks to stay at Salamis, VIII. 56–63; secret message to Persians, VIII. 75; interview with Aristides, VIII. 79, 80; exhortation before Salamis, VIII. 83; meeting with Polycritus of Aegina, VIII. 92; his policy after Salamis, secret message to Xerxes, and extortion of money from islanders, VIII. 108–112; honours paid him by Greeks after Salamis, VIII. 123–125

Theocydes, an Athenian, VIII. 65

Theodorus, a Samian artist, his work at Delphi, I. 51; for Polycrates, III. 41

392

INDEX

Theomestor of Samos, his services to the Persians at Salamis, VIII. 85; despot of Samos, IX. 90

Theophania, a festival at Delphi, I. 51

Theopompus, a Spartan king, VIII. 131

Thera, one of the Cyclades, once called Calliste, IV. 147; its original settlement, *ib.*; reason of its sending a colony to Libya, IV. 151; story of Battus of Thera, IV. 155; Theraeans with Dorieus in Libya, V. 42

Therambos, a town in Pallene, VII. 123

Therapne, near Sparta, a temple of Helen there, VI. 61

Theras, a Cadmean of Sparta, his colonisation of Thera, IV. 147, 148

Thermodon, (1) a river in Boeotia, near Tanagra, IX. 43. (2) A river in Cappadocia, II. 104; near Themiscyra, IV. 86; victory on it of Greeks over Amazons, IV. 110, IX. 27

Thermopylae, description of the pass, VII. 176, 198–200; story of the battle, VII. 210–225; visit of Persian forces to the field of Thermopylae, IX. 24, 25 (other mentions in VIII. and IX. refer to the battle)

Theron, despot of Acragas, his expulsion of Terillus from Himera, VII. 165; victory with Gelon over Carthaginian confederacy, VII. 166

Thersandrus, (1) son of Polynices, ancestor of Theras, IV. 147, VI. 52. (2) A man of Orchomenus, his presence at a Persian banquet at Thebes, IX. 16

Theseus, his abduction of Helen into Attica, IX. 73

Thesmophoria, a Greek festival in honour of Demeter, in Attica in the autumn, II. 171; its celebration by Ephesian women, VI. 16

Thespia, a town in Boeotia, burnt by the Persians, VIII. 50; Thespians allies of Thebans, V. 79; their refusal to submit to Xerxes, VII. 132; their steadfastness at Thermopylae, VII. 202, 222, 226; Sicinnus made a Thespian, VIII. 75; Thespians in Pausanias' army, IX. 30

Thesprotians, in N.W. Greece, neighbours of the Ampraciots, VIII. 47; their practice of necromancy, V. 92; Thessalians from Thesprotia, VII. 176

Thessaly, Pelasgians formerly there, I. 57; Darius' European tribute from nations east of it, III. 96, VII. 108; Thessalian allies of Pisistratus, V. 63; Lacedaemonian invasion of Thessaly, VI. 72; Aleuadae of Thessaly at Xerxes' court, VII. 6; description of Thessaly, VII. 129; its submission to Xerxes,

INDEX

VII. 132; Greek force there, VII. 172, 173; danger to Phocis from Thessalians, VII. 191, 215; Xerxes' march through it, VII. 196; Thessalian cavalry inferior to Asiatic, *ib.*; defeats of Thessalians by Phocians, and Thessalian revenge, VIII. 27–32; Mardonius in Thessaly, VIII. 113, 133; Thessalians in his army, IX. 31; Artabazus in Thessaly, IX. 89 (other less important reff.)

Thessalus, a Spartan companion of Dorieus, V. 46

Theste, a spring in Libya, defeat there of Egyptians by Cyrenaeans, IV. 159

Thetis, Magian sacrifice to her to abate a storm, VII. 191

Thmuite province of Egypt, inhabited by one of the warrior tribes, II. 166

Thoas, king of Lemnos, killed by women, VI. 138

Thon, of Egypt, referred to in the Odyssey, II. 116

Thonis, warder of the Nile mouth, his reception of Paris, II. 113

Thorax, an Aleuad of Larissa, his support of Mardonius, IX. 1; Mardonius' address to him, IX. 58

Thoricus, a deme of Attica, near Sunium, IV. 99

Thornax, a mountain in Laconia, Apollo's temple there, I. 69

Thrace, Phocaean migration thither, I. 168; conquest by Sesostris, II. 103; Thracian contempt of peaceful occupations, II. 167; Thracian rivers, IV. 49; use of hemp there, IV. 74; Darius in Thrace, IV. 89–93; population and customs of Thrace, V. 3–8; Histiaeus there, V. 23; Aristagoras killed by Thracians, V. 126; their attack on Mardonius, VI. 45; Thrace conquered by Mysians and Teucrians, VII. 20; Persian supremacy, VII. 106; Xerxes' route through Thrace, VII. 110; reverence of Thracians for road of Xerxes' army, VII. 115; Thracians in his army, VII. 185; Thracian theft of Xerxes' chariot, VIII. 115; Artabazus' retreat harassed by Thracians, IX. 89; human sacrifice there, IX. 119

Thracians of Asia (Bithynians), their conquest by Croesus, I. 28; tribute to Persia, III. 90; in Xerxes' army, VII. 75; their former migration from Thrace into Asia, *ib.*

Thrasybulus, despot of Miletus, his deception of Alyattes, I. 20–23; advice to Periander of Corinth, V. 92

Thrasycles, a Samian, IX. 90

Thrasydeïus, an Aleuad of Larissa, Mardonius' address to him, IX. 58

Thrasylaus, an Athenian, VI. 114

Thriasian plain, near Eleusis in Attica, Dicaeus' vision there,

INDEX

INDEX

Tisandrus, (1) an Athenian, father of Isagoras, v. 63. (2) An Athenian, father of Hippoclides, vi. 127

Tisias, a Parian, vi. 133

Titacus, a legendary Athenian, his betrayal of Aphidnae, ix. 73

Tithaeus, a cavalry officer in Xerxes' army, vii. 88

Tithorea, a peak of Parnassus, retreat of Delphians thither, viii. 32

Titormus, an Aetolian, his strength and solitary habits, vi. 127

Tmolus, a gold-producing mountain in Lydia, near Sardis, i. 84, 93, v. 100

Tomyris, queen of the Massagetae, her proposal to the invading Persians, i. 205, 206; her victory over Cyrus and revenge for her son, i. 212–214

Torone, a town in Chalcidice, on the Sithonian peninsula, vii. 22, 122

Trachis, the coastal region closed to the E. by Thermopylae, several unimportant reff. to it, vii. 175–226; its town of the same name, vii. 199; Xerxes' passage from Trachis into Doris, viii. 31

Trapezus (later Trebizond), a town on the S.E. coast of the Euxine, vi. 127

Traspies, a Scythian tribe, iv. 6

Trausi, a Thracian tribe, v. 3

Travus, a river in Thrace flowing into the Bistonian lake, vii. 109

Triballic plain (in modern Serbia), iv. 49

Triopian promontory, S.W. point of Asia Minor, i. 174, iv. 37; temple of Apollo there, i. 144

Tritaea, a town in Achaea, i. 145

Tritantaechmes, (1) a Persian, son of Artabazus, his governorship of Assyria, i. 192. (2) A Persian, one of the generals of Xerxes' army, vii. 82, 121

Triteae, a Phocian town burnt by the Persians, viii. 33

Triton, (1) a deity of the sea, his guidance of Jason, iv. 179; his cult in Libya, iv. 188. (2) An alleged river in Libya, flowing into the "Tritonid lake," iv. 178; the lake itself, *ib.*, and iv. 186 (neither river nor lake is identified)

Troezen, in Argolis, entrusted with the island of Hydrea, iii. 59; mother-city of Halicarnassus, vii. 99; its contingent in the Greek fleet, viii. 1, 43; in the force at the Isthmus, viii. 72; in Pausanias' army, ix. 28, 31; Troezenians in the battle of Mycale, ix. 102, 105

INDEX

INDEX

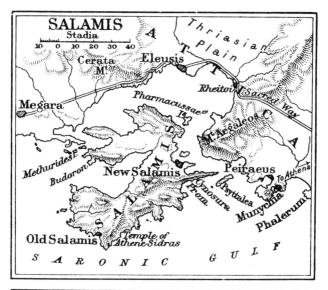

SALAMIS

Stadia

10 0 10 20 30 40

Cerata M^t.

Eleusis

Thriasian Plain

A T T I C A

Rheitoi

Sacred Way

Megara

Pharmacussae Is.

Methurides Is.

Budoron

New Salamis

M^t. Aegaleos

Peiraeus

Psyttalea

Cynosura Prom.

Munychia

To Athens

S A L A M I S

Phalerum

Old Salamis

Temple of Athene Sidras

S A R O N I C   G U L F

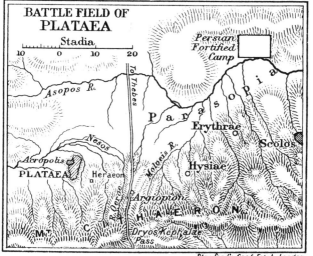

BATTLE FIELD OF PLATAEA

Stadia

10 0 10 20

Persian Fortified Camp

Asopos R.

To Thebes

P a r a s o p i a

Erythrae

Scolos

Nesos

Acropolis

PLATAEA

Heraeon

Molois R.

Hysiae

Argiopion

M^t.   C   I   T   H   A   E   R   O   N

Dryos Kephalae Pass

Stanford's Geog. Estab., London.